Napoleon

From 18 Brumaire to Tilsit
1799–1807

GEORGES LEFEBVRE

THE FRENCH REVOLUTION

(*In two volumes*)

I. From Its Origins to 1793

II. From 1793 to 1799

NAPOLEON

(*In two volumes*)

I. From 18 Brumaire to Tilsit, 1799–1807

II. From Tilsit to Waterloo, 1807–1815

Napoleon

From 18 Brumaire to Tilsit

1799–1807

BY

Georges Lefebvre

TRANSLATED FROM THE FRENCH
BY HENRY F. STOCKHOLD

COLUMBIA UNIVERSITY PRESS
NEW YORK

Published 1969 by Routledge & Kegan Paul Ltd, London

This book is a translation of the first three parts of *Napoléon,* by Georges Lefebvre, Volume XIV of the series 'Peuples et Civilisations,' published by Presses Universitaires de France. The original work was published in 1936 and this translation is based on the fifth (1965) edition.

Clothbound editions of Columbia University Press books
are Smyth-sewn and printed on permanent
and durable acid-free paper.

ISBN 0-231-02558-0

Library of Congress Catalog Card Number: 68-29160

Printed in the United States of America

10 9 8 7 6

Contents

v

CONTENTS

III. IMPERIAL CONQUEST TO THE TREATY OF TILSIT (1802–1807)

Translator's Foreword

THIS BOOK is a translation of the first three parts of Georges Lefebvre's history of the Napoleonic Era. The original work was published in 1935, and this translation is based on the fifth (1965) edition.

Throughout, my primary object was to fashion a clear and readable English translation. This was not always an easy task. By confining himself to a one-volume history, Lefebvre was forced to compress an enormous quantity of factual material into relatively little space. He was impatient in his attendance to narrative detail, often reducing the findings of his massive research efforts to a succession of clipped, laconic statements. This sometimes made it difficult for me to convey a sense of continuity because parts of the historical narrative were insufficiently developed. However, it is only fair to point out that it was not the author's purpose to describe at length that which could readily be found in many another period history. Lefebvre was an historian's historian, and he simply assumed that his readers would possess an easy familiarity with his subject. His demands upon his readers were as severe as his sweeping synthesis and vision of the whole through its variegated parts were magnificent.

In endeavouring to strike a just balance between readability and strict adherence to the original, I felt compelled to take certain minor liberties with the text. Interminably long paragraphs were broken up, and in a few instances the order of sentences was rearranged for the sake of greater clarity. Occasionally a connective was added, when dictated by reasons of sense and style. Christian names of lesser known personages were frequently supplied, and obvious errors involving names, dates, and quotes were 'silently' corrected. Attempts, although not always successful, were made to reproduce quotes in their original wording whenever they emanated from an English source. Certain foreign terms and expressions were thought better left in the original, whether by virtue of their acceptance into contemporary English usage or because they defied translation into precise English equivalents: *Sturm und Drang, Aufklärung, corvée, octrois, receveurs généraux, rescriptions, biens nationaux, amalgame.* In such cases, explanatory footnotes were provided wherever deemed necessary.

I wish to express my profound gratitude for the invaluable assistance I received from my dear friend Wilson Robert Augustine of York University. For his painstaking scrutiny of the entire manuscript, for the countless hours which he devoted to it, and for his many penetrating criticisms and expert suggestions, I am indeed deeply indebted. I am also indebted to Professor Leon Smolinski of Boston College for his generous help on passages dealing with fiscal and monetary policy, and to Dr. James Friguglietti of Harvard University for his thoughtful letters in which he called my attention to numerous textual errors in the French printings of this work. Finally, I owe a great debt of gratitude to my mother, Rose Ruth Stockhold, without whose constant encouragement and support this translation might never have been completed.

HENRY FREDERIC STOCKHOLD

New York
January 1968

Introduction

AT THE TIME when Napoleon Bonaparte assumed control of France, Europe and the French Revolution had been at war for over seven years, and except for a brief interruption, this conflict was to last until 1815. The 18 Brumaire did not in itself mark the end of an epoch. It might be more logical to say that the period of peace which followed the Treaty of Amiens was the dividing point between two eras. True, when considering the internal history of France, one sees that the coup d'état of Brumaire opened the way for the restoration of personal power. In this respect, the contrast between the Napoleonic and Revolutionary periods is well defined, but their essential unity cannot be ignored. It was to the Revolution that Bonaparte owed his marvellous destiny. He was able to force himself upon republican France precisely because an internal necessity fated that country to dictatorship as long as the partisans of the Old Regime strove to re-establish the monarchy with the help of foreign powers.

In his methods of government, Bonaparte had more in common with the Committee of Public Safety than writers are generally willing to admit. It was because he respected the social legislation of the Constituent Assembly that he was able to remain the leader of France. His military victories assured that the work of the Constituent Assembly would endure and become permanently rooted in French society. More than that, his victories enabled French ideas to sweep over the Continent with a rapidity and an efficacy which neither propaganda nor spontaneous diffusion could have equalled. Had he not implanted the fundamental principles of the modern state and society in all the countries which he dominated, no trace would have ever been left of his smashing campaigns. In vain did he attempt to create a new legitimacy and a new aristocracy. His contemporaries always saw him as the soldier of the Revolution, and it was as such that he made his mark upon European civilization.

All this notwithstanding, from the moment that Bonaparte became master of France, he was elevated to a place in the very centre of universal history. And so, despite the fundamental unities linking his reign with the tragedy that was the Revolution, the traditional dividing point—his accession—has much to be said for it, and is the one used in this work.

It is hardly necessary to point out that this book is not a biography of Napoleon. As in the other volumes of this general history, an attempt has been made to cast light not only on the essential features of the collective life of the French people and those who were subjugated by the Emperor, but also on the operation of forces independent of his will and on the distinguishing characteristics of nations which escaped his domination. England and the United States maintained their liberal tradition; capitalism continued its progress; and the bourgeoisie, growing in strength, was well on its way to assuming complete political power. Religious life followed its course, and Napoleon was unable to modify it. Nations reacted against the universal empire whose foundations he was laying. Above all in Germany, Romanticism fostered new ways of feeling, thinking, and acting; and Latin America threw off the Spanish yoke. Even the Far East, in a negative way, experienced repercussions of the great conflict, for it would have been subjected to European assaults much earlier had not the Napoleonic Wars monopolized the energies of Europe. The nineteenth century, so shifting and varied in its character, was visible beneath the apparent uniformity which Napoleon's genius tried to impose. But during the course of this period, otherwise so brief, everything seemed to yield before him. It was he who dominated history. What then could be more natural than that this volume should bear his name.

I

THE LEGACY
OF THE
REVOLUTION

CHAPTER ONE

The Conflict between the Old Regime and the Revolution

THE PASSAGE OF TEN YEARS, and above all, war, had profoundly modified the course of the French Revolution. The map of Europe had already undergone noticeable change, and the expansion of French territory to the 'natural frontiers' had clearly upset the European equilibrium. Such was the legacy of Bonaparte, and it weighed heavily on his policies. It would be advisable therefore to describe some of the features of that heritage, even if we disagree with Albert Sorel's contention that Bonaparte was more the creature of his destiny than its maker.

Of these features, the most deep-seated was the conflict which had been going on since 1789 between the Revolution and Europe. Above all, a social conflict existed between the privileged classes and the bourgeoisie, who were supported by the rest of the Third Estate. A political conflict existed also because royal despotism, like privilege, had been condemned, and kings, having taken the aristocracy under their protection, ventured the risk of perishing with it. Finally, there was a religious conflict arising from the common understanding of the Revolution as the offspring of Cartesian rationalism, whose merciless critique had destroyed the mysteries and traditions which were regarded as comprising the foundation of the Old Regime. The rivalry

3

of nations, each aspiring to leadership, blurred these conflicts but did not obliterate them from the consciousness of contemporaries. Unyielding, they dominated the history of the Napoleonic era.

THE SOCIAL AND POLITICAL CONFLICT

The ebbing of the Revolution had been evident since 9 Thermidor. The Constitution of Year III (1795) had brought to power a bourgeoisie sincerely attached to the new order, yet hostile to democracy, which it did not distinguish from Jacobinism. Along with Madame de Staël and the *Idéologues*, it envisaged an oligarchy more modern than that of England but essentially analogous to it—an oligarchy which would strike a balance between the interests of the rich and men of talent. Meanwhile, the bourgeoisie gradually set about destroying the work of the Mountain, and did not even spare that of the Constituent Assembly. They abolished family courts and courts of arbitration, and reinstated imprisonment for debt and notary fees. The retroactive features of the inheritance laws of Year II disappeared, and the rights granted to bastards were fiercely attacked. The sale of the *biens nationaux** no longer benefited anyone but the rich, and in Year VII those who held mortgaged biens nationaux were gratuitously given an unencumbered title. The division of communal lands was suspended, and attempts were once again made to drive the peasants from the forests, which they had used freely since 1789.

But what basic significance did all this have for the European nobility? Strive as the Revolution might for bourgeois ideals, it nevertheless remained a revolution for civil equality. Wherever its armies had penetrated—Belgium, the Rhineland, Holland, Switzerland—the Revolution had undertaken the destruction of the Old Regime. The Pope was a prisoner; the Prince of Orange, the Rhenish Electors, and the Swiss patricians were in flight. Suvorov's victories alone had reconquered Italy and had restored its legitimate princes. The states neighbouring France were being secretly permeated with subversive propaganda and the news of the liberation of French peasants and the vic-

* Literally, national property. The property confiscated by the state from the clergy, nobility, and others during the Revolution. TRANSLATOR.

4

tories of the Sans-culottes was spoken of everywhere. Less effective were the efforts of writers and journalists, most of whom had been either disillusioned by the excesses of the Terror or else forced to be silent. One could point to men everywhere who wished to make a compact with the French, as for example, in South Germany. Even in Prussia the refusal to perform *corvée* and to pay feudal dues became more frequent. It was rumoured that the king would abolish these exactions, and Frederick William III was besieged with petitions on his accession. Across the sea, Antonio Narinõ had translated the Declaration of the Rights of Man, and in the United States, Washington's party suspected Jefferson and the Republicans of having been contaminated by the egalitarian mania.

Everywhere, even among the great Whig families, the aristocracy was frightened and rallied around the throne; everywhere, governments tightened their controls. Except for Russia, stooped under the atrocious despotism of Paul I, the prize went to Austria, where henceforth Colloredo became the living spirit of an obscurantist police state for which Metternich later claimed credit. In Prussia, Wöllner, who up until the death of Frederick William II had attempted to install the same system, nearly escaped being dismissed. At Jena, Fichte, accused of atheism and abandoned by the Duke of Weimar, had been forced to surrender his chair in 1799. In England, habeas corpus had been suspended since 1794, and 'seditious' associations and publications had been prohibited. In 1799 Pitt made printers profess their allegiance, and he had members of illegal societies sent to penal colonies for seven years. In America, the Federalists, profiting by their rupture with the Directory, voted an Alien Bill aimed at French democrats, and a Sedition Act to deal with associations and newspapers. In Latin America, the cause of liberty already had its martyrs. While not entirely groundless, the fears inspired by 'Jacobins' were exaggerated. The rare admirers of France, like Kant, Fichte, and the youthful Hegel, who set out to criticize the Bernese patriciate and the oligarchy of Württemberg, took great care to stipulate that they placed their faith solely in legal and peaceful progress. No nation imitated France spontaneously; rather, it was her armies that spread the principles of the Revolution.

Lively though the reaction was, it could not be said to have

The Conflict between the Old Regime and the Revolution

condemned all reform. Enlightened despotism had shown that some reforms were reconcilable with absolute monarchy and an aristocratic society. Recognizing that not all of the work of the Constituent Assembly was contemptible, governments of the Old Regime envied France for its administrative unity and for its suppression of fiscal privilege. The example of England further demonstrated to the agricultural countries of the Continent the advantages of enclosure and the drawbacks of serfdom. Nevertheless, it was only in Germany, notably in Bavaria and Prussia, that reforms were undertaken which would permit Western influences to combine with national traditions.

The *Aufklärung*, while it had lost its prestige among the literati, had nonetheless schooled the bourgeoisie and officialdom. Count Montgelas, who had recently come to power in Bavaria, was one of its disciples. In Berlin, the Austrian ambassador bitterly remarked that the Prussian bureaucracy reproached the enemies of France for wanting to 'banish from the earth the rule of reason', to which Prussia owed her greatness. The Prussian high civil service, which was organized into colleges and recruited by co-optation, maintained a strong esprit de corps. It had watched with displeasure the ceaseless royal extension of cabinet power, whereby everything was decided by the king and his 'camarilla'; such personal administration of Silesia and the Polish provinces by crown and nonministerial advisers ('cabinet') had incurred disastrous results in the reign of Frederick William II. These lofty civil servants would have willingly subjected their king to the rule of law, and Wilhelm Carmer, who finished drafting Frederick's Law Code in 1794, included provisions for personal liberty, permanency of tenure for judges, and religious toleration. They also realized that the Frederickian state, with its peasant serfdom, its provinces jealous of their particular institutions and divided from each other by customs barriers, each considering itself autonomous, did not form a single nation. Finally, like all riparian Baltic states, Prussia had been for a quarter century a major exporter of grains and textiles, and enlightened individuals took notice of the introduction into Denmark of English agricultural methods by Albert Thaer, the Saxon agronomist. The Prussian civil servants were equally interested in the economic liberalism of Adam Smith, which was taught in Hamburg by Johann Büsch, in Vienna by Watteroth,

6

and notably in Königsberg by Christian Kraus, who exerted a great influence on two eminent administrators of the monarchy, Schön and Schrötter. The people most inclined to accept new ideas, however, were officials whom Prussia had drawn from Western Germany or abroad: the Franconian Karl Altenstein; the Hanoverian Karl von Hardenberg, who governed Ansbach and Bayreuth; Johann Struensee, who came from Denmark; and most important of all, Heinrich Baron von und zum Stein, a scion of the Rhenish *Ritterschaft*, who before taking office in 1804 had administered the provinces of Cleves and Mark where the 'Prussian system' had never been introduced.

Nor was this all. Contrary to certain historical accounts, Stein and other statesmen examined the French experience closely and concluded from it that the government could increase its power and prestige by giving the nation some voice in questions of law, taxation, and administration. Nevertheless, since they defined the 'nation' as the nobility and rich bourgeoisie, it was on England that they concentrated their attention. Under Pitt's guidance that nation appeared to have reconciled royal prerogative with constitutional law, party rivalry with the maintenance of order and stability, aristocratic supremacy with bourgeois ambition, and the interests of the nobility with those of the whole commonwealth. Pitt humoured the Lords, whose 'pocket' and 'rotten' boroughs assured him a parliamentary majority, but he did not share their prejudices. Among the ninety-five peers he appointed were a number of 'new men', captains of banking and commerce who rejuvenated the aristocracy and helped it to remain rich and able. Thanks to Burke, this miracle of balance and wisdom had won the adherence of numerous enemies of the Revolution, particularly those of middle class and protestant origin, like Mallet du Pan and François d'Ivernois. There were admirers of England even among the French émigrés. German anglophilia naturally abounded in the Hanseatic towns, and in Hanover it flourished at the University of Göttingen. August Rehberg and Heinrich Brandes acquainted Stein with English ideas, and he used them in his own political thought. One can find evidence of them in the individualistic teachings of Wilhelm von Humboldt, who would have left the state with only police and military power, abandoning the other spheres of government, as in England, to the spontaneous organization of society.

This, he believed, would have served to subject the social order to the patronage of the aristocracy.

The great majority of the privileged classes abhorred these bureaucratic reformers as much as they did the 'Jacobins'. In the face of their protests, sovereigns faltered or fell back. Pitt himself was an example. Without repudiating his early projects, he deferred them until a later time. In Austria, the agrarian reforms of Joseph II had been suspended by Leopold II, and in 1798 his successor Francis II ended by retaining the feudal dues and the corvées. In his Livonian provinces, Paul I contented himself with wresting certain mitigations of serfdom from the Diet, and his commissioner in the Danubian Principalities, Paul Kiselev, went no further. In Prussia, the Junkers had already imposed a revision of Frederick's Code upon Frederick William II, and Frederick William III soon renounced his plan to suppress fiscal privileges, a reform which he had contemplated in 1798. True, he resolutely continued to liberate peasants and reform the agrarian economy in his vast personal domains, but he did not dare extend these enterprises to the seignorial *Gut*. The Prussian nobility retained its monopoly of high positions and ranks. In 1800 there were only 695 commoners out of 6,000 or 7,000 officers. Stein himself was unable to effect more than technical reforms in finance, and he failed to abolish the internal customs barriers.

Thus the reformers outside France were almost as ineffectual as the Jacobins. It was the ruling hand of Napoleon, or the rude impact of his armies, that would rejuvenate the Old World. And France had never ceased to be the bête noire of European monarchies and aristocracies. 'I am not, nor can I ever be, sympathetic to the French,' wrote Maria Carolina of Naples; 'I shall always regard them as the assassins of my sister and of the royal family, and as the oppressors of every monarchy.' Stolberg called them the 'Western Huns', and Nelson, although he was not born noble, contemptuously referred to them as the 'French villains'. The conservatism of the Consulate and Empire never succeeded in appeasing them except superficially.

The anti-French Coalitions have been traditionally explained in terms of national interests, and the entire drama has been reduced to the question of the balance of power, or, as Pitt said, of security. This conclusion is not unreasonable since ill will

8

toward the French never once prevented sovereigns from dealing with France when they found it expedient; but for all that, they did not cast off their inflexible enmity, and their entourages persisted in proclaiming their hatred of France. This is an incalculable factor which cannot be disregarded. Only in order to conciliate the Whigs did the Tories publicly deny the intention of imposing on France a government of their own choice. Lord Grenville was revealing his real feelings when on December 22, 1795, he included amnesty for émigrés and the restitution of their estates among the numerous conditions of the peace. In January 1800, he added the restoration of the monarchy. This noble lord was revolted by the necessity of negotiating with republicans, whom he could not even regard as gentlemen. Nor would Pitt rejoice at having to stomach the man of whom he would speak on February 3, 1800, as 'this last adventurer in the lottery of revolutions'.

THE CONFLICT OF IDEAS

Political and social reaction naturally found their reflection in the world of thought. Authority and tradition once again came into fashion, and an increasing number of writers and publicists passionately applauded its return. Some were motivated by conviction, others by self-interest—for governments recognized the value of propaganda and appropriated money for that purpose. Important among the voices of reaction were French and Genevan émigrés like Rivarol and Abbé Barruel, François d'Ivernois and Mallet du Pan. In England, Canning joined the list with the publication of his periodical *The Anti-Jacobin*. Usually, events in France were exploited in order to terrify the population. Abbé Barruel resumed Hoffman's charges against the *Illuminati* and Freemasons with never-failing success. But certain writers made it a point of honour to raise the level of the debate by offering a new apology for traditional thought in opposition to the rationalist critique.

There was nothing original in this, for during the course of the eighteenth century, English empiricism, having become conservative with Hume and even more so with Bentham, had aspired to restore authority and moral conventions. It was argued that just as reason was able to govern the physical world

9

by searching for natural law and conforming to it, so reason could observe social life and discover that traditional institutions, by virtue of their prolonged existence, were in harmony with the 'nature of things'. In Burke, this pragmatism had been complicated by the addition of a social vitalism borrowed from medical science, such as had been taught in eighteenth-century France at the school of Montpellier and by Marie François Bichat during the period of the Directory. Man was thought to be the fruit of a spontaneous and progressive germination caused by an irrational force called life. Similarly, Burke spoke of society as a plant or animal, the individual being only one of its organs, so that social authority was imposed on him as a condition of his existence which he could no more repudiate than his physical needs. This experimental rationalism, mingled with a mysticism which gave it some affinity to romanticism, passed from England to Germany, where it made a strong impression on Rehberg and Brandes. It has been said that Friedrich von Gentz, who translated Burke's *Reflections* as early as 1793, and even Metternich derived their political philosophy from this school of thought.

Very close to these ideas were two French political philosophers, Louis de Bonald and Joseph de Maistre. In 1796 there appeared the simultaneous publication of the former's *Théorie du pouvoir politique et religieux* and the latter's *Considérations sur la France*. They too subordinated the individual to society, and Bonald frequently referred to the nature of things, but they substituted the working of Providence in place of the vital life source. According to the autocratic and authoritarian Bonald, who cherished the royalist tradition as much as he did Catholicism, the structure that God had set for society remained immutable. For Joseph de Maistre, who had a sense of history and who, as a good Ultramontanist, was somewhat indifferent to forms of temporal government, the Creator limited himself to preserving society by infinitely wise and flexible means. Thus man had to bow before the facts.

On occasion, even political economy was not above attacking lofty reason. Observing the England of his time, Malthus in 1798 maintained that the notion of unlimited human progress was but a chimera, because in spite of technological efforts, population tended to increase much faster than the means of subsistence. Thus every social improvement which helped to increase the species merely resulted in aggravating the evil; it was disease, 'vice', famine, and war which redressed the balance. Yet Malthus, who was fundamentally liberal, found an escape by advising that the poor resign themselves to chastity. The traditionalist thinkers, however, were unanimously convinced that he had struck a fatal blow at the hopes of Condorcet and Godwin.

Having identified the Revolution with rationalism, the traditionalists did not delay in turning against it the most dreaded enemy that rationalism had ever encountered, namely the movement inimical to the primacy of reason. This movement, which had inspired Rousseau and the *Sturm und Drang*, was in the process of flowering, toward the closing years of the century, into what is usually called the first German Romanticism. Cartesian rationalism had promised that intellect would be able to solve the riddle of the universe, and it commanded that reason defend its freedom against instinct and feeling, which were under the sway of matter operating atomically and mechanically. It was a philosophy of endeavour in which science and happiness were the rewards. But there are always mystics waiting to experience the mystery of an inspiration which is pure grace; there are always unruly spirits hoping that chance may bring them happiness, or taking pleasure in risk itself; and there are always artists with an inclination for imagination and fantasy. The wheel of time now brought forward a new generation in quest of something original in order to win its place in the sun. So it rehabilitated the emotions and outlined a metaphysics that endowed emotion with the ability to attain the absolute through intuition while denying reason such access. There were philosophers who were entirely of the same opinion. Kant, in particular, destroyed the Cartesian metaphysic, after which he constructed another by predicating the existence of an ethical sense, which was divine intuition in essence.

Mysticism, which had never been stifled by rationalism, enjoyed an extraordinary vogue at the end of the century. It achieved popularity through the occultism of Swedenborg, de Pasqualis, and Saint-Martin, and began to seep into Freemasonry and Illuminism, since it pretended to rest on scientific theories and discoveries. From medicine it, too, borrowed vitalism, and from physics it borrowed magnetism, which was also considered to be an irrational force. Mesmer's tub, like somnambulism, brought the mind to a state of entranced unconsciousness, at which point it made contact with the supernatural world. Even Catholicism was unable to protect so loyal a son as Joseph de Maistre from its seductive lure.

Nevertheless, the depth of any such movement is not readily evident if its ideology alone is considered and if no allowance is made for the temperament and social condition of its adherents. For the most part, these mystics were either unable to adapt themselves to the social milieu or had not yet succeeded in doing so. They included the sick, or unstable, whose helplessness doomed them to melancholy and even to suicide; the young, thirsting for independence and pleasure and incensed by social restrictions; and yet others who were trying to make their way in the world and who collided with the privileges of rank, fortune, or established reputations. It is not surprising that these people tended to idealize the 'Robin Hood' figure, the righter-of-wrongs, nor that with age or success many of them became wiser. There have always been 'romantics', but the eighteenth century witnessed their proliferation because the rise of the bourgeoisie dislocated social groupings and a growing number of talented but poor young men became irritated and desperate.

Literature and art more or less capitulated to the antirationalist reaction. In the name of reason, the French imposed tyrannical aesthetic rules which greatly restricted opportunities for originality. French works became models everywhere, and critics, especially in Germany, had every opportunity to denounce this 'classic' art as a foreign importation. In this domain, the successes of undisciplined individualism far outweighed risks, while actually promising renown. Originality was sought everywhere—in nature, in little known islands, in the Orient, China, America, and in the works of the forgotten past. The English and Scots ecstatically welcomed the spurious poems of Ossian, and the French invented the troubadour style. Shakespeare was used to justify all the attacks on the three unities of time, place, and action in French classic drama, as well as the attacks on the distinction of literary genres. Even Hellenism, which was just being discovered, was invoked in order to repudiate seventeenth-century tastes.

The plastic arts, less flexible, did not enjoy the same degree of emancipation. The end of the century again witnessed the triumph of the classic spirit, which sought its sources in antiquity and in the Italian Renaissance. It was owing to the genius of David and Canova that this triumph was possible. On the other hand, the new spirit was given a powerful stimulus by the development of instrumental music, a modern art form which created its own rules, and which was pre-eminently romantic in that it suggested rather than described, and was essentially sensual and emotional in its appeal.

In many ways it seemed that the revolutionary upheaval ought to favour this new spirit. The Revolution had emancipated the individual, declared war on all traditions, proclaimed freedom of the press and theatre, and suppressed the privileged groups whose task it had been to assure the maintenance of classical disciplines. It had inflamed human passions, and its numerous and terrible vicissitudes affected a good many people who were to develop a morbid taste for the unstable and the horrible—as the success of Anne Radcliffe's novels aptly demonstrated. Finally, it revived a sense of tragedy arising from the spectacle of so many misfortunes and of man's struggle against the implacable forces of nature and fate. Nevertheless, the effects of the movement were not everywhere the same.

For the time being, Southern Europe was scarcely affected; even in France and England Romanticism had not made much headway. Despite William Cowper and the Lake Poets, it was the classicism of William Hayley which set the fashion in England around 1800, while George Crabbe remained faithful to a discreet and restrained realism. In France, the revolutionary fever had inspired the writing of speeches and hymns, but it had revitalized neither the theatre, poetry, nor the novel. The most likely explanation is a political and social one. In both countries young men found spheres of action other than the realm of thought and the arts. In England, they were attracted to business and politics, and the struggle against France gradually reinforced the trend toward conformity. Wordsworth, Coleridge, and Southey finally gave in under the pressure of the social ostracism inflicted on them. In France, youth either entered the service of the Revolution or emigrated. Until 1815, war captivated their imagination and their craving for fame and fortune. Napoleon himself was a romantic poet who became a

13

man of action, and it was not for lack of trying that Chateaubriand did not undergo the same metamorphosis.

Things were different in Germany, still imprisoned within its medieval casing. The enthusiastic and impulsive Friedrich Schlegel was a kind of Vergniaud who would have nothing to do with revolution, and even the war did not attract him. German patriotism, which was not yet political, was the affair of princes and nobles. Germany's two outstanding poets, Goethe and Schiller, settled down after a hectic youth: the former became minister to Charles Augustus of Weimar, and the latter, professor at Jena. They claimed by studying Greek antiquity to have discovered how man's divergent inclinations could be brought to harmony in the realm of art—the *élan vital* and passion reconciled with reason. Their new humanism summoned the individual to isolate himself in order to develop his own 'totality'. It approached a pantheistic position in philosophy and exercised a keen attraction for a while. Works like *Wilhelm Meister* (1794–1796), the *Wallenstein* trilogy (1798–1799), and *The Song of the Bell* (1799) enchanted the reading public. Wilhelm von Humboldt joined the classical movement, and Friedrich Hölderlin was no stranger to it.

Nevertheless, the attraction was short lived, and quite naturally so, for in no other country was mysticism so powerful. It stood at the very core of Lutheranism, and through Pietism and the Moravian Brotherhood one could trace the connection between Jacob Böhme, the shoemaker and theosophist of the seventeenth century, and the Romantics. Böhme had been read by scholars like Abraham Werner, Karl Ritter, and Franz Baader, who in turn imparted the most unexpected symbolic interpretations to their own positive understanding of his works. After Kant, intuitionism had continued to occupy an ever increasing place in German philosophy, and had finally brought that philosophy to a position of transcendental idealism. In his *Theory of Science (Grundlage der Gesammten Wissenschaftslehre)* which appeared in 1794, Fichte had, in a spiritual insight, seized upon *ego* as the unique reality, which manifests itself in pure activity. He then erected *non-ego* in order to provide ego with a motive for seeking to absorb non-ego. Later, Schelling endowed non-ego with an independent, albeit purely idealistic existence. He believed that nature and ego were but two aspects of the absolute, whose unconscious unity was disassociated by reflection, but which artistic genius could grasp through intuition, and to which it could give expression in its works. Finally, music flourished in Germany as never before. The art of Haydn, who was then producing his greatest works, *The Seasons* and *The Creation*, still breathed the radiant and confident optimism of the eighteenth century. On the other hand, the tragic spirit of Beethoven was already stirring in some of his first sonatas.

The century had not yet come to a close when a group of men, separating themselves from Goethe, and still more from Schiller, took as their banner the words *romantic* and *romanticism*, and thereby derived their success. In 1798 Friedrich Schlegel, together with his brother August, launched a review in Berlin called *The Athenaeum*. It lasted three years. In Dresden in 1798, then in Jena in 1799 (where August taught), they met with Novalis (whose real name was Baron von Hardenberg), Schelling, and Tieck. Tieck had just published *The Outpourings of a Lay Brother Friend of the Arts* (*Herzensergiessungen eines Kunstliebenden Klosterbruders*), which had been left to him by his friend Wilhelm Wackenroder, who had died while still young. Together they outlined a philosophy which Friedrich Schlegel incorporated into his literature course in 1804, but which never took a systematic and coherent form. Inasmuch as they were disciples of the classics, they at first conceived of the world as an inexhaustible flux, continually changing the creations of the life force. Under the influence of Schelling and other savants, they introduced into their philosophy the concept of a 'universal sympathy', which manifested itself, for example, in chemical affinities, magnetism, and human love. Having been moved by the religious effusions of Schleiermacher, they later borrowed from Böhme the idea of a *Centrum*, which was the soul of the world and the divine principle. In any event, it was only the artist of genius who had access to the true reality, through his powers of intuition or even by means of dreams and magic. In him, this mysterious experience transmuted itself into a work of art. This was a philosophy of miracles in which the poet was high priest. Unfortunately, it cannot be said that the miracle was ever really accomplished, since these Romanticists left no great works, the best being those of Novalis, chiefly his *Hymns to the Night* (1798–1799).

They did, however, sow some fertile ideas. A major role was played by August Schlegel's lectures, given in Berlin between 1801 and 1804, in which he defined Romanticism and proclaimed art the highest form of expression in the life of a nation —the very symbol of its spirit. Schlegel taught history a valuable lesson: that beauty knows no universal, and that art must be studied and appreciated primarily in relation to the circumstances under which it is created. Nations, for their part, deduced the corollary that nothing is more valuable to the process of attaining complete national self-consciousness than the study of the monuments of their past. It was through the Romantic Movement that Germany, already on the threshold of a political and social revival, became, in addition, one of the centres of European thought. Its effects on France came at a later time, but its influence in England was immediate. Coleridge, who had already discovered the virtues of intuition, came into contact with the philosophy of Romanticism while travelling in Germany and embraced it wholeheartedly.

Romanticism in itself was not a political doctrine, but since it relied on sentiment in politics as in every other area, its adherents were left without clear principles to follow. With reaction triumphing, and the careers of the Romanticists still ahead of them, they were not long in becoming ardent counter-revolutionaries. Moreover, looking into the past, they discovered the Holy Roman Empire and the papacy, as well as the moving quality of Catholic liturgy and music. As early as 1799, Novalis extolled the Christian unity, which had done so much credit to the Middle Ages, and composed a hymn to the Virgin. He himself remained Protestant, but since Austria had many posts to fill, and offered a sterner resistance to Napoleon, many of Novalis' friends entered the Austrian service and were converted to Catholicism.

However interesting these ideas may be, their influence on public opinion must not be exaggerated. The majority of those who abhorred the Revolution were not inspired by philosophical motives, and if they felt any such need, they looked for it in religion. The closing years of the eighteenth century witnessed a religious renaissance which conservative pragmatism and sentimental intuitionism favoured, but which had its own origins. Aristocracy, just as it had rallied to the side of monarchy, increased its solidarity with state churches and concurred in the opinion that the first of the Jacobins had been none other than the Devil himself. Besides, great catastrophes and protracted wars have always brought the restless and frightened masses back to the altar.

The revival of religion filled a pressing need of Catholicism, which had been the principal victim of disaffection. Both France and the countries she occupied were no more than 'mission lands'. In Germany a new disaster was imminent: the treaties of Basle and Campoformio presaged a general policy of secularization, and Protestants, even counter-revolutionaries, enthusiastically envisaged 'driving the black army from the Rhine'. In addition, enlightened despotism maintained its tutelage. In Germany and Austria, it was the state which trained the clergy in its universities and regarded the *curé* as an instructor rather than a priest. In Spain, Godoy's successors, Francisco de Saavedra and Mariano Luis de Urquijo, had been posing as *philosophes* ever since 1798; in 1799 appeals to the papal court in Rome were forbidden, and there was some thought of seizing ecclesiastical properties in order to procure money. Pius VI had just died a prisoner of the Directory, and Austria scarcely concealed her eagerness to divide the temporal domain of the Holy See with the Kingdom of Naples. Yet contrary to the expectations of her enemies, the misfortunes of the Church turned to her advantage, for they brought her sympathy. England welcomed with open arms the deported French priests, who were to sow the first seeds of an English Catholic Renaissance. Then, too, in order to conciliate the Irish, Burke had never stopped urging that they be granted religious liberty. In Münster, a small zealous group gathered around Franz Fürstenberg and Bernhard Overberg. It was called the 'Holy Family', and in it, such personalities as Princess Galitzin and the Marquise de Montagu (sister of Madame de Lafayette) occupied a shining place. For them, Stolberg's conversion in 1800 portended much. Emperor Paul I of Russia also inspired great hopes. He had been persuaded by Joseph de Maistre and Father Gruber to insist on the re-establishment of the Jesuits, and he had taken under his protection the Order of Malta, to which he was elected Grand Master.

Protestantism, which until then scarcely had been touched by the Revolution, derived nothing but benefit from the religious renaissance. In Germany, Schleiermacher revitalized its mystical fervour in his *Reden über die Religion*, which appeared in 1799, while Wilhelm Wackenroder and the Romanticists were finding their way back to religion by way of aesthetic intuition. At Emkendorf in Holstein, Fritz von Reventlow was the guiding spirit of a circle of piety which was the counterpart to Münster's 'Holy Family'. Stolberg stayed there before his conversion, and even Portalis, a Catholic and future Minister of Cults after the Concordat, was associated with the group. In England, Wesley, who died in 1791, had brought Methodism closer to the Church of England by creating, alongside the lay preachers, a hierarchy which co-opted its members. In 1797 this resulted in the first schism within Methodism, but the sect nevertheless continued to grow by encouraging mysticism among the masses. Methodism exercised a profound influence over the Dissenters. The Baptists advanced by copying Methodist ways, while the Socinian and rationalist Presbyterianism of Priestley and Price were rapidly disappearing. Even in the Anglican Church there formed a small core of evangelicals who tried, although unsuccessfully, to revitalize the church, the most notable of them being Wilberforce. The Dissenters now abandoned their sympathies for the Revolution, and even if their conservative influence over the masses has been exaggerated, it still appears to be indisputable.

France seemed to remain the bastion of rationalism in the world, at least in the critical sense, hostile to tradition and Christianity as in the eighteenth century. Its spokesmen—Destutt de Tracy, Cabanis, Daunou, Volney—were entrenched in the *Institut* and in the great establishments of higher learning, which had been founded by the Convention. They controlled the *Décade Philosophique* through Ginguené, and their disciples taught in the *écoles centrales*, which had been organized in almost all of the *départements*. Rationalism, however, was undergoing changes. Most of the few remaining materialists among the Idéologues were no longer concerned with metaphysics. Influenced by the sciences, they limited themselves to the study of phenomena, and leaned toward experimental positivism.

The sciences were flourishing in France because the Revolution had given them a prominent place in public education.

The Conflict between the Old Regime and the Revolution

Destutt de Tracy and Cabanis intended to formulate a science of the mind, a psychology detached from metaphysics but linked to physiology. Political economy, under Germain Garnier and J. B. Say, laid a less well-founded claim to the dignity of an experimental science. It was a movement fertile in ideas, but did not make great strides until much later. Moreover, this positivism, reflecting as it did the spirit of the Encyclopedists, differed greatly from English empiricism. It appears again in Laplace's *Système du Monde*, in Lamarck's attack on vitalism, and in Charles Dupuis' *Origine de tous les Cultes*. Although the government and the republican bourgeoisie tried to become socially conservative, they in no way lessened their hostility to Christianity. Among the masses, religious habits were certainly very much weakened, for Ercole Consalvi would write at the time of the Concordat that 'the majority of the people are indifferent'.

It should not be forgotten, however, that the philosophy of rationalism in the eighteenth century, far from being embraced by all Frenchmen, had been attacked by numerous writers generally lacking in talent but not in readers. Instead of abandoning their convictions in the revolutionary turmoil, the champions of tradition had become firmer in their beliefs. Their ranks were swelled by a part of the old bourgeoisie, which had been ruined by the inflation and so had developed an aversion for new ideas.

Nor was France spared from mystical and sentimental doctrines of intuition. Occultism had collected its faithful there, and began to flourish around 1800 notably in Lyons with Jean Willermoz and in Alsace where Jean Frédéric Oberlin combined it with German influences. It was in France, in fact, that Romanticism found its most illustrious and by far most influential protagonist, for Rousseau's spell had never lost its force. On the contrary, those who repudiated his political theories were precisely the ones most eager to grant sentiment a leading place in literature and religion, Chateaubriand being a celebrated example. Finally, like everywhere else, some Frenchmen returned to Catholicism, whether from feeling like Joseph Joubert, from conservative convictions like Louis de Fontanes, or simply to find comfort like Bancal des Issarts, the friend of Madame Roland. When at a later time Bonaparte did an about face, these men would provide him with support for

19

concluding the Concordat, in spite of the opposition of those who had brought him to power, and against the will of his own army.

If rationalism had thus reached its limits, the cause is not to be found in counter-revolutionary pragmatism, since the works of Bonald and de Maistre, appearing abroad, had not made any inroads in France. The same was true of German thought. Romanticism in France had no philosophy; it had not even supplanted classicism in art. Literature of the North was read only to discover themes to exploit, or for its picturesque elements, or for its emotional content. The current fashion was Ossian, who had been translated into French by Marie-Joseph Chénier, and from whom Antoine Arnault had drawn his *Oscar* and *Chants Galliques*. Bonaparte, too, became infatuated with Ossian. But in 1800, Madame de Staël for the first time contrasted the literature of the North with that of the South, and advised French classicists to borrow from the former its mood of melancholy and sadness. The better part of the French public continued to be indifferent to the conflict between philosophical rationalism and tradition, and surely nothing can better account for Bonaparte's success. The new bourgeoisie of nouveaux riches, who had risen to wealth through the sale of the biens nationaux, speculation, and government contracts, and who were totally ignorant, cared but little for what Beugnot called 'the sickness of principles'. In this respect, former nobles in the government, like Barras and Talleyrand, who were avowed embezzlers and experts in the art of treachery, displayed a cynical disdain. The high society that haunted the fashionable salons—those of Mmes Tallien, Hamelin, or Récamier—thought only of pleasure. More serious still was the fact that the younger generation, which had grown up in the midst of turmoil, was poorly informed and did not trouble itself about it. The members of this generation were realists, and dreamed only of making their careers. The military provided the path to success, and courage was a sufficient qualification. But even if these realists gave Bonaparte a free hand, as long as he was victorious, they by no means wished for a return to the Old Regime. Indifferent to ideas, they accepted the achievements of the Revolution as a fait accompli, at least to the extent that they profited from it. Thus the majority of the nation remained loyal to the work of the Revolution, and the gulf between France and Europe continued to exist.

The Conflict between the Old Regime and the Revolution

THE AWAKENING OF NATIONALITIES

There was a universal quality in the conflict between the Revolution and the Old Regime. It was a war of class against class, and at first national sentiments did not appear to have been brought into play. Such feelings, moreover, were not considered important in the eighteenth century. Monarchs and the diverse elements of the aristocracy formed a cosmopolitan society of rulers who parcelled out peoples among themselves like flocks, without regard for their national origins. There existed states, but no nations. Although the enlightened bourgeoisie was well aware that the human race admitted of variety, fundamentally they envisaged it as one, capable of attaining a common civilization; and although rationalism had secularized the concept of Christendom, it had also perpetuated it. The Revolution once begun, Louis XVI made an appeal to the solidarity of all monarchs, and the émigrés made an appeal to all aristocracies. This call was not made in vain. Ever since 1790 Burke had advocated a crusade, and so did François d'Ivernois around 1800. By the same token, all men were brothers to the revolutionaries, and all tyrants were their enemies. Until 1815 the struggle retained something of this quality. France maintained friends abroad up to the very end, while at home, irreconcilable enemies remained.

Having called upon men to govern themselves, the Revolution, according to the same canon, summoned nations into being. Partisans of the Revolution proudly styled themselves 'patriots', and to them France was 'the nation'. At first, however, they believed that all would welcome France's gospel, and that in this way civilization would preserve its universal character. Steeped as they were in the belief that tyrants alone made wars and that democracy would bring peace and brotherhood to all people, it never occurred to them that nations might become enemies. Conversely, monarchs and aristocracies were hostile to the national idea, because it seemed to be tied to principles of popular sovereignty and civil equality—'*Nation, das klingt jacobinisch*' ('Nation, that sounds Jacobin'). In the Low Countries, the nobility and the clergy preferred to fall back under the yoke of Austria rather than lose their privileges. Similar fears weakened the national cause in Poland. In Hungary, the magnates remained faithful to the Hapsburgs, even allowing themselves to be partly Germanized once they were allowed a free hand over the peasantry. As for monarchs, they continued to pursue their own anti-national interests. They succeeded in partitioning Poland. The Hungarian Diet in vain asked for concessions from Vienna: Magyar as the official language, customs advantages, and access to the sea through the annexation of Dalmatia or Fiume. But despite the recommendations of the regent Archduke Joseph, Emperor Francis II turned a deaf ear to these demands. In Ireland, the insurrection of 1798 persuaded Pitt to end what remained of her independence, and the government and parliament in Dublin were suppressed. One hundred Irish members and thirty-two Irish Lords were henceforth to sit in Westminster. The island kept its debt and its domestic taxes, but was to contribute two-seventeenths of the imperial expenditures. It was given reason to hope for the opening of the English market. Above all, Pitt, with the support of the lord-lieutenant, Cornwallis and the first secretary Robert Stewart, Viscount Castlereagh, disclosed his intention of repealing the Test Act, which prohibited Catholics from sitting in parliament. He even hinted at the possibility of 'establishing' the Catholic Church in Ireland, provided the government had the right to supervise the choice of bishops—to which ten bishops concurred. This alone sufficed to turn a number of Irish Protestants against the union, men who had at first rallied to the project out of fear. Pitt was forced to resort to bribery by distributing peerages and large sums of money which were, moreover, charged to the Irish debt. Union was finally voted in Dublin on February 5, 1800, and ratified in London in May.

It was the war which gradually brought about a change from cosmopolitanism to nationalism. Attacked on all sides, the French were the first to develop a sense of their own uniqueness. They scorned those who would remain enslaved, and prided themselves on being *La Grande Nation*. The Republic, when it turned to conquest, exploited these feelings by appealing to pride and self-interest. But thus severed from their revolutionary idealism, such sentiments lost some of their purity. From the very beginning, Bonaparte favoured this development, which so greatly contributed to his ascendancy.

England, too, finally caught the national fever from warring with France. At first, the remnants of the Whig Party under the leadership of Fox had ranged themselves on the side of popular sentiment, and had regarded the war as the affair of Pitt and the Tories. But when France made preparations for a descent on Ireland, and when she conquered Egypt, feelings began to change. The invasion of Switzerland converted Coleridge who, in *France: an Ode*, condemned the impious and perfidious enemy, the fickle and cruel race. From then on, Pitt was able to ask of the nation an effort which was greater than prudence would have allowed prior to the change in public feeling.

Meanwhile, France was establishing the principle of territorial and national unity by uprooting the remnants of the Old Regime in Holland, the Cisalpine, and Switzerland. This did much to promote the awakening and growth of local national sentiments. The French intervention benefited Italy in particular, where the nationalists, more numerous than is often believed, suddenly became aware of themselves. But pressed by the necessity of war, France treated these countries like military marches. Charged with the burden of supporting the French army, they soon came to realize the price of independence. Thus, by a fatal reversal that Robespierre had once predicted, France brought about their hostility. When the Russians and Austrians invaded Italy in 1799, they were hailed as liberators.

The danger was still not great, because Germany had not yet been affected. Although the magnificent flowering of arts and letters, and the return to the past which Romanticism had aroused, had succeeded in exalting a feeling of national consciousness in the literate public, it had not yet assumed political form. In contrast to politically organized peoples and their barbaric struggles, Germany, the *Kulturnation*, was by her very weakness considered superior and endowed with a divine mission. This proud attitude did not survive the invasion.

In France, the nation rested to all intents and purposes on a contract. With due allowance for the natural and historic conditions which influence individual preferences, the nation had established its federation on the basis of free choice. In contrast to this revolutionary concept of the nation, a different view evolved in Germany. Herder, and after him the Romantic Movement, regarded the German nation as a living being, born like all others out of the unconscious operation of a life spirit—

23

the *Volksgeist*. Customs, traditions, language, folk songs, and art were but manifestations of this force. Once again we find Germany the centre of future European development. She would become the rallying point against revolutionary France, not only through her emergence as a nation, but also by preaching a different concept of nation—a collective being in which the individual loses all claim to autonomy, and in which freedom, as with the mystics, lies in the cheerful acceptance of submission, and which, repudiating a rationalist and a universal civilization, places a supreme value upon its own needs and passions.

A similar development was taking place in Japan at about the same time. There, Chinese mandarins had previously imparted a critical and rationalistic strain to their teachings. They contested the solar ancestry of the Mikado, and they declared that the gods did not recognize differences among men. But ever since the middle of the eighteenth century, under the leadership of Kamo Mabuchi and his disciple Motoori Norinaga (who died in 1801), there had developed a mystical and romantic revival which had a high regard for Buddhism and its moral precepts and which restored Shintoism and the prestige which the nation had enjoyed in the past. The political consequences of this movement were most significant. According to these innovators, the emperor once again became the son of the gods, the shogun a usurper, and the Japanese a chosen race destined to dominate over a world empire. After the authoritarian and reforming regency of Sadanobu Matsudaira, which ended in 1793, the shogun Ieharu achieved a reconciliation with the court in Kyoto. Nevertheless, the seeds of an imperial revolution had been sown. It is not surprising to find once again the alternation of two eternal courses in the history of human thought. Since, however, there existed as yet no intellectual relations between Europe and the Far East, this similarity between the two ends of the world is well worthy of notice.

CHAPTER TWO

The Consequences of the War and the Terms of the Peace

QUITE APART from the issue of national enmities, there were traditional aspirations of states which, from the beginning, complicated the conflict between France and the rest of Europe. In going to war, the Coalition was not aiming merely to crush the Revolution. The Continental Powers planned to dismember France, while England hoped to seize her colonies and destroy her commerce and navy. This would advantageously terminate the Anglo-French duel begun in the time of Louis XIV and restore British hegemony upon the seas—a superiority that had been recently compromised by the American Revolution. But not all of the problems which had brought the powers into conflict during the eighteenth century were resolved as yet: the Prussian-Austrian alliance would eventually founder over the Polish question; Russian designs in the East and in the Mediterranean worried Pitt; and Spain continued to be apprehensive about England. The allies never succeeded in co-ordinating their efforts, and the disparity of their separate gains only served to accentuate their division. The Continental Powers were beaten, and France was able to negotiate with Prussia, win Spain over to an alliance, and attain and surpass her 'natural boundaries'. The Second Coalition had recaptured Italy and a part of Switzerland in 1799, but like the First Coalition, it

The Consequences of the War and the Terms of the Peace

was already disintegrating. And while England might triumph on the sea, lacking an army she could not by herself subdue France. Nor was her economic position without its weaknesses. The question was whether France, profiting from these European divisions, could achieve victory and secure a lasting peace that would preserve her 'natural boundaries'. All historians of Napoleon regard this as the fateful issue controlling his destiny.

THE CONTINENTAL POWERS

The European monarchs were a singularly mediocre lot. In Austria, Francis II was a solemn nonentity who kept his brother Charles in the background and insisted on conducting all affairs with his devoted but not very intelligent chief *Kabinetts minister*, Count Colloredo. In Prussia, Frederick William III was honest, well-meaning, and not too bright; and although indecisive, he was very jealous of his authority. In Russia, there was Paul I, half mad, inconstant, and cruel. Even the war had not taught these monarchs anything. Austria, for example, still recruited soldiers by impressment, or by drawing lots among the peasants, and they were still enlisted for life. The officers, almost all of them nobles, continued to purchase their posts. In 1798, Archduke Charles had planned to regroup his regiments into divisions, but the war had forced him to give up the project. Neither tactics, nor strategy, nor logistics had undergone any changes.

The Continental Powers were not lacking in men. It has been estimated that between 1792 and 1799 their losses numbered 140,000 killed, 200,000 wounded, and 150,000 prisoners —a large figure no doubt, but their manpower remained far from being exhausted. What was mainly lacking was money. In Austria, despite an increase in taxes, the annual deficit soared from 20 million guldens (or florins)* at the end of Joseph II's reign, to 90 million in 1796. The government had to resort to forced loans, and the debt rose from 390 million in 1793 to 572 million in 1798. England granted subsidies to Austria, and in addition, guaranteed or authorized private loans in London. Nevertheless, financial solvency could be maintained only by issuing paper money, the *Bankozettel*, the value of which had to be pegged by decree in order to finance the campaign of 1800.

* This monetary unit was worth about 50 French sols. AUTHOR.

The amount of paper money in circulation rose from 27 million in 1793 to 200 million in 1801. From then on, the Austrian florin began to depreciate. In 1801 it had lost 16 per cent of its par value on the Augsburg exchange. Weaker still was the Russian rouble, which was being exchanged at 60 per cent of its par value in Leipzig. The Russian debt, which had been contracted primarily in Holland, rose from 43 to 132 million florins under Paul I, and the government issued 14 million new paper roubles every year. Sweden also resorted to printing paper money, which lost over 25 per cent of its value in 1798. It would have indeed been difficult for the Coalition to keep the war going without English subsidies. But did a coalition still exist?

Paul I made a great show of his hatred for the French Revolution: he sheltered Louis XVIII at Mittau, and supported Condé's army. But it had taken the Egyptian campaign to convince him to enter the war. This was because the Eastern question was coming to assume an ever greater importance for Russian foreign policy. Catherine II, not content with dismembering the states of the sultan, had won a privileged position in them—certain rights over the fate of the sultan's Christian subjects, and free passage for her merchant ships through the Dardanelles. This privilege was accorded to England only in 1799, and to France in 1802. The disintegration of the Turkish Empire promised fresh gains. Since 1793, Selim III had striven to organize a modern army, but in many provinces he exercised only nominal authority. Ali Pasha (Tepelini) was carving himself a fief in Albania and Epirus; Pasvan Oglu had seized Vidin, named himself pasha, and was marching on Adrianople; Djezzar controlled Syria; and Abdul-Aziz, leader of the Wahabis, had conquered the entire Nejd and now threatened the holy cities and the Pasha of Baghdad. The Greeks, and particularly the Serbs, were also causing concern. The former, taking advantage of the war, were spreading throughout the Mediterranean, thanks to Turkish neutrality. They penetrated the Black Sea in Russian ships and began forming colonies in every large port. They had heard about the French Revolution through the writings of Adamantios Koraés and Rhigas Pheraios, and they had seen the tricolour streaming over the Ionian Islands. The call of Hellenism had indeed been aroused. The Serbs, exasperated by the depredations of the Janissaries, had given their assistance to Austria in the last Turkish war. Their leaders, Kara George and Nenadovich, were only waiting for an opportunity to resume hostilities on the side of Russia.

Russia gained access to the Mediterranean Sea as a result of Bonaparte's Egyptian expedition. Paul I became an ally of the sultan, and had the Straits opened to his warships. Together with the Turks and the Pasha of Janina, he occupied the Ionian Islands, making them a republic under his protection. Elected Grand Master of the Order of Malta, Paul planned to rule over the island, and on November 3, 1799, Grenville had to promise him that should England seize Malta from France, she would not remain there. Paul also coveted Corsica, landed his troops in the Kingdom of Naples, and promised to restore the King of Sardinia. Thus by reversing traditional Russian policy towards Turkey, he was able to acquire a degree of influence in the Mediterranean never again equalled by his successors. England, intent on recapturing Egypt, was willing to ignore the spread of Russian influence. But Francis II had no intention of letting the Russians have their way in Italy, and Paul, ascribing Suvorov's defeat at Zurich to Austria's treachery, recalled his army. This put an end to Russian participation, since Rostopchin, hostile to the idea of a Coalition, had triumphed over Panin and had been named head of the department of foreign affairs. Paul's defection resulted in isolating Austria, but, more than that, the way was now open to a conflict with England, should she in the future consider herself free to retain Malta. Had not Catherine II once before mobilized the neutrals against England's naval hegemony and prevented her access to the Baltic, which was of paramount importance to British commerce?

Meanwhile, Austria had to bear the brunt of the war alone. Officially, the Reichstag supported the war, but ever since the Peace of Basle, the Holy Roman Empire seemed no more than a shadow. Prussia guaranteed the neutrality of Northern Germany and Hanover. To the north of the line of demarcation—the 'enchanted circle' as it was called by the Austrian Hudelist—the German states enjoyed the advantages of peace and large commercial profits. Prussia's prestige was much enhanced, and Frederick William was rapidly becoming a 'lodestar', an 'antiemperor'. It was quite unnecessary for Gentz, in 1799, to advise Frederick William that he persist in this policy of neutrality, for he was already well set on the idea. Indeed, he counted on becoming the leader of a North German confederation, and he dreamed of territorial expansion. He waited impatiently for secularizations, coveted Hanover, and manœuvred to annex Nuremberg. Austria then, driven from the north, felt discredited in the south by the loss of the left bank of the Rhine; and she also felt betrayed in her designs on Bavaria, although Maximilian Joseph, who succeeded Charles Theodore in 1799, momentarily feared for his succession. As for the Duke of Württemberg, Frederick II, he was embroiled in a chronic conflict with the provincial estates who, on their own account, had already dispatched emissaries to Paris. In these circumstances, the South German princes followed Austria out of fear alone, and they were only waiting for an opportunity to accommodate themselves with France. A union of the German states against France thus became impossible, and the very disappearance of the Holy Roman Empire seemed so likely that Görres had already ironically drawn up its death certificate. Chancellor Thugut of Austria was not worried about it, and he regretted the loss of the Low Countries even less. He did not neglect to seek indemnification in Poland, but like his eighteenth-century predecessors, his interests were cast primarily in the direction of Italy. After absorbing the Venetian states, he hoped to supplant the French in the peninsula from which they had just been driven. In that case, he calculated, not without reason, that Austria would have little cause for complaint in the end.

Would the French win over the Russians and neutralize Austria by abandoning Italy to her? If so, the least that could happen to England was that she would be left without allies.

THE ENGLISH WAR EFFORT

Britain's administration had undergone no changes. It remained antiquated, complex, encumbered by sinecures, and inclined to corruption. Nevertheless, parliamentary government attested to a stability and continuity of purpose that continental despots might well have envied. England's ruling oligarchy did not abound in talent, but it regarded the nation as its patrimony and defended it with tenacity and discipline. Their leader,

The Consequences of the War and the Terms of the Peace

William Pitt, had been unlucky in his undertakings, but they admired his perseverance and cautious empiricism, which had spared England constraints and sacrifices. Recognizing the danger at last, they began to cry out for a reversal of policy. England began to impress sailors and recruit soldiers for the war effort, both drawn from the poorer classes of society. These men were then led by volunteers from the aristocracy, who purchased their commissions. Bodies of fencibles were formed for home service, and the militia was gradually raised to 100,000 men. In principle, they were to be chosen by lot, but in practice, those chosen were allowed to purchase substitutes, and parishes generally bought their contingents for a price. So common had this practice become that the recruitment of regulars eventually dried up. Between 1794 and 1799 the latter were used in the colonies, and the allies, encouraged by English subsidies, were left with the burden of creating a continental diversion which would further England's interests. Grenville frankly admitted that he much preferred to pay the Continental Powers than to send them reinforcements, which would have deprived industry of its manpower. Besides, the money was not lost since it was spent on the British market for supplies which the armies needed.

This was a costly policy. Expenditure rose from £26* million in 1792 to £91 million in 1801. Pitt effected a slight increase in indirect taxes, which in 1797 provided 75 per cent of the revenue, but this was insufficient. Revenues covered 68 per cent of expenditures in 1792, and less than 29 per cent in 1797. The Bank of England discounted exchequer bills only cautiously: £8·5 million in 1792, £17 million in 1797. With the suspension of gold payments, the Bank became more obliging, so that this floating debt surpassed £24 million in 1801. But the most important resource was the consolidated bonds, whose principal rose from £9 million in 1792 to £36 million in 1801. Pitt's ability to maintain the rate of exchange while amortizing the debt shows to what degree the English aristocracy had confidence in its own future, and it also proves that England was already drawing vast sums from her trade and her colonies.

* In 1791 £1 sterling equalled 20 francs (1 Louis d'or), 13 marks, 11 Dutch florins, 8 roubles and 4½ American dollars. The 1791 £1 would be the equivalent of about £5 5s. today.

Nevertheless, England's staying power depended on credit. Since the activity of her capitalists also depended on it, it is understandable that this hitherto unknown system appeared artificial and rickety to the French. It was on the basis of that judgment that France waged its economic war during the entire period.

When, after 1794, war on the Continent took a turn for the worse, the British government made every effort to urge the nation on to new sacrifices. The decisive change did not come, however, until after the Treaty of Campoformio, when England found herself isolated, attacked in Ireland, and threatened in Egypt. With the suspension of gold payments in 1797, Pitt insisted on financial reforms to limit inflation. This time the landed gentry and the middle classes were not completely spared: the land tax was increased and an income tax was introduced. Direct taxes brought in £10·5 million in 1801, compared to £3 million in 1792. But their importance must not be exaggerated, for in 1801, indirect taxes still represented 65 per cent of receipts, and loans over 65 per cent of expenditures. It became evident at this time that a renewed effort would be required to continue the war.

Recruitment proved far more difficult to improve. In 1794 it was easy to find home volunteers by the tens of thousands, for until an actual invasion they remained in their homes and were excused from service in the militia. They were organized by private initiative, and they agreed to fight within a certain radius fixed by themselves. It was expected that they would wage war as in the Vendée, but, in fact, the only thing they had in common with the volunteers of the French Revolution was their name. Luckily for England, they were never put to the test. Meanwhile, the situation in the regular army became so critical that in 1796, country parishes were required under penalty of fine to provide 15,000 regulars drawn by lot. The attempt failed completely, because they preferred to pay the fine. Finally in 1798, it was proposed that militiamen enlist in the regular army in consideration of a bounty. But the idea encountered strong opposition from the lord lieutenants of the shires, who named the officers of the militia and maintained it on the revenues of the land tax, and thus considered the militia their preserve. Nevertheless, this system was finally adopted on

July 12, 1799, and it lasted until 1815. The militiamen answered the call and took part in the expedition to Holland, and later in Egypt. Pitt went no further, not daring to institute compulsory military service.

Nor did he put an end to the confusion in the military administration, which was divided between Dundas, Windham, the Duke of York, and the Home Office. In reality, operations were directed by Pitt, Grenville, and the king. But some progress was made in military technology: mounted batteries were created in 1797, and the artillery was made an independent corps in 1799. Apart from garrisons, the English expeditionary force numbered only about 10,000 men, and, not counting the expedition to Holland, which failed pitifully, the army fought only in the colonies between 1794 and 1807. First the French islands, then the Dutch, then Trinidad; and in 1801, the Swedish and Danish Antilles fell. But 7,500 men perished in San Domingo, which had to be evacuated in 1798, when Toussaint L'Ouverture allied with Sonthonax to drive the English from the island. These successes were naturally due to the action of the fleet, which constituted England's main contribution to the Coalition.

The fleet had grown much larger, although not without difficulties, since the merchant marine was expanding at an even swifter rate. As early as 1793, it became necessary to permit 75 per cent of the crews of English vessels to consist of foreigners. Sailors of all nations, prisoners of war, convicts, strikers, and political suspects were all impressed indiscriminately. Since shipboard life remained unbearable, mutinies were frequent. In 1797, they degenerated into a widespread revolt, which was put down by setting a few examples, but chiefly by increasing pay and prize money. Naval technology scarcely changed. The standard ship of the line remained 200 by 50 feet at midship beam, equipped with 74 guns, two fighting decks, and a 600-man crew; still, the number of towering three-deckers gradually increased. Lord Spencer, First Lord of the Admiralty until 1801, encountered no major obstacles in construction. The English oak and the fir or Norway pine of Scotland were still accessible. Timber from the Baltic region, which the French could no longer buy, as well as American white pine, were also used.

Until 1796, the naval war was pursued ineffectively. Howe and Bridport kept their ships in port during the winter months, thus suspending the blockade. Then the rupture with Spain led to the abandonment of Corsica and the Mediterranean. A resurgence began in 1798 when Admiral Jervis, Earl of St. Vincent, organized permanent cruises at a short distance from the coasts, coupled with a supply service and staggered reliefs. The cruising fleet was ordered to rally at the entrance to the Channel if the French attempted to run the blockade. In the same year, Pitt decided to force his way into the Mediterranean to save Naples. He failed, but managed to seize Sicily and Minorca. Meanwhile, the British fleet was joined by the Neapolitan and Portuguese navies. The Dutch fleet was captured in 1799, and Nelson had already destroyed Brueys' squadron at Abukir. The Army of Egypt was bottled up, and Malta was besieged. It looked as if, barring intervention by Paul I, the Mediterranean would fall to England. But the French had not yet been eliminated: in April 1799, Admiral Bruix was able to leave Brest, reach Toulon, and return to his home port. At least the British admirals were able to safeguard their lines of communication, put a check on the activities of the corsairs, and destroy the enemy's merchant marine. Thanks to the use of convoy escorts, shipowners lost only 500 ships in an average year. This constituted 3 per cent of the total British complement, hardly more than the usual hazards at sea. Marine insurance rates, which had climbed to 50 per cent during the American War of Independence, did not now exceed 25 per cent, and after the peace in 1802, dropped to 12 per cent. England captured 743 privateers and, as early as 1798, held 22,000 sailors as prisoners. The French were left with 200 merchant vessels of more than 200 tons, only one-tenth of their effective strength in 1789.

Of all the Coalition powers, England alone had achieved her ends. Her allies realized this and reproached her for not having sent them troops; this did not strengthen the Coalition. But England had yet to learn that her navy alone could not force France to capitulate, and that ultimately victory would have to be won on the Continent.

FRANCE AND HER ALLIES

With the Coalition powers disunited, France certainly occupied a very strong position on the European Continent. In addition to Avignon, Montbéliard, and Mulhouse, she had annexed Belgium, Maastricht and Dutch Flanders, the left bank of the Rhine (at least up to a line which, leaving the Rhine below Coblenz, reached and followed the course of the Roer), the ancient Bishopric of Basle (which comprised Porrentruy, the valleys of St. Imier and Moutier, and Bienne), Geneva, Savoy, and Nice. France was still the most populous country in Europe. The war had cost her around 600,000 casualties, dead and missing. These losses, however, which were considered unparalleled, had not compromised her strength, which, used sparingly, could undoubtedly repulse any assault. Moreover, France was no longer isolated as in 1793.

Compulsory military service, which had been adopted as a temporary expedient under the name of *levée en masse*, was now established as a permanent principle of recruitment by the Jourdan Law of 19 Fructidor, Year VI (September 5, 1798). Except in the case of invasion, this law limited its demands to a fixed body of men, chosen either by lot or by conscription. But in Year VII, young men who were about to be drafted were given the opportunity to evade the law by jointly recruiting volunteers to make up the contingent of their communes. Bonaparte would add only the privilege of individual replacement, a measure which had been granted and later suppressed by his predecessors. The Directory had, in addition, perfected the *amalgame*,* appreciably improved the cavalry, and reorganized the officer corps: the election of officers by soldiers was greatly reduced by the Law of 14 Germinal, Year III (April 3, 1795).

The spirit of the army had undergone a change. As in civilian life, love of glory and even of money had gradually replaced revolutionary ardour. Yet, despite mutinies instigated by royalist propaganda, the army continued to be the shield of the Revolution. As an instrument of war, it was incomparable. Rapid promotion for bravery remained the popular symbol of

---

* A process whereby raw recruits were immediately mingled with seasoned veterans and were expected to learn the essentials of war while marching on their way to the front. Thus, by dispensing with formal military training, the French armies were able to obtain the men needed to fill the ranks in the shortest possible amount of time. This principle, first tried in 1793, was used with increasing frequency by the later republican governments and during the time of the Consulate and Empire. TRANSLATOR.

34

equality, and attracted the ambitious and fighting young men. The importance given to individual worth, which the Revolution made the essential principle of the modern world, showed its value; this superior social principle gave the French army a decided edge on those of the Old Regime.

For France, no less than for her enemies, the weak point lay in the increasing difficulty of financing the war. Bankruptcy had forced the Directory to liquidate paper money and revert to specie. Reduced to tax receipts alone, the Directory was also ever increasingly exposed to the usual embarrassments of deflation: changing prices, economic paralysis, and a decline in revenues. This financial situation, for which it was not responsible, prevailed throughout its history, and accounted for its unfortunate reputation. The Directory actually made great efforts to improve the financial situation. It ameliorated the direct tax base and even created a new one; it urged, with some degree of success, the drawing up of tax rolls; and it tried to expedite methods of collection, without, however, going so far as to deprive the elective municipal and provincial bodies of those functions. It also increased indirect taxes, and placed them in Year VII under the permanent regulation of the registration, stamp, and mortgage departments. Finally, it established a tax on the use of public conveyances, instituted highway tolls on wagons and beasts of burden, and provided assistance to the towns by authorizing them to institute *octrois*.* The Directory fully realized that important consumer goods (salt, for example) would have to be taxed in order to secure abundant and regular revenues, but these were measures which it did not consider itself strong enough to risk. Consequently, it was left with no alternative but to cut expenditures, which in turn forced it to repudiate two-thirds of the public debt and to neglect public services.

Had the Directory succeeded in balancing the regular budget, it would still have been obliged to finance the war, and this could have been done only on credit. For political reasons, however, forced loans were the only means of borrowing. There were no bankers willing to advance the government the money necessary to keep the treasury going. Since the tax

---

* Taxes on commodities which were brought into towns. Hence, municipal tolls. TRANSLATOR.

collectors kept their funds as long as possible in order to turn them to profit, there was talk of re-establishing *rescriptions*, that is to say, promissory notes made by the tax farmers of the Old Regime against future tax receipts. But who would discount them? The bankers did indeed propose the creation of a state bank, but one which would discount their own paper. In short, the Directory was compelled to pay the *rente*,* pensions, and salaries in bearer bonds, which made it thoroughly detested, and it was forced to abandon the provisioning of the military to private companies who fleeced the government, and who were reimbursed in shares of biens nationaux, timber, future taxes, or in drafts that no bank could cash.

These expedients, which constituted disguised inflation, provoked a wave of frenzied speculation. They also demoralized many government officials and politicians to whom contractors offered bribes in the hope of getting paid. The army suffered terribly, and was enraged at these 'intercessors'. Since the police lacked the means to combat thievery, law and order became increasingly compromised as the economic crisis steadily worsened. The life and morals of the nation were not the only things affected: the penurious Directory exploited Holland and expanded into Italy and Switzerland in order to support its armies. Purveyors, generals, and war commissioners zealously pursued their own selfish interests. The army, and even the state, lived on war; this was the origin of a war party whose incarnation was Bonaparte.

The restoration of public order and finances required time, as the Consulate would demonstrate, but most important of all, a strong hand was needed. The Directory organized its work well (its 'secretariat of state' was later taken over by Bonaparte, as was its Ministry of Police, which Fouché had joined in Year VII), but it failed to consolidate its power. In the first place, the Constitution of Year III had re-established decentralization on a wide scale, and had created a separation of powers in Paris which deprived the national executive of the initiative that war demanded. The executive did not have control of the treasury, and was impeded in its work by insoluble

---

* Various kinds of government obligations, such as bonds, annuities, and other securities (and the interest paid on them)—all of which constituted the public debt. TRANSLATOR.

36

conflicts with the legislative chambers, or between the chambers themselves. In the second place, as long as the former privileged classes resisted the new order, there survived in France a stubborn core of seditious opposition, civil war, and treason, which weakened the government or drove it to violence. In Year VII, the west of France had again taken up arms, the south-west was in rebellion, and an uprising in Provence and Franche-Comté was being prepared for the spring, with foreign connivance and English money.

The counter-revolution could not be expected to subside as long as it retained the support of part of the Catholic clergy. On September 18, 1794, the Civil Constitution of the clergy had disappeared along with the religious budget. Priests were required only to swear loyalty to the Republic, but many of them refused. These were hunted down and interned on the prison ships at Rochefort or Île de Ré, and then deported to Guiana. They were to some degree in contact with Rome and with the former refractory bishops, most of whom lived in England and were subsidized by Pitt. Whether they so desired it or not, their faithful followers were likely recruits for the insurrection.

The priests who had submitted to the laws, and the former constitutional clergy who had reorganized their churches after the Reign of Terror, were unfavourably disposed to the Directory, for, like the bourgeois republicans and the Idéologues, the Directory had lost no opportunity in showing its hostility towards Catholicism. It had sold many churches, imposed the observation of the *décadi* (Tenth Day), forbidden by law all public religious observances, and introduced into the churches themselves Tenth Day worship and theophilanthropy in rivalry to Catholicism. After 18 Fructidor, the Directory began to attack the 'free schools', which were chiefly Catholic. They were to be closed down unless instruction in civic virtue was assured, and public officials were forbidden to send their children to these schools. Had the Republic abandoned this hostile attitude and practised a sincerely neutral policy toward religion, it would undoubtedly have won over the constitutional and the juring clergy and weakened the prestige of the refractory priests. This, however, would have required a far-sighted policy. It would have been necessary to come to terms with the Pope to obtain immediate results, but having already imprisoned and deported him, the Directory would have had too much ground to regain. In any event, its supporters would never have permitted it. The state might have found a bulwark in the attainment of national unity, real or apparent, but such an ambition presupposed a state already strong.

Among France's allies, Spain, who alone truly deserved the name, did what she could; one of her squadrons was even anchored at Brest. But the war was proving disastrous for her. Her fleet, defeated at Cape St. Vincent, had been unable to prevent the loss of Minorca and Trinidad, and the silver of the Indies arrived only with difficulty. There were fears for the Americas, and the fate of the Pope and the Bourbons of Parma and Naples saddened Charles IV. Meanwhile, the Directory increased its demands. It had nothing but contempt for the home of the Inquisition and for a king cuckolded by his foreign minister, Godoy. It coveted Louisiana, and it protested against the consideration shown to Portugal—without even noticing that Talleyrand, having been bribed by the Portuguese, was a responsible party. Exasperated, Spain ended by listening to English proposals. All was not yet lost, but it would have been necessary to conciliate this Old Regime monarchy, whose means were limited, and which was capable of acting only very slowly. Her finances were also in a pitiful state: in 1799, a fixed rate of exchange was given to the *vales reales*,* which were being quoted at 50 per cent off par. With the help of François de Cabarrus, founder of the Banco de San Carlos in Madrid, the French financier Ouvrard had already contracted to provision the Spanish fleet, and he dreamed of grandiose speculative schemes in that country, which the French regarded as an Eldorado.

In addition to the Spanish ally, there were the vassal republics. The Italian ones were lost, and at the battle of Zurich, Masséna was able to save only half of the Helvetic Republic. The Batavian Republic had narrowly missed being lost, and the English had seized its ships. Both of these satellites provided supplies for the French troops and offered important strategic positions. To provide more than this would have required the

---

* Interest-bearing royal bonds circulated as legal tender and issued by the Spanish government to meet its current obligations. TRANSLATOR.

existence of stable governments, something the Directory failed to establish.

There was also a social problem. The privileged classes either emigrated or kept aloof because the French had proclaimed the end of the Old Regime. The bourgeoisie was more disposed to participate in the government on condition that it be granted political power, which was also claimed by the only true francophiles, the Jacobins. Both these parties intrigued with the representatives of the French Republic to bring about coups d'état. Schimmelpenninck, the leader of the moderate Dutch bourgeoisie, wished to create a government which would be agreeable to France, until the time when peace would bring independence. It was only in July 1798 that he was able to organize a definitively constituted Batavian Directory, and it was still not stable. In Switzerland, La Harpe had been able to impose his dictatorship, thanks to the war, but the moderates were planning his overthrow.

Burdened by the military occupation, the masses were hostile in Holland and hesitant in Switzerland. To win them over, it would have been necessary to favour the peasantry, as in France. In Holland nothing was done. In Switzerland, the personal feudal rights of the gentry and the lesser tithes were abolished without indemnity in 1798, but feudal dues and the great tithes were made redeemable. Although the state undertook to pay a share of the indemnity, it planned to do so in biens nationaux, which could therefore hardly pass into the hands of the peasantry. In addition, a land tax was introduced before the old feudal dues were abolished. Finally, French rule annoyed everyone. In these countries, too, government reform was deemed desirable. This was what the Directory thought, and it even proceeded to make certain attempts in this direction that it would never have dared try at home. But it did not have the authority to carry them through. What France lacked most of all in its struggle with Europe, was a government with the energy of the Committee of Public Safety.

THE BLOCKADE AND THE NEUTRALS

The war on the Continent ended French hopes of successfully contesting England's hegemony of the seas. Consequently,

France gave the economic struggle a new direction: she tried to turn against the English the very methods that they had previously perfected. During the eighteenth century, while a blockade might prove bothersome to an enemy, it could hardly paralyse him. In accordance with the principles of mercantilism, the maritime powers saw the blockade primarily as a means of suppressing the enemy's exports in order to seize his markets and corner the supply of specie. Even so, there were still advantages to be had in buying certain raw materials or, given the opportunity, foodstuffs from the other side. Nor, according to mercantile theory, were there any reasons for refusing to sell goods to the enemy, apart from the contraband of war. Thus England applied the blockade with a judicious empiricism, granting licences when convenient even for ports actually closed by her squadrons. Since the number of these ports could never be great, the neutrals had every opportunity to get around the blockade. England had also worked out a maritime law in her own inimitable fashion: enemy goods were declared fair prize even when carried in neutral bottoms, and all or any part of the enemy coast was considered to be under a 'paper blockade' —so that any vessel coming from or sailing toward it was regarded as a blockade runner. Finally, the system was enforced by boarding all merchantmen on the high seas. Thus, the ocean was turned into an English imperium.

The neutrals particularly resented the regulations aimed at the colonies. Colonial traffic had always been foremost in international commerce, and in time of peace every mother country claimed a monopoly of trade with her colonies. But France, and later Spain, being at war with England, renounced these exclusive rights and opened their colonies to neutral shipping. After 1793, as in 1756, England forbade neutrals to reap the benefits of this windfall, intending to bring her own ships to the enemy colonies. Nevertheless, in order to pacify the Americans, who considered themselves the most injured party, England permitted neutrals who were destined for neutral, non-European ports, to load in the West Indies and later re-export the cargo once it had become their own property. This was known as the 'circuit'. Soon thereafter, the British Navigation Act was suspended, owing to a shortage of ships and a desire to use neutrals to export goods to France. In 1798, neutral vessels were granted permission to carry on trade in the West Indies for England or for their own countries. Thus, while retaining a virtual monopoly over colonial products, England turned the neutrals into auxiliaries.

England also granted licences to neutrals in keeping with her needs. In this way her commerce assumed, to a certain extent, the aspects of a controlled economy. Despite their grievances, the neutrals—Scandinavians, Prussians, Hanseatics, and Americans—made huge profits. Hamburg took the place of occupied Holland as the intermediary between England and Germany, and became the largest banking centre on the Continent. It was through the House of Parish that subsidies reached the Coalition. American sales, of which half were in colonial products, rose from $20 million in 1790 to $94 million in 1801. They supplied the Antilles and Spanish America, carried wood and grain to England, and won an important place in the French market and in Hamburg. Americans were perfecting the science of naval construction, and the Baltimore clipper came to be regarded as a model. Finally, because the neutral nations prospered, their businessmen and financiers became resolute anglophiles.

It was now up to France whether she should preserve a large part of her maritime commerce, even with England; all the more so, since the neutrals did their best to evade the British regulations. During the American Revolution, France had accepted the formula which stated that except for contraband, a neutral ship had the right to protect merchandise (*le pavillon neutre couvre la marchandise*). This had allowed her to continue trading, and had won her the Dutch alliance at a time when the League of Armed Neutrality was being formed against England. The Convention had later reversed this policy, the underlying reason being the Treaty of 1786, which had subjected French industry to English competition. The war had provided an excellent opportunity for a countermove. The cotton manufacturers clamoured louder than anyone for a return to protection, and Fontenay, the great merchant from Rouen, became their spokesman. They guided the Convention just as they would later guide Napoleon. Furthermore, the belief persisted that England's economy, and consequently her credit, depended on exports, and that the hardest blow one could strike would be to deprive her of France, her best customer. Such was the reasoning of Brissot and Kersaint in January 1793, and such would be the reasoning of the Emperor at a later time. On May 9, a decree declared enemy property in neutral holds to be lawful prize, and on October 9, a prohibition was placed on English goods.

As long as neutrals were allowed to trade with France, these measures were illusory, since England permitted the neutrals to do so precisely in order to dispose of British goods. Besides, the people regarded the neutrals with disfavour since their purchases forced prices to go up. An embargo was declared in August, and France thereby gave the blockade an airtight character which the English themselves did not.

Shortages of colonial products and raw materials, beginning with cotton, were not slow in making themselves felt. This was not what the businessmen had intended. The blockade was supposed to be flexible like that of the enemy, for the convenience of the mercantile interests. Anxious about provisioning the army, the Committee of Public Safety reopened the ports to neutrals, and the Thermidorians restored their treaty privileges. English goods immediately reappeared. But after the Treaty of Campoformio, when England remained the only enemy and when overland trade was resumed, the protectionists returned to the offensive. The Directory once again forbade British products, and on 29 Nivôse, Year VI (January 18, 1798), adopted an unprecedented measure against the neutrals: their vessels were to be considered lawful prize if they were found carrying any items whatsoever of British origin or if they had merely called at an English port. Neutral vessels no longer appeared, but the United States broke off diplomatic relations with France.

Smuggling, however, continued actively, and France's allies also engaged in it. It was partly in order to check the flow of contraband that Geneva and Mulhouse were annexed in 1798. France and Holland, which together absorbed 18 per cent of British exports in 1792, still accounted for 12 per cent in 1800. The Directory was fully aware that for such an economic policy to be both effective and bearable, France would need a vast continental market. Conquest became in part a necessity of the economic struggle. The occupied countries and Spain were closed to the English, and it was pointed out that the occupation of the Hanseatic towns would insure control over the German market. The continental blockade was beginning to take shape, and the world was already being divided into two very unequal parts: France and her allies on the one hand, England and all other countries on the other. The two principal belligerents were now forced to consolidate their respective positions in order to survive.

France had suffered serious losses. The most terrible blow had been the loss of her colonial trade, which had accounted for a third of her imports and a fifth of her exports in 1789. A part of the Continent remained closed to her, and she had not been able to recover her former position elsewhere. Despite the fact that she had increased in size, her sales fell from 441 million livres in 1789 to 272 million in 1800. The revolutionary crisis had affected every industry, and some had recovered only with difficulty. More than half the looms were idle in Lyons, and cloth manufacture had been reduced by more than two-thirds since 1789. After having succumbed to a runaway inflation, France now found herself a prey to the ills of deflation, which added to the general feeling of insecurity. Metallic currency continued to be scarce, and credit was nonexistent. Interest rates varied from 3 per cent to 7 per cent per month. The decline in prices paralysed industry. A succession of good harvests, which in itself should have had a calming effect, provoked a further decline in prices, and reduced the buying power of the peasantry. The Directory could do nothing except redouble its encouragements. But this was only a passing crisis. Given a government with renewed strength, and given the re-establishment of peace on the Continent, metallic currency would gradually reappear, new avenues of trade would emerge, and production would recover.

The French Revolution had created conditions favourable to economic progress: freedom, thanks to the abolition of guilds, and unity of the national market, through the suppression of internal customs duties, the reduction of tolls, and the adoption of the decimal system. It had also opened new vistas in the annexed lands, where French metallurgy, for example, could avail itself of the resources of Belgium and the Saar. There was still an abundance of labour in the countryside. The blockade, if it had been applied with expediency rather than for purely warlike ends, would have had only salutary results, by providing the protection necessary for nascent capitalism. It did in fact exercise a favourable influence on the metallurgical, chemical, and especially the cotton industries. Cotton continued to be the most innovating industry, and the most alluring for capitalists. The manufacture of spinning jennies increased greatly, and Christopher-Philip Oberkampf had already begun operating the first calico printing machine in 1797. Several captains of industry made their appearance and founded factories: Boyer-Fonfrède in Toulouse, Richard and Lenoir in Charonne, and Bauwens in Passy and Ghent. Machinery was only in its infancy, and was still unknown in the manufacture of cloth; William Cockerill, an English mechanic who had crossed over to the Continent, had only just been called to Verviers. Silk was still being spun by Vaucanson's method, and Jacquard had not yet perfected his weaving loom. Metallurgy registered no progress. Except in the Anzin mines, no use was made of steam power until Bauwens adopted it in Ghent in 1799. But since France was sheltered from English competition, she could afford to mechanize at leisure.

In any event, the French Republic—where the great majority of the population were peasants who practised mainly a form of natural economy—could have lived, if necessary, from her own resources. Agriculture, which had also been released from its fetters, improved, but slowly. The rural community retained its practices of compulsory crop rotation, common pasturage, and other time-worn rights. In fact so strong was this attachment that no one in the revolutionary assemblies ever dared to suggest that a redistribution of land be imposed to uproot these customs. Nor had much of the common land been divided. While artificial meadows, tobacco, chicory, and potatoes made small gains, land reclamation, irrigation, and planting declined; roads continued to be in bad repair, and a rural police simply did not exist. Yet the social structure of the countryside had improved, and thus increased the country's powers of resistance. The number of small landowners had grown considerably, at least in certain regions: by 13,000 in the Moselle, by 20 per cent in the Côte-d'Or, and by 10,000 in the Nord. At the same time, large-scale farming generally declined in favour of more moderate holdings. Naturally there remained many landless day labourers, more or less condemned to begging, and the stability of the rural population depended on the harvest as always. But ever since the disappearance of the tithe and feudal dues, the government had no more to fear than passing disturbances.

England could no more defeat France with the blockade than with the guns of her fleet. Moreover, should the Republic succeed in restoring peace on the Continent, her economic position could once again become satisfactory. The question of knowing whether England was, in this respect, exposed to collapse is far more complex.

THE STRENGTH AND DANGERS OF BRITISH CAPITALISM. EUROPEAN EXPANSION IN THE WORLD

England profited from an enormous advance in capitalistic production. Its growth continued to be favoured by the rise in prices, which had begun around the middle of the eighteenth century and which persisted throughout the Revolutionary and Napoleonic periods until the second decade of the nineteenth century. The basic cause for this rise is to be found in the great increase in currency, due first to the increased production of the American mines, but also to the appearance of fiduciary money in a number of countries such as Denmark, Sweden, Russia, Austria, France, Spain, and the United States. The emission of paper money was generally accelerated by the war.

By driving out fortunes, the revolutionary crisis caused the metallic supply of foreign nations to increase. Much French specie found its way to England, Holland, Prussia, and Hamburg. An international syndicate (with which Napoleon would later have to cope) involving Baring of London, Hope and Labouchère of Amsterdam, Parish of Hamburg (not to speak of Boyd, established in both England and France), and foreign bankers in Paris, notably Perregaux, were making enormous profits by speculating on the *assignat*, usually selling it short. Little is known about the consequences of the inflation on the European Continent. The prices of colonial products increased greatly in Hamburg from 1793 to 1799, but it appears that the abundance of money operated to increase speculation rather than production. In any case, it was England who most profited from the inflation.

The Bank of England was the only bank issuing notes that inspired confidence, and after the occupation of Holland, England became the surest refuge for capital. In 1794, the Bank purchased £3·75 million worth of precious metals, instead of the average £650,000. Its banknotes in circulation rose from £11 million in 1790 to £15 million in 1800. Until 1795 it discounted commercial paper at less than 3 per cent. The rate increased only after the suspension of the gold standard in 1797: in 1800 it rose above 6 per cent. Moreover, England was the only country where banking developed in the provinces. In 1792 there were 350 banks issuing notes without any sort of control. They financed local businesses, so that the monetary inflation was accompanied by an inflation of credit. Momentarily compromised during the panic of 1793, these banks prospered afterwards more than ever. In 1804 they numbered nearly 500. Prices rose almost continuously. Taking as an index 100 for the year 1790, they reached 156 in 1799. Wheat, priced on the average at 45 shillings a quarter between 1780 and 1789, leaped to 55 shillings in the following decade. Wages rose proportionally far less, so the margin of profits increased. Since the inflation made money cheap, everything stimulated the spirit of business enterprise.

The rise in prices might have resulted in hindering exports, but for the suspension of the gold standard. The abundance of money had made it possible for Pitt to obtain loans, and he had thus been able to deal with the Bank. But he was still forced to make the Bank discount an increasing quantity of exchequer bills. In 1795 the Bank held exchequer bills totalling nearly £13 million at a time when its cash reserves were less than £5·5 million. Then too, since Pitt was forced to pay in cash for the expense of the expeditionary forces, for the grain purchases of 1796, and for the foreign subsidies (a total of more than £28 million from 1793 to 1799), he compelled the Bank, despite the law, to advance him a part of its cash reserves which, early in 1797, did not exceed much more than £1 million. Its banknotes were then declared inconvertible, and remained so until 1821. Since the Bank of England was the keystone of the entire credit structure that sustained the economy, the consequences of this action could have been disastrous. But there was no panic. The people, unacquainted with the methods of John Law or the assignats, never realized that the pound was in danger. Pitt also reassured the capitalists, persuading them by means of an energetic fiscal reform that he had no intention whatsoever of resorting to paper money. With peace restored on the Continent, he spent only £2 million in 1797 and 1798 for the support of the armed forces in Europe, and for foreign subsidies. The pound sterling was at a premium, and the Bank's cash reserves were brought to £7 million in 1799. In fact, the Bank henceforth accepted a far larger quantity of exchequer bills, and there was some governmental inflation, but it was moderate enough not to ruin the currency as in France, and it spared England the deflation which had overwhelmed the Directory. But this was only a lull in the storm. In 1799 the war was resumed on the Continent, and scarcity compelled the government to make new grain purchases which cost nearly £3·5 million. The Bank's reserves fell off, and this time the rate of exchange dropped. The pound lost 8 per cent of its face value in Hamburg and 5 per cent in Cadiz in 1799. Although it was not long before this crisis impaired the nation's morale, the decline of the pound in itself, benefited the capitalists: they were paid in cash for exports, while they themselves paid wages in depreciated paper currency. England's monetary and financial policy, by its empirical methods, attested to a degree of expertness of which no other country was then capable.

The industrial revolution owed its progress to this policy, but it advanced more slowly than has sometimes been believed. In the cotton industry, which was the most advanced, weaving was still done by hand. Edmund Cartwright's power loom was first adopted only in 1801 in Glasgow, and its use spread only after William Radcliffe's invention of the dressing machine around 1804. The woollen industry was still in its trial stage; it made little use of the spinning jenny, and Cartwright's machine for spinning wool combings was not perfected until 1803. Coal mining remained backward despite the growing expansion of rails and the use of steam engines. With the exception of a few cotton mills, the steam engine was not yet used in industry. Most cotton mills were still content with the water-frame. In communications, interest was still centred on canal construction, and there were few good roads. The slowness of transportation and the constant decline in wages enabled traditional manufactures to hold out energetically, and capital continued to be concentrated in commerce rather than in the creation of factories. Some contemporary captains of industry like David Dale, who was the father-in-law of Robert Owen, and Radcliffe of Stockport, began with the putting-out system. But Crompton's spinning mule, although not in use everywhere, gave to cotton spinning an irresistible force. Knitted goods and loom-made lace prospered. Metallurgy was extensively modernized, and engineers, the most famous of whom was Bramah, inventor of the hydraulic press, were rapidly increasing the number of machine tools. In all branches of production where it became established, the machine guaranteed England world supremacy.

According to official valuations of the customs house, based on a scale of prices which had prevailed at the end of the seventeenth century, Britain's balance of trade should have been constantly favourable. In 1799, for example, the balance of payments surplus comes to £5 million. Industrial progress has always been cited as the cause. In reality, reference to the real value of imports and exports suggests the contrary conclusion, that except for a very few years—only one, 1802, between 1798 and 1815—Great Britain's balance of trade showed a deficit: £10·5 million in 1799, and almost £20 million in 1801. If industrial exports increased in quantity, their prices also declined, a factor, moreover, which allowed England to retain and win new markets in spite of the difficulties presented by the war. England became nonetheless wealthier. The balance of accounts was redressed by freight charges, insurance, commissions, and above all by the exploitation of overseas territories—the Negro slave trade, the funds invested in plantations, the salaries and pensions of officials of the East India Company, the colonial speculations of private traders, the riches which the 'nabobs' brought back from the colonies, and the return on capital invested there.

The rise in prices also benefited agriculture. England at this time no longer produced enough grain for its home consumption, and the war made purchases so expensive that the Corn

Laws lost their effectiveness, as long as wheat prices remained so high. The result was that more wheat was planted, since it became more profitable than stock farming. Enclosures were also extended on a scale larger than ever before, making this a golden age for landlords as well as for farmers. Improvements in agricultural methods continued, and in 1793 Sir John Sinclair and Arthur Young were placed at the head of a Board of Agriculture. The agrarian revolution had also affected Scotland. There the clan chiefs, who were landlords and who wished to devote their estates to stock raising, evicted the Highland tenant farmers, who were left with no choice but to emigrate. In regard to her food supply, this agricultural prosperity strengthened England and made her less vulnerable. It also enabled small landowners to hold out and even increase in numbers in certain counties. Actually there were not many left, but at least they were content with their lot, and along with the farmers they constituted an element of stability.

English capitalism, despite its progress, did not yet entertain the idea of free trade. Far from renouncing the Corn Laws, both landowners and farmers demanded that they be strengthened. Manufacturers remained faithful to mercantilism to the point of prohibiting the exportation of machinery. But at home they increasingly evaded the regulations limiting the number of apprentices and authorizing the establishment of a minimum wage. Workers, on the other hand, continued to invoke the statutes of labourers and backed up their demands with blacklists and strikes, which were forbidden in principle, but which the justices of the peace were reluctant to condemn—inasmuch as the employers themselves set the example in breaking the law. Also worthy of note was the Combination Act of July 12, 1799. Enacted at a time when the authorities allowed the laws favourable to workers to fall into abeyance, the act punished every kind of strike, as well as working men's associations and collections of funds intended to support strikes. The employment of foundlings, women, and uprooted peasants, plus the advances made by mechanization depressed wages, which trailed far behind rising commodity prices. In addition, the truck system and the imposition of arbitrary fines helped to reduce wages even more. Beginning in 1795, however, wages were supplemented out of the receipts of the poor tax, such assistance being calculated in relation to the price of bread. This accounts for the relative resignation of the working classes.

Aside from France, English industry was almost unrivalled. Except for a few mining works and the great Silesian metallurgical industry—a monopoly of a few magnates, or of the state —capitalism on the Continent ignored the steam engine and remained commercial. The cotton industry prospered in Saxony, Switzerland, and Swabia, but it was not until 1786 that the spinning jenny was introduced in Chemnitz, and the knitting machine appeared only in 1797. Besides, the war affected traditional industries, such as Silesian linen, which was completely ruined.

In agriculture, the Baltic states, which produced for export, began to imitate England. Above all this meant dissolving the village community and reconstituting the divided land strips into unified plots capable of escaping the system of obligatory crop rotation and common pasturage—in short, working toward enclosures. The states also sought to abolish serfdom and to arrange the redemption of the tithe, feudal dues, and corvées so as to transform the peasant into a landowner or a wage-earning day labourer. This reform had been operating in Denmark ever since 1781, and it was extended in principle to Schleswig-Holstein in 1800. In Prussia the king applied it to his own domains.

As an importer of grains, England could not help but profit from these reforms. She likewise regarded favourably the advances made in the United States, still purely agricultural, and was particularly pleased by the progress of sea-island cotton, which had been brought over from the Bahamas in 1786. It had been introduced in Glasgow for the first time in 1792, and had been immediately acclaimed by cotton spinners. No sooner had the problem of ginning been solved by Whitney's invention in 1793 than exports reached 8 million pounds in weight, and by 1798 this figure had already doubled. It was a development of far-reaching significance to the United States, for slavery thenceforth became a fundamental institution in the South, and planters began to covet Florida and Louisiana. For the time being, however, the North saw in it only an opportunity to put its capital and ships to work. The introduction of English technology was still in its very beginnings, and the great fortunes of the Astors and the Girards were being built by trade, shipping, and speculation in land.

Deprived of the markets controlled by France, yet relieved of French competition, England compensated at the expense of her allies and the neutrals. It was through the Hanseatic ports that she entered upon the economic conquest of Germany. Her exports to Bremen and Hamburg increased sixfold between 1789 and 1800. At the Frankfurt and Leipzig fairs she came into contact with Swiss, Austrians, Poles, and Russians. Her cotton goods and her yarn in particular drove out Swiss and Saxon products. The world of finance looked to London. The elector of Hesse invested his capital there, and it was by helping him to do it that Meyer Amschel Rothschild of Frankfurt extended his business; in 1798, his son, Nathan, established himself in England, and became wealthy soon after. The Baltic region also became an English preserve of great importance for supplies of naval stores, grains, and textiles. At the beginning of the nineteenth century, 72 per cent of British imports came from Prussia and Russia, 75 per cent of her grain from the port of Danzig alone. French resistance fared better in the Mediterranean. She embarrassed England by conquering Italy, but she failed to eliminate her. After 1798, however, France was driven from the Levant.

The naval struggle increased the importance of the continental routes between the Mediterranean and the northern seas. The closing of the Rhine had seriously imperilled communications across France, Italy, Switzerland, and Holland, which, until then, had been more or less secure. Ever since 1790, France had interrupted traffic along the left bank by bringing her customs posts to the river, and the occupation of the Rhineland and Holland was a new blow to this trade route. With the mouth of the Rhine closed, Cologne's trade was reduced to less than a third of its previous volume by 1800; only a portion trickled through Emden to Frankfurt. To the south, Switzerland was cut off from Genoa. As in the time of Louis XIV, the transcontinental route receded toward the east. Henceforth it would pass through Hamburg and Leipzig in order to reach Venice, or preferably Trieste.

We possess only problematic estimates based on customs house valuations (*official values*) to indicate the fluctuations of

British commerce up to 1798, but the trend is clear. Exports would have risen from £20 million in 1790 to £35 million in 1801, and taken together with imports, the volume would have increased from £39 million to £67 million. In terms of *real values*, exports rose from £42·6 million in 1798 to £52·3 million in 1800, and taken together with imports, the volume increased from £99·1 million to £118·8 million. The tonnage of departing ships increased by a third, reaching almost 2 million tons. It was during the war that the London docks were constructed and equipped with bonded warehouses. The cotton industry, more than any other, profited from this rise. Its exports soared from £1·5 million to £6 million in 1800; and imports of raw cotton rose from £734,000 in 1797 to £1,663,000 in 1800. That same year (1800) 2 million tons of coal and 1½ million tons of wrought and cast iron were exported.

England also doubled her shipments to the United States. Like the latter, her eyes remained fixed on Spanish America, where her occupation of Trinidad served primarily for smuggling. The unrest there promised great prospects. United States independence, the suspension of the *exclusif*,* and the abolition of slavery in the French Antilles had shaken the whole colonial system. Above all, the Creoles wanted freedom of trade, as did Belgrano in Buenos Aires, and Spain had been forced to admit neutrals into her colonial ports. Some of the colonies were also beginning to aspire to political independence. In Mexico and in Venezuela, conspiracies resulted in bloody repressions. After first having made his appeal to France, General Francisco Miranda turned to England when Spain changed sides in the war. In London he met Nariño and O'Higgins, and was to have founded a 'Lautaro Lodge' to prepare a general insurrection. In any case, in 1798 he solicited the aid of Pitt in the name of a committee formed in Spain at his instigation, but Pitt referred him to the United States, which had for the moment broken with France.

England, mistress of the seas, was now in other parts of the world the only nation capable of imposing the authority of

---

* A term denoting a system of exclusive colonial trading rights, whereby a mother country prohibited its colonies to raise or manufacture anything that might compete with its own goods, to trade with other countries, or to use any ships other than its own in foreign trade. TRANSLATOR.

the white man. It was a task to which she was not much disposed. Although the mercantile view had not adopted Bentham's hostility toward colonies, the example of American independence did not encourage further colonizations. Rather, England's imperialism was commercial. Still, the British Empire continued to grow. The French Antilles were yet good for the taking. Enormous amounts of capital were invested in Dutch Guiana, resulting in a tenfold increase in production. The navy needed anchorages like the Cape of Good Hope. Colonial administrators, who descended from the nobility, satisfied their yearning for action by spontaneously pushing for further conquests. In Africa, the colony of Sierra Leone was founded in 1792, Mungo Park explored the Niger as far as Timbuktu, and the Cape was taken from the Dutch. In Australia, Captain Arthur Phillip had landed the first gang of convicts at Sydney in 1788.

But it was in India above all that the English expanded, after the arrival of Richard Colley, Earl of Mornington, afterwards Marquis Wellesley. He annexed part of Mysore following the death of Tippoo Sahib in 1799, and in 1800 established his protectorate over the Nizam, sovereign of Hyderabad, who had obtained the rest of Mysore. Then he attacked the Marathas. He kept a close watch over the Punjab, where Ranjit Singh had forced the Afghans to cede Lahore in 1794. Finally he attended both to Persia, where Sir John Malcolm secured a treaty in 1801 that opened the gulf coast to the English, and to the Red Sea, where Perim was occupied in 1798 and where Sir Home Popham was later dispatched to obtain the Arabian coffee monopoly and to prepare an expedition of sepoys against Egypt.

Had it not been for the war in Europe, the Far East would very probably also have fallen prey to European encroachments. In Indochina, Bishop Pigneau de Béhaine helped Nguyen Anh recapture Cochin China from the rebellious Tayson mountaineers, and he remained Nguyen's counsellor until he died. Nguyen then gradually reconquered Annam and Tonking, where the Le-Loi dynasty had been dethroned, and he assumed the crown in 1803 taking the name of Gia Long. Nevertheless, French influence had fallen to nothing. In China, the Manchu dynasty reached its peak under Ch'ien Lung, who died in 1799 after having conquered the frontier provinces. Not content with colonizing these provinces, the Chinese were already spreading in numbers into Cochin China and the Philippines. They reached as far as Siam and Bengal, and were the only foreigners admitted into Japan. At home they traded with Europeans only at the Portuguese trading post of Macao, which was frequented by hardly any but the English and Americans after the dissolution of the Dutch East India Company. Sent to Peking in 1793, the Englishman George Macartney was unable to obtain any concessions. But after the death of Ch'ien Lung, his cruel and crapulent son Chia Ch'ing (1796–1820), who was threatened by revolts fomented by secret societies, was no longer in a position to resist anyone attacking in force. The English, however, were busy elsewhere. Japan was even more tightly closed. Unable to feed her population, which was continually being decimated by famine, Japan nevertheless prohibited the importation of grain and forbade emigration. Each year she admitted only a few Chinese junks and one Dutch vessel to which she sold some copper at Nagasaki. Quite weak militarily, Japan witnessed with misgiving the arrival of English and especially Russian ships in the Sakhalin, Kuriles, and even at Yezo in 1792.

Missionaries have often paved the way for merchants and soldiers, but at this time they were primarily concerned with America. In China, Ch'ien Lung persecuted the Lazarists, who were successors to the Jesuits, and their mission, whose recruitment had been interrupted by the Revolution, disappeared in 1800. A new development was the entry into the lists by the Protestants, who had hitherto been represented by only a few Moravian Brothers. It was, in fact, England which changed the situation. The first incursions were made by the Baptists in 1795; and in 1799 Joshua Marshman landed in Bengal, where he was given a very bad reception by the East India Company.

Emigration among the whites came almost to a standstill. It was rather through an excess of births that the settlers of North America multiplied and advanced towards the West, pushing back the forest. In the United States, Kentucky and Tennessee were admitted as states in 1791 and 1796, Ohio in 1803. But in 1800 the West still numbered only 370,000 inhabitants out of more than 5 million. Vancouver explored the Pacific coast from 1790 to 1795, and the Russians had begun to appear there, but between the Atlantic and Pacific there existed no connection other than the trading posts of the Hudson's Bay Company, which had reached as far as the Columbia River. In 1793 Alexander Mackenzie still preferred to venture into the solitude of the Arctic regions.

With Latin America no more than a hope, Europe and the United States constituted the markets on which the existence of England depended. That these markets might sooner or later be threatened was considered not entirely impossible. On the Continent, industry could not help but feel the effect of British competition. To save their spinning industry, Switzerland and particularly Saxony were forced to modernize their equipment—the first water-frame machine appeared at Chemnitz in 1798. Thus an embargo on British goods would have been as useful to them as it was to France. Then too, the British blockade continually gave rise to diplomatic difficulties. In 1794 Denmark and Sweden had drawn up a new league of neutrals. Alone they were powerless, but if Russia joined, Prussia and North Germany would follow suit, and the Baltic would be closed. The United States presented an even more obvious danger to British commerce. To the question of the blockade had been added that of the American sailors that England purposely confused with the nationals she sought out and impressed from aboard neutral vessels. Washington and the Federalists confined themselves to protests, but in 1800 Jefferson became president, and it was likely that he would prove less accommodating.

Nor must it be forgotten that, because of the war, the conditions of world trade were not entirely sound. In London, Amsterdam, and Hamburg, speculation on colonial commodities took the form of reciprocal credit arrangements, and capital was immobilized in stock accumulation. As the Elbe froze over and shipments stopped late in the winter of 1799, prices rose to dizzy heights in Hamburg. When the thaw set in before the spring fairs, ships began to pour in and a drop in prices followed, reaching as much as 72 per cent in sugar. At the same time the war resumed, and in August, on the eve of the invasion, Amsterdam bankers cut off credit. In Hamburg 136 firms failed, and the House of Parish lost over a million marks. The crisis had its repercussions thoughout Europe, and especially in

London, where at least twenty merchants went bankrupt. The cotton industry was considerably shaken, and factories either shut down or cut wages. It was in order to curb the labour unrest that the Combination Act was then passed. As it happened, the financial and monetary situation was growing worse, and finally the harvest of 1799 and 1800 proved exceptionally bad. The quarter of wheat rose from 49 shillings at the beginning of 1799 to 101 shillings in February 1800.

France failed to attain her goal by shutting out the English, for British commerce found new markets and prospered more than ever. In believing England's economic structure to be weak and artificial, the French were mistaken because they overlooked the wonders of the credit system. Yet it is true that England's economic structure was a delicate mechanism, automatically subject to intermittent checks, and capable of breaking down through a combination of external circumstances such as the policies of other states and bad harvests. Precisely such a threat was looming in England, and it was quite possible that a time would come when, disheartened, she would consent to make peace.

THE TERMS OF THE PEACE

To profit from such an occasion, the Republic had to restore peace on the Continent. She would have to fight and conquer once again, and then, when the treaty was signed, re-establish internal order and disarm the counter-revolutionary forces. Otherwise, their persistent appeals abroad would bring about a renewal of hostilities at the first crisis. Success also depended, however, upon just which of its conquests France intended to keep.

After 9 Thermidor, French policy had gradually turned to the acquisition of natural frontiers. In the Constitution of Year III, the Thermidorians had forbidden the surrender of any territory whatsoever. At that time (August 1795), French territory had included, by reason of conquest, only Savoy and Nice. But on 9 Vendémiaire, Year IV (September 30, 1795), the Convention annexed Belgium, and this acquisition was held to be sanctioned by the constitutional plebiscite. Henceforth, the plebiscites of 1793 were also invoked to justify France's claim to the left bank of the Rhine, contrary claims to which were abandoned by Prussia at Basle, Austria at Campoformio, and by the Holy Roman Empire at Rastatt. Carnot, a member of the Directory until 18 Fructidor, did not approve such aggrandizement, and the Idéologues, who propelled Bonaparte to power, were of virtually the same opinion. On November 1, 1799, one of them, probably Daunou, declared in the *Décade Philosophique* that the Constitution of Year III, by fixing the territorial limits of the Republic, had decreed 'eternal warfare and the total annihilation of the French people'. This did not mean that the republicans would have to negotiate on the basis of the 'old limits', as the royalists were made to promise by France's enemies. France could still expand into Walloon Belgium and into the Saar.

The majority of the nation would surely have approved this moderation. What it wanted above all else was peace, as the article in the *Décade*, which was destined to prepare the coup d'état, indeed proves. Nevertheless, the difficulties of such an attitude must not be disregarded. In its struggle against royalism, the Directory had never ceased to appeal to national feeling, so that the republicans developed the habit of identifying the Revolution with the conquest of the natural frontiers. Consequently, they prided themselves on having completed the work of the monarchy. The army would not have looked favourably upon the loss of its conquests. If the army secured peace by means of fresh victories, how could the government be less demanding than its predecessors?

The Directory had let Bonaparte set a dangerous precedent by his formation of the Cisalpine Republic beyond the natural frontiers. It was an act which he subsequently repeated in Rome and Naples. He established himself in Piedmont, made the canton of Valais a republic in order to control the Alpine passes, and behaved like an overlord in Holland and Switzerland. Still, it could be argued that the war justified such a policy. With the peace signed, France would assuredly not lose interest in what took place along her natural frontiers, but it did not follow that she would have to maintain her armies in these adjacent lands. She might well content herself with guaranteeing their independence in conjunction with the other powers. There is no doubt that public opinion would have supported the government in this respect. After so many disappointing experiences, the Girondins' enthusiasm for revolutionary propaganda had faded, and no one would blame Bonaparte for not having re-established the Roman or Parthenopean Republics.

A lasting peace was impossible as long as France went beyond her natural frontiers, but assuming she went no further than that, would the Continental Powers have granted her even that much? It has been denied, but without convincing reason. For Prussia, only the promise of indemnities in Germany mattered, and Russia had not gone to war for the sake of the left bank of the Rhine. Austria would be the most recalcitrant, but would have been pacified by territorial compensations, especially by a renunciation of French claims in Italy.

There remained England. Pitt had stated at various times his refusal to negotiate without a full guarantee of England's security, and that this could not be obtained as long as France occupied the Low Countries. He further stated that France would have to be deprived of at least the major part of the left bank of the Rhine which, added Grenville in 1795, would then be reunited with a Belgium in Austrian hands. While it was not true that England's security was their only concern—they also wished to deprive France of Savoy—nevertheless it cannot be denied that one of the cardinal points of England's foreign policy had always been to preserve the Low Countries from French domination. Only now the Low Countries would have to be recaptured, and this was an undertaking in which England could not succeed without the help of her continental allies. If France came to terms on the Continent, it would then be a matter of a war of attrition. Economic circumstances might then induce England to resign herself to the situation, especially if the seas and the colonies were left to her uncontested. The crisis of 1797 had forced Pitt to suggest such an accommodation, and in 1799 all signs were pointing in the same direction. The danger, however, was that France might attribute England's difficulties to nothing other than the blockade she had imposed to counter that of her rival. In such a case the temptation might arise to contest England's rule of the seas as well, by increasing the pressure through an extension of the blockade to all of Europe. Then the war on the Continent would have begun anew and would have truly become a *'guerre éternelle'*, not because France would have reached her natural frontiers, but because she would have overstepped them.

If wisdom had prevailed in France, it would have meant that Europe, so intensely hostile to the regicidal Republic, would have forever renounced the idea of recovering all or part of France's prodigious conquests. But this is not the way to look at the question. In 1799, as always, the problem for a statesman was not how to arrest the course of history. Rather, it was a matter of knowing whether France had a chance to secure peace for a decade or two, while retaining her so-called natural frontiers, and to regain her strength in order to prepare to defend them with still more energy than before. That the answer was 'yes' cannot be doubted; but would the republican members of the Directory have been capable of it? This is by no means certain, but at the end of 1799, the decision was no longer theirs. They had placed it by their own choice in the hands of a single man.

CHAPTER THREE

The Coming of Napoleon Bonaparte

THAT THE FRENCH REVOLUTION turned to dictatorship was no accident; it was driven there by inner necessity, and not for the first time either. Nor was it an accident that the Revolution led to the dictatorship of a general. But it so happened that this general was Napoleon Bonaparte, a man whose temperament, even more than his genius, was unable to adapt to peace and moderation. Thus it was an unforeseeable contingency which tilted the scale in favour of 'la guerre éternelle'.

THE DICTATORSHIP IN FRANCE

For a long time the republicans had wanted to strengthen the central authority. One need only look at the constitutions they gave to the vassal states: in Holland, the members of the Directory controlled the treasury; in Switzerland, they appointed government officials; in Rome, they appointed judges as well. In the Helvetic and Roman Republics every department already possessed a 'prefect'. All this is not to mention the Cisalpine Republic, which was Bonaparte's personal fief. Unfortunately, in France the amending procedure prescribed by the Constitution of Year III required a delay of at least seven years. The coup d'état of 18 Fructidor had provided the occasion sought by Sieyes, Talleyrand, and Bonaparte, but they let the opportunity slip. In Year VII, however, they hoped to bring about a new one. Without realizing it, the republicans were giving way to a tendency which, ever since the start of the civil and foreign wars, was pushing the Revolution in the direction of a permanent and all-powerful executive, that is to say toward dictatorship. It was this social revolution that drove the dispossessed nobility far beyond insurrection. Subsidized by enemy gold, it exploited the wartime hardships—that inexhaustible source of discontent—and particularly the monetary and economic crisis, thereby intending to turn the people against the government. The French did not want a return to the Old Regime, but they suffered and they held their leaders responsible for it. At every election the counter-revolution hoped to regain power. It was awareness of this danger that led the Mountain in 1793 to declare the Convention in permanent session until the peace. The Thermidorians had intended to restore elective government, but they immediately returned to Jacobin expediency by passing the Decree of the Two-Thirds. Next, the Directory, overwhelmed by the elections of 1797, re-established the dictatorship on 18 Fructidor. Yet as long as the Constitution of Year III continued to exist, this dictatorship, put to the test each year, required a host of violent measures and could never be brought into working order. So it was still necessary to revive the principle of 1793 and invest it with permanence until such time as peace, settled once and for all, would persuade the counter-revolution to accept the new order. It was in this respect that Napoleon's dictatorship became so much a part of the history of the French Revolution. No matter what he may have said or done, neither he nor his enemies were ever able to break this bond, and this was a fact which the European aristocracy understood perfectly well.

In 1799, as in 1793, the Jacobins wished to establish a democratic dictatorship by relying on the Sans-culottes to push it through the councils. Taking advantage of the crisis preceding the victory at Zurich, they succeeded in forcing the passage of several revolutionary measures: a compulsory loan, the abolition of exemptions from military service, the law of hostages, a repeal of assignments on public revenues which had been granted to bankers and government contractors, withholdings on the rente and on salaries, and finally, requisitions. These measures constituted a direct attack on bourgeois interests and brought that class to action. Thus it was symbolic that assignments on public revenues were restored the very night of 19 Brumaire. The Idéologues who gathered around Madame de Condorcet at Auteuil or in the salon of Madame de Staël wanted neither a democratic dictatorship nor even a democracy. Writing in 1799 on the means to 'end the Revolution' and on 'the principles fundamental to the Republic' (*Des Circonstances actuelles qui peuvent terminer la révolution et des principes qui doivent fonder la république en France*), Madame de Staël expressed their desire: to devise a representative system of government which would assure power to the moneyed and talented 'notables'. Sieyes, who had become a Director, took his inspiration from the Decree of the Two-Thirds. Together with his friends he wanted to select the membership of the newly constituted bodies which would then expand themselves by co-optation, leaving to the nation only the role of electing candidates. Furthermore, those already in office saw in this plan the chance to keep themselves in power.

The people having been eliminated as an obstacle to the dictatorship of the bourgeoisie, only the army remained. The Directory had already sought its help on 18 Fructidor, Year V, and had managed to keep the upper hand, despite serious incursions. Now, however, the situation was very different in that steadfast republicans, not royalists, were to be driven out. Only a popular general could have carried it through, and Bonaparte's sudden return destined that it should be he. The will of the nation which was invoked to justify 18 Brumaire played no part in the event. The nation rejoiced at the news that Bonaparte was in France because it recognized an able general; but the Republic had conquered without him, and Masséna's victory had bolstered the reputation of the Directory. Consequently, the responsibility for 18 Brumaire lies on that segment of the republican bourgeoisie called the Brumairians, whose leading light was Sieyes. They had no intention of giving in to Bonaparte, and they chose him only as an instrument of their policy. That they propelled him to power without imposing any conditions, without even first delimiting the fundamental character of the new regime, betrays their incredible mediocrity. Bonaparte did not repudiate the notables, for he too was not a democrat, and their collaboration alone enabled him to rule. But on the evening of 19 Brumaire, after they had hurriedly slapped together the structure of the Provisional Consulate, they should not have harboured any more illusions. The army had followed Bonaparte, and him alone. He was complete master. Regardless of what he and his apologists may have said, his rule was from its origins an absolute military dictatorship. It was Bonaparte alone who would decide the questions on which the fate of France and Europe hinged.

NAPOLEON BONAPARTE

What sort of a man was he? His personality evolved in so singular a manner that it defies portrayal. He appeared first as a studious officer full of dreams, garrisoned at Valence and Auxonne. As a youthful general, on the eve of the battle of Castiglione, he could still hold a council of war. But in the final years as Emperor, he was stupefied with his own omnipotence and was infatuated with his own omniscience. And yet distinctive traits appear throughout his entire career: power could do no more than accentuate some and attenuate others.

Short-legged and small in stature, muscular, ruddy, and still gaunt at the age of thirty, he was physically hardy and fit. His sensitivity and steadiness were admirable, his reflexes quick as lightning, and his capacity for work unlimited. He could fall asleep at will. But we also find the reverse: cold humid weather brought on oppression, coughing spells, dysuria; when crossed he unleashed frightful outbursts of temper; over-exertion, despite prolonged hot baths, despite extreme sobriety, despite the moderate yet constant use of coffee and tobacco, occasionally produced brief collapses, even tears. His mind was one of the most perfect that has ever been: his unflagging attention tirelessly swept in facts and ideas which his memory registered and classified; his imagination played with them freely, and being in a permanent state of concealed tension, it never wearied of inventing political and strategic motifs which manifested themselves in unexpected flashes of intuition like those experienced by poets and mathematicians. This would happen especially at night during a sudden awakening, and he himself referred to it as 'the moral spark' and 'the after midnight presence of the spirit'. This spiritual fervour shone through his glittering eyes and illuminated the face, still 'sulphuric' at his rise, of the 'sleek-haired Corsican'. This is what made him unsociable, and not, as Hippolyte Taine would have us think, some kind of brutality, the consequence of a slightly tarnished *condottiere* being let loose upon the world in all his savagery. He rendered a fair account of himself when he said, 'I consider myself a good man at heart', and indeed he showed generosity, and even kindness to those who were close to him. But between ordinary mortals, who hurried through their tasks in order to abandon themselves to leisure or diversion, and Napoleon Bonaparte, who was the soul of effort and concentration, there could exist no common ground nor true community. Ambition—that irresistible impulse to act and to dominate—sprang from his physical and mental state of being. He knew himself well: 'It is said that I am an ambitious man but that is not so; or at least my ambition is so closely bound to my being that they are both one and the same.' How very true! Napoleon was more than anything else a temperament.

Ever since his military school days at Brienne, when he was still a poor and taunted foreigner, timid yet bursting with passion, Napoleon drew strength from pride in himself and contempt for others. Destined to become an officer, his instinct to command without having to discuss could not have been better served. Although he might on occasion have sought information or opinion, he alone was master and judge. Bonaparte's natural propensity for dictatorship suited the normal practice of his profession. In Italy and in Egypt he introduced dictatorship into the government. In France he wanted to put himself forward as a civilian, but the military stamp was indelibly there. He consulted often, but he could never tolerate free opposition. More precisely, when faced with a group of men accustomed to discussion, he would lose his composure. This explains his intense hatred of the Idéologues. The confused and undisciplined, yet formidable masses inspired in him as much fear as contempt. Regardless of costumes and titles, Bonaparte took power as a general, and as such he exercised it.

Beneath the soldier's uniform, however, there dwelled in him several personalities, and it is this diversity, as much as the variety and brilliance of his gifts, which makes him so fascinating. Wandering about penniless in the midst of the Thermidorian festival, brushing past rich men and beautiful women, the Bonaparte of 1795 burned with the same desires as others. Something of that time never did leave him: a certain pleasure in stepping on those who had once snubbed him; a taste for ostentatious splendour; an over-tender care for his family—the 'clan'—which had suffered much the same miseries as himself; and a few memorable remarks of the citizen-turned-gentleman, as on the day of his coronation when he exclaimed, 'Joseph, if only father could see us!' But even much earlier there lived in him a nobler trait, a passionate desire to know and understand everything. It served him, no doubt, yet it was a need which he fulfilled for its own sake, without any ulterior motive.

As a young officer he was a tireless reader and compiler. He also wrote, and it is obvious that had he not entered the royal military academy at Brienne, he could have become a man of letters. Having entered into a life of action, he still remained a thinker. This warrior was never happier than in the silence of his own study, surrounded by papers and documents. In time he became more practical, and he would boast that he had repudiated 'ideology'. Nevertheless, he was still a typical man of the eighteenth century, a rationalist, a philosophe. Far from relying on intuition, he placed his trust in reason, in knowledge, and in methodical effort. 'I generally look ahead three or four months in advance to what I must do, and then I count on the worst'; 'all work must be done systematically because left to chance, nothing can succeed'. He believed that his insights were the natural fruit of his patience. His conception of a unitary state, made of one piece according to a simple and symmetrical plan, was entirely classical. At rare moments his intellectualism revealed itself by his most striking characteristic: the ability to stand off from himself and take a detached look at his own life, and to reflect wistfully on his fate. From Cairo he wrote to Joseph after having learned of Josephine's infidelity, 'I need solitude and isolation. I find grandeur tiring, my feelings drained, and glory dull. At twenty-nine I am completely played out.' Walking with Girardin at Ermenonville, he would exclaim shortly thereafter, 'The future will tell if it would not have been better for the sake of world peace had Rousseau and I never been born.' When the state councillor Roederer remarked, while visiting the abandoned Tuileries Palace with Napoleon, 'General, this is all so sad,' Bonaparte, already First Consul for two months, replied, 'Yes, and so is grandeur.' Thus by a striking turnabout, this firm and severe intellect would give way to the romantic melancholia characteristic of Chateaubriand and de Vigny. But these were never more than flashes, and he would pull himself together at once.

He seemed to be dedicated to a policy of realism in every way, and he was, in fact, a realist in execution down to the slightest detail. During the course of his rise, he made the rounds of human emotions, and well did he learn to play upon them. He knew how to exploit self-interest, vanity, jealousy, even dishonesty. He knew what could be obtained from men by arousing their sense of honour and by inflaming their imagination; nor did he for a moment forget that they could be subdued by terror. He discerned ever so clearly what in the work of the Revolution had captured the heart of the nation and what fitted in with his despotism. To win the French people, he declared himself both a man of peace and a god of war. That is why he must be ranked among the great realists in history.

And yet he was a realist in execution only. There lived in him an alter-ego which contained certain features of the hero. It seems to have been born during his days at the military academy out of a need to dominate a world in which he felt himself despised. Above all he longed to equal the semi-legendary heroes of Plutarch and Corneille. His greatest ambition was glory. 'I live only for posterity,' he exclaimed, 'death is nothing, but to live defeated and without glory is to die every day.' His eyes were fixed on the world's great leaders: Alexander, who conquered the East and dreamed of conquering the world; Caesar, Augustus, Charlemagne—the creators and the restorer of the Roman Empire whose very names were synonymous with the idea of a universal civilization. From these he did not deduce a precise formulation to be used as a rule, a measure, or a condition of political conduct. They were for him examples, which stimulated his imagination and lent an unutterable charm to action. He was stirred less by the accomplishments of his heroes than by the consuming spiritual zeal which had engendered their work. He was an artist, a poet of action, for whom France and mankind were but instruments. How well he expressed his sense of grandeur when, in St. Helena, he evoked memories of the victory at Lodi and the awakening in his consciousness of the will to power! 'I saw the world flee beneath me, as if I were transported in the air.'

That is why it is idle to seek for limits to Napoleon's policy, or for a final goal at which he would have stopped: there simply was none. As for his followers who worried about it, he once remarked, 'I always told them that I just didn't know', or again, more significantly, despite the triteness of his expression, 'To be in God's place? Ah! I would not want it; that would be a cul-de-sac!' Here, then, we see that dynamic temperament which struck us at first glance in its psychological manifestation. It is the romantic Napoleon, a force seeking to expand and for which the world was no more than an occasion for acting dangerously. But knowing the disposition of one's means alone is not the mark of a realist. On the contrary, the realist also fixes his goal in terms of the possible, and although his imagination and his flair for grandeur push him on, still he knows where to stop.

That a mind so capable of grasping reality in certain respects should escape it in others, as Louis Molé* so accurately observed, can only be due to Napoleon's origins as much as to his nature. When he first came to France, he considered himself a foreigner. Until the time when he was expelled from Corsica by his compatriots in 1791, his attitude had been one of hostility to the French people. Assuredly he became sufficiently imbued with their culture and spirit to adopt their nationality; otherwise he could never have become their leader. But he lacked the time to identify himself with the French nation and to adopt its national tradition to the point where he would consider its interests as a limitation upon his own actions. Something of the uprooted person remained in him; something of the *déclassé* as well. He was neither entirely a gentleman nor entirely common. He served both the king and the Revolution without attaching himself to either. This was one of the reasons for his success, since he could so easily place himself above parties and announce himself as the restorer of national unity. Yet neither in the Old Regime nor in the new did he find principles which might have

* Comte Louis Mathieu Molé was prime minister of France from 1836–1839. Under Napoleon I he held various important prefectural and ministerial posts, and he was an *auditeur* in Napoleon's Council of State. TRANSLATOR.

served as a norm or a limit. Unlike Richelieu, he was not restrained by dynastic loyalty, which would have subordinated his will to the interest of his master. Nor was he motivated by civic virtue, which could have made him a servant of the nation.

A successful soldier, a pupil of the philosophes, he detested feudalism, civil inequality, and religious intolerance. Seeing in enlightened despotism a reconciliation of authority with political and social reform, he became its last and most illustrious representative. In this sense he was the man of the Revolution. His frenzied individuality never did accept democracy, however, and he rejected the great hope of the eighteenth century which inspired revolutionary idealism—the hope that someday men would be civilized enough to rule themselves. He did not become cautious through a concern for his personal safety, as were other men, because he was indifferent to it. He dreamed only of greatness through heroism and danger.

What about moral limits? In spiritual life he had nothing in common with other men. Even though he knew their passions well and deftly turned them to his own ends, he cared only for those that would reduce men to dependence. He belittled every feeling that elevated men to acts of sacrifice—religious faith, patriotism, love of freedom—because he saw in them obstacles to his own schemes. Not that he was impervious to these sentiments, at least not in his youth, for they readily led to heroic deeds; but fate led him in a different direction and walled him up within himself. In the splendid and terrible isolation of the will to power, measure carries no meaning.

Unaware of Bonaparte's romantic impulse, the Idéologues believed him to be one of their own. Perhaps they could have succeeded in restraining this elemental urge by keeping him in a subordinate position under a strong government. But by pushing him to supreme power, the Brumairians precisely renounced any such precaution.

II

THE PACIFICATION OF
FRANCE AND EUROPE
(1799–1802)

CHAPTER FOUR

The Organization of the Dictatorship in France

HAVING SEIZED POWER, Napoleon immediately set about organizing his dictatorship. A part of his work was destined to endure, and still forms the administrative backbone of France today. The fruits of this long and exacting labour which continually preoccupied him until his downfall, could only appear gradually. Meanwhile, preparation for the campaign of 1800 brooked no delay. Napoleon was therefore forced to improvise at whatever risk. These two features would continue up to the very end. He never stopped building for the future, but bent as he was upon doing the impossible, he was forever condemned to improvising every one of his enterprises.

THE PROVISIONAL CONSULATE AND THE CONSTITUTION OF YEAR VIII

On the evening of 19 Brumaire, Year VIII (November 10, 1799), several deputies hastily sanctioned the establishment of a provisional government, which was charged with the task of drafting a new constitution. Both executive and legislative power was placed in the hands of three consuls: Bonaparte, Sieyes, and Roger-Ducos. On the 20th they agreed to take turns presiding, but actually Bonaparte took complete control from the very beginning. Two commissions of twenty-five members, each divided into three sections, were substituted for the Council of Ancients and the Council of Five Hundred and were to assist only in the preparation of the new constitution.

This development did not give rise to any serious opposition, since neither the Revolution nor the Republic seemed to be called into question. It was just another coup d'état. A barely enthusiastic France watched Bonaparte at work—who even knew whether he would last? Still, a leftist and a rightist minority began to take shape immediately. The Consulate was anti-Jacobin in its origin, since the motive for the Brumaire coup had been, after all, an alleged 'anarchist' plot. It was the left which had opposed the meeting of the Councils at Saint-Cloud and offered resistance in certain sections of the country. Sixty-one deputies had been excluded from that sitting, fifty-six of them Jacobins, of which twenty were later exiled to Guiana and the Île de Ré, and many others had been arrested. The terroristic measures of 1799—the compulsory loan, the law of hostages, and the requisitions—were rescinded; it was a victory for the merchants and the bankers. Now that 'respectable citizens' professed their satisfaction, so too did the royalists in their publications and in the theatre. In Bonaparte they hoped to find a second Monk, a restorer of the monarchy, and a strong clerical upsurge was evidenced everywhere as the refractory clergy no longer remained in hiding. But Bonaparte lost no time in repudiating the counter-revolution, and he was able to repress it without much trouble since the departmental administrations of the Directory were retained and placed under the control of delegates appointed by the consuls. Fouché, the Minister of Police, from the first took the side of the left; he rescinded the proscription of the Jacobins. True to the spirit of Brumaire, Bonaparte ruled along with the notables, who were either allied or committed to the work of the Revolution.

Meanwhile, the drafting of the constitution continued under the care of the two sections of the legislative commissions who were specifically assigned to this task. They consulted Sieyes, but the Oracle, as he was called, declared that he had not yet prepared anything. He voiced his views, however, the essence of which has been preserved by Boulay de La Meurthe, Daunou, and Roederer. Even though their reports differ to some extent as to what was actually said, two points are worth noting. First, the Brumairians were to be installed in the constituted bodies, which would then proceed to recruit additional members by co-opting from among the notables. Public officials would likewise no longer be elected, since authority, said Sieyes, would have to come from above. He added, however, that since confidence must come from below, the people—who were to be made sovereign by virtue of universal suffrage—would be allowed to choose candidates from among the notables to make up the electoral lists. This would not in any way have impeded the realization of the idea which had given birth to 18 Brumaire —a dictatorship of the notables. Power, on the other hand, was to be thoroughly divided. The legislature was to consist of three assemblies; and executive power was to be divided between a Grand Elector appointed for life, but subject to 'absorption' by the Senate, and two consuls appointed by him—one for domestic affairs, the other for foreign affairs. Within their respective spheres of authority, both consuls and their separate ministers and the state council were to enjoy complete independence. Here then were Sieyes' real intentions. By designing these complex provisions he sought to protect freedom of individual action from state despotism. But in so doing, he belittled the need to strengthen the authority of the government, which had been the second motive for the coup d'état, and he also underestimated the extent of Bonaparte's ambitions.

Bonaparte naturally offered no objection to the disappearance of elective government or to the creation of numerous assemblies, but he categorically demanded executive power for himself alone. A meeting of Bonaparte and Sieyes, arranged by Talleyrand, only served to embitter the conflict between the two consuls. The members of the two sections dealing with the constitution put an end to the dispute by pronouncing themselves against Sieyes. They declared themselves in favour of a First Consul who, although assisted by two lesser consuls, would be invested with pre-eminent authority and the power to appoint all officials. They did not even spare the rest of Sieyes' plan, and they decided to re-establish both a limited suffrage based on property qualifications and the elective principle, probably realizing that the assemblies would otherwise be left powerless before Bonaparte.

The Organization of the Dictatorship in France

As soon as the draft had been written down by Daunou, Bonaparte assembled the members of the two commissions in his apartments. New deliberations ensued, during which Sieyes managed to restore into the constitution the principle of co-optation, the Lists of Notability, and universal suffrage, apparently without any trouble since Bonaparte could not but approve them. Bonaparte in turn considerably increased his own powers. His two colleagues found themselves reduced to a consultative voice, and he alone acquired the power to promulgate laws. The Tribunate was deprived of any legislative initiative. The final product thus appeared to be a compromise, but in fact, what Sieyes had obtained could only have benefited Bonaparte, once the latter had concentrated complete executive power in himself. Doubtlessly, some of the Brumairians went along with him in order to tie themselves to his rising star; others, however, supported him out of principle, sincerely believing that the well-being of the Revolution necessitated a strong leader.

Because of the informal nature of these proceedings, legal debate should now have been left to the Council of Five Hundred and the matter then referred to the Council of Ancients. But the general feeling was to terminate these deliberations, and when, on the night of 22 Frimaire (December 13), Bonaparte requested the deputies to indicate their assent by signing the articles, and proceeded then and there to insert the names of the three consuls (Bonaparte, Cambacérès, and Lebrun), no one protested this new coup d'état. The constitution offered to the French people for approval was carried in a national plebiscite by a vote of 3,011,107 against 1,562. Having already undergone irregularities in its preparation, the constitution was subjected to yet another illegality by being put into effect on 4 Nivôse (December 25), before having been ratified.

This Constitution of Year VIII, comprising ninety-five articles hastily tossed together, made no mention of the rights of the citizen other than a guarantee against nocturnal house searches, and it was very incomplete in its organization of public powers. In its brevity and obscurity, the constitution conformed to Bonaparte's desire to preserve a free hand for himself. Above all, it established the omnipotence of the First Consul, and except for the right to make peace or war, which was of little conse-

74

quence at this time, Napoleon held complete executive power. He appointed the ministers and the other high government officials; only the justices of the peace were to be elected. His ministers, being responsible, were subject to prosecution by the Legislative Body, but this only increased his control over them. The First Consul and his handpicked functionaries, except for the ministers, were responsible to no one, and could only be prosecuted by the Council of State, whose members Bonaparte himself appointed. He alone possessed the right to initiate legislation. The legislative power was reduced to a mere deliberative process and to a 'yes' or 'no' vote on bills introduced by Bonaparte after listening to the opinions of the Council of State. Even so, discussion and voting were kept separate: the 100-membered Tribunate discussed, while the Legislative Body—the 300 'mutes'—voted. Finally Bonaparte exercised without a check decree powers which revolutionary assemblies had accorded in the past to the executive for applying the law, the details of which were left for him to fill in and to interpret. Another body, the Conservative Senate, could annul laws deemed unconstitutional, but in reality the office of senator was a sinecure since its functions were mainly electoral.

It has rightly been said that the constitution reflected the work of Bonaparte, but there is another factor of major importance which serves to explain the complete ineffectiveness of the assemblies—namely, the abolition of the elective principle. Henceforth, members of the assemblies were chosen without popular participation. The two departing Provisional Consuls and the new Second and Third Consuls appointed the first thirty-one senators who, in turn, chose the other twenty-nine senators; in the future, the Senate would continue to recruit its full complement of members by co-optation. The Senate was to name the tribunes and legislators as well as the consuls at the expiration of their ten-year terms. Subsequently, however, all of these nominations were supposed to be made from among the notables who were to be elected in a number of stages by universal suffrage. In each 'communal district' (*arrondissement communal*) the electors chose a tenth of their number, and these candidates on the 'communal list' of notables then selected a tenth of their number to form the departmental list. The same procedure was again applied by the notables on the

75

departmental list to form a national list of candidates eligible for public office. Just what the 'communal district' was intended to be no one now knows. In any event, the system turned out to be inapplicable, and the lists finally prepared in Year IX were, for all they were worth, hardly used at all.

The nation was sovereign, of course, but it was no longer consulted. The Brumairians were satisfied—they now sat as the government. Yet they represented no one but themselves, and Bonaparte wasted little time in telling them, 'I alone represent the people.' Although they formed so-called representative bodies, they remained a group of notables which was summoned by the executive to collaborate in government only to the extent to which it might suit him. The king, under the Restoration, admitted as much. At first the Brumairians thought differently. Since they fully mastered the Senate, which Sieyes had filled with handpicked candidates, they also controlled the Tribunate and the Legislative Body, and so believed themselves in a position to force their collaboration upon Bonaparte. And in fact, the assemblies did manifest a tendency to resist, but since the constitution offered no means of resolving these conflicts, they evolved by way of successive coups d'état, which only Bonaparte had the means to carry through. The history of the Consulate and even of the Empire is in part the steadily increasing subjection of the legislative power. From the very first, Bonaparte encroached upon its rights. On 5 Nivôse, Year VIII (December 26, 1799), he empowered the Council of State with the function of interpreting laws by issuing 'opinions'. Nor did he hesitate at times to modify or circumvent the laws according to his need by means of executive decree. The Constitution of Year X permitted him to deprive the Tribunate and Legislative Body of all authority by investing the Senate with consultum powers. Thus, by abusively enlarging the scope of his regulatory power (*pouvoir réglementaire*), Bonaparte eventually began to legislate directly by decree.

The contention has been advanced that Bonaparte and Sieyes filled the assemblies with Jacobins—the so-called 'safe Jacobins'. Not so at all. Rather, they favoured the moderates far more. Second only to the Institute, the Senate became the bastion of the Idéologues. The Tribunate was membered with writers and orators such as Daunou, Chénier, Ginguené, Say, and above all Benjamin Constant. Those less known were diverted to the Legislative Body. A total of 330 members had previously occupied seats in the councils of the Directory, 57 in the first three revolutionary assemblies. The Jacobins and the loyal nobility numbered but a small minority. Under these circumstances—this being the personnel upon which Bonaparte himself depended—it would have been impossible for him to impart a significantly different colour to the Council of State and ministries. It explains the fact that even the Council of State tended toward a certain degree of independence. In his choice of the two junior consuls however, Bonaparte revealed his true inclination. Cambacérès had been a member of the Plain in the Convention. Stately and ceremonious, he was loyal and he did his best to exercise a moderating influence on Bonaparte. Lebrun, a former secretary under Chancellor Maupeou, had kept himself aloof during the Revolution, and Bonaparte knew him to be a royalist. In finance, he called upon the services of Gaudin and Mollien, both of whom had been employed in the office of the *Contrôle Général*. The result was a symbolic fusion of the revolutionary bourgeoisie and the men of the Old Regime who were now reconciled to the new order. Then, by gradually increasing the proportion of ex-royalists in the government, Bonaparte aligned his personnel in harmony with the evolution toward monarchy.

THE ORGANIZATION AND EXTENSION OF BONAPARTE'S POWERS

Bonaparte moved into the Tuileries Palace on 30 Pluviôse, Year VIII (February 19, 1800), and immediately retired to his private study so as to work undisturbed. The only people permitted access to his presence were his secretaries for dictation, Bourrienne at first, then Méneval or Fain. Whenever he wished to confer with his collaborators, he would move to an adjoining room. The very thought of the Old Regime monarchy, however, filled him with a mistrust for ministers and their encroaching ways. He accustomed them to communicate with him in writing. It was not long before he had in his hands reports periodically submitted to him in the form of ministerial 'portfolios', information on the state of affairs in the Ministry of War, and at a later time, the accounts of the *domaine extraordinaire* (the extraordinary internal and external receipts). He retained the office of the Secretariat of State, which had been created by the Directory, and changed it into a ministry, placing it under Hughes-Bernard Maret. It acted as a central bureau for collecting the dossiers of the various governmental departments and offices, and it communicated to them Bonaparte's orders, which Maret received day and night. Thus the ministers were transformed into mere clerks.

Bonaparte also increased their number: to the existing Ministry of Finance he added a separate Ministry of the Public Treasury in 1801; while alongside the Ministry of War, he created a separate Ministry of Military Affairs in 1802. Moreover, he established within certain ministries themselves independent bodies* entrusted to councillors of state who acted as his direct agents and were to deal with public worship, public education, national property, forests, and bridges and highways. This was the origin of our present-day department heads (*directeurs*). The ministers took offence, but these rivalries delighted Napoleon, as they had Louis XIV before him. Only Talleyrand, the Minister for Foreign Affairs, enjoyed the privilege of working together with the master. On his part he affected an air of downright adoration of Bonaparte. Although Napoleon scorned him, he was also reluctantly deferent toward Talleyrand—the deference of a parvenu for the blue-blooded aristocrat steeped in the kind of etiquette which inspires respect by its very loftiness and makes one feel the presence of a great personage. Since the ministers were shorn of the authority to make decisions, and since they did not in themselves constitute an organized body, Bonaparte alone, as Beugnot remarked, 'kept everything together'. Like Frederick II, he ruled from the depths of his study.

Having never been schooled for this kind of work, Bonaparte lacked much of the requisite technical know-how for it. Tales of his instant, all-pervading comprehension are pure legend. He managed to teach himself a great deal, but his real talent lay in the ability to recognize the value of the men who had ruled

---

* The author is referring to the General Boards (*Directions Générales*), which were established partly to minimize the importance of the ministers and partly to facilitate the business of administration. TRANSLATOR.

during the Revolution, to consult them frequently, and to use them for his own purposes. From the inception of his term as consul, these were the kind of men he chose to make up the majority of the 29-membered Council of State. Except for Brune and Réal, the backgrounds of these men marked them as moderates. Their ranks numbered but three ex-members of the Convention, of which only one, Berlier, had been a regicide, and even he had favoured a postponement of execution. Alongside these were men like Champagny, Fleurieu, and Moreau de Saint-Méry, who left no doubts about their royalist sympathies and who had regarded the passing of the Old Regime with considerable regret. These two groups grew unevenly during the years to follow: to the former were added Thibaudeau and Treilhard; to the latter, Barbé-Marbois, Portalis, Dumas, Bigot de Préameneu, and Muraire. They did not all enjoy their master's trust. When Bonaparte returned from Marengo on 7 Fructidor, Year VIII (August 25, 1800), he effected a change which enabled him to dismiss without public scandal any councillor who might have incurred his displeasure, for he considered it politically unwise to attract too much attention to such situations. Henceforward, Bonaparte prepared two lists every three months, one containing the names of councillors engaged in ordinary service, the other, the names of councillors extraordinary, that is to say charged with specific missions and thus kept out of the meetings of the Council of State, although retaining both title and honours. Their mission accomplished, nothing dictated that they should be reinstated, and so it sufficed to transfer a councillor from one list to the other to conceal a disgrace.

The Council of State was divided into five sections which functioned separately but which periodically assembled at general meetings, usually under the presidency of Bonaparte. It also had a General Secretariat which was placed under the direction of Locré. Appointed as they were by the First Consul and subject to dismissal, the councillors lacked the kind of independence which in the royal Council of State had resulted in venality, fixity of tenure, and an esprit de corps engendered by social and professional ties. Since the Council lacked decision-making authority, it merely expressed opinions which were in no way binding on Bonaparte.

The Organization of the Dictatorship in France

The role of the Council of State was none the less considerable, especially during the first years. It boasted many famous administrators, such as Roederer, Chaptal, Cretet, Fourcroy, Portalis, Berlier, and Thibaudeau, and it was in the Council that the great organic laws and codes were drawn up. As a court of supreme administrative jurisdiction, the Council, sitting in disputation, was in a position to regulate little by little the operation of the entire administrative machine. Bonaparte took great pleasure in this work. He allowed the councillors to express themselves freely and, feeling very much at home, would himself expatiate with inexhaustible verve. He excluded from these discussions only political questions, notably the Concordat and the Law of 18 Germinal, Year X, which he knew would encounter strong resistance.

Bonaparte never granted the Council a monopoly on advice, however. He also provided a stimulus to other advisory groups whose gatherings were improvised at first but later became more regular. To these so-called 'administrative councils' he would summon the interested ministers and their department heads, several state councillors, and even certain officials, specially invited, from the provinces. Although not as well-known as the Council of State, these last-mentioned groups played a role almost equal in importance.

The new government, like the Directory, was from the very first day haunted by the deplorable condition of the treasury, which it had found almost empty. Consequently, the government was forced to make almost daily appeals to bankers for loans by mixing threats with soft words. Then, too, administrative reforms were first introduced in the realm of finances, and it was in this area that centralization scored its first success. Early in Frimaire before the completion of the constitution, Gaudin, the new Minister of Finance, undertook certain decisive measures to raise revenues and to replenish the treasury. His first act, initiated on 3 Frimaire (November 24, 1799), was to deprive local officials of the power to assess and in part collect direct taxes, reserving this responsibility for agents of the central government. At the head of the new central organization stood a general director for direct taxation and deputy directors for each département. Below them were auditors (*contrôleurs*) and inspectors (*inspecteurs*) in charge of apportioning taxes among the taxpayers in each commune. Although these deputy directors appointed local tax assessors (*répartiteurs*) to aid them, they alone were responsible for drawing up the tax rolls. But no one gave much thought to the new assessments for the time being, and the auditors set about preparing the tax lists in arrears and those of Year VIII (the current year) by copying the previous ones. Other government appointees included a treasurer and a paymaster in each département, revenue agents called *receveurs généraux* and *receveurs particulier,** as well as tax collectors (*percepteurs*) in towns where the tax rolls exceeded 15,000 francs. Elsewhere, municipalities retained the right to collect taxes and generally awarded the office to the lowest bidder. Finally, on 6 Frimaire, the annual rescriptions of the receveurs généraux were re-established.† They were to be issued in twelve monthly instalments, but were actually made payable over a period of twenty months. The chief bureau in the Ministry of Finance— those dealing with property, customs, and the debt—rapidly acquired directors, the treasury department being the first to do so; on 1 Pluviôse (January 21, 1800), it was placed under the direction of Dufresne, who had been a treasury employee before 1789 and at the time of the Constituent Assembly. A separate Ministry of the Public Treasury was created in the Year X and was placed under Barbé-Marbois.

The great problem was to market the promissory note issued by the receveurs généraux. In order to back them up, Gaudin established a Security Bank (*Caisse de garantie*), which he funded by returning to the practice of bonding officials of the fisc and by putting the bank in charge of warehouses and consignments. Placed under Mollien's direction, this bank was also to maintain the price of government bonds by carrying out open market purchases in order to reduce the rate of interest and place the treasury on a better footing. Thus it soon came to be known as the Sinking Fund. The discounting of promissory

* *The receveurs généraux des finances* were a traditional agency surviving from the Old Regime. They comprised important government officials who acted as representatives and banking agents of the treasury. The *receveurs particuliers des finances* were created on March 18, 1800. They too acted as treasury agents and were in charge of collecting direct taxes, fines, etc. TRANSLATOR.

† These rescriptions were advances based on anticipated revenues, and issued by the receveurs généraux to the treasury in the form of notes promising payment at a future date. The notes were then discounted for the treasury by bankers. TRANSLATOR.

notes, nevertheless, still depended on the bankers' good will. The Revolution had made it possible for them, in agreement with leading manufacturers, to organize several emissory institutions for their personal needs. Chief among these were the Bank of Current Accounts (*Caisse des comptes courants*) established in Year IV and run by Perregaux, Récamier, and Desprez, and the Commercial Discount Bank (*Caisse d'escompte du commerce*) founded in Year VI. The former possessed the funds to come to the aid of the treasury, although a state bank would have been preferable. This was precisely what the directors of the Bank of Current Accounts wanted—a state charter which would enable them to expand their business. It was in this manner that their final agreement with the regime was sealed. On 24 Pluviôse (February 13, 1800), their bank was transformed into the Bank of France with a capital of 30 million francs in 1,000-franc shares. The two hundred leading stockholders elected fifteen governors (*régents*) and three directors (*censeurs*); the governors then appointed three out of their number to be in charge of granting commercial loans and establishing the discount rate. The Bank of France contracted to include in its portfolio rescriptions amounting to 3 million francs. In return, half of the Sinking Fund's security bonds were placed into Bank of France stock, and the other half was made available to the Bank outright. Finally, the Bank was to manage government annuities and pensions. Nevertheless, the Bank was not granted a monopoly of issuing notes on the belief that it might then choose to discount notes only for its own shareholders, thus forcing businessmen everywhere to come to its counters. That, in fact, was one of the tacit assumptions upon which the agreement was based.

Much as Gaudin's work deserves to be admired, to forget that for months it constituted but a mere façade would be to misconstrue the history of the Consulate. The tax rolls were not prepared until the end of Year VIII, and only a small part of the rescriptions was in fact ever discounted by the Bank. Had the Bank accepted all of the rescriptions that were issued, the proceeds would still not have been sufficient to cover the state's expenditures. Like the Directory, Bonaparte remained for a long time at the mercy of the bankers and purveyors.

The reform of the provincial administration, which was an

indispensable adjunct to that of the central government, produced results more quickly. It was initiated by Bonaparte in January and culminated in the Law of 28 Pluviôse (February 17, 1800), prepared under the chairmanship of Chaptal. The départements, cantons, and communes were retained—these last regaining their divisional autonomy owing to the abolition of the cantonal municipalities which had been created in Year III. Between the communes on the one hand and the départements on the other, the new intermediary administrative unit became the *arrondissement*, a revived district, but of larger area. Every administrative division was placed under the direct responsibility of a single magistrate. A prefect assisted by a general secretary replaced the older 'central administration' in every département; a subprefect was dispatched to every arrondissement; and a mayor together with one or more deputies was sent to every commune. As with the central government, the main point of the reform was to abolish popular election. Henceforth all officials were appointed by the government. The authority to choose mayors and deputies in communes with less than 5,000 inhabitants was delegated to the prefects. Although local councils were retained on the departmental, district, and communal levels, their members were also chosen by the central government or by a prefect. Furthermore, their sessions and functions were vastly reduced: local councils listened to financial reports, and on the departmental and district levels they assessed direct taxes, voted additional sums of moneys (centimes) to meet local needs, and were permitted to formulate resolutions; on the municipal level, they regulated the use of communal lands and provided for the upkeep of municipally-owned buildings. As for questions relating to the centime and to loans, the municipal council was to register only an opinion. Thus the communes were reduced to a state of tutelage. The administrative divisions which had been created for the large municipalities in Year III were abolished. Lyons, Marseilles, and Bordeaux were to be administered by a single council, but until Year XIII they remained with several mayors. In Paris, the twelve districts and their municipalities were retained, almost all of the administrative powers were transferred to the Prefecture of the Seine, and a General Council took the place of the Municipal Council.

The Organization of the Dictatorship in France

Bonaparte did not know enough about the political personnel to draw up the list of prefects himself. That task was left mainly to his brother, Lucien, the Minister of Interior, or more accurately, to Lucien's secretary, Beugnot, a former member of the Legislative Assembly. But Cambacérès, Lebrun, Talleyrand, and Clarke also interjected proposals, as did certain members of the assemblies, like Chauvelin and Cretet for the Côte-d'Or. As a rule, Bonaparte followed Lucien's choice of candidates. Most of the prefects were appointed on 11 Ventôse (March 2). Once again, the choice fell principally on the moderates, of whom about half had served in former revolutionary assemblies. Letourneur had even been a Director of the Committee of Public Safety, and Jeanbon St. André—whose Jacobin views offered a marked contrast to the general tenor of choices and who was assigned the annexed département of Mont-Tonnerre —had been an active member of that committee. To the prefectures were added generals and diplomats. All of the prefects were men of wide experience, and most were very capable. The prefectoral corps, which did so much to enhance Bonaparte's reputation, was one of the legacies of the French Revolution. As in the case of the central bureaucracy, it was destined to take on characteristics of the Old Regime.

In no instance were these prefects recruited locally—unlike the minor officials and members of local councils who were actually appointed by prefects and local politicians. Generally, the prefects too observed a preference for moderate notables who had sat in the local assemblies or headed technical bureaus during the Revolution. In the département of Seine Inférieure, half of the members who had participated in the general council of 1790 were restored in 1800. It was the villages that presented the greatest problem. The Revolution had unearthed but few villagers well enough educated and cultured to possess a sense of integrity and of public interest. The fact that the prefects encountered the same difficulty was frequently used as an argument for handing over the communal administration to the nobility.

Although the principle of centralization of power constituted the single most important feature of Bonaparte's reform, it was also a step toward the division of bureaucratic functions among officials who were independent of each other and were directly responsible to the central authority. Their technical proficiency was bound to increase at the expense of a further weakening of local autonomy. The Revolution had given administrative bodies control over matters in litigation, direct taxation, and the police. The Law of 28 Pluviôse now conferred the first upon the council of prefecture, over which the prefect in effect presided. Gaudin took away the administrative bodies' power to tax; and the municipality soon lost the power to judge over infractions of the law.

The logic of the system was such that Bonaparte also separated the police from the administration in order to transform the police into a centralized institution. Toward this end he retained the Ministry of General Police, which was reorganized by Fouché with the help of Desmaret, a former revolutionary priest and functionary during the Directory, who as head of the secret section of the Ministry of General Police became Fouché's indispensable assistant. In Paris, the restoration of the former Lieutenancy of Police under the name of Prefecture of Police on 17 Ventôse (March 8, 1800), provided Fouché with a co-adjutor. The Prefect of Police was charged with maintaining order in the capital, and was later subordinated to the Municipal Guard, created on October 4, 1802. Dubois, a former attorney in the parlement and a tool of Fouché, became the first Prefect of Police for Paris. In the provinces, the Ministry of General Police did not have permanent representatives. The creation of general commissioners of police in the large towns and on the frontier, which replaced the local authorities, did not begin until 5 Brumaire, Year IX (October 27, 1800). Several special commissioners were also created, as in Boulogne. Other than that, in most of the départements the only permanent agents of the ministry were the prefects, who possessed the authority to issue search and arrest warrants as had the *intendants* in times past. They were not, however, responsible to the Minister of Police alone. Furthermore, since prefects lacked trained subordinates, they often received their directions from the minister himself, or from agents which he dispatched to the provinces. The *gendarmerie*, which was carefully reorganized under the command of General Moncey, functioned separately alongside the police.

These sundry institutions wielded excessive powers from the

start. Fouché scattered a blanket of police spies and informers everywhere, who were recruited from within even the highest classes of society. The *cabinet noir*, headed by Lavalette, kept a close surveillance over correspondence. Arbitrary arrests became widespread, and the prefects themselves issued *lettres de cachet* not only against political suspects, but also against persons charged with having violated the law who were either guiltless or had already been acquitted, and also in the interests of certain influential families. That the police system lacked the degree of unity and centralization which characterized the rest of the government was undoubtedly due to Bonaparte's mistrust of Fouché, who was the most invaluable, feared, and independent of ministers. Asking little in the way of a budget, he had his own sources of revenue which he derived from the closing down of gambling houses, the rights to issue passports and firearm permits, confiscations of conspiratorial funds, and many kinds of arbitrary contributions exacted from brothels. Thus, in order to keep him in check, Bonaparte favoured the existence, side by side, of several police organizations. He had his own private police, not to mention a host of informers like Fiévée, Madame de Genlis, and Montlosier; and he also allowed Dubois to dabble in politics and set himself up as a rival to Fouché. As a result, these competing police bodies strove to outdo each other at the expense of a citizenry deprived of all recourse.

The reorganization of the administrative system had hardly been set into motion when that of the judiciary system was also effected by the Law of 27 Ventôse, Year VIII (March 18, 1800). On the civil side, the commune retained its local magistrate (*juge de paix*), and every arrondissement received a court of the first instance—as had formerly been the case with the district. A novelty was the establishment of twenty-nine courts of appeal, which brought back memories of the parlements. As to the criminal courts, the instrument of justice became the police court, while the court of the first instance and the court of appeal were given the authority to pronounce sentence. The criminal court of the département was to be retained, but henceforth staffed with its own judges. The law also provided for the retention of grand and petty juries, commercial, military, and maritime courts, as well as the court of cassation. The manner in which legal officials were to be chosen was subsequently worked out. Bonaparte continued to appoint the notaries (*notaires*); and he reserved to himself the choice of bailiffs (*huissiers*), except those of the justices of the peace, and the choice of *procureurs* to whom he restored the title *avoués*, without, however, making their employ compulsory. The profession of *avocat* alone remained open.

Changes in the judiciary hierarchy did not constitute the most important feature of the Ventôse Law, however. In the first place, except justices of the peace and those of the commercial courts, judges were no longer elected. Aside from the court of cassation magistrates, who were appointed by the Senate, the First Consul named all other judges. True, they were irremovable, but they depended nevertheless upon the state for their salaries and promotion. It must have pleased Lebrun to have seen the realization of Maupeou's reform, and it is likely that he had a hand in it. In the second place, the office of the public prosecutor (*ministère public*) was entirely reconstituted. Here lay the real basis of public order which had brought about the reform. The question was not merely one of purging the judicial personnel and of assuring its loyalty, but was also one of intensifying the use of repressive measures in a troubled land. The functions of the prosecuting magistrate (*accusateur public*) were merged with those of government commissioners who had always been representatives of the central power; that is, the prosecutor was to manage the judicial police officials. The justice of the peace and the officer of the gendarmerie retained their authority to issue warrants and to initiate pretrial hearings. Then, as in the past, these preliminary judicial inquiries were taken up by the president of the court of first instance who was head of the grand jury but nonetheless appointed by the state. The process of consolidation was still incomplete, but it did not remain so for long.

The choice of magistrates entailed greater difficulty than that of the prefects because they were considerably more numerous and had to be recruited locally. Therefore Bonaparte was obliged to rely on the advice of others. Circulars requesting nominations were sent to the regional assemblies, and many very different persons of distinction were solicited for information. Abrial, Minister of Justice, prepared the lists of candidates according to districts; Cambacérès then examined them with the assistance of regional politicians. But despite these precautions, the formation of the courts was attended by a certain degree of disorder and resulted in certain choices which were to be regretted. Here, too, men of the Revolution were favoured and made irremovable, thanks to which the judicial personnel evolved less rapidly than others in the direction of the Old Regime.

The administrative and judicial reforms of Year VIII occupy a position in the history of France second in importance only to the work of the Constituent Assembly of 1789, to which it was greatly indebted, however. The Constituent Assembly had abolished privileges and intermediary bodies, and it had achieved national unity. Bonaparte had but to affix his stamp, and that is why he was able to succeed so rapidly. After all, he did no more than resume the precedent set in Year II. The Committee of Public Safety had not had the time to carry out the policy of centralization as thoroughly, but its intention had been the same. Saint-Just had envisaged a single magistrate in every département or district, acting as agent of the central authority, and Chaptal spoke as Robespierre might well have done when he said, 'The strength of an administrative system lies completely in the certainty that the laws and acts of the government will be executed without reservation. . . . The chain of execution extends downward without interruption from minister to those who are to be administered and transmits the laws and orders of the government to the very last branch of the social order with the speed of electricity.' This was the comparison which the Sans-culottes were so fond of making.

The laws of Year VIII have often been ascribed to a design on the part of Napoleon to increase his own authority, and not without reason. No mention had ever been made in the constitution about the repudiation of popular elections for local assemblies, and Bonaparte's contemporaries were fully aware that his dictatorship had made a giant step forward. And yet behind these laws there lay deeper causes which discouraged resistance to them. The policies of decentralization carried out by the Constituent Assembly had imperilled France during the war, and had created a state of affairs which continued as long as the war lasted. It was in response to this situation that the Committee of Public Safety had seized the reins of government—reins that had slackened under the Thermidorians until finally Bonaparte seized them once again. He turned a temporary expedient into an ideal of government. That he should have thus satisfied his personal instinct for domination was made possible only because the ideal fully tallied at that time—and the Brumairians were as one in this opinion—with the interests of revolutionary France.

While occupied with the task of reshaping the nation, Bonaparte nevertheless felt compelled to defend himself against criticism. The notables had been delivered from the 'democratic' danger and were in possession of all the important positions. But since they no longer decided anything, they nurtured a discontent which Madame de Staël, who had hoped to govern France through the intermediacy of Bonaparte or at least Benjamin Constant, did not bother to hide. It was in the Tribunate, which certainly offered the means for it, that opposition broke out. The Tribunate sat permanently, elected its executive officers (*bureau*), and chose Daunou as its president. It could make resolutions, discuss petitions, lay charges against ministers, and denounce government measures which it deemed unconstitutional to the Senate. Above all, the Tribunate was a place for making speeches, and Benjamin Constant took full advantage of this opportunity starting on January 5, 1800, when the very first bill was presented to the Tribunate for discussion. Upon hearing of this, Bonaparte became enraged and everyone took cover. Sieyes departed for his country house, accepting an endowment, much to his discredit. To tame the moderates, Bonaparte had only to ask, 'Do you want me to abandon you to the Jacobins?' The Jacobins naturally felt even more disaffection. Throughout the countryside and especially in the west of France they were kept in check by the menaces of the 'Whites'. The installation of prefects took away support for the Jacobins in former administrative bodies. They frequently rioted, as in Dijon and Toulouse, and were not really put down until the summer. As for the royalists, they changed their tune because Bonaparte, during an interview with their representatives Hyde de Neuville and d'Andigné, refused to accede to any of their demands. Controlling as they did most of the newspapers, they made a great outcry against the new assemblies, demanding an immediate purge. But on January 17, 1800, Bonaparte took advantage of this disturbance to shut down in one blow sixty out of the seventy-three existing newspapers. Others stopped publication later, and by the end of 1800 there were only nine. The *Moniteur* had become the official government organ after December 27, 1799, and was under the direction of Maret. Censorship, although not officially re-established, was in fact carried out by Fouché, and on April 5, 1800, Lucien Bonaparte instituted it in the theatres. Of course the leftist press was also swept away by the purge.

With legal opposition impossible, extremists began to think in terms of violence. During the month of Germinal, there was again talk of a Jacobin plot. But the only serious danger could have arisen from the army, where there were still many republicans and even more malcontents, for there was no general who did not feel himself cut out to be First Consul. Bonaparte used circumspection. He appointed Carnot Minister of War, and he greatly increased the number of concessions to Moreau, who commanded the Army of the Rhine. His most fearful enemies remained the royalists, at least those who were resolved to turn down all concessions. Yet they could neither agree on principles, since some advocated constitutional monarchy, nor on a method of action. Living in Mittau with d'Avaray and Saint-Priest, Louis XVIII combined negotiation with conspiracy. A royal agency in Paris, in which Royer-Collard figured, was instructed to sound out Bonaparte, and handed him two letters from the pretender which were left unanswered. In Swabia, a bureau directed by Précy and Dandré and subsidized by Wickham was preparing an invasion of Provence by émigrés. Moreover, this bureau corresponded with royalists in Lyon, Toulouse, and particularly Bordeaux where the *Institut Philanthropique* of Year V had struck deep roots. The Count of Artois, who resided in England, maintained agencies both in Jersey and in Paris where the plots of Hyde de Neuville were uncovered in May. The royalists' main strongholds were in the west, however. There the *Chouannerie* had resumed in Year VII, but soon degenerated into a form of brigandage which, with the arrival of government troops in October—Hédouville north of the Loire and Travot in the Vendée—was promptly reduced. Hédouville entered into negotiations with the *Chouan* chieftains, and they agreed to an armistice on January 4, 1800. Bonaparte, who wished to turn all of his forces against Austria, was very anxious to pacify the west. Unlike the Thermidorians, however, he had no intention of dealing with the rebels as equals, and he was determined to disarm the peasants. Consequently, he offered amnesty to those who would lay down their arms. But receiving no answer, he dispatched Generals Brune and Lefebvre to the west, suspended the constitution in those départements, and ordered anyone apprehended with arms or preaching rebellion to be shot. Actually there was little fighting. The nobles d'Autichamp and Bourmont surrendered in January. The popular leaders held out somewhat longer in Brittany, Cadoudal being the last to submit on February 14. In Normandy, Frotté, who had come to Alençon to negotiate under promise of safe conduct, was arrested during the night of February 15–16. At Verneuil on February 18, the detail which was taking him to Paris encountered a courier with orders to set up a court martial, and Frotté was executed that same day along with six of his companions. In his struggle against partisanship, Bonaparte continued to act in the tradition of Year II: he was a terrorist pure and simple. 'Not since the time of Robespierre have laws been so severe,' noted an annalist from Chinon.

Bonaparte took good care not to make a habit of these methods, however. He was more skilful than the Jacobins in these matters, and he did not go beyond making examples; at the same time he welcomed all offers of surrender. Not waiting for the peace to disarm the counter-revolution, he undertook measures to hasten his summoning of the nation. Thus he was sure to please a great many people, for an end to disorders would bring a return to prosperity and would calm those who had profited from the Revolution. True, it was to be feared that the rallying together of the diverse elements of French society was not all that genuine, and Bonaparte never harboured any illusions on that score. But what did it matter so long as he continued to be victorious?

The great difficulty was to make the republican bourgeoisie and particularly the army accept measures which were favourable to the refractory clergy and émigrés. Until Marengo, however, Bonaparte kept to moderate enough enactments. On December 28, 1799, he confirmed to Catholics the full use of non-alienated churches. He also granted them freedom to worship every day, even Sundays, except on the décadi—a reservation which turned out to be of little importance since he abandoned in effect the religion of patriotism and almost all the revolutionary festivals. He merely demanded from the priests a promise of loyalty to the Constitution of Year VIII. It seems that for a time he believed they would seize this opportunity to submit. Nothing came of it, however. The majority of those who had refused the earlier oaths continued to do so now, despite the advice of Abbé Émery. Religious worship in secret continued and the ringing of church bells and religious processions remained the subject of numerous conflicts. Bonaparte quickly realized that in order to break the resistance of the clergy, he would have to come to terms with the Pope. Moreover, the Council of State declared that the constitution implicitly abrogated the exclusion of ex-nobles and parents of émigrés from public office. However, it also decided to retain the laws proscribing the émigrés themselves. But on March 3, 1800, it was decided that only those who had fled before December 25, 1799, were to be included on the émigré list, and a commission set up with the object of reviewing émigré applications for re-entry into France accepted a great many such requests. The ex-terrorists Barère and Vadier, those who had been proscribed in Fructidor, and members of the old 'patriotic' party of the Constituent Assembly, such as Lafayette, were all recalled without argument. The émigrés on the list numbered 145,000, however, and the work of the commission proceeded slowly. Fouché himself advised the recall of émigrés en bloc, aside from a few exceptions. But the time was not yet. To undertake such a risk, and as in arranging a concordat, Bonaparte would first have to enhance his prestige by achieving both victory and peace.

THE IMPROVISATION OF THE CAMPAIGN OF 1800

Bonaparte prepared energetically for the campaign on which the retention and extension of his power depended. Manpower was not a problem, for on March 8 the entire yearly contingent of recruits was placed at his disposition. But he opposed the methods used by the Jacobins and the Directory. This was decidedly not the time to imitate the great military conscription of Year VII; besides, money was lacking. Moreover, Bonaparte realized, if we are to believe an historian who was very partial to him, that a 'nation's enthusiasm for war grows inversely to the number of soldiers called upon to go to war', and so he contented himself with 30,000 men. The well-to-do were easily managed, since they were given the right by law to find substitutes. The Army of the Rhine having been made ready, it remained to put together a fresh Army of Reserve. This entailed making use of all available means, emptying military depots, recalling the veterans of the Army of the West, creating an Italian Legion, and marching conscripts who had not yet learned to load their rifles. Bonaparte employed little in the way of cavalry, and even less artillery. Given these conditions, it required an incredible amount of audacity and self-confidence for Bonaparte to plunge into the conquest of Italy.

The main problem was to finance the campaign. About 65 million francs were needed. The irregular war subsidy, which had taken the place of the compulsory loan, and the measures used to expedite the collection of revenues did not meet the immediate needs; all the more so since obligations could be discharged in notes and drafts which had been issued by the Directory and were now valueless. In addition, private contractors who were again entrusted with the commissariat ensured their deliveries with chattel mortgages. Gaudin wished to resort to indirect taxation, but Bonaparte, still somewhat unsure of his strength, limited himself to standardizing municipal tolls (octrois), which were to be earmarked for hospices and the municipalities themselves. Expenses were cut to the limit, but the Consulate was obliged in the end to resort to the same expedients as the Directory. The government discontinued the contracting system and re-established requisitions. But this scrip could not be used to discharge tax obligations. The government then decided on a partial deferment of payments: every ten days the little that was left over in the treasury was distributed to the various ministries. Other than that, the government issued drafts which were irredeemable. In the end it resorted to bankers and contractors who agreed to discount the notes at 5 per cent per month. The government also turned to financiers abroad, such as in Geneva and Hamburg, who, under pressure and compulsion, advanced $6\frac{1}{2}$ million francs.

The Organization of the Dictatorship in France

The only novel feature instituted by this authoritarian government in its financial dealings was its high handedness. The private contractors, who were not being paid, were nevertheless alerted to hand over 52 million francs if they wanted to be reimbursed in new debt certificates (*assignations*), which immediately lost 50 per cent of their face value. Gabriel Ouvrard, the famous financier who had been thrown in prison, was forced to give the government 14 million francs. Consequently, survival became a daily problem. Although the government's efforts were indeed prodigious, it would be a mistake to delude oneself about the results. The Army of the Rhine, which received preferential treatment for political reasons, was granted altogether 6,200,000 francs, and in Pluviôse was owed 15 million francs back pay. The Army of Reserve ambled on without pay or provisions other than those gotten along the way from the peasants. As in the Revolution, the enormous gaps in the preparation of the campaign were made up at the expense of the troops. In finance, as in politics, everything hung on victory. The war effort could not be kept up for long without demanding from the nation the kind of sacrifices which had made the Convention and the Directory so unpopular.

This, at least, was how people reasoned, and everyone prepared himself accordingly. When Bonaparte left Paris on May 6, the Brumairians began contemplating the range of possible solutions in the event he should fail to return. Sieyes reappeared in Paris, and there was talk of a directory, of a new First Consul —Carnot, Lafayette, Moreau. Mention was also made of the Duke of Orleans. Bonaparte's brothers, Joseph and Lucien, were burning with desire to be of service. Given the situation, some speculation was to be expected; but it is difficult to believe that there were not many prominent persons who looked forward to defeat with complacency. The liberals and certain Jacobins were left with no other hope. 'I wished for Bonaparte's defeat because it was the only means left to stop the advance of his tyranny,' wrote Madame de Staël some time later. The royalists, for their part, did their best as usual to help the enemy: Cadoudal returned from England on June 3 to revive the Chouannerie. The defeat of Bonaparte would have surely meant the fall of the nation and of the Revolution. France could no longer hesitate to choose between Napoleon and his rivals.

CHAPTER FIVE

The Pacification of Europe

MUCH AS IT WAS in Bonaparte's interest to wage battle and dictate peace, it was just as important for him to convince the French people that he was not responsible for the war. He would willingly have concluded an armistice in order to complete his preparations, and above all to rescue the army in Egypt, whose loss would constitute an irreparable setback for France in the Mediterranean and in the East. But to make peace on the basis of the natural frontiers was for him unthinkable. He later remarked that to abandon Italy 'would have dampened imaginations', that is to say, undermined his prestige. Nor would he listen to the proposals of the King of Prussia who told Beurnonville that the conditions of a genuine desire for peace would be the evacuation of Holland, Switzerland, and Piedmont. Perhaps *The State of France in Year VIII*, which was shortly to be published by d'Hauterive, Talleyrand's right-hand man, best reflected the political ideas of Bonaparte. It proposed that Europe substitute for the traditional policy of balance of power a kind of league of continental states under the hegemony of France.

The enemy, however, did Bonaparte the service of rejecting his peace offers. Actually, Thugut, the Austrian Chancellor, was diplomat enough to inquire into the conditions for peace, but when Talleyrand mentioned the territorial limits established at Campoformio, Thugut objected vehemently; and when the present limits were suggested as a basis of understanding, he dodged the entire question. For as long as he remained in power, Thugut longed to win back Nice and Savoy in order to force the King of Sardinia to cede in return part of Piedmont to Austria; the Austrian Archduke Charles, who counselled treating with France, lost the command of the Army of Germany. To the English, Thugut gently hinted at conquests in France which could serve as currency against the restoration of the monarchy. At least he had the intelligence not to say anything publicly. Pitt and Grenville, however, committed the blunder of openly disclosing the secret aspirations of the aristocratic Coalition. They declared before the House of Commons that a treaty with Bonaparte would not guarantee the future, and they pronounced, with impertinence to the French Republic, that the best assurance would be 'the restoration of that line of princes which for so many centuries maintained the French nation in prosperity at home, and in consideration and respect abroad'. The Prussian publicist, Friedrich von Gentz, who was in their pay, suddenly became possessed with an intense zeal for a counter-revolutionary crusade. Consequently, there was nothing left for France but to fight.

THE CAMPAIGNS OF 1800 AND THE TREATY OF LUNÉVILLE

Russia had withdrawn from the struggle, and Frederick William III could not have wished for better than to reconcile her with France, thereby securing himself from all risk. But it could not have suited Bonaparte to have chosen him as a mediator. Resuming the policies of Dumouriez and Danton, themselves heirs to the anti-Austrian tradition in French diplomacy, Napoleon offered Frederick instead an alliance which would have turned Prussia into an auxiliary. The king refused, and so the war became a duel between France and Austria.

Thugut, whose mind was fixed on Italy, kept General Kray in his defensive position behind the Rhine. To General Melas in Italy, whose forces were reinforced with great difficulty to something over 100,000 men, he issued orders to attack the

French, who had withdrawn behind the Apennines in the vicinity of Genoa since November, and to march into Provence where Willot and the Marquis of Puyvert were to provoke an insurrection. The Austrians counted on the help of the English in Minorca, but as usual, Dundas was unable to gather a sufficient force. Sir John Stuart, having been given only 5,000 men, tendered his resignation, and his successor, Sir Ralph Abercrombie, did not arrive until after the battle of Marengo. Melas now scattered half of his forces across the plain and below the Alpine passes. Seizing the offensive with the other half, he split the French forces in two on April 6, laying siege to Masséna in Genoa and driving Suchet back to the banks of the Var. The result of Thugut's military strategy, based as it was on purely political considerations, was that the Austrian army drove the French toward the south-west, and obtained nothing decisive. The French, on the other hand, remained in control of Switzerland and were consequently in a position to take the two Austrian armies from the rear.

At first Bonaparte deployed the various parts of his Army of Reserve between Chalon and Lyon. In March, he attempted to persuade Moreau to cross the Rhine near Schaffhausen with his entire force in order to cut Kray's communications and so beat him in detail.* According to this plan, the Army of Reserve would then have entered Switzerland and, reinforced by a part of the victorious Army of the Rhine, would have carried out the same operation against Melas, crossing the Alps as far east as possible, no nearer than by the Saint Gotthard Pass. But Moreau completely failed to grasp the value of this thunderbolt strategy, and in the meantime, Melas began his attack. Leaving Moreau to his own devices, Bonaparte concentrated his Army of Reserve in the lower Valais region toward the end of April. The 27th of that month, on the basis of information gathered by his engineers, he decided to lead the army to the Great Saint Bernard Pass which, having been crossed in 1798 and 1799, was a passage familiar to French armies. On May 5, he ordered Moreau to send him General Moncey with 25,000 men by way of the Saint Gotthard. Moreau, however, was unwilling to send more than 15,000 men. This

---

* Divide the enemy into separate, isolated pockets, and then defeat each one successively. TRANSLATOR.

did not weaken him any the less during his offensive which had just begun, and the decisive blow was reserved for Bonaparte. It was the starting point of their falling out.

The crossing of the Great Saint Bernard, begun on the night of May 14–15, was completed on May 23. Since the troops were forced to defile laboriously past the great guns of the Fortress of Bard, only ten cannons were able to get through, and until the army reached Milan this made up the entire artillery. Lannes, who was in the vanguard, captured the fort and town of Ivrea located at the head of the plain of the Po. From there, Bonaparte could have rallied Turreau's forces which were descending the Mont Cenis and Mont Genèvre passes and marched on Genoa. But then Melas would have been free to concentrate his men and to fall back on Lombardy if he were beaten.

The alternative course was to march on Milan and so cut his line of retreat. A victorious encounter would then be decisive and would deliver Italy to the French. Yet the risk was great. As long as the army in Milan had not secured a line of operations—an assured retreat across the Saint Gotthard—Melas would be in a position to cut its communications by undertaking an offensive north of the Po. Bonaparte needed a victory, an immediate victory. He therefore chose the latter course, perilous, but bound to produce a stupendous effect if successful. The main army, covered by Lannes, turned eastward and reached Milan on June 2, where it was joined by General Moncey and his reinforcements. The Austrian General Vukasovich had fallen back behind the Oglio River and the Austrian forces found themselves separated into two very unequal masses. The French divisions then headed south, crossed the Po, converged toward the west, seized the defiles of the Stradella Pass where Lannes took Montebello on June 9, and then debouched onto the plain of Marengo. On June 13 the advance guard, led by Victor, reached the banks of the Bormida within view of Alessandria. Bonaparte had combined the advance of his divisions with a sureness that was truly amazing. He arranged their grouping into autonomous corps, keeping them as concentrated as possible. Meanwhile, Masséna had been obliged to evacuate Genoa on June 4, and had rejoined Suchet, who was driving back Elsnitz and inflicting great losses on the Austrians. Bonaparte thought that they would be able to take Melas from the rear. Although they failed to do so, they were nevertheless able to draw off a sizable part of the enemy's cavalry.

Out of the 70,000 men still left to him, Melas concentrated only 30,000 at Alessandria. He had taken a great gamble by leaving himself without cavalry, but he still had almost 200 cannons. Bonaparte was ignorant of his precise whereabouts, but he realized that the Austrian force might try to cross the Po or slip away along the Apennines. Consequently, on June 13 he dispatched one division north of the river and two more under Desaix's command toward the south, keeping only 22,000 men and 22 or 24 cannons. Moreover, he committed a cardinal mistake by failing to cut the bridges of the Bormida. On June 14, at 9 A.M., his advanced guard was attacked by 20,000 Austrians. Two divisions hurried to the rescue, but were outflanked by the enemy's left, and the French fell back in disorder, leaving their artillery behind. Fortunately for them, the Austrian divisions on the left and on the right were advancing separately in marching column, concerned only with what lay before them and not seeking to envelop the French forces. Bonaparte hastened to recall the divisions which he had sent out to bar Melas' escape, but only Boudet's force (5,000 men and 5 cannons) was brought back by Desaix in time. Having rallied together the remnants of the French army, Desaix attacked the front of the advancing Austrian column. The battle was still undecided when Kellermann with 400 cavalry charged the Austrian flank. The enemy panicked and broke into a rout, but the Austrian left and right kept order and covered the retreat. Desaix had been killed in the midst of the fighting, unnoticed.

This, then, was the victory which Bonaparte had wanted. It was indeed the crowning point to an admirable campaign, but considering the manner in which the battle began, he should have lost; he later took pains to spread a falsified account of the battle which misled historians for a long time. Had he lost, the army could have extricated itself because it had maintained a line of retreat, but Bonaparte's career would undoubtedly have been finished. Never in war as in the life of man (genius or not) has the unforeseeable been more clearly manifest.

The defeat did not bring the Austrian army to the point of despair, because the French forces were exhausted and short of munitions, but Melas became totally demoralized. 'His appearance was as doddering as his physique,' said Count Neipperg, a man who was destined to gain some renown as one of the Austrian officers sent to negotiate with the 'rabble'. Under the terms of the armistice, which was signed on June 15 at Alessandria, the Austrians withdrew to the line of the Mincio River, thus keeping Tuscany and the Papal Legations.

Moreau, meanwhile, was slowly advancing in Germany. After his left wing made a diversionary feint on Kehl, the main army crossed the Rhine at various points from Breisach to Schaffhausen on April 28–May 1. He then proceeded to march across the Black Forest in the direction of General Lecourbe, who commanded the French right wing. This entailed a considerable loss of time, and the separate forces failed to concentrate for combat. Only Moreau, with the centre, managed to support Lecourbe. Kray had been surprised, however, and was unable to collect his army to take advantage of the disarray. At Engen and at Stockach on May 3, and at Messkirch on May 5, Moreau kept the upper hand, thanks to the steadfastness of his soldiers. He continued his advance toward the Iller River and the Vorarlberg, driving a wedge between Kray and his left which occupied the Tyrol. Kray then fell back on Ulm. Moreau, who was weakened by the loss of 15,000 men whom he had sent to Italy, had only 90,000 soldiers against the Austrian's 140,000, and so began to manœuvre his forces, not daring to attack. Finally on June 19, Moreau forced a crossing of the Danube at Hochstädt, compelling the Austrians to abandon Ulm from the north. The enemy made their way back across the Danube, trying to establish a line of defence on the Isar, but the French dislodged them by occupying Munich, throwing them back on the Inn. On July 15, an armistice was signed at Parsdorf.

Since June 16, Bonaparte had again written to Francis II inviting him to negotiate a peace. But the proposal came at a bad time. On June 20, Thugut concluded a treaty with Lord Minto in which England granted Austria a subsidy provided she did not sign a separate peace. In order to gain time, the Austrian court nevertheless dispatched Count Saint-Julien on an unofficial mission to Paris, the purpose of which was to make inquiries into the proposed conditions for peace. Outwitted by Talleyrand and threatened by Bonaparte, Saint-Julien allowed himself to be induced into signing a preliminary draft of a treaty ceding the entire left bank of the Rhine in return for certain unspecified compensations in Italy. Upon his return to Vienna, he was discredited and thrown into prison. Meanwhile, in order to play along with Austria's game, England declared herself ready to participate in a conference, at which point Thugut agreed to negotiate officially. Since the armistice conventions were nearing their term, Bonaparte took advantage of this offer to demand a general suspension of hostilities and the right to reprovision Malta and reinforce his position in Egypt. This Grenville refused; besides, Malta capitulated on September 5. The price of this stalemate was paid for by Austria, since Bonaparte had only agreed to prolong the armistices on condition that she surrender Phillipsburg, Ulm, and Ingolstadt. Meanwhile in Vienna, there raged a fierce struggle between the advocates of war and those for peace, viz., between Thugut, who was supported by Maria Carolina of Naples and the Empress on one hand, and the Archduke Charles on the other. Thugut refused to ratify the agreement signed by Saint-Julien and he resigned as chancellor. He was succeeded by Louis de Cobenzl, who had negotiated the two last partitions of Poland in St. Petersburg. Thugut nevertheless maintained his influence through the instrumentality of Colloredo, since Cobenzl personally departed for Lunéville to negotiate the treaty. Having first been summoned to Paris by Napoleon, Cobenzl was unable to begin his talks with Joseph Bonaparte, France's representative at Lunéville, until November 5, 1800. Anyway, these conferences in Lunéville came to naught because the First Consul remained vague on the subject of French concessions in Italy. All the while, Napoleon proceeded to establish himself in the Cisalpine Republic, Genoa, and in Piedmont. It was there that Murat led the Third Army of Reserve. In addition, General Dupont occupied Tuscany under the pretext that the English were in Leghorn. With this act, which was in direct violation of the armistice, the winter campaign began.

The French forces in Italy now numbered 100,000, of whom

only 57,000 were under General Brune, the new commander-in-chief of the army in Italy. Brune held the line of the Mincio opposite the Austrian General Bellegarde, who commanded 80,000 men deployed between the Vorarlberg and the Po. Macdonald, who with the 18,000 soldiers of the Second Army of Reserve occupied the Grisons, had received orders to cross the Splügen Pass, thereby extending Brune's left in an attack through the Tyrol. In Bavaria Moreau led an army of 95,000 men, which the Austrians opposed with 100,000, who were nominally under the command of the young Archduke John, but in reality were led by General Lauer. On the Main stood Augereau with 16,000 French and Dutch troops. It would have been only natural to have combined the forces of Augereau, Macdonald, and even Murat with those of Moreau for a drive on Vienna, but Bonaparte counted on dealing the mortal blow himself in Italy.

The campaign was decided in much less time than Bonaparte had thought possible. Preparing to cross the Inn with 60,000 men, Moreau had deployed his divisions along the river when suddenly Lauer, with 65,000 men, took the offensive, manœuvred to the right, and skilfully began threatening the French left at Ampfing. As the two armies turned to face each other, Moreau rushed to gather together all the available forces along the edge of the forest of Hohenlinden. There the battle took place on December 3. The Austrians, advancing through the woods in separate, unconnected columns, found themselves unable to debouch from the defiles of the forest into the clearing. Meanwhile Decaen and Richepanse flanked and turned the Austrian left. Then Richepanse went on to take the Austrian centre from the rear, causing them to break into a rout. The Austrians lost 12,000 to 15,000 men and 100 guns. This time Moreau hurried to the pursuit, chasing after the dislocated enemy and capturing 25,000 prisoners. In order to avoid losing Vienna, Austria signed an armistice at Steyer on December 25, and agreed to conclude a separate peace. While this was taking place, Macdonald had reached the upper Adige after a remarkable campaign across the mountains, and Brune was finally able to begin his attack. Brune, however, handled the crossing of the Mincio very badly, and at Pozzolo on December 25, General Dupont escaped disaster only because the enemy forces were equally poorly commanded. With the Adige and Brenta having been crossed, the armistice signed at Treviso on January 15, 1801, pushed the Austrians back behind the Tagliamento River. Thus it was Moreau who had put an end to the war, and for this Bonaparte never forgave him. As for Murat, he invaded Tuscany and at Lucca, drove out the Austrians, and compelled the Neapolitans to sign a convention at Foligno.

In Lunéville, Cobenzl did his best to resist Bonaparte's demands, giving in step by step as the news grew steadily worse. Having agreed to negotiate in the name of the Holy Roman Empire and having abandoned Mantua, he attempted to salvage Tuscany. But England was powerless to help in this matter, and Paul I had definitely broken with England and begun his *rapprochement* with France. The peace was finally signed on February 9, 1801, exactly as dictated by the First Consul. The Holy Roman Empire consented to cede, pure and simple, the entire left bank of the Rhine, subject to certain indemnities which were to be distributed among the dispossessed princes at the expense of lands belonging to the Catholic Church. The Duke of Modena was awarded the Breisgau, and the Duke of Tuscany was also compensated in Germany. France seized control of northern and central Italy: the boundary of the Cisalpine Republic was extended to the Adige thereby including the territories of Verona and Polesina; the territory of Novara, taken from Piedmont, had already become part of the Cisalpine Republic so as to open the route of the Simplon Pass; finally, the Papal Legations were also incorporated into the republic. The treaty made no mention of the kings of Sardinia and Naples, nor of the Pope. Hence their respective fates were left to Bonaparte's discretion. True, the treaty did guarantee the independence of the Cisalpine and Ligurian Republics, Holland, and Switzerland. But then, what was this promise worth?

Precisely what was going to be in store for Italy soon became apparent. Even then the Cisalpine Republic was reorganized by Bonaparte, who gave it first a *consulta* or legislative assembly and then a triumvirate of his own making. In Genoa he established a governing commission. The refusal of Charles Emmanuel IV, King of Sardinia, to return to Turin led to

Bonaparte's establishment of a provisional government in Piedmont. The Russian negotiations with the French ambassador Saint-Marsan over the future of Piedmont—negotiations which had been pursued out of deference for the tzar—were broken immediately after the death of Paul I. Piedmont was transformed into a French military province, divided into départements, and subjected to the same administrative and financial rule as France. King Ferdinand IV of Naples signed the Treaty of Florence on March 28, according to which he evacuated Rome, ceded the island of Elba and the principality of Piombino, agreed to close his harbours to English vessels, and authorized the occupation of Otranto and Brindisi for one year by French garrisons who could use them as ports of embarkation for Egypt. Lucca became a republic. Tuscany was to be Bonaparte's trump card in his Spanish and colonial politics. On March 21, 1801, the Treaty of Aranjuez awarded the Grand Duchy of Tuscany (which had been converted into the Kingdom of Etruria at Lunéville) to the Duke of Parma's son, who was the nephew of the Spanish queen and husband of a Spanish infanta. This gift to Spain was considered payment for her retrocession of Louisiana to France, made on October 1, 1800. In addition, France was to obtain Parma from Spain, but the ageing Duke of Parma turned a deaf ear on the bargain and Bonaparte did not press matters until his death. Bonaparte's representatives carried great authority everywhere: Brune in Milan, Jourdan in Turin, Dejean in Genoa, Salicetti in Lucca, Clarke in Florence, Moreau de Saint-Méry in Parma, Alquier in Naples, and Murat in Rome where Pope Pius VII, elected in February 1800 by the Venetian conclave, had established himself the summer before. Like the other princes of the peninsula, the Pope lay at Napoleon's mercy, and Marengo, like Marignano 285 years before, would open the way to the negotiation of a concordat under advantageous circumstances.

Bonaparte had slashed the Gordian knot with a single blow. The victory over Austria had done far more than confirm and consolidate the conquest of the natural frontiers. As the creator of the Cisalpine Republic, it would have been personally difficult for Bonaparte not to have recaptured it. But far from stopping there he clearly indicated that he intended to keep Austria out of Italy altogether. Finally, the Treaty of

Lunéville provided the means for contesting the Austrian claims in Germany. The pacification of Europe, pursued along these lines, could only result in a temporary truce.

THE LEAGUE OF ARMED NEUTRALITY AND THE ENGLISH CRISIS

While Bonaparte was depriving England of her allies, he also strove to threaten her directly, and with the help of Paul I he began making plans for an anti-British federation of continental states—preliminary shades of the system later adopted at Tilsit.

During the course of the year 1800, Bonaparte began reorganizing the naval administration and developing the armament, especially at Brest. After Lunéville he formed a camp at Boulogne with the intention of invading England. In England, public opinion, if not the government, immediately reacted with alarm. In August 1801 Nelson attacked the French flotilla commanded by Admiral Latouche-Tréville on two separate occasions, but he was repulsed with heavy losses. With Holland unable to do any more on the sea, Bonaparte redoubled his demands on Spain. It was partly in order to better control that country that he extended himself in Italy, for Bonaparte himself later declared that whoever held Italy also held Spain. It was all very reminiscent of eighteenth-century politics and of the Family Compact of 1761, but it was not Bonaparte's fault that the Bourbons of Naples were not committed to the revival of this policy. However, in 1802 the occurrence of a double marriage between the son of Ferdinand IV and a Spanish infanta on one hand, and the Prince of the Asturias and Marie-Antoinette of Naples on the other, offered some hopes in this respect.

Bonaparte unfortunately had no other ideas on Spain than had the Directory before him. He too despised that country of the Inquisition, along with its king and queen and their favourite, Manuel de Godoy—Godoy had just recovered his control over the affairs of state by having his cousin Don Pedro de Ceballos installed as First Secretary of State after Urquillo's disgrace on December 13, 1800. Bonaparte therefore treated them with contempt. Believing the kingdom enormously rich, his demands on it were great, and he attributed its traditional dilatoriness to bad will. Meanwhile, his entourage looked on Spain as an object of prey. Talleyrand extorted immense bribes which he divided with Berthier, never missing an opportunity to manifest his hatred of Charles IV, who had not been able to conceal his contempt for him. Ouvrard was also looking out for fortunes to be made in Spain and maintained close contact with Hervas, a Spanish banker residing in Paris whose daughter married Michel Duroc, the future Duke of Friuli. The Spanish fleet by itself would have been ineffective against England, and its principal squadron, commanded by Admiral Gravina, continued to remain at Brest. Beyond Spain, however, Portugal, a British 'fief', was vulnerable, and Lucien Bonaparte was sent to Madrid to persuade the Spaniards to undertake a joint expedition. The affair turned out to be sheer comedy. Godoy, who harboured his own suspicions, did not bother to wait for the French army. He captured the fortress of Olivenza on May 16, 1801, laid siege to Elvas on May 18, and having thus brought to an end the 'war of the oranges', he immediately proceeded to sign a peace, the conditions of which were the cession of the province of Olivenza by Portugal and the promise to pay Spain an indemnity of 15 million francs. As an accessory to this scheme, Lucien returned to Paris with an enormous booty. Talleyrand was also involved, being in the pay of Portugal and a former lover of Madame de Flahaut, who was at the time remarried to the Portuguese ambassador. Even England was prepared to profit from the situation, if necessary, by seizing Brazil. She had refused to grant military assistance to Prince John, who was Regent of Portugal in the name of his insane mother, and to his minister, Coutinho, counselling them to sue for peace in order to avoid occupation. Befooled from every quarter, Bonaparte raged, but to no avail as he was unable to do more than raise the amount of the indemnity to 20 million francs.

Assistance came principally from Paul I, whose hostility toward England was steadily mounting, and also from the neutrals who followed in Russia's wake. Toward them, Bonaparte exhibited a degree of moderation which contrasted with the policies of the Directory and which in no way portended the continental blockade. From the month of December on he abolished the radical measures of his predecessors, returning to the attitude adopted by France during the American War of Independence. He also made certain changes in the area of laws governing prizes at sea. The emissaries from the United States, whom President Adams had agreed to send in his anxiety to avoid war, soon arrived in France. Since France recognized the principle of freedom of enemy goods in neutral ships, except contraband (*le pavillon neutre couvre la marchandise*), an agreement was easily reached and concluded at Mortefontaine on September 30, 1800. The Americans were especially desirous that Bonaparte no longer insist on the alliance of 1778, so that they might be free to pursue the policy of no entanglements which Washington had always advocated. Bonaparte's attitude made that of England appear much more irritating to the Scandinavians, the Prussians, and the Russians. Besides, Paul I was growing increasingly worried about the fate of Malta. On August 29 he declared an embargo on all English vessels in Russian ports, and did so again upon learning that Malta had capitulated; in addition, Grenville, on October 17, decided in favour of keeping Malta. Finally on December 16, 1800, Sweden and Denmark, following Russia's lead, formed, together with her, the Second League of Armed Neutrality, Prussia joining on December 18. England was now shut off from the Baltic Sea; the Danes entered Hamburg, and Prussian troops occupied Hanover, on the pretext of preventing a French occupation. British shipping was thus effectively barred from the German rivers and the Hanseatic towns. England was now deprived of its two essential markets, Germany and the Baltic states.

It was Bonaparte's treasured hope that Paul would consider these steps as only preliminary to a more far-reaching alliance between France and Russia which would officially unify the Continent against England. Ever since July 1800 he had offered to restore to the tzar, without ransom, the Russian prisoners who had been detained in France, and not on a basis of exchange, since the Russians held no French prisoners. Towards this end General Sprengporten was dispatched to France. In December, a simultaneous exchange of friendly letters passed between Paul and Bonaparte: the latter ordered the suspension of hostile acts against Russian vessels; the former expelled Louis XVIII from Mittau. Then in March 1801, Kolychev was sent to Paris to sign the peace and to discuss terms for an alliance. Paul, very much at odds with England, decided to embark on the conquest of India, and marched off an advance guard of cossacks toward the steppes of Central Asia. But for all that he had no intention of renouncing the gains which he had already won or even those which he contemplated, such as Rostopchin's proffered European project entailing the partition of the Turkish Empire between Russia and Austria and the creation of an immense Greek state under Russia's protection. Paul still coveted Malta; he expected that the Kingdom of Naples would be evacuated and the King of Sardinia restored; and he also maintained his protection over Germany. But Bonaparte, who had refused to surrender Italy to Austria (it would have assured the peace), was not about to hand that country over to Russia. Nor was he about to deliver her the Grand Turk. How then was Bonaparte to win Russia over to his side without in effect granting her anything? The problem was all the more difficult since Kolychev, like Markov who succeeded him in July, was the inflexible representative not only of Paul I but of a Russian aristocracy still very hostile toward France, and he had made it a point of honour to defend the interests of the Italian princes. A choice had to be made. But as far as England was concerned, the prospects were not becoming any the less perilous.

England was experiencing severe difficulties. Her industry had suffered from the crisis of 1799, and famine had been rampant ever since the harvest of that same year. Between 1800 and 1802 England imported nearly 3½ million quarters of wheat. Neither of these blows, however, was as harsh as the one dealt her by the League of Armed Neutrality. The stoppage of shipments from the Baltic caused a panic on the corn exchange, and the quarter rose to 151 shillings on April 25, 1801. A pound of bread sold for up to more than five pence, or the equivalent of seven French sous. Even though Parliament decreed the usual measures for such eventualities, disturbances erupted here and there which were blamed on speculation, and the farmers did in fact unite to keep prices high. Threatening placards, which were ascribed to Jacobinism and to French propaganda, such as those calling for 'bread or blood', inflamed public opinion. At the same time the financial situation appeared disquieting: gold was at a 9 per cent premium in 1801, and silver at 17 per cent; the cash reserves of the Bank of England fell once again to £4½ million; subsidies amounting to £5,600,000 together with the cost of maintaining garrisons (£2,800,000) and grain purchases accounted for £23 million which flowed out to the Continent in 1800 and 1801. The rate of exchange on the pound lost nearly 16 per cent in Spain in 1801, and 13 per cent in Hamburg. And yet neither the aristocracy nor the merchants countenanced the idea of raising the income tax. Given these conditions, peace, as in 1797, soon became the cry of the day, and Fox took advantage of it. On October 9, 1800, William Grenville's brother, Thomas, wrote: 'the scarcity of bread and the consequent distress of the poor, if it continues, will I believe, force you whether you will or no to make your peace with France'. And the *Monthly Magazine* (October 1800) pointed out that 'as the humane and laudable policy therefore of starving the French nation cannot be realized, perhaps it would be sound policy to try to prevent our own people from starving by making peace'.

It would have been difficult for Pitt and Grenville to accept this fact had not an incident in domestic politics spared them that humiliation. The Union with Ireland having been accomplished, it still remained to honour the promise tacitly given to the Catholics to abolish the Test Act. On September 30, however, the Lord Chancellor, Loughborough, had declared himself opposed to its abolition. His sentiments were promptly echoed by the entire Protestant coterie, and the king pronounced himself publicly as being of the same opinion. The cabinet became divided over the issue, and Pitt tendered in his resignation on February 5, 1801. The king then called on Addington, a man of mediocre talents, to form a government, thereby assuring himself more influence in the conduct of affairs. As a result of these troubles, George III succumbed to another fit of insanity, but he quickly recovered and blamed Pitt for his illness. Eager to resume his office, Pitt unabashedly promised never again to raise the Catholic question during the king's lifetime. Grenville, however, refused to have any part in this palinode, and since Addington was not willing to step down, Pitt was forced to resign on March 14. Political circumstances being what they were, it may be assumed that Pitt's disappointment was to some extent mitigated. Lord Hawkesbury, the new foreign secretary, had approached France with offers to open peace negotiations as early as February 21. And although Addington's administration, which in fact depended for its continued existence on Pitt's tolerance, received Pitt's approval on its policies as far as the signing of the Peace of Amiens, it is quite possible that Pitt, seeing that a peace was inevitable, was only too happy to have escaped the responsibility for its making.

The negotiations between Hawkesbury and Talleyrand immediately ran afoul over the question of Egypt. Hawkesbury was not opposed to letting the French stay there; he even sent a countermand to the expeditionary force already on its way to Egypt, which arrived too late, however. But as compensation he wanted to retain most of the British conquests, whereas Talleyrand calmly contented himself with offering India! Actually, England's willingness to treat only reinforced the hopes of Bonaparte, who counted on crushing her with the help of Russia. Addington, on the other hand, although resolved to negotiate, hoped for a somewhat better settlement should the ventures then in progress turn out favourably. As it happened, the respite benefited Great Britain.

THE PEACE OF AMIENS (MARCH 25, 1802)

Two events occurring almost simultaneously shattered the dream of a continental coalition. During the night of March 23, 1801, Paul I was assassinated. That should not have come as a surprise. The Russian nobility, already exasperated by his sanguinary fickleness which threatened all of the officials, had been driven to it because the break with England would have deprived them of a market for their grains and timber. The plot was engineered by Count Nikita Panin and Count Peter Pahlen in collusion with Alexander. It appears that the grand duke had stipulated that no bodily harm should befall his father, and he was later overcome by grief, but his illusions, if that were the case, were naïve to say the least. One of the first things Alexander did was to seek an accommodation with England.

The other event occurred on March 28 when a squadron

under Sir Hyde Parker, with Nelson second in command, forced the passage of the Sound. Copenhagen was shelled, and the Danish fleet severely damaged. Denmark concluded an armistice, and upon hearing of the tzar's death, signed a peace on May 28; Sweden had already done as much on May 18, and Alexander followed suit on June 17. The Second Armed Neutrality was no more. Formed during the course of the winter, it had not inflicted great material losses on England, but it did leave an impression not soon forgotten. There was nothing left for Bonaparte to do but come to terms with Russia. On October 8, Alexander agreed to re-establish the peace officially. He secured recognition of the situation which his father had acquired, both in the Mediterranean where he retained a protectorate over the seven Ionian Islands and a garrison at Corfu, and in Turkey where Bonaparte accepted him as the sultan's mediator. France also consented to evacuate Naples after a settlement of the Egyptian question and to treat the King of Sardinia with the consideration called for by the situation. Finally, the affairs of Germany were to be arranged by common agreement. In short, Bonaparte conceded to Alexander very nearly all that he had wrangled out of Paul, and that, without obtaining in exchange anything more than a peace treaty. For Napoleon it was a resounding failure.

The Egyptian venture turned out to be another setback. On departing from Egypt, Bonaparte had appointed General Kléber to succeed him. The latter was determined to follow Bonaparte back to France as soon as possible by signing a convention of evacuation. Kléber, the Grand Vizier Yussef, who commanded the Turkish army advancing through Syria, and Sir Sydney Smith, an English commodore, met at El-Arish on January 24, 1800, where they negotiated an agreement; but Admiral Keith, the commander of the English fleet, refused to ratify it. The grand vizier resumed his advance on Cairo, but Kléber completely routed the Turkish army at Heliopolis on March 20. Unfortunately, Kléber was assassinated on June 14. His successor, General Jacques-Abdallah Menou, lacked Kléber's authority, and his conversion to Islam had not increased his prestige. He continually quarrelled with his subordinates, and used his soldiers as judges. In an effort to save the Army of the Orient, Bonaparte sent a squadron under

Admiral Gauteaume to reinforce Menou. It sailed from Brest on January 23, 1801, and would have encountered little in the way of enemy opposition, but Gauteaume timorously put in to port at Toulon. When he resumed the attempt toward the end of March, the British expeditionary force had already set sail for Egypt, and Gauteaume once again begged off. In a final attempt he put out to sea at the end of April and tried to land his reinforcements in Tripoli, whose pasha had consented to a treaty, but confronted there by Arab hostility Gauteaume abandoned the whole project. At that moment the fate of Egypt was already decided. Shortly after the capture of Malta, Henry Dundas, the Secretary of State for War, had ordered preparations for the sending of an expeditionary army to Egypt under the command of Sir Ralph Abercromby. It landed on March 6 and repulsed Menou's attack on March 21 at Canopus. With Popham's fleet now in control of the Red Sea, 6,000 sepoys sent from India by the Marquess of Wellesley landed at Kosseir; meanwhile, 25,000 Turks emerged by way of the Isthmus. Cairo fell on June 28, and Alexandria on August 30.

Late in July, after the break up of the Second Armed Neutrality and the failure of his attempt on Portugal, Bonaparte held out new peace proposals according to which the belligerents were to restore each other their respective conquests. The only exception was that Holland would lose Ceylon and would open the Cape to international traffic. In short, France was to relinquish Egypt—a condition about which Bonaparte affected calm acceptance, but which made its loss nonetheless certain. On the other hand, France would retain all her continental conquests. England was to abandon Malta, Minorca, Elba, Trinidad, the French Antilles and, in effect, Egypt, keeping only Ceylon. Although her position had already become favourable enough to make this glaring inequality appear offensive, England was content to demand only the retention of Trinidad in addition to Ceylon. Concerned over her relations with Alexander, England raised no objection to the restitution of Malta, although she could have pleased him by demanding guarantees for Naples and Sardinia. No efforts were made toward that end, however. Only in regard to Holland did Lord Hawkesbury try to obtain assurances, and he also demanded that Malta be given a garrison furnished by a Great Power, which would thus become the guarantor of its neutrality. This provided France with an excellent opportunity to advance the candidacy of Russia and so revive her rivalry with England. But Bonaparte spurned the chance, and when he threatened to break off negotiations if these preliminaries of peace were not signed, Hawkesbury gave in on October 1, 1801, without so much as demanding an indemnity for the Prince of Orange or a commercial treaty.

It has been argued that this capitulation was caused by Addington's incompetence as Prime Minister, but that reason is simply not adequate. After all, the British government continued to labour under the pressure of the crisis which had characterized the early months of the year and whose effects were still being felt throughout the country. More than anything, the government wanted to economize, and it believed that peace would provide a return to prosperity. The intense rejoicing with which the public reacted to the news of peace attests to the fact that such was the dominant opinion. Nevertheless, there were protests and reservations made both in Parliament and in the press. William Windham cried out against the 'fatal treaty' which he regarded as 'the nation's death warrant' and which, he claimed, would allow Bonaparte to undertake fresh conquests. Addington retorted that since a new coalition was for the moment impossible, it would be better to try a policy of peace which a contented France might after all take to heart. Should the case prove different, England would always find allies again. Castlereagh, in a letter, expressed the same opinion. Pitt, who had approved the government's policy, defended it on November 3 on the surprising ground that Trinidad constituted a more valuable gain than Malta, the retention of which would have made peace impossible anyway, and that Ceylon seemed more preferable than the Cape. He placed great value on Trinidad for the sugar it produced and as an important base for the contraband trade with Spanish America. Here one can distinguish an expression of the mercantilistic attitudes on the objectives of war which had always dominated the policies of Britain's ruling oligarchy. In England the peace was regarded not only as a truce but also as a businessmen's experiment.

It was not long before perspicacious individuals realized that the chances for a lasting peace were indeed quite poor. Bonaparte was already engaged in sending an army to San Domingo (December 1801), and in January he became President of the Cisalpine Republic whose name was changed to that of 'Italian Republic'. In discussing the final settlement of the treaty, Bonaparte refused to consider a commercial agreement, and he laid claim to certain colonial concessions, the opening of India to free trade, and a station in the Falkland Islands. These demands were rejected, but created quite a sensation. Nevertheless, Addington persisted in his course. It is quite certain that in the negotiations which followed at Amiens, British interests suffered once again from the incompetence of the government and its representative, Cornwallis—an honest man, a good soldier, but a pitiful diplomat. France's allies, who bore the cost of the peace, and particularly Schimmelpenninck, would have gladly lent Cornwallis their support; but it was not until they had agreed to the preliminaries that Bonaparte admitted them to the conferences.

The discussions centred principally on the French conquests and Malta. Bonaparte wanted England to recognize the new republics, a gesture to which she was not altogether opposed provided that some concessions were granted to the King of Sardinia. Obtaining nothing on that score, England refused. Bonaparte then declared that she should have no grounds for complaint if 'in consequence her commerce suffered' and if one of these states should choose to incorporate itself 'with a major continental power'. It was a bad omen! As for Malta, England accepted Talleyrand's proposal for a collective guarantee of the Great Powers, but refused to agree to a general dismantling of its fortifications, insisting that the island receive a Neapolitan garrison until such time as the reconstituted Order of St. John could itself procure adequate forces to maintain its independence. Having torn Malta away from England, Bonaparte saw his success confirmed. Still, Malta's surrender was made dependent on so many conditions that England too should have been reasonably satisfied and could await developments. Cornwallis had been instructed to hold fast on two other points: the cession of Tobago in exchange for the cost of maintaining French prisoners, and an indemnity for the Prince of Orange. However, Bonaparte was adamant in his refusal to surrender any French territory, and as for the 'Orange-Nassaus', he observed that negotiations regarding an indemnification were going on in Berlin. The heir to that house, a great admirer of the First Consul, displayed his willingness to deal directly with Bonaparte and left England. Cornwallis then signed the peace on March 25, 1802.

Public opinion in England, although somewhat cooler than before, remained satisfied, and a great many islanders flocked to France out of curiosity for a country transformed by such momentous developments and ruled by such an astonishing figure. Although critics in political circles were rapidly becoming more numerous, Parliament still accorded the government its confidence.

As chief of state, Bonaparte had attained the crowning achievement of his destiny by signing the Peace of Amiens. Europe had agreed to lay down its arms without contesting his claim to the natural frontiers. But his indomitable will to power, which he was unable to bridle with each succeeding opportunity, prevented him from ever being satisfied in a way that France might have been, had she but been her own mistress guided by national tradition and interest alone. Still, all would not have been lost had Bonaparte stopped harassing England on the seas and in her colonies, agreed to reopen the French market to English trade, and consented to exercise in neighbouring countries that legitimate amount of influence which his power allowed and which the security of France's frontiers required. Even before the Peace of Amiens had been concluded, however, Napoleon had given proof that this was not the way he understood matters to be.

THE REORGANIZATION OF THE VASSAL STATES

Actually, France could not abandon her neighbouring states and those she occupied to their own devices without first making sure that they were in a position to defend and govern themselves. Now, after the political and social changes to which she had subjected them, they would have been hard put to organize themselves on their own. In many of the vassal republics, the unionist advocates of strong central government were unable to agree with the federalists on the very principles of government. Such was the case in Holland, in the Cisalpine—where the inhabitants of the département of Olona, that is to say, the Milanese, who followed Count Melzi, quarrelled with the *Ottrepadani* (the inhabitants of the states south of the Po), also known as Emilians, led by Aldini—and above all in Switzerland, where the cantons longed ever so passionately for their autonomy.

More serious still was the social conflict. Jacobin democrats were becoming very active, agitating in their clubs and jeering at nobles and priests at every opportunity. Being but a minority, they were on the best of terms with the French, to whom they had appealed for help, and were quite willing to do their bidding. Representatives of the bourgeoisie, like Schimmelpenninck in Holland, Usteri and Rengger in Switzerland, Corvetto in Genoa, and those of the nobility who were reconciled to republican government, like Count Melzi d'Eril in the Cisalpine, approved with more or less vigour the unity and the new social order; but they were hostile to democracy and hoped that, as in Consulate France, the notables would be assured a position of pre-eminence. Nevertheless, they were not always at one—in Switzerland especially—on accepting the Constitution of Year VIII in so far as it suppressed the normal functioning of elective government. If they felt the need to depend on France, they were also less obedient. In Holland and in Switzerland they appealed to France to preserve the integrity of their country; everywhere, they wished for the evacuation of French troops and for independence. As for the aristocracy, they hoped for the downfall of France so that they might restore the Old Regime. To achieve this they would have delivered their country without scruple to other foreigners, but since the French were there, they played the role of patriot. They were willing to keep quiet for the time being as long as Bonaparte left them alone.

In addition to this kind of party strife, normal government was also made impossible by budgetary difficulties. The cost of the war and the occupation had from the very start ruined finances and crippled economies. The Cisalpine, with its 4 million inhabitants, paid 33 million francs to the French army, and it furnished French troops with requisitions in kind whose total amount was estimated at 160 million francs. Then, too, the military arrogated to itself additional levies at will, and generals, notably Murat, subjected the authorities to high-handed treatment. The same can be said of civilian officials, like the Marquis de Sémonville in Holland. Both the military and civilian officials intervened in local politics and supported this or that candidate according to his preferences. Consequently, petitioners came to Bonaparte from every direction requesting that he reorganize the state as he saw fit or that he lighten their burden and bring his own subordinates to justice. Bonaparte was as free to act among these factions as he was in France. He hated the democrats, distrusted the moderates whom he considered too independent in regard to France, and he did not want to re-establish the aristocracy. As long as the Concordat remained to be concluded with the Pope who, for his part, still hoped to recover the Papal Legations, and as long as the war with England continued, Bonaparte acted with circumspection, and this he did to advantage. For as the situation worsened, so did his task become easier, and as long as the occupation lasted, his troops cost him nothing. It was only after the preliminaries of the maritime peace were signed that the changes began.

In Holland, where there appeared some signs of disobedience, Sémonville, the French representative, prepared a constitution with the approval of the Dutch Directory. It was designed to place power in the hands of trustworthy men. He submitted it, on his own prerogative, for popular ratification, but the legislative chambers refused to sanction it on the ground that the procedure had been illegal. General Augereau then dissolved the two chambers, and the constitution was placed before a national plebiscite. A majority vote was obtained by declaring that the abstentions had been taken as a sign of approval, and the constitution was promulgated on October 6, 1801. It created a *Staatsbewind* or reigning council invested with legislative initiative and executive power, including the nomination of officials, and a legislative body to be renewed one-third at a time by means of elections in two stages. In fact, the Directory itself named seven of the twelve regents, the remainder being co-opted; it also chose the members of the legislative chamber. The new government, just as Bonaparte had hoped, worked to unify factions, but it did so by getting rid of the democrats and by giving all of the official posts to the notables.

In Italy, which Bonaparte himself intended governing, the work of reorganization took a little more time. During the month of July 1801 a deputation from the Cisalpine Republic arrived in Paris to complain about the intolerable situation at home. In October it was arranged that a 'commission' gather in Lyon in order to establish a new government. The commission was made up of lawyers, representatives of the army and of the national guard chosen by the government, and of elected members of the courts, chambers of commerce, universities, and departmental and municipal administrative bodies. In addition, these choices were made under the watchful eye of Murat. On December 29, 1801, 442 deputies met in Lyon. Talleyrand, who arrived on the eve of the meeting, divided them into regional sections for the purpose of studying the constitutional project and drawing up lists of trusted candidates from which the new personnel would be chosen. In so doing, he fanned the flames of particularism so that Bonaparte might step in and arbitrate over a divided assembly. The latter made his appearance on January 11, 1802. He proceeded as usual to make his personal inquiries, and settled everything himself. He considered Joseph for the presidency of the Cisalpine, but that important personage refused because he was not being offered Piedmont as well. On January 21, the committee in charge of selecting chief magistrates chose Count Melzi and Count Aldini. They both refused. On January 24, Bonaparte was offered the presidency and he accepted, taking Melzi as vice-president. Two days later, he substituted the name 'Italian Republic' for that of 'Cisalpine', thus giving rise to great hopes. The date set for the official installation of the new government was February 9, 1802. The executive authority was accorded the same prerogatives as in Paris; it included a secretary of state and various ministers. In addition, the executive chose the members of the legislative council from among the candidates nominated by the three electoral colleges. On this occasion however, Bonaparte himself elected the members of the legislative council and the colleges. Finally, the Italian Republic was given an original institution called the State Council: it was irremovable and was to deal with foreign affairs and matters of state security. In Genoa, a constitution drawn up by Salicetti in October 1801 was promulgated in June 1802. There, Bonaparte named the members of the Senate and a Doge which formed the executive authority. A consulta, which should have been chosen by three electoral colleges, was never formed. Lucca submitted to a similar reorganization on December 28.

The history of the Helvetic Republic was considerably more turbulent. The coup d'état proposed by Frédéric-César de La Harpe to his colleagues in the Directory in November 1799 did not receive their approval. The legislative councils, having been warned, countered by voting the dissolution of the Directory on January 7, 1800, entrusting power to an executive committee in which Dolder exerted the leading influence. The executive committee soon also fell to quarrelling with the councils and appealed to Bonaparte. On August 7, 1800, the councils, surrounded by French troops, capitulated and formed a provisional government from among their own ranks, charged with the task of preparing a new constitution. The coup was the work of moderate unionists, that is to say, that party which favoured strong central government and a unitary state. Above all, they were advocates of government by notables. As enemies of the Jacobins, they sought the support of the aristocracy and reintroduced tithes, ground rents, and feudal dues which had previously been abolished. True, these were made redeemable, but at the expense of the peasantry. In January 1801, these moderates submitted to Bonaparte a constitutional project markedly unionist in character, according to which the members of the constituted bodies were to be co-opted. Seeing that the unionists were intent upon laying claim to the Valais and to the Bishopric of Basle (the Bernese Jura), the federalist-minded representative of the French government in Switzerland, Reinhard, suggested fomenting a new revolution with the support of the aristocracy. This, however, Bonaparte would not permit. He simply rejected the constitutional proposal, and on April 29, 1801, substituted for it a counter-project called the 'Constitution of Malmaison', which foreshadowed the later Act of Mediation. Bonaparte felt that federalist sentiment was too deeply rooted not to grant a large degree of sovereignty to the cantons. It is also likely that since he intended to evacuate Switzerland in order to benefit from its neutrality, he was not favourably disposed to the creation of a centralized Switzerland which would have made that country too powerful. By the Constitution of Malmaison, the seventeen cantons were given considerably autonomy, and were authorized to frame their own constitutions with a proviso that suffrage be limited to property holders. The federal Diet elected a Senate consisting of twenty-five members who in turn chose two leading magistrates from among themselves bearing the title of *Landammann*: one presided over the Senate; the other formed, along with four other senators, a small council which was to exercise the executive authority. The central federal authority now possessed extensive powers, particularly in its appointment of the cantonal prefects (*statthalters*).

This solution pleased no one. The unionists assured themselves a majority in the Diet, and excluded from the Senate the federalists who seceded. The unionists then refused to apply the Constitution of Malmaison, voted for a new one, and, to crown it all, openly defied Bonaparte by accepting into their ranks the deputies from the Valais. On October 28, 1801, the French agent, Verninac, and General Choin de Montchoisy declared the Diet dissolved and set up a provisional government under the rule of Aloys Reding, the ablest of the aristocrats. Reding purged the administration, suppressed freedom of the press, amnestied the émigrés, abolished the land tax, and reopened the monasteries. Bonaparte refused to recognize him, demanding that he make a place for the moderates. This naturally created discord within the council. Reding journeyed to Paris, but received nothing for his trouble; he returned to Switzerland, and proceeded on his own authority to promulgate a new constitution on February 26, 1802. During the Easter recess however, Verninac took advantage of Reding's absence from Bern to have it annulled by his enemies. An assembly of notables was summoned, and it finally approved the Constitution of Malmaison on May 29, 1802, and appointed Dolder Landammann. The Valais was constituted as an independent republic, and the Valley of Dappes was ceded to France.

There exists an obvious connection between these changes and those which took place in France. Everywhere, the Constitution of Year VIII had encouraged notables to lay claim to

The Pacification of Europe

authority by much the same processes. Everywhere, the executive power had undergone strengthening, thus holding out the promise of order and stability. And everywhere, Bonaparte demanded that democrats be brushed aside and that efforts be made to reconcile moderates and well-intentioned aristocrats. But it was in Italy, where he regarded himself as master rather than arbiter, that Bonaparte revealed his secret predilections, such as he would never have dared presume openly in France and even less in Holland or Switzerland, where he was to maintain genuine elections in the future. In the Italian constitutions, the electoral colleges were not in any way founded on suffrage, even of a kind limited to property holders. They were simply professional groupings: the first consisted of a certain number of landed proprietors (*possidenti*), the second of merchants and manufacturers (*commercianti*), and the third of members of the professional classes (*dotti*). The first two of these colleges co-opted their members; the third, being naturally suspect of harbouring 'ideology', i.e., subversive ideas, was limited to offering the government a list of candidates. To perfect the scheme, only one step remained to be made: simply to confer upon the chief of state the power to appoint the members of the colleges.

In itself, the reorganization of the states that neighboured France did not offer Europe any cause for concern. Quite the contrary, it was to be hoped that France, having made it possible for these states to govern themselves, would recall her troops and give them the independence which she had promised them—barring the details—in the Treaty of Lunéville. Bonaparte did in fact give the order to evacuate Switzerland in July 1802; and he also consented to reduce the number of soldiers stationed in Holland—the Prince of Orange having renounced his claims to the stadholdership on May 24, in exchange for the cession of Fulda and Corvey to his son. At any rate, it was good enough to pass as a promise of future evacuation. Melzi, in the Italian Republic, hoped to obtain a similar advantage sooner or later: Bonaparte's presidency could only be temporary. How very illusory these hopes appear to us today! But without these illusions, the road upon which Addington and Pitt decided to venture would have lacked all raison d'être.

CHAPTER SIX

Bonaparte Consul for Life

VICTORY AND PEACE made Bonaparte a hero of the nation, and he used the occasion to increase his personal power and to further his personal ambitions. The country, satisfied with his accomplishments, was willing to follow him; but there were feelings of regret and anxiety when he heightened his dictatorship at the very moment when peace promised a return to liberty. In any event, opposition increased, and it was only by fresh applications of force that Bonaparte was able to subdue the resistance.

THE CRISIS OF YEAR IX

After Bonaparte's departure for Italy, France experienced a period of anguish. His defeat would probably have resulted in an invasion by foreign troops, and most certainly in new uprisings inasmuch as bread prices had risen ever since the harvest of Year VII; during the course of a riot in Toulouse, the mob forced merchants to lower the price of grain. On the Paris exchange, prices were falling. Then suddenly, as if by magic, the news of the military victory at Marengo restored public confidence and magnified Bonaparte's popularity a hundredfold. Appreciating the power of the press and possessing an instinct for public relations, Bonaparte had assumed that such indeed would be the effect. In his mind, pride and ambition spontaneously transformed truth into legend. He published a *Bulletin of the Army of Reserve* which, along with the *Moniteur* and other more or less official newspapers, glorified his entire campaign. Moreau's victory at Hohenlinden came too late to attenuate his prestige, and besides, he took good care to stifle its repercussions. Ironically, had the truth about Marengo been known, Bonaparte's halo would surely have been even brighter, for men are seduced still more by the workings of chance than by sheer genius (and it inspires in them a certain superstitious awe). The throw of the dice at Marengo could hardly have detracted from a man who, on two occasions, had miraculously escaped the English cruisers.

In the meantime, Bonaparte, having heard what was being said and plotted during his absence, hastened to return to Paris, and he entered the city on July 2, 1800. He returned an embittered man, full of rancour against his entourage, with a hostile distrust for the generals who had been waiting for the chance to succeed him. And he was seized with a feeling of melancholy now that the effort was spent and the danger past—and now that the tragic side of the adventure dawned on him with the full realization of how close he had come to disaster.

The royalists collapsed at once. Only a few bands of brigands remained from their preparations for an insurrection. Wickham returned to England, and the agency in Augsburg dispersed; some of its members tried to regroup in Bayreuth, but Fouché had them thrown into prison by the Prussian police. England stopped subsidizing Condé's corp of émigrés, which had entered into its pay, and disbanded it. On September 7, 1800, Bonaparte at last made his reply to Louis XVIII saying, 'Your return to France is not a thing to be wished for; it could only be accomplished over the bodies of 100,000 men.' Expelled from Mittau, the king took refuge in Warsaw, then later went to England. Their rupture was complete.

The republicans, too, were well aware that Bonaparte's victory would rivet their chains. There were many in his entourage who had secretly contemplated his death or downfall. Now they became all the more anxious to convince him of the necessity to stabilize his authority by restoring the hereditary monarchy to his own advantage. Most illustrious among them were Roederer and the *Feuillants*. They had rallied to the Republic, but remained monarchists at heart. Talleyrand naturally supported them. Lucien Bonaparte, always turbulent, fearlessly said what no one else dared to say when he launched a pamphlet entitled *A Comparison Between Caesar, Cromwell, Monk, and Bonaparte*, which was probably written by Fontanes. The path of fortune had been marked for Fontanes ever since the First Consul had returned to France and designated him to deliver a eulogy on the occasion of Washington's death, not to mention the fact that he was already Eliza Bonaparte's lover.

Nevertheless, all these manœuvres encountered resistance. Fouché remained hostile to all monarchical projects until 1804. For Fouché, although widely connected and valued even in the Faubourg St. Germain for personal services rendered sub rosa, was still regarded as the leader of the left. And not without good reason. True, he was a sceptic who bore no illusions about men, an egotist whose passions were money and power. But his attachment to his revolutionary past was greater than one might suppose. Witness his domestic life, simple and familial, his cool vigour and determination, and his preference for terroristic methods, which, although wisely tempered, quite naturally suited his functions as Chief of Police. Then there was his sincere desire to save what he could of the work of the Revolution and to prevent the aristocracy from regaining control of the state. Finally, and above all, there was his hot temper, concealed under a phlegmatic exterior, resulting in his habitual irreverence, his caustic tongue, and his nostalgic regret for the time when, as Representative on Mission of the Convention, he too had spoken with absolute authority in the name of the sovereign people. Bonaparte valued his talents and feared him, feeling that Fouché might assert his independence at any time.

Fouché found support in Bonaparte's immediate circle. Josephine, having failed to produce an heir, feared that the establishment of a hereditary line of succession would lead to a divorce. Bonaparte could hardly have been pleased by the insatiableness of his family clan; he fully expected a raging tempest if circumstances forced him to choose between his brothers. But he did not intend to have his hand forced, and he considered any talk of monarchy premature at this time: the peace had not been concluded, the reorganization of the country had to be completed, and the parliamentary bodies still had to be cowed. And so Lucien was dismissed; he ceded his post as Minister of Interior to Chaptal, and became an ambassador.

Bonaparte was waiting, nonetheless, for the chance to increase his own power. The uncovering of several conspiracies furnished him with just such an opportunity. These plots were still another consequence of the victory at Marengo: after that battle, the Jacobins and royalists lost all hope, and some became desperate enough to try their hand at assassination. In the closing days of Year VIII and shortly thereafter, three Jacobin plots were uncovered: on September 14 three persons were arrested; this was followed by the arrest of Aréna, Topino-Lebrun, and two others on October 10; and finally, Chevalier and an alleged accomplice on November 8. Whether or not these conspiracies were genuine has never been solved. The second seems to have been uncovered behind Fouché's back, and Fouché, feeling his position endangered, made a great fuss about the third so-called conspiracy. Just as the government was working on a project to proscribe the Jacobins, the royalists came on the scene and greatly facilitated this task. In June, Cadoudal had sent several Chouans from Brittany to organize a plot in Paris. The police, who kept track of their movements, were only able to apprehend a certain Chevalier de Margadel, whom they shot. Three of the conspirators—Saint-Réjant, Limoélan, and Jean Carbon—managed to construct an infernal machine which they exploded in the Rue Saint-Nicaise the evening of December 24 on Bonaparte's route from the Tuileries to the Opéra. Twenty-two people were killed and fifty-six were wounded, but Bonaparte escaped unharmed. The consensus was that this had been the work of Jacobins. Bonaparte, who was already near enough to the throne to loathe regicides above all else, also appears to have believed it. On December 25, while the parliamentary bodies were congratulating him on his fortunate escape, he thundered furious imprecations on 'those who have dishonoured the Republic and sullied the cause of liberty by all kinds of excesses, and especially by the part they played in the September days and the like'. 'Blood must run,' he declared in the Council of State on December 26. And indeed, the previously accused Jacobins were either shot or guillotined on January 13, 20, and 31, 1801.

The upshot of the affair was the wholesale arrest of Jacobins which now followed, and their subsequent deportation without trial. Fouché had laid the blame on 'English gold' ever since the night of the attempt—indeed, he knew who the true culprits were. Limoélan was kept in hiding by the Jesuit Clorivière and by the sister of Champion de Cicé until he finally managed to escape to America where he became a model priest; Carbon was arrested on January 8, and Saint-Réjant, on January 28. But it was too late to save the victimized Jacobins, and besides, Bonaparte could not have been swayed from his goal. The Council of State refused to pronounce on the proscription, declaring that it was not a legislative matter. Then on January 5, the Senate was called upon to ratify the act as a 'measure tending to preserve the Constitution'. Among the 130 deportees were Choudieu and two former deputies, Talot and Destrem, whose vehement opposition on 19 Brumaire Bonaparte had never forgiven. There were also some well-known revolutionaries: Fournier l'Américain, Rossignol, and Lepeletier. Fouché managed to save about a third of them by playing for time. Twenty-six were not sent to Guiana until 1804, and sixty-eight were shipped out to the Seychelles after 1801. More than half died in exile. In addition, many more republicans were placed under surveillance. Fouché also arrested about a hundred royalists, whom he condemned to prison or interned without trial. Carbon and Saint-Réjant were tried at last, and succumbed to the guillotine on April 21.

The Bonapartist terror had once again struck the left and the right. 'It was the only kind of impartial justice from which he never wavered,' wrote Madame de Staël, 'thus he made friends out of those to whose hatreds he ministered.' The blow had been directed primarily against the left, and one might even say that it had been completely crushed. But the Jacobins were not the only ones affected. The assemblies had not been summoned to vote on the law of proscription, because it was not absolutely sure that they would accept it. Bonaparte's pronouncement on December 26, that 'the metaphysicians are the cause for all our troubles', very clearly constituted a threat to the assemblies. After that, he turned to the Senate which, as 'guardian of the constitution', invested itself tacitly with the power to modify or violate that constitution. Consequently, the decree of 13

Nivôse, Year IX (January 5, 1801), stands as the first in a series of *senatus-consulta* which were to make it possible for Bonaparte to legislate personally without the legal assistance of the assemblies, and so to revise to his own advantage the Constitution of Year VIII, which had not provided for any such procedure.

During and after the month of November 1800, while the proscription of the Jacobins was going on, Bonaparte contemplated certain repressive measures which, although less spectacular, would exercise a still much greater influence on the general condition of the country. The problem, as he saw it, was to put an end to the Chouan uprisings and to brigandage with one blow. Cadoudal, having revived the Chouannerie, was scouring the countryside in Brittany. He was continually being hunted down and was forever eluding capture. Using the good offices of the royalist Bourmont, Fouché finally succeeded in bribing certain persons involved in the Chouannerie to kill or deliver Cadoudal to the police. But the Breton royalists had an extremely active counter-espionage network which extended into the government ministries. Thus, when the two renegade Chouans, Becdelièvre and Duchatellier, were sent to murder their former leader, Cadoudal, informed of the situation, had them killed. The Prefect of Ille-et-Vilaine, Borie, may himself have betrayed Duchatellier.

The exploits of the Chouans exasperated Bonaparte. On September 23, 1800, Clément de Ris, former administrator of Indre-et-Loire, Senator, and important purchaser of the biens nationaux, was kidnapped from his château at Azay-sur-Cher, while on November 19, Audrein, Bishop of Finistère, was assassinated. Convoys carrying treasury funds were continually being raided and pillaged by various bands of insurgents. As in Year VIII, Bonaparte had recourse to extreme measures. On 18 Floréal, Year IX (May 8, 1801), three columns accompanied by military tribunals were dispatched under the command of General Bernadotte. The mopping-up operations proceeded rapidly. By the end of the year, Cadoudal returned to England. Even so, there still remained some isolated bands of Chouans. Aside from a few sincere individuals, the majority were irregulars who looked upon rebellion as a way of life.

Whether or not the brigands invoked the name of religion

or the king, they existed to some extent everywhere. Certainly they were not restricted to mountainous regions, such as the Alps and Apennines where the 'Barbets' carried on a smuggling trade; they were also to be found in wealthy places such as Nord and Beauce. People called them *chauffeurs* (furnace men) because they tortured their victims by fire to extract their money. This was nothing new; the rural population abounded in day labourers, who were unemployed part of the year, and peasants who were unable to live on the meagre harvest from their lands, especially during the bad years. The countryside was always swarming with beggars and vagabonds, and it was inevitable that some of them became outlaws. The evil had been seriously aggravated by internal troubles as well as the war, which upset the economy and disorganized the rural police. The peasant has always valued his security even more than the urban dweller, because he has always been more exposed. And since security is the basic condition of sustained and productive labour, nothing could have been of greater service to the nation than its re-establishment. Consequently, nothing could have heightened Bonaparte's reputation more, as was indeed the case with Henry IV and Louis XIV.

The problem was not just one of apprehending the brigands —that could have been done by letting the army reinforce the gendarmerie—but of obtaining their conviction. Both witnesses and juries knew that they were open to reprisals, and so the one kept quiet and the other acquitted the culprits. Numerous cases of misdemeanours had already been brought before the courts in Year VIII, and prefects had been given the right to supervise the choosing of juries by the justices of the peace. The results remained poor. Moreover, the slowness with which the repression was carried out deprived it, in part at least, of its efficacy. Under analogous circumstances, the monarchy had had recourse to the provostal court, a special legal instrument which summarily condemned and executed: 'caught and hung'. As an exceptional measure, Bonaparte resorted to military tribunals in the west, in Provence, and in the Rhineland. He had not the slightest intention of renouncing them, but he also wished to revive the expeditious methods of the Old Regime on a permanent and regular basis.

Such, then, was the object of the law of 18 Pluviôse, Year IX

(February 7, 1801). It authorized the government to establish, in each département where Bonaparte thought it advisable (he decided on thirty-two), a special criminal court composed of a president, two judges issuing from the regular criminal court, and five other persons (three from the military, two civilians) all appointed by the First Consul. They were to pronounce final judgment, without appeal, on vagrants and habitual criminals, *ratione personae*, and on a great number of crimes pertaining to brigandage: burglary, highway robbery, murder, arson, counterfeiting, seditious assembly, and illegal possession of weapons. The following year, on 23 Floréal, Year X (May 13, 1802) another special court was established in every département dealing with crimes of forgery, but which, in the absence of a special criminal court, could also take cognizance of many crimes of brigandage.

On 26 Vendémiaire, Year XI (October 18, 1802), the jury system was suspended in a large number of départements by a senatus-consultum; henceforth, criminal court judges were set up into a kind of special court without any intervention on the part of the military, however. In short, Bonaparte did away with the jury system in a great many parts of France, and these newly created judicial bodies continued to function until his downfall. The same law did away with the grand jury, since the special courts now delegated the preliminary judicial inquiry to one of their members. Finally, the regular judicial process, wherever it continued to exist, was given new strength by a change in the office of public prosecutor and by a reform in procedure. On 7 Pluviôse, Year IX (January 27, 1801), a 'criminal magistrate' (*magistrat de sûreté*) took the place of the government commissioner in the courts of first instance, and he was empowered to draw up the indictments; the judicial inquiry became in part secret, witnesses being heard in the absence of the accused. Thus the grand jury had to decide from indirect evidence, since the accuser and witnesses were excused from appearing in court so that they might be kept out of reach of the felons' vengeance.

Despite all of these measures, one should not conclude that Bonaparte succeeded in immediately re-establishing perfect order in the country districts. Regardless of what he may have thought or done, the suppression of mendicity and vagabondage did not depend on him entirely. It was a long time before outright banditry was overcome. In the Rhineland, it was a difficult task to capture Schinderhannes, a veritable 'Cartouche'* whom people regarded with some complacency because he was particularly fond of attacking Jews. Nevertheless, by the early years of the Empire it was apparent that conditions had become incontestably better. Since the special courts were not used for political ends—they touched only the abject and delinquent members of society—they were not condemned by public opinion. As for political suspects, Bonaparte dealt with them through the military tribunals of which he made much use. Although the judicial reforms were severe with respect to professional criminals, they also served to check the poverty-stricken elements that despair might otherwise have driven to riot, as in 1789. 'Decent', law-abiding citizens drew no distinction between starving mobs and felons, nor did the law of Year IX. Such must have been Bonaparte's wish surely, for according to Chaptal, he feared nothing quite so much as a bread riot.

The establishment of the special courts, coming on the heels of the proscription of the Jacobins, caused a good deal of concern among the republicans in the assemblies. Debate in the Tribunate became very heated, and a vote in the Legislative Body, resulted in 88 'nays' as against 192 'ayes'. No longer bearing any illusions about Bonaparte, the republicans did not miss this opportunity to remonstrate. Nevertheless, one must do them justice: these notables had favoured strong government, but not an arbitrary one, and they were unable to regard these exceptional measures as being any more consonant with principles under the Consulate than at the time of the Convention under the Mountain. Bonaparte, however, would not be blocked by any law, not even a constitutional one. Speaking before the Council of State in Year X, he came straight to the point: 'A constitution must not interfere with the process of government, nor be written in a way that would force the government to violate it. ... Every day brings the necessity to violate constitutional laws; it is the only way, otherwise progress would be impossible.' 'Government does not have to be tyrannical ...;

* Cartouche was the leader of a notorious band of robbers in the early eighteenth century. TRANSLATOR.

but it cannot avoid committing certain arbitrary acts.' Briefly then, the Constitution was a screen for enlightened despotism. Debates in the Tribunate also aroused Bonaparte's fury. 'In the Tribunate are a dozen or so metaphysicians only fit for the garbage heap. They are vermin on my clothes. I am a soldier, a son of the Revolution, and I will not tolerate being insulted like a king.' The crisis of Year IX thus rendered official the breach between Bonaparte and the republican bourgeoisie, which had carried him to power. But now he wanted them to ratify the Concordat, and of all his projects, it was precisely this one that they least approved.

This parliamentary opposition found no support in the rest of the country. The various interest groups were satisfied, and peace and public order favoured a resumption of business. A new bank of issue was created in Paris: a commercial bank known as the *Caisse Jabach*. Notes issued by the Bank of France and its rivals permitted speculators to dispose of currency in the provinces where it stimulated the economy. A series of bad harvests brought about an unprecedented increase in the price of agricultural products, and so strengthened the buying power of the landowning peasantry or farmers. After the deflation, which had made them so unhappy under the Directory, they were delighted with this windfall. They were grateful to the First Consul who exhibited, moreover, an avid interest in the national output, and so they spared him no encouragements. An amelioration in the condition of public finance was also becoming noticeable. The military conquests had helped to lighten the burden on the budget, since the French armies were now able to maintain themselves outside France. Taxes were being collected regularly, and in Year X the budget actually revealed a small surplus of receipts over expenditures. In large towns the tax on movable personal property was gradually being replaced by municipal tolls (octrois), to the satisfaction of the rich. As for taxes on landed property, a study was being conducted to determine ways of arriving at a more equitable distribution of the burden among the communes. Later, in Year XI, cadastral surveys of the extent of cultivations, land boundaries, and valuations of soil productivity were under-taken in a number of communes in every département.

The state of the treasury continued to be a matter of concern.

An attempt was made to eliminate some of the middlemen (*faiseurs de services*) in the ministry's operations by creating, on August 18, 1802 (30 Thermidor, Year X), an association or syndicate of receveurs généraux. The idea was to force them to discount their own obligations, but the attempt failed. The notes continued to be negotiated at a loss. For the public, however, the major event was the liquidation of the debt. As in the time of the Directory, it was achieved by means of bankruptcy. The highly depreciated 'two-thirds' bonds issued in 1797 were freely exchangeable at one-twentieth of their face value for consolidated government annuities bearing 5 per cent interest, unless the bearer chose to redeem them, as before, for payments in biens nationaux. Bonds issued in Year VI and paper obligations in arrears were consolidated into government bonds at 3 per cent and 5 per cent interest with extreme slowness. Still, creditors were happy that this enactment of 30 Ventôse, Year IX (March 21, 1801), had at least brought them something; but the main impression resulted from the resumption, at the end of Year VIII, of the cash payments of government salaries and annuities. Purveyors to the state continued to be paid at Bonaparte's pleasure.

This is not to say that confidence in French finances was fully restored. In spite of manœuvres on the part of the Sinking Fund, the value of government bonds on the bourse remained weak. After the Peace of Amiens, the 5 per cent French consolidated government bonds were quoted at 48 to 53 francs, while the 3 per cent British Consols fluctuated between 66 and 79. Still, if the bourgeoisie felt itself at the mercy of any new crisis that might have arisen, it did not wish to precipitate one by creating difficulties for Bonaparte. The lower classes alone suffered. After the harvest of Year VIII, the price of a four-pound loaf of bread rose to 13 sous (65 centimes) in Paris, and by 1801, the rise in prices affected all commodities and so lessened the good feeling brought about by the Treaty of Lunéville. The harvest of Year XI was quite poor, even in areas of large-scale farming; during the course of that winter, bread rose to 18 sous in Paris, and as high as 7 sous per pound in small towns and the countryside—as much as in England. Brittany, no longer able to export, remained the only exception.

In order to meet the crisis, Bonaparte turned to methods

which had been used by the Old Regime. The prefect of police reorganized the bakers along corporate lines, and compelled them to set up a reserve granary. This resulted in driving many small bakers out of business. On November 17, 1801, Chaptal was instructed to purchase grain abroad, but since the government was short of money, it again became necessary to approach the bankers: five were commissioned to procure 50,000 quintals monthly. This turned out to be insufficient, and in Floréal, Year X, Bonaparte brought the financial wizard Ouvrard out of disgrace and obtained his promise to do what was necessary to relieve the situation. Success was such that Paris was kept supplied, and the price of bread was maintained at 18 sous. A million quintals of grain and more were needed to do this, at a cost of over 22 million francs; the grain was then resold at a loss of 15½ million francs to the state. Outside the capital, the countryside was once again dotted with familiar scenes: bands of beggars, requisitions on farmers, incendiarism, and raids on markets. That this agitation did not become so menacing as in 1789, when bread was almost as expensive, was due only to the absence of political and social troubles and to the efficient reorganization of the repression that had just been introduced. Here, then, were the fruits of the law of 18 Pluviôse, Year IX. In any event, popular disturbances could only have brought about a still closer attachment of the propertied classes to Bonaparte. He became the bulwark of society. The crisis attained its height during the summer of Year X, at the very moment that Bonaparte was preparing to assume the Consulate for Life, and so served his purposes well.

THE CONCORDAT

In order to re-establish order once and for all, it was still essential that the counter-revolution in France be disarmed, and Bonaparte had long considered that this could be done only through a reconciliation with the Roman Church. The refractory clergy continued to be intractable. 'Peace with the nonjuring clergy is not to be expected,' wrote de Redon, one of the Consul's special commissioners.

One might well ask what the future of France would have been had church and state remained separate? The Roman

Catholics would not have recognized the secular character of the state or liberty of conscience; at best, they would have resigned themselves to tolerance at the price of a privileged position. Only on these terms would they have agreed to disarm, at least temporarily. And so Bonaparte decided to make the best of it. On 30 Thermidor, Year VIII (August 17, 1800), in the presence of Roederer, he began reproving those who 'believe that the priests should be ignored as long as they keep still, and arrested whenever they step out of line. It is as if one were to say: You see these men with torches camped around your house? Leave them be. If they set fire to it, arrest them.' What was to be done? 'Win the leaders over by appealing to their interests,' but first and foremost, choose them well. 'Fifty émigré bishops subsidized by England,' he would later say to Thibaudeau, 'are now running the French clergy. Their influence must be destroyed, and to accomplish this requires the Pope's authority.' This, then, was the reasoning behind the Concordat.

To call upon the Pope to dismiss the French bishops, as Louis XIV had once thought of doing, was tantamount to dealing a death blow to ecclesiastical Gallicanism, one of the oldest of French traditions. This tradition was totally foreign to Bonaparte, whose sole interest was monarchical, not clerical, Gallicanism. The only argument which might have moved him had been Thibaudeau's remark: 'You will never truly win them over to the Revolution.' Bonaparte overrode this judgment. Like all others who had invoked the assistance of the Roman Church, he believed himself strong enough to keep it under his control.

Disarming the royalists by denying them the support of the clergy was not the only advantage to be gained from the Concordat. Although there was no issue of counter-revolutionary affection for the Bourbon cause, in such newly acquired provinces as Belgium and the Rhineland, the support of the local clergy was still much to be desired. These people had no national political institutions, and their primary loyalties lay with their priesthood. Consequently, to win over the priests was to win over their flocks. Another point that did not escape Bonaparte's attention was that even among ardent supporters of the Revolution, there were many who retained their ties with traditional religion and who deeply regretted the schism.

Would they not have covered with gratitude the man who would effect a reconciliation, even an apparent one, between the Church and the principles of 1789? And what possessor of Church lands would not have been overjoyed to hear that the clergy had forever renounced its attempts to reclaim them?

Bonaparte also foresaw an advantage to be reaped in the future. Wishing to win the aristocracy and counter-revolutionary bourgeoisie to his side, he could hardly ignore the religious renaissance they were now experiencing. At the beginning of 1801, Father Delpuits-Bordier founded *La Congrégation de la Vierge*, which was to acquire much renown; it was not long in attracting such personages as Mathieu de Montmorency and his brother, as well as Laënnec. Charitable congregations also began to reappear; they were readily patronized by Chaptal in Paris, and certain prefects such as J.-A. De Bry in Besançon. Religion was once again considered good form in society, and it was reflected in the literature of the day. Writers were delighted at the opportunity to renew religious themes and give direction to the intellectual fashion. Madame de Genlis, the self-styled 'mother of the Church', was prolifically turning out her novels of virtue; Chateaubriand, sensing the trend, was in the process of writing *Le Génie du Christianisme*, which would appear on the eve of the Easter Te Deum of 1802 celebrating the conclusion of the Concordat, and would prove the truth of Catholicism by its aesthetic merits. Writers like Fontanes, who were more political in their thinking, saw a good deal more deeply into the situation: restoration of the cult was socially significant in that it would support the new class division. And since it was precisely Bonaparte's intention to consolidate this class division, he fully agreed with them. As he told Roederer and would later repeat to Molé: 'There can be no society without material inequality, and there can be no material inequality without religion. A starving man watching another stuff himself cannot accede to their differences if there is no authority to tell him "God wills it so"; the world must consist of rich and poor alike; but there will come a day when for all eternity, man's lot shall be decided differently.' Fontanes, too, sharply observed that the government would also benefit from an agreement. 'No religion, no government,' he wrote to Lucien on April 18,

1801, 'successful conquerors have never quarrelled with priests. They can be kept in check and made use of. . . . One may laugh at the augurs but it would be impolitic not to join them in eating the sacrificial birds.'

Although winning over the Pope did not seem to be the most difficult of tasks, it was really not an easy thing to do. While passing through Vercelli on June 25, 1800, Bonaparte had made overtures to Bishop Martiniana, who in turn transmitted them to the Pope in Rome. Pius VII was not the fighting pope that his predecessor had been; he was a gentle soul and somewhat weak-willed. Still, he baulked at making peace with the Revolution and especially at abandoning the old episcopate who proclaimed that they had sacrificed themselves for the pontiff. Then, too, there was the risk of alienating Louis XVIII and the Catholic powers. In August, 1800, the cardinals, who regarded the prospect of a concordat with little favour, declared the oath of fidelity to the constitution illicit. It was a decision that Pius VI had never dared to make, and which Pius VII wisely kept secret. On the other hand, it seemed impossible to reject an offer so advantageous to the Church and so profitable to the papacy. This last consideration was most assuredly a weighty factor in its favour. In the first place, the French army could still come to Rome, and Pius VII distrusted both the Neapolitans who occupied his capital and the Austrians who were still in possession of the Legations. Secondly, by deposing the Gallican bishops, the Pope would gain an unprecedented victory over Gallicanism.

This point having already been granted by Bonaparte for his own reasons, Cardinal Spina left for Paris with instructions to demand, as a preliminary, the restoration of Catholicism as the 'dominant religion'. Arriving on November 6, he immediately met with Abbé Bernier, Bonaparte's negotiator. The former spiritual leader of the Vendéans, Bernier had just crossed over to Bonaparte's camp in the firm hope of becoming Archbishop of Paris and being elevated to the office of cardinal. Naturally the French proposals made no mention of a state religion, but at Spina's insistence, Bernier gave way and Bonaparte saw no harm in it. There was a misunderstanding, however, for Bonaparte had failed to realize the technical implications of such an avowal. By calling Catholicism the state or dominant religion, he only intended to confer on the Church an endowment and a privileged position over all other sects. Talleyrand and Hauterive quickly opened Bonaparte's eyes to the fact that this would do away with such basic revolutionary gains as the liberty of conscience and the secular character of the state. From then on Bonaparte recognized Catholicism only as the religion of the majority of Frenchmen, a position from which he refused to budge.

The other point of contention was that the nonjuring French prelates were to be forced to resign their dioceses. The Pope, despite his scruples, had too much at stake for Spina not to have finally ceded to Bonaparte's demands. If the negotiations dragged on, it was because the curia was awaiting the outcome of the war; but the occupation by the French armies of the Legations and of Rome itself left no alternative but to yield. At the end of February 1801, the tempo of the negotiations increased, and Bonaparte sent Cacault to Rome to pursue the matter. Since the curia procrastinated, Bonaparte directed Cacault on May 19 to demand an unreserved acceptance of the French terms and to break off negotiations in case of a refusal. The cardinals had already rejected the French proposals, however, and Pius VII had just sent the First Consul a letter suggesting certain modifications when Cacault, returning to Paris, took it upon himself to bring Cardinal Consalvi, the Papal Secretary of State, back with him. Arriving on June 2, Consalvi proceeded to dispute the treaty article by article, but finally signed it on July 16, 1801, at two o'clock in the morning.

According to the terms of the Concordat, Catholicism was declared the religion of the majority of the French people as well as that of the consuls. It was further stipulated that should a non-Catholic accede to the head of the government, negotiations would have to be opened for a new concordat. The Church was to enjoy freedom of public worship, subject to certain police restrictions which the temporal authority might deem necessary in the interest of public safety. The state, for its part, agreed to pay salaries to bishops and to as many parish priests as there were justices of the peace (3,000–3,500 by the law of 8 Pluviôse, Year XI—January 28, 1801); it authorized the restoration of cathedral chapters and diocesan seminaries, without, however, being obliged to endow them; and it granted

Catholics permission to make pious foundations. The Pope undertook to exhort refractory bishops to renounce their sees, failing which he would dismiss them. Bonaparte was to make identical demands of the constitutional clergy, thus putting an end to the schisms. No mention was made of the monastic orders, which, therefore, remained completely under the direct authority of the Pope. The power of the bishops was also considerably increased, in the spirit of the Edict of 1695: they were given the right to appoint parish and chapel priests—a privilege which they had not enjoyed under the Old Regime. In return, Bonaparte obtained a new episcopate of his own choosing, an oath of fidelity to be taken by the clergy, public prayers for the Republic to be recited at the end of divine services, the promise of the Church not to contest the sale of its confiscated lands, and to accept a redrawing of ecclesiastical boundaries. Bishops were to be nominated by the First Consul and canonically instituted by the Pope. This was the essence of the matter for Bonaparte: he believed that by controlling the bishops he would be controlling their priests and, fearing the refractory element, he preferred placing the parish clergy under the thumb of the episcopate rather than watching over them himself. As for the monastics, he intended to tolerate their independence only to the extent that it would prove profitable for him to do so.

The Pope ratified the Concordat and sent Cardinal Caprara to Paris as his legate to supervise the practical details of its application. Meanwhile, on October 7, Bonaparte appointed to the post of Minister of Public Worship his Councillor of State, Portalis—a man whose fervent piety was combined with definite Gallican leanings, but who nevertheless lost no time making numerous further concessions. The constitutional bishops, who had held a council in 1801, submitted without resistance despite the severe criticism of the Concordat by their most illustrious representative, Abbé Grégoire. Such, however, was not the case with the nonjuring bishops: thirty-six of the eighty-two refused to submit, as did one of the thirteen bishops from the newly annexed territories (*pays réunis*). These recalcitrants protested against the dispossession of their sees, and in this they were followed by a number of their faithful. The result was that in several dioceses there continued to exist, and does to our own day, a church opposed to the Concordat—the so-called *Petite Eglise*—although its adherents were never numerous.

In spite of the opposition, a list of new bishops was immediately prepared. Since the provisions of the Concordat did not specify any specially reserved places for the constitutional bishops, Rome claimed the right to refuse their institution, and it took all of Bonaparte's firmness to carry through the appointment of twelve ex-constitutionals, among whom Grégoire was noticeably absent. Also appointed were sixteen of the former refractory bishops who had sent in their resignations, which included Champion de Cicé at Aix, Boisgelin at Tours, and d'Aviau at Bordeaux. To these were added thirty-two new bishops drawn largely from among the priests who accepted the agreement. The entire settlement was imperilled at the last moment by Caprara's insistence that newly appointed ex-constitutional bishops retract their late errors and by the latter's staunch refusal to make amends. Bernier, who was negotiating for the French government, managed to save the situation by making use of an equivocation, as had been done in 1668 to reconcile the Pope with the Jansenist prelates: he simply assured Caprara that the schismatics had made a satisfactory oral declaration of their errors. It should be added that this over cunning individual only received the bishopric of Orléans for his services.

All that remained now was to have the treaty ratified by the assemblies. The Council of State was frankly hostile to it, and its session on October 12 was very stormy. Bonaparte had just prohibited all gatherings of theophilanthropists, a move hardly calculated to assuage feelings. On November 22, the Legislative Body elected as its president, Dupuis, author of the anti-religious book, *L'Origine de tous les cultes*; on November 30, the Senate chose the constitutional bishop Grégoire to fill a vacancy. In the Tribunate, opposition to the Concordat was fairly unanimous, and the Idéologue Volney was subjected to a celebrated dressing-down by Bonaparte. Opposition in the government found two opportunities to manifest its annoyance: in the peace treaty with Russia which the opposition criticized roundly because the text made mention of 'French subjects' rather than 'French citizens', and in the Civil Code, of which the first 'Titles' were voted down on December 28 except for the one dealing with the public registry because it explicitly excluded any state religion. There was not the least doubt as to the sentiments of the army, and on July 20, the morrow of the signing of the Concordat, Fouché directed that recalcitrant priests were to be sought out and arrested; Bonaparte had to make him withdraw the order. It seemed as if the Concordat was headed for certain defeat.

Talleyrand advised making some concessions to the opposition, and he himself pointed the way, observing that the literal execution of the Concordat would necessitate certain supervisory regulations. Appearing as *Articles organiques du culte catholique*, these regulations were then added to the Concordat without the knowledge of the Pope, who, upon hearing of their inclusion, did not dare protest. The articles made Gallicanism a general law of the state: seminarists were to be taught the four Gallican articles of 1682; and the publication of bulls, the holding of general councils, the ordination of priests, the creation of seminaries, and the editing of catechisms were all made subject to the approval of the government. The temporal authority further arrogated to itself the right to regulate bell ringing, processions, and priestly dress. The articles also fixed the new ecclesiastical divisions and the salaries, from which pensions granted by revolutionary laws were to be deducted. Communes were permitted to grant lodgings or to pay chapel and parish priests if they so desired.

This was not all. In order to ensure that Catholicism would not again become the state religion, provisions for Protestants were drafted under the title of *Articles organiques des cultes protestants*. Reformed and Lutheran ministers were also to be salaried; Calvinists were to be administered by local consistories comprising the most heavily taxed members of the congregation and placed under the presidency of the oldest pastor; Lutheran Churches were to be provided with general consistories. This Protestant charter was joined to the Concordat, framed by the 'Organic Articles', and so constituted a single and unique law. It was not certain that even so modified, the agreement with the papacy would have found favour in the assemblies. But Bonaparte had taken precautions, especially since he harboured other designs which were sure to encounter opposition. A new coup d'état sufficed to bring about the capitulation of the assemblies.

On January 4, 1802, Bonaparte withdrew all the bills that had been submitted to the assemblies, and put them, as Portalis had predicted, on a 'diet of laws'. Three days later the Council of State declared that the session of the assemblies should therefore be considered terminated, and that it would now be possible to proceed with the first renewal of a fifth of its representatives, which had been scheduled for Year X. Since the method of selecting the outgoing members had not been defined in the Constitution, the matter was referred to the Senate. Clearly, these members should have been chosen by lot, and one might well have thought that the Senate would have acted accordingly since it, no less than the other assemblies, entertained certain qualms. But the Senate was probably threatened with force, and it may have been promised new advantages as an inducement to submit. In any event, the Senate itself decided, by a vote of 46 to 13, to designate the members who were to be retired, and in so doing, it removed the most prominent Idéologues in the Tribunate, to wit: Benjamin Constant, Marie-Joseph Chénier, Daunou, Ginguené, Laromiguière, and Jean-Baptiste Say. They were replaced by men of lesser consequence, officers and civil servants. Carnot alone remained. Lucien Bonaparte became a tribune, and so re-entered politics to play the same role as in Brumaire. He presented to the Tribunate a measure which was adopted on 11 Germinal, Year X (April 1, 1802), dividing that body into three sections which were henceforth to deliberate *in camera* on laws and articles of the Civil Code. This was soon followed by a consular decree which ruled that the laws under preparation were to be examined first by competent section heads and state councillors in special councils presided over by the First Consul. Thus it was highly improbable that any disagreement would ever be aired at an open session. 'There must not be any opposition,' said Bonaparte. 'What is government? Nothing, if it does not have public opinion on its side. How can it hope to counterbalance the influence of a tribune if it is always open to attack?' The Council of State, likewise suspect, was also affected by these changes since it no longer exercised control over the final drafting of laws; in short, it was in the specially created councils composed of his trusted appointees that Bonaparte now set about preparing his ambitious programme, the results of which were only submitted to the Council of State as a mere formality.

The assemblies having been subdued, there remained only the danger of a military revolt. Advantage had been taken of the peace to scatter and purge the dangerous elements of the several armies; a corps destined for Portugal had been supplied by the Army of Italy; troops sent to San Domingo had been provided by the Army of the Rhine. Nevertheless, a good deal of discontent persisted, for the army's pay was not being met regularly, and soldiers, especially in these times of scarcity, longed for the profitable adventurous life which was so much a part of every campaign. Paris was literally swarming with idle generals who envied their chief. They were the men who least believed in his military genius and would only admit to the workings of chance. 'There is not one among them who does not fancy himself as deserving as I,' Bonaparte would say. They all put themselves forward as republicans, but their civism was open to great doubt. They spoke of dividing France into separate commands; had they succeeded, they would have soon fought among themselves and the country would have fallen into a state of anarchy. Given the fact of military dictatorship, a single dictator was the only logical possibility, and the French nation, on this score too, endorsed Bonaparte.

Foremost among the generals hostile to Bonaparte were Moreau and Bernadotte. Moreau was definitely on bad terms with his rival. His wife and mother-in-law even urged him to break off all social contact with Bonaparte; the *Moniteur*, for its part, insinuated that Moreau had been malfeasant in Germany. But he was even more indecisive in civilian matters than in military life. Bernadotte, on the other hand, was more energetic, and as commander of the western forces at Rennes, he would have been in a position to issue a manifesto. Actually, in spite of his blustering ways, he was much too concerned for his own interests not to have carefully weighed the risk involved in such an act. As Minister of War, he had missed his chance to seize power in the summer of Year VII, and circumstances now were much less favourable. Before he would compromise himself, he insisted that the Senate take the first steps. In Paris, from March to June, numerous secret conspiratorial meetings were held, and certain civilians were sounded out, including Fouché. Meanwhile, three officers were arrested on May 7, one of whom was General Donnadieu. On May 20, General Simon, Bernadotte's chief of staff, secretly dispatched two inflammatory proclamations to the army, attacking Bonaparte. These fell into the hands of Dubois, the Prefect of Police in Paris, who rejoiced at having caught his minister napping. Fouché then arrested General Simon and his accomplices in the 'libel plot'. Bonaparte hushed the matter up for he did not want it said that the army was against him. The officers in question were kept in prison without trial; the 82nd regiment of the line was shipped out to San Domingo and remained there permanently; and the generals Richepanse and Decaen were sent to the colonies —Lannes to Lisbon, and Brune to Constantinople. General Lahorie was retired and General Lecourbe was put on half-pay. Bernadotte continued to be spared out of consideration for his wife Julie Clary, Bonaparte's former fiancée whom he had abandoned for Josephine, but he nevertheless lost his post. Nothing ever did more to heighten Bonaparte's so-called antimilitarism, which was only a distrust for his former comrades. This wariness dated from his famous declaration to the Council of State on May 4, 1802, when he said, 'Pre-eminence lies incontestably with the civilian authority.' And on this occasion, he regarded himself as such. Politicians who found themselves compromised were advised by Fouché to take cover. Madame de Staël left Paris for her château at Coppet in Switzerland, and when, in 1803, she attempted to return, Bonaparte ordered her expulsion from France.

Bonaparte's misgivings could not have been too serious, for in no way did they slow down the course of events. The Peace of Amiens, signed on March 25, 1802, acted like a signal. In less than two months, from April 8 to May 19, the regime underwent a complete change: the Republic was transformed into a monarchy, the counter-revolution was officially won over, and the power of the notables was increased. On 18 Germinal, Year X (April 8, 1802), the law comprising the Concordat and the

Organic Articles was passed by the Legislative Body. Ten days later the performance of a Te Deum at Notre Dame celebrated the reconciliation of the Revolution with the Roman Church. This was followed on 6 Floréal (April 26) by a senatus-consultum (actually prepared fifteen days earlier in a special council) granting amnesty to émigrés provided they returned to France before 1 Vendémiaire, Year XI (September 23, 1802), and agreed to swear fidelity to the Constitution. Only the most compromised émigrés, a number not exceeding one thousand, were to be denied amnesty. On 11 Floréal (May 1) a law reorganizing the system of public education authorized the establishment of *lycées*. It was hoped that a distribution of grants would promote the growth of a body of civil servants and of the professional classes in a direction favourable to the government. Then, on 29 Floréal (May 19) a law created the Legion of Honour. It was to consist of fifteen 'cohorts', each numbering 350 legionaries appointed by Bonaparte from among the notables, both civil and military. A grant of 200,000 francs to each 'cohort', defrayed out of the biens nationaux, held the promise of salaries, lodgings, and convalescent homes for legionaries who in turn swore 'to dedicate themselves to the service of the Republic', 'to combat . . . all attempts at restoring the feudal order', and 'to unite . . . in the preservation of liberty and equality'. The Legion of Honour was indeed a host of meritorious citizens, and not a national decoration, as its members were not even given a distinctive medal at this time. Finally, between May 8 and 14, the rule of Bonaparte was transformed into the Life Consulate.

Although the capitulation of the Senate and the purge of the Tribunate robbed the Brumairian bourgeoisie of all hope, a certain amount of resistance continued to make itself felt. The Legion of Honour was harshly criticized in the Council of State, and the law by which it was created passed in the Legislative Body by a vote of only 166 to 110. As for the Constitution, Bonaparte succeeded in overthrowing it, but only by means of successive violations of his own authority and with the collaboration of the monarchist-minded members of his entourage—Cambacérès, Roederer, Talleyrand, and Lucien. On May 6, the Treaty of Amiens was sent to the Senate, and that body was asked to determine what token of the 'nation's gratitude' could most fittingly be bestowed upon the First Consul; but on May 8, when a senator proposed consulship for life, the assembly contented itself by passing a resolution that 'Napoleon Bonaparte' be re-elected for an additional period of ten years. This, incidentally, marked the first appearance of Bonaparte's famous praenomen in official documents.

The attempt to circumvent the constitution having proved a failure, Bonaparte, acting upon the advice of Cambacérès, picked up the thread again by replying, on May 9, that he would accept the Senate's generous offer 'if the will of the people' directed him to do so. A special council then drafted two questions which were to be submitted to the French people for a vote. Framed by Roederer, the resolution proposed, in addition to the Life Consulate, that Bonaparte be granted the right to designate his own successor. Although there was nothing to justify such a procedure legally, the Council of State, to which the matter was referred, passed the resolution; Fouché did not attend the session, and five or six councillors absented themselves. Presented with the draft referendum, Bonaparte cautiously struck out Roederer's provision for the succession. The Tribunate and Legislative Body, having no power to intervene in the revision of the constitution, approved the plebiscite on the Life Consulate. The Senate, thus pushed aside, ironically saw itself charged with the task of counting the popular vote which, as in Year VIII, was cast publicly. On 14 Thermidor (August 2), the Senate proclaimed Bonaparte Consul for Life.

Without wasting any time, Bonaparte dictated a new constitution which was approved by the Council of State and the Senate, without discussion, on August 4. One of its articles empowered the First Consul to present for the Senate's approval his choice of a candidate for the succession. This could be done by testament, or for that matter, at any time. In the event that the Senate did not agree, Bonaparte could name two other candidates, seriatim, of which the third only could not be rejected. Bonaparte had thus arrogated to himself a right which he had declined to ask from the people. The difficulties initially inherent in choosing a likely successor have often been cited as an explanation for this tortuous course of events. As long as Bonaparte remained childless, Joseph and Lucien quarrelled over the succession as if, Lucien remarked, it had been 'their own late father's inheritance'. To have favoured a Brumairian would have incurred the bitter resentment of others. The problem might have found its solution in Charles, son of Louis Bonaparte and Hortense de Beauharnais. Napoleon had in fact contemplated the possibility of eventually adopting a nephew from that marriage; but Charles was not born until October 10. It would therefore seem that, notwithstanding his subjection of the press and the assemblies, Bonaparte saw danger in submitting to a plebiscite a proposal altogether too monarchical. Consequently, he took by force what he had not dared solicit. It has also been argued that the men of the Revolution, who had linked its destiny to that of Bonaparte and who looked upon him as the only man capable of defending the natural frontiers, found themselves logically obliged to make him a monarch in order to obtain the stability to which they aspired. But, as Thibaudeau foresaw only too well, the Life Consulate and the hereditary succession were no more than illusory guarantees. Bonaparte's rule—essentially a military dictatorship founded on victories—had no real need of these measures as long as he remained triumphant on the field of battle. As Bonaparte himself remarked, 'What meaning would these senatus-consulta have' if ever the Coalition powers entered Paris? And once dead, who would care about his will? 'Had the testament of Louis XIV ever been respected?' France, which revered him, and the Brumairians, who were his prisoners, yielded to his demands. Neither the glory that comes from being the nation incarnate and the foremost of its citizens would gratify Bonaparte, who alone conceived the desire to become king, without even deceiving himself about the ephemeral nature of his improvised greatness.

Still, it must be noted that the republican bourgeoisie, while a party to his demands, continued to remind him discreetly of the pact made in Brumaire. Roederer himself, among others, had spoken of important bodies representing the predominant social interests which would be linked to the government and given constitutional guarantees; no doubt this meant granting the assemblies, and especially the Senate, some real control. These republicans also pointed out that the executive power was now strong enough to restore to the citizenry a certain degree of liberty. Chabot de l'Allier made a timid allusion to this necessity when he presented Bonaparte with the law on the plebiscite (it was the same Chabot who had moved in the Tribunate to reward the First Consul on behalf of the nation): 'The greatness and munificence of Bonaparte's conceptions will not let him depart from the liberal principles which made the Revolution and established the Republic. His devotion is too great ever to permit him to blemish with abuses of power the immense glory which he has already acquired.' The Idéologue Camille Jordan expressed his thoughts more plainly in *The True Meaning of the Plebiscite for the Life Consulate*, a pamphlet which was promptly confiscated.

The master would not forgive. Fouché fell into disgrace on 26 Fructidor (September 13), and his ministry was reattached to the Department of Justice. Roederer was eventually deprived of both the presidency of his section in the Council of State and of his direction over matters of public education. For the time being, Bonaparte emphasized the necessity for dictatorship: in England, the opposition had a place in the constitutional order; in France, it was to become the province of the counter-revolutionaries and the Jacobins. Now that he had restored to the former their civil rights, Bonaparte could fairly remind the republicans that a return to elections would not necessarily benefit them. 'Government must remain in the hands of the men of the Revolution; that is the only thing they have.' Bonaparte's collaborators did not contest this, but they pointed out that it had been their understanding that they would be sharing the business of government with him.

The Senatus-Consultum of 16 Thermidor, also known as the Constitution of Year X, reduced the extent of their participation instead. The First Consul invested himself with the power to make treaties and grant pardons, with the exclusive right to designate candidates to the Senate, the Court of Cassation, the office of Second and Third Consul, and to select justices of the peace from among candidates proposed by the electors. Above all, he reserved the right to define or interpret the constitution by organic senatus-consulta. This would later permit the establishment of the Empire to proceed without any of the difficulties which had been incurred in the creation of the Life Consulate. He also assumed the right to suspend the constitution, dissolve the Tribunate and Legislative Body, and annul decisions of the courts by regular senatus-ccnsulta. Draughted by a privy council which he created and whose members he appointed before each sitting, these senatus-consulta provided him with the sole power to initiate legislation. The Senate, invested with this exorbitant authority, was appropriately reconstituted. Although its members continued to be co-opted, the First Consul was given the right to present candidates for seats created by the Constitution of Year VIII and the right to appoint forty additional senators directly. Presently, on 14 Nivôse, Year XI (January 4, 1803), Bonaparte secured their appointment. At the same time, he created a *senatorerie* in each of the administrative districts of France, which were themselves based on the territorial jurisdiction of a Court of Appeal. These senatoreries were endowed with national lands and seigniorial residences which Bonaparte bestowed upon the more compliant senators as a bonus to their existing salaries. Finally, the new constitution authorized senators to hold, in addition to their seats, ministerial positions and various high government posts. The powers of the other assemblies, on the other hand, were reduced. The Legislative Body lost the right to hold regular sessions and to elect its own president. The Tribunate was reduced to fifty members, and a provision that condemned it to silence was incorporated in the constitution. The Council of State yielded its precedence to the Senate, and saw itself rivalled by the Privy Council. Although Bonaparte did not cease to submit new laws in the Council of State, he could now dispense with it and legislate by senatus-consulta.

Another major change was the abolition of the *Listes de Notabilité*, which the Senate had only just published in March. Bonaparte's pretext was the difficulties which had been encountered in drawing them up, while in fact he felt that they allowed too great a latitude of choice to the assemblies. No doubt he also wished to please the notables by restoring to each département its own body of representatives. He therefore instituted a system of electoral colleges to take the place of the Listes de Notabilité. At its base, the cantonal assembly, composed of all citizens in the canton, presented candidates for the office of justice of the peace and for seats on the municipal councils. It also nominated the members of the district and departmental colleges from among the 600 most highly taxed citizens, so that the tax rolls finally appeared. The district colleges nominated two candidates for each vacancy in the Tribunate and Legislative Body; the colleges of the départements nominated two candidates for each vacancy in the Legislative Body and Senate. The assemblies were thus made regionally representative. Since the colleges were obliged to choose at least one of the two candidates outside their own ranks, they were not completely oligarchical. The First Consul exercised a powerful influence on these colleges since he not only appointed their presidents but could add ten members to the district college, twenty to the departmental college, and he authorized public functionaries to take part in their proceedings.

Given the fact that the members of the assemblies were chosen for life terms, and that vacancies were not filled until an assembly fell below a third of its original number, elections were reduced to a minimum. Moreover, until Year XII, notables who had recently been chosen to the communal lists alone made up the cantonal assemblies, and the colleges which they in turn constituted continued to function without change until the end of the Empire. The monopoly of the notables was thus confirmed and even strengthened. Hearken to Lucien as he lectured to the college of the département of Seine on March 24, 1803: 'The principles of our new electoral law . . . are no longer founded on chimerical concepts but on the very basis of society, property, which arouses in us a desire to preserve public order. Today, the electoral privilege has by gradual and temperate means become the exclusive prerogative of the most enlightened and civic-minded class of our society.' But in reality, it was to Bonaparte that this class would henceforth owe its place.

BONAPARTE'S SOCIAL POLICY

The major enactments of Year X were not just limited to the extension of Bonaparte's personal power; they also foreshadowed the social schemes which were taking shape in his mind. Speaking before the Council of State, Bonaparte lashed out against the individualistic society which had been born out of the French Revolution. He characterized it as so many 'grains of sand', and he stressed the necessity 'to erect some pillars of granite upon the soil of France', so as to 'give the French people a sense of civic direction'. Plainly stated, Bonaparte wanted to create clusters of interests attached to the regime, who, in return for advantages and honours, were expected to secure the loyalty of the populace by virtue of their influence upon the wage-earning classes. This was tantamount to a revival of the kind of intermediate or corporate bodies that had been prevalent under the Old Regime, with the added safe-guard that they should no longer be able to oppose the state or degenerate into oligarchies. Bonaparte cleverly pointed out that this would directly benefit the bourgeoisie. He argued that 'while we lack unity', the aristocracy was a block bonded by blood, class prejudice, and ecclesiastical hierarchy, and that the Legion of Honour would serve 'to bring together the partisans of the Revolution'. The creation of these social bodies, however, would be left to him and to him alone; the penal code even went so far as to subject all organizations numbering more than twenty persons to his authority. So it was perfectly clear to everyone that his power would grow.

The assemblies constituted one such body, the Legion of Honour another, the electoral colleges yet another. Added to these was the newly swollen bureaucracy, graded according to a table of ranks. Drawing initially from the financial middle class, Bonaparte created, by a decree of 19 Germinal, Year XI (April 9, 1803), a new set of officials: the *auditeurs*.* Sixteen were appointed at first, but this was only a beginning. They were attached to the ministries and to the Council of State and were to form the nucleus of a high administration free from ties with the Revolution or the Old Regime. Judges occupied a place of honour in this scheme. Being poorly paid, they were drawn perforce exclusively from the well-to-do middle class. The Con-stitution of Year X gave them a hierarchy and a discipline that was professional. Officials of the legal establishment were also organized into corporations: chambers of solicitors (avoués) had

* These *auditeurs* were groomed for positions as future state councillors, judges, and other high administrative officials. As such, they provided an administrative link between the ministers and the Council of State on the one hand, and the assemblies on the other. They were charged with presenting reports to the meetings of the sections of the Council of State. They were also allowed to attend sittings of the general assemblies, but were denied the right to speak other than in answer to points requiring explication. TRANSLATOR.

existed since Year VIII; notaries (notaires) and public auction-eers (*commissaires-priseurs*) had been associated since Year IX. Nor were the businessmen forgotten: chambers of commerce and manufacture, brokerage houses, and the reappearance of commercial agents were not only a response to technical needs but part of a definite social plan. Had it been left entirely to Bonaparte, one would surely have witnessed the rebirth of guilds.

As Bonaparte conceived it then, the social hierarchy was to be founded on wealth. It could not have been otherwise, since he had seized power with the sanction of the bourgeoisie. True, by making free education available to all, the Idéologues had in-tended to introduce men of talent, as well as men of fortune, into leading government positions. But wealth once acquired tends naturally to reserve this privilege for itself. Moreover, Bonaparte shared the distrust of the rich for 'men of talent' as long as they were poor, regarding them as revolutionary tinder; and so it was generally agreed that they would only be em-ployed in technical positions, as in the time of the former aristocracy and absolute monarchy. Whenever Bonaparte pro-claimed himself the representative of the Revolution, he always reduced that movement to the abolition of privileges of which the rise of the propertied bourgeoisie was a direct consequence. One only has to remove his personal despotism to appreciate the fact that the social enactments of Year X laid the foundation for the July Monarchy.

The Civil Code became the bible of the new society. On August 12, 1800, a committee of four legal experts—Tronchet, Portalis, Bigot de Préameneu, and Maleville—was appointed to prepare a draft of the *Code Civil*. The project was completed in January 1801, but Bonaparte's conflict with the assemblies led to the suspension of open debate on the laws until 1803. The various articles were finally promulgated as a single law on March 21, 1804, under the title of the *Civil Code of the French People*, and only later became known as the *Code Napoleon*. Bona-parte took personal part in the preparation of the Code, but only on those sections dealing with family law. He was intent on strengthening the authority of the father and the husband in the home, on depriving illegitimate children of their heritage unless they had been legally recognized (in which case their share was to be reduced anyway), and on retaining divorce, for his own reasons.

Like all of Bonaparte's achievements, the Code was dual in character. On the one hand, it confirmed the disappearance of the feudal aristocracy and adopted the social principles of 1789: liberty of the individual, equality before the law, secularization of the state, freedom of conscience, and freedom to choose one's profession. This is why it swept through Europe as the symbol of the Revolution, and heralded, wherever it was introduced, the fundamental laws of modern society. Tarnished though this quality may have become in our time, the failure to depict the Code in all of its original freshness would play false the history of the Napoleonic years, and it would prevent us from ever grasping the full significance of the French hegemony. But, on the other hand, the Code also confirmed the reaction against the democratic accomplishments of the Republic. Conceived in the interest of the bourgeoisie, it was concerned primarily with consecrating and sanctifying the rights of property which it regarded as a natural right, anterior to society, absolute and belonging to the individual, and it gave the possessor the title to ownership. Sections regulating contracts dealt almost exclusively with property, with services being relegated to two articles. To a large degree, the family itself was regarded in this light. Consequently, the scrupulously detailed regulations governing the marriage contract made of it a moneyed transaction, and behind the Code's extensive interest in filiation lay the question of inheritance.

The idea that the laws should promote the interest of the state, as understood by Bonaparte and his jurists, was the other guideline employed in the preparation of the Code. It was Bonaparte who, in a certain measure, limited the rights of landed proprietors in matters of subsoil use and eminent domain, and above all in their freedom of testamentary disposition. The family was of great value to the state, for it constituted one of those social entities which disciplined the behaviour of individuals. The *patria potestas*, which had been weakened by the Revolution, was thus restored once again: a father could imprison his children for six months on the strength of his word alone; he had complete control over their property; similarly, he could administer his wife's property and, joint ownership being part of the common law, he could dispose of it as often as not. But, as with all groups, there was always the possibility that the family might become too powerful as against the state, and especially so since its cohesiveness was by nature very strong, thus giving rise to the restoration of an independent aristocracy. For this reason, the state placed the family under its tutelage: the testamentary powers of the father were modified by re-establishing the principle of 'legitimacy', and the question of inheritance was declared to be a matter of public interest and was made subject to the regulation of law. Viewed in this light, the Code was bitterly criticized by the former nobility and by a part of the bourgeoisie, whose powers it limited in that it assured the division of patrimonies.

As regards those who possessed nothing, the Code kept silent except to protect their personal freedom by prohibiting the lease or hire of services in perpetuity. Proclaiming the freedom of labour and the equality of citizens before the law, it in fact abandoned the wage earner, as had been the wish of the Constituent Assembly, to all of the hazards of economic competition, and it treated labour as just another commodity. It repudiated the idea, conceived in 1793, of recognizing the citizen's right to a livelihood. Since only the employer was taken at his word in matters of wage disputes, the Code even departed from the principle of juridical equality by discriminating against wage earners. Moreover, the state used its police powers to enforce labour discipline, because the Code could not offer sufficient protection to employers: since the poor possessed nothing, they would have been effectively immune to punitive law suits. The law of 22 Germinal, Year XI (April 12, 1803), renewed the ban on workers' associations, and on the following December 1, a decree obliged workers to carry a workbook supplied by the local authorities, without which it was forbidden to employ them.

The Code, then, was the product of the evolution of French society insofar as it created the bourgeoisie and carried it to power. When one considers the Code in its detail, the imprint of history upon it becomes even more apparent. The Napoleonic jurists drew largely from the works of Domat and Pothier, both of whom had already embarked upon a rational codification, the latter devoting himself to the written Roman Law of the

Midi, the former to customary law. By combining this legacy with the work of the Revolution and weeding out the contradictions, they succeeded in making the Code a compromise. Another manifestation of the Code's historic character was its extensive preoccupation with landed property, which was still the principal form of wealth, whereas it neglected industrial wealth, business organizations, and credit. In short, it cannot be said that the Code was a product of theoreticians who wished to impose arbitrarily on a society an abstract set of laws remote from living reality, and the criticisms levelled by Savigny and other German jurists were completely unfounded. These critics were inspired by aristocratic sentiments of which the Code was the very negation.

Bonaparte's idea of public education was that it should be in keeping with the established social order and the authoritarian nature of the regime: it must, he said, 'embrace the nation' and be the 'first concern of the government'. The decree of 11 Floréal, Year X (May 1, 1802), drafted by Fourcroy, whose proposal was substituted for that of Chaptal (which was thought too ambitious), left the elementary schools (*écoles populaires*) to the care of the municipalities, just as under the Old Regime. Like Voltaire before him, Bonaparte and a large number of the middle class believed that to educate the poor was politically and socially inconvenient. Not so with regard to secondary institutions of learning which were to educate future leaders. These were patterned on the Prytanée, formerly known as the Collège Louis-le-Grand and the only such school preserved by the Revolution: under the Directory it had again become a school of resident students, unlike the écoles centrales, and it was remodelled in Year VIII (March 22, 1800) by Lucien Bonaparte, the then Minister of Interior. Every Appeal Court district was to have a state supported lycée. It was also anticipated that there would be secondary schools, privately administered but government authorized and controlled; in Year XII, the state began appointing their teachers. Six thousand four hundred scholarships were created for the lycées, of which 2,400 were awarded to the sons of military officers and government officials, and the remaining 4,000 were set aside for the best pupils in the secondary schools. To a degree, these grants met the wishes of the Idéologues; but being in fact beyond the reach of the poor, they constituted an endowment only in favour of civilian and military officials and were an inducement to bind the *petite bourgeoisie* to the notables and to seduce its most talented elements: as public servants or as leaders in the nation's economic life, they would no longer be a ferment of unrest. Institutions of education which were not administered by the state continued to exist in principle, although in Paris at least, Frochot, Prefect of the Seine, claimed the right to authorize and supervise them. The Catholic clergy immediately benefited from this tolerance; the *Frères des Écoles Chrétiennes* became active once again and founded an institute at Lyons in Year XII. Bonaparte never created any obstacles for the clergy when it came to primary education, and because he attached no importance to the education of women, he permitted the restoration of several sisterly teaching orders. The lycées and the clerical secondary schools for boys soon came into conflict with each other, however, and in the end, Napoleon was driven toward the establishment of a government monopoly over all forms of public instruction.

Even as he sanctioned its social ascendancy, Bonaparte evidenced his distrust of the middle class. In the Council of State he spoke harshly of wealth: 'Affluence carries no merit. The rich are often a pack of undeserving idlers, and a rich merchant usually gets his wealth either by selling dear or by outright thievery.' More critical still was his attitude toward men of finance. Clearly, his was not an attack upon all forms of wealth, but one directed against the masses of liquid capital which were precisely the origin of bourgeois fortunes. First, it was a wealth not readily seizable, be it to tax or to confiscate. Then, too, it produced at every turn individuals who, taking pride in not being indebted to anyone but themselves and being all the more determined to preserve their independence, tended to shatter the social structures which Bonaparte strove to establish. In his pursuit of the throne, Bonaparte evidently contemplated a monarchy based on the support of a landed aristocracy, in return for which the monarch would guarantee the servitude of the peasantry. This ideal was not to be realized, and Bonaparte did not even consider restoring a nobility at this time; but he found himself guided by preference even more than by the national interest in bringing about a reconciliation with the counter-revolution. In the months following the establishment of the Constitution of Year X, what struck contemporaries most was the very progress of this reconciliation. The application of the Concordat followed its course. Caprara, the papal legate, was conciliatory, and Portalis endeavoured to please him without completely concealing his own attachments to Gallican traditions. By the nature of things, the refractory priests began to play an increasingly important role in the new clergy. The government recognized the inevitability of the situation and forced the constitutional bishops to accede to it, for even had circumstances been otherwise, they would have been unable to find a sufficient number of priests who had taken the oath. In the département of Bas-Rhin, for example, the bishop Saurine was unable to appoint more than 16 'constitutionals' out of 351 priests to parishes and chapels, making less than 5 per cent; as for the former refractory bishops, La Tour d'Auvergne in the Pas-de-Calais and Caffarelli in the Côtes-du-Nord, they awarded the 'constitutionals' 78 positions out of 634, and 43 out of 340, respectively, or about 12 per cent. Then again, a number of bishops imposed an oath of submission, which amounted to a retraction, on the juring clergy of 1791, and when the prefects objected, they succeeded at best in making the wording of the formula somewhat less precise. The constitutional bishops were exposed to the effronteries of their subordinates, and the case was worse for ordinary priests.

Fouché insisted in his circulars on maintaining liberty of conscience, and he presumed, not without impertinence, the right to treat bishops as if they were government officials or police auxiliaries, a sort of spiritual gendarmerie. He fell into disgrace, however, and Portalis, the Director of Cults, almost always sided against the prefects. In order to pacify the bishops, the prefects of the Pas-de-Calais and Bouches-du-Rhône were at last removed. The Organic Articles, no sooner promulgated, encountered many a snag. Prelates were addressed as Monseigneur; ecclesiastical garb reappeared; religious processions and bell-ringing were freely restored; and bishops were allowed to add to their title, 'by divine mercy and by grace of the Holy See'. Contrary to his personal feelings, Portalis refused to make the observance of Sunday obligatory, believing that habit would see to it soon enough. He did, however, permit the revival of marriage banns, and above all he supported bishops in their efforts to secure the right to watch over government officials. 'You are in a better position than anyone else,' he wrote to Champion de Cicé, 'to inform the government on all that touches upon the public interest.' The Subprefect of Boulogne, Masclet, although distrustful of the clergy, nevertheless instructed his mayors that no matter what their personal convictions, they were still obliged by virtue of their office to conform to religion.

The lower (nonbeneficed) clergy immediately complained of their wretched condition. The peasants were not hostile to them, merely indifferent, and no one wished to support them. Although the Organic Articles made religious worship free of cost, charitable donations were to be divided among parish priests (curés) and curates (*vicaires*), and this practice was promptly revived. Bishops began to publish schedules of expected contributions, and they set about establishing church councils which were intended to assure the material well-being of the parishes. But the nonbeneficed clergy still were accorded neither lodgings nor salaries by their congregations, and Bonaparte in Year XI began to press the administrative bodies to deliberate upon these matters; he also restored to parishes nonalienated Church lands. These measures were not truly effective but under the Empire the state became increasingly open-handed to the Church. And so the Concordat became a point of departure for a development which prepared the Catholic clergy for the later triumphs of the Restoration.

The return of the émigrés did not give rise to any debates such as those generated by the Concordat, but it made a deeper impression still, and it is worth mentioning that if Bonaparte did receive numerous compliments on the occasion of the Life Consulate, he did not receive a single one apropos the amnesty. The amnesty put the émigrés under the surveillance of the police for the next ten years, and they, like others, could be incarcerated by simple administrative action. Consequently, the émigrés exercised great caution as a rule, but this did not stop them from behaving like masters in the villages nor from seeking to force upon the purchasers of their alienated properties a restitution or a settlement. The purchasers of national lands took alarm, especially since Bonaparte ordered an audit of the accounts on July 23, 1803, to determine the balance of their payments outstanding. This provoked all manner of chicanery and even some frantic speculation, the impression being that the sales themselves might be called into question. Had the choice been left to Bonaparte, the decree of July 17, 1793, which had abolished without indemnity the feudal seigneurial dues (*rentes foncières*), might have been revised so as to have provided a compensation to former landowners as well as revenue to the treasury—these landed rents being largely tied in with the national lands. However, Bonaparte did not venture to override the decision of the Council of State which declared on February 19, 1803, that the law could in no way be revised. Already a number of émigrés had taken positions in the regime: Louis-Philippe Séguier had been appointed to the Council of State; Séguier sat in the Court of Appeals of Paris, and the duc de Luynes sat in the Senate; and in 1804, Joseph-Marie Gérando became chief of a department in the Ministry of Interior. Bonaparte also married several of his top-ranking officers—Junot, Ney, Lannes, Augereau, Savary—to daughters of the nobility. Others, Duroc and Marmont for example, preferred money.

The reconciliation was most apparent at the court of the First Consul. The Tuileries Palace, more than Malmaison, rapidly took on the flavour of the old monarchy. Duroc was already Governor of the Palace. In November 1802 Josephine received an official rank and was henceforth surrounded by four ladies-in-waiting chosen from the old nobility. It was in this company that she travelled with Bonaparte to Belgium. There seemed to be no end to the minute refinements of etiquette. The populace was again dazzled by the spectacle of costumes, carriages, liveried attendants, festivities, and fancy-dress balls at the Opéra. When General Leclerc, Pauline Bonaparte's husband, died in San Domingo in January 1803, ceremonial mourning was reintroduced at the court. A new saint's day, the festival of St. Napoleon, was instituted on August 15, 1802, and the republican holidays of July 14 and 1 Vendémiaire were celebrated, until 1804, only for the sake of appearance. Finally, in 1803, coins were struck in Bonaparte's effigy.

The salons eagerly followed the tone set by the court. This newly emerging aristocracy kept the nouveaux-riches and men of finance at a distance. Bonaparte prescribed for it a certain decorum which had not been characteristic of the pre-revolutionary aristocracy. He took Josephine away from her former friends, Mme Tallien and Mme Hamelin, and he recalled women to a sense of propriety. But this austerity of morals was never more than a façade, and Bonaparte was never one to deny himself the pleasures of indulgence. His sole concern was that outward appearances be maintained, and in this he himself set the prime example. The fact of the matter was that this society was still thoroughly middle class, and it condemned the ease and abandon of the eighteenth-century nobility for its lack of 'considerateness'. Moreover, its transformation was far from complete, as the fate of the Legion of Honour clearly demonstrated: having violated his own law by appointing the members of the Legion's 'Grand Council' (they should have been elected), Bonaparte proceeded to postpone the nomination of the legionaries. Already this institution which he had designed seemed to him too closely tied to the Revolution.

By the end of 1802, many indications left no doubt as to Bonaparte's real intentions. Thus from the standpoint of national policy Bonaparte reached his pinnacle with the Treaty of Amiens. More than anything the French people wanted peace, and Bonaparte gave it to them; they were attached to the social accomplishments of the Revolution; and Bonaparte had preserved them. Satisfied and proud of their leader, they had not yet begun to realize that he was abusing his power and that he contemplated objects inimical to their own interests. But they did not want their leader to become king, and they wanted still less that he create a nobility, while Bonaparte in his heart had broken with the Republic and with the notion of *égalité*. Pleased with having secured the natural frontiers, they did not in the least desire to go beyond them, but their master had already done so, making war inevitable. The French people still saw him as a hero of the nation at the very moment that he had ceased to be one.

III

IMPERIAL CONQUEST TO THE TREATY OF TILSIT (1802–1807)*

* For a brief account of the various interpretations of Napoleon's foreign policy in French historical writing, turn to p. 302 of the bibliography at the back of this book.

CONTEMPORARIES AND EARLY CHRONICLERS of Bonaparte attributed the imperial conquests and the Empire itself to what they called the 'ambition' of Napoleon. Not that ambition was the only factor. Opportunities did present themselves, but even then the national interest would have counselled a prudent refusal. For many historians of a later time, such an interpretation seemed too simple. Some wished to see him only as the defender of the 'natural frontiers': they argued that the republicans had made him a consul and then an emperor for this very purpose, but that this task, the baleful legacy of the Revolution, compelled him to conquer Europe and at last destroyed him. These historians were merely transposing, in an obvious way, the idolatrous myth of the Old Guard, to which Napoleon himself, while at St. Helena, gave wide currency— a soldier of the Revolution, he had done no more than to defend himself against monarchy and Old Europe. Other historians, loath to diminish the role of the individual in history and refusing to regard Napoleon as simply an instrument of destiny, persisted in seeking in his character the wellspring of his policy, thinking it could be found in some grand unifying design. There were those for whom the thematic idea was the struggle with England over maritime supremacy; and for these, the period after the rupture of the Treaty of Amiens was the apotheosis of the struggle begun under Louis XIV and had its roots in the old history of France. There were others for whom it was the 'oriental' mirage that lured him toward the precipice. For still others, Bonaparte was more European than French, and endeavoured to recreate the Carolingian, and later the Roman, Empire—the well-ordered world of Western Christian civilization.

In each of these interpretations there is a piece of the truth, but all are insufficient. It is true that Bonaparte's sponsors wished to hold on to the 'natural frontiers', and that to defend them one might have been tempted to venture beyond them; but this was neither the surest nor the only means of protecting them; nor is it clear that he had only the interests of the nation in mind in extending his conquests. It is true that England was his constant and tenacious enemy, and that in beating him, she triumphed over France once and for all; but if, in accordance with a maturely considered plan, he was aiming at England alone, his continental policy would have been greatly different —the blockade itself, of which so much has been made, was much more the offspring of the Grand Empire than its cause. Nothing would have pleased the new Alexander so much as a thrust towards Constantinople or India, but most of his enterprises were only ephemerally connected with this dream. It is a fact that he compared himself to Charlemagne and to Caesar, and that he aimed at a political federation of the Western world, but it was not an intellectual desire to restore the past which drove him to action. The legend of the hatred of the Coalition powers for the soldier of the Revolution contains a keen insight, and it is surprising that so many historians should have forgotten it. But there was more to Bonaparte's policy than justifiable self-defence.

The truth is, no unifying concept can be found that will rationally explain Napoleon's foreign policy; he simultaneously pursued ends that were contradictory. In the last analysis, we must return to his 'ambition'. Contemporaries were blinded by the crude and gaudy theatrical apparatus, the wanton adventures, the quarrels of a rapacious family, and the malversations of officials. While appreciating Napoleon's genius, they depreciated his ambition to the common level of humanity. With time's perspective, the dimness of his image has been brought to focus and his mystery unveiled: the heroic urge to take risks, the magic lure of the dream, the irresistible impulse of his flashing temperament.

CHAPTER SEVEN

France and England: The Struggle Renewed
(1802–1805)

AT NO TIME were the traits of Napoleon's personality better revealed than in the critical years between the Treaty of Amiens and the War of 1805. The treaty with England did not last much over a year. But so long as the struggle on the Continent was not renewed, the political arrangement which had been possible in 1799—a victorious but peaceful France, facing England, mistress of the seas—had not been completely discarded. After the Peace of Pressburg, this solution was no longer possible.

BONAPARTE'S ECONOMIC POLICY AND THE RUPTURE OF THE TREATY OF AMIENS

It would be difficult to disprove Prime Minister Addington's serious resolve to try the experiment of peace and his faith in its substantial duration. He repealed the income tax and cut naval expenditures by £2 million. Saint Vincent, First Lord of the Admiralty, suspended ship construction and dismissed the workers in the naval dockyards. The timber trust broke with him after he initiated an investigation of their peculations, and supplies to the dockyards dried up. Nevertheless, the government encountered opposition in its own party. Convinced that the peace would permit France to rearm for a new assault against the British Empire, the Tory dissidents preached war to the death, as had the Whigs a hundred years earlier. The Tories controlled part of the press, and the French émigré Peltier assisted them in vituperating the Revolution and the military dictatorship of Bonaparte.

The business community hesitated between these two policies. Peace endangered many interests: the war industries were grinding to a halt; English merchants were on the point of losing their monopoly of commerce in the Baltic and in Germany, not to mention the harm to the colonial trade; the restitution to France of her lost colonies was a material loss to England, the trade of Dutch Guiana alone being valued at £10 million. Finally, after the signature of the Treaty of Amiens, world prices fell to such a point that even the neutrals, and especially the United States, regarded the peace as a calamity. Nevertheless, it was generally thought that these evils were only temporary. The tocsin rung by the Tories left some impression, but on the sea and in the colonies, the peril did not seem imminent. As for the Continent, English opinion was not over concerned. The relevant question was whether Bonaparte would open the vast market of France and her satellites to British commerce, for England would not tolerate the treaty for long if profitable business relations did not quickly ensue. In May 1802, the Foreign Minister Hawkesbury stated that it would be necessary to hasten the re-establishment of commercial relations in order to win over the greatest possible number of people to the peace. The key to the problem thus lay in the economic policy of the First Consul.

Like all enlightened despots, Napoleon always devoted great attention to economic progress; not, indeed, because it improved the lot of mankind and permitted the common people to share in the fruits of civilization, but simply for political reasons. He was interested in sound finance, in the growth of population and the consequent fresh supply of recruits to the army, and in 'order', that is, a minimum of idleness and an abundance of commodities. Yet he was more receptive to some branches of production than to others. Military by nature, he distrusted business and finance, which were cosmopolitan and closely linked with England. He was interested in industry, especially to the extent that it consumed native raw materials. He was inclined to regard agriculture as the strength of a great military state, of a Sparta or a Rome. Thence came the soldiers, and thence the capacity, if necessary, to be economically self-sufficient. In this his ideas were physiocratic, and to the extent that he turned from the bourgeoisie and envisaged the re-creation of a landed aristocracy, he approached that school of thought from a second direction. But, as always happened when he ran into concrete difficulties, he did not trouble himself with pursuing a single theory. Although he favoured agriculture, he continually carped at the right to export grain, because the masses stirred with every increase in the price of bread as the experience of Year X had confirmed. For reasons of state, he shared the popular prejudice against speculators in the grain trade and cultivators who sought to reap undue profits. Industrial crises, when they threw workers out of jobs, caused similar problems; and so it was necessary for him to keep a close watch over the cotton industry, despite the fact that it utilized an imported raw material.

Of all the practical considerations which Bonaparte faced, it was the monetary problem which demanded his greatest attention. While England was giving way to a mild, controlled inflation, one which kept prices at a high level and stimulated production, France, apart from the limited issuances of banks, was saddled with a metallic currency that was persistently being hoarded, and she experienced a continued shortage of Louis d'ors. This inconvenienced her economy because capital continued to be scarce and expensive. Bonaparte never ceased reproving the Bank of France for its extreme caution in discounting commercial paper, and he would have wanted to see it branch out into the provinces making credit widely available. The scarcity of coin also affected public finances adversely by placing a great burden on the treasury. After the fiasco of the assignats, Bonaparte was loath to return to paper money; such an attempt would surely have incurred a loss of prestige. Like Colbert in analogous circumstances, he was converted to mercantilism and so to the belief that France had to protect her supply of specie by purchasing little from abroad and by creating metal inflows either through increased exports or simple conquest.

The Consulate also took pains to encourage manufactures, particularly of luxuries. A Bureau of Statistics, created in 1800, resumed the investigations begun by the Committee of Public Safety and François de Neufchâteau. Working through the prefects, it undertook an economic and demographic census of France, and in the course of the following years, a substantial part of its findings was published. An attempt was made to unify the French economy by adopting the decimal-metric system which, however, only gradually gained acceptance. On 17 Germinal, Year XI (April 7, 1803), the ratio between silver and gold was set at 1 to 15·5, but due to a lack of resources an insufficient number of coins were struck to replace the old currency. The new regime stood firmly behind its money; the franc was legally defined in terms of silver (4·5 grams of pure silver, or 5 grams of silver $\frac{9}{10}$ pure). Since the livre had never been legally defined, money of account and metallic currency became identical in value for the first time.

The regulation of commerce was entrusted to a general council, and with the advent of the Empire it was brought under the jurisdiction of a section of the Council of State. On March 19, 1801, the exchanges were reorganized; on December 24, 1802, Chambers of Commerce reappeared; on April 28, 1803, sixteen seaports were designated as ports of international trade and were accorded the right to establish bonded warehouses. At the close of 1801, a 'Society for the Encouragement of National Industry' was formed under the presidency of Chaptal; as Minister of Interior, he revived the practice (begun at the time of the Directory) of holding industrial exhibitions. On April 12, 1803, Chambers of Manufacture appeared. The Paris Agricultural Society had already been reconstituted in 1798.

Like Colbert, Bonaparte was by nature inclined to regulate by means of corporations. Artisans would gladly have recovered their monopoly, and certain merchants would have welcomed regulations against cottage industry and hired labour. Using 'public order' as an excuse, the Prefect of Police managed to reorganize the bakers and the butchers along guild lines. The First Consul did not dare go further for the moment, however, because the bankers and leading industrialists, supported by the Council of State, were strongly opposed to any restrictions on freedom to work. The Law of 22 Germinal, Year XI (April 12, 1803), confined itself to the establishment of a system of copyright for trade-marks and designs. Then, too, the state of the fisc did not permit public works to be undertaken as would have been desirable. Nor did it allow scope for the encouragement of private enterprise. Even later when funds were available, Napoleon refused to give direct assistance to industry; he only gave them contracts and in times of crisis, loans, in order to avoid stoppages in the production of goods. All that remained to complete a Colbertian system was the addition of a protective tariff.

There were many powerful reasons recommending this last step. Laissez-faire economics, as preached by Jean-Baptiste Say, was far from being universally accepted. In a work published in 1805, *Du gouvernement considéré dans ses rapports avec le commerce*, Ferrier remained faithful to the mercantilism of Colbert. Even before the Peace of Amiens, English smuggling was constantly denounced, and more so when the war ended. The cotton manufacturers were vociferous in stating that a return to the Treaty of 1786 would engender a repetition of the grave crisis which followed it. Weaving continued to prosper, and although spinning was making some progress (the annual importation of cotton bales rose from an average of 5 million kilos in the preceding decade to nearly 11 million kilos in Year XII), it fell short of expectations. For high-count thread especially, English manufacturers defied all competition. Bonaparte had not revoked the ban against English merchandise pronounced by the Directory; what is more, on May 19, 1802, he authorized a temporary raising of tariff rates, and taxed colonial articles of English origin at least 50 per cent higher than similar articles from the French colonies.

On the other hand, Bonaparte had not yet discarded the possibility of a commercial agreement with England. Coquebert de Montbret and a number of other commercial agents were sent to London and were offered a return to the Treaty of 1786 along with safeguards which would permit France to take temporary measures to protect its home industry. In the summer of 1802, the Council of Commerce came out firmly against the prohibition of English imports, and Chaptal advised the government to accept London's offers and to demand that the English market be opened to French silks as well as wines on the same basis as port and sherry. He also counselled against a high French tariff. 'I am waiting,' he said, 'for our manufacturers to begin screaming.' This plan could have been withstood by dispensing appropriate favours. Coquebert, on the contrary, advised that British cargo be accepted only to the extent that French products of equal value were admitted to the British market. Chaptal replied that such a proposal would mean issuing licences and creating a monopoly of foreign trade for the benefit of a few private individuals. This system of licences which Chaptal characterized as 'absurd', was in fact instituted in 1811. Between the extremes of free trade and embargo there was room, given English consent, for a policy of moderate protection as advocated by Chaptal, and of which French industry was so much in need. Between the demands of industrial entrepreneurs and the national interest (which called for peace), it remained for Bonaparte to decide. In the end, he chose to support the side of total protection.

Bonaparte was simply not interested in keeping the peace. 'A First Consul,' he told Thibaudeau, 'cannot be likened to these kings-by-the-grace-of-God, who look upon their States as a heritage. . . . His actions must be dramatic, and for this, war is indispensable.' He was careful not to speak these thoughts in public, for the nation would have disapproved. 'I have too much at stake to let foreigners take the initiative,' but, he added, 'they will be the first to take up arms.' With such an attitude it was natural that he should encourage them. In any event, by assuring an accumulation of coin, the embargo hastened the military build-up to the point where it became a weapon of war—as it had been during the Revolution.

It seemed more than ever before that the economy and financial structure of England, based on borrowing and inflation, were vulnerable. Such sentiments were repeated by Hauterive in Year VIII, the Chevalier de Guer in 1801, Lassalle in 1803, and by the *Moniteur* itself. Although there existed no doubt of the perils menacing France, the mistake of believing that France, unassisted, could bring the English to economic ruin, was again committed. Bonaparte was overready to share this illusion, since he, a soldier and a dictator, held in contempt this oligarchy of merchants who were without an army and without a government. He would have played both Cato and Scipio to England's Carthage. No more was said of a commercial treaty: vessels were seized because they were found carrying articles of British origin. Meanwhile, France's foreign trade rose from 553 million francs in 1799 to 790 million in Year X. The English capitalists learned that the economic struggle would continue, and they became disgusted with a peace which profited them nothing.

Since colonial goods were essential to her foreign trade, it became incumbent upon France to salvage the Antilles which were still left to her. The Peace of Amiens had not yet been signed when Bonaparte dispatched an expedition to San Domingo. Toussaint L'Ouverture was by now in control of the entire island, and had, on May 9, 1801, promulgated a constitution granting himself governing powers under the purely nominal authority of France. Although he surrendered in good faith to General Leclerc, who headed the French expedition, he was arrested on June 7, 1802, and deported to France, where he died in the fortress of Joux on April 7, 1803. At the same time, Richepanse reoccupied the smaller West Indian islands. If these Antillean conquests were not worth troubling about, the English were nevertheless truly concerned over Bonaparte's Louisiana project: an expedition was being prepared on the coast of the North Sea to send General Victor to the Mississippi. The flotilla was scheduled to depart in March 1803, but it was delayed. In the meantime, Spain closed the Mississippi to American traffic. Since France and Spain were allies, and Holland a French satellite, the Gulf of Mexico appeared to be at Bonaparte's disposal. And, consequently, so did the contraband of the Spanish Indies, where the French were now in a position to extract advantageous concessions. Nevertheless, these prospects vanished without England having to interfere. The United States, which had for some time coveted Spanish Florida, had no wish to see the French established in New Orleans. The newly elected president, Jefferson, with his secretaries Madison and Gallatin, tried to pursue a Republican programme of peace, disarmament, and reduced expenditures. Even though Jefferson was well disposed towards France, and had been pleased with the signing of the Treaty of Mortefontaine, he could not hold back the tide of public opinion. And so he let it be known that if France remained in Louisiana, the United States would join England in the coming war. On April 12, 1803, Jefferson's ambassador, James Monroe, arrived in Paris with a proposal to which Bonaparte had already decided to agree: the purchase of the Louisiana Territory. The ensuing treaty, signed on May 3, brought Bonaparte 80 million francs, of which only 55 million remained after deducting indemnities owed to the United States and the commissions paid to Hope and Baring, the bankers who handled the transfer.

Insurrection, resulting from the re-establishment of slavery, had already become widespread throughout San Domingo. In Bonaparte's immediate circle, where the advocates of the white planters were many (not to mention Josephine herself), the slave system was being upheld as the most expedient way to revive production quickly in the colonies. However, it was not imperative that there be slavery, since even in the colonies where the decree of 16 Pluviôse, Year II, had been applied, both the commissioners of the Directory and Toussaint L'Ouverture himself had already instituted forced labour. Bonaparte was at first inclined to keep this system, limiting himself to the retention of slavery in the islands where it already existed—the Mauritius island group where the Convention decree was considered a dead letter, and Martinique which, having been under English occupation, had never received the decree. Finally, Bonaparte gave in. Indeed, the law of May 20, 1802, explicitly stated that slavery would be 'maintained' in the colonies, from which one might have deduced that it was not to reappear in places where it had been abolished. But Bonaparte, deciding otherwise, commanded Richepanse to reintroduce slavery in Guadeloupe, thereby provoking a revolt. In San Domingo, Leclerc declared the measure premature. But the blacks could see what was in store for them, and in September, Toussaint's lieutenants, Christophe and Dessalines, had no trouble raising the island in revolt. The French force, decimated by yellow fever, was rapidly exhausted. Leclerc died. His successor, Rochambeau, a supporter of the planters, lost everything by attacking the mulattoes, whom Bonaparte had already alienated by prohibiting them entry to France and marriage with whites. Port-au-Prince fell on November 19, 1803, and a few besieged garrisons managed to drag out a miserable existence until 1811.

If the English were displeased to see France re-establishing her colonial empire, they might nevertheless have delayed going to war to prevent her from doing so. But to threaten English possessions was altogether another matter, and this was precisely what Bonaparte did. A new grand concept prompted him in the direction of the Mediterranean, that is to say, Egypt. The Treaty of Amiens had at last convinced the Turks to make peace with the French (June 26, 1802) and to open the Dardanelles to French trade. A French agent, Ruffin, immediately set about restoring the consulates in the Levant. Also, pacts had been concluded with the Pasha of Tripoli in 1801 and with the Bey of Tunis in 1802. In August 1802 a flotilla compelled the Dey of Algiers to follow suit. Constantinople was already very concerned about French intrigues in the Peloponnesus, in Janina, and among the Serbs, and there were fears of a possible partition. At the end of August, Colonel Sebastiani embarked on a mission of observation to Egypt, by way of Tripoli, and then went on to Syria, seeking everywhere to establish ties with the native chieftains. Cavaignac had been sent to Muscat, and Decaen sailed for India on March 6, 1803, with an important staff capable of forming sepoy regiments. All this led England to conclude that Bonaparte was planning to launch a new attack against Egypt and India, and that prudence demanded that he be stopped from completing his preparations. Under the circumstances, a British surrender of Malta was unthinkable. But that decision was a clear violation of the Treaty of Amiens.

Bonaparte's continental policy gave the English the pretext they needed. Despite Schimmelpenninck's repeated demands, Bonaparte refused to evacuate Holland, alleging that the conditions of the treaty had not been fulfilled. Although he abandoned the Neapolitan ports and the Papal States, he annexed Elba in August 1802, Piedmont in September, and occupied Parma in October, following the death of its duke. In Switzerland, the last of the French troops had no sooner withdrawn when Alois Reding led a rising of the small mountain cantons

France and England: The Struggle Renewed (1802–1805)

on the night of August 27, 1802. A rebel diet was gathered at Schwyz. Zurich, Berne, and Fribourg fell under its sway. The legal government, seeking refuge in Lausanne, desperately granted the rebel peasants of Vaud the abolition of feudal dues, and promised to compensate the proprietors out of public lands: but in vain. The government was thus forced to appeal to Bonaparte for help. The First Consul intervened as mediator on September 30, and imposed a general disarmament. Ney marched into Switzerland, and the diet, obtaining nothing more substantial than fine words from England and Austria, dispersed. Reding was arrested. A consultative assembly was summoned to Paris on December 10, and a commission of ten of its delegates was appointed to discuss Bonaparte's project for a constitution with four French senators. Bonaparte ordered the commission to draft constitutions for the several cantons, and these were then embodied in the final product, the Act of Mediation of February 19, 1803. Each of the nineteen cantons received its own constitution providing for a limited, property-based suffrage in most cases, particularly in the old aristocratic cantons where it ensured that the rule of the pre-revolutionary urban patriciate would continue. The cantons recovered a large measure of autonomy, the freedom to dispose of public lands, and the right to regulate feudal dues and religious affairs. Reaction was thus enabled to triumph nearly everywhere, religious liberty being guaranteed only in the districts where it had previously existed. All that remained of unity was the equal rights of the cantons, which were forbidden to form alliances, the liberty of the Swiss to dwell and own property throughout the confederation, and the abolition of internal tariff barriers. The feeble central government was composed of a diet, where each canton had one or two votes depending on its importance, and a chief magistracy, the office of Landammann, which revolved among the leaders of the six main or 'directorial' cantons, viz. Berne, Basle, Lucerne, Zurich, Fribourg, and Solothurn. Bonaparte appointed the first Landammann, Louis d'Affry, a former officer of the French Swiss Guards, who represented Fribourg. On September 27, 1803, the Helvetic Confederation signed a defensive treaty of alliance with France for fifty years and renewed the stipulations for the recruitment of four regiments of 4,000 men each.

But the confederation was left without a standing army, and Bonaparte did not even permit the formation of a general staff.

Meanwhile, in Germany, French influence was making giant strides towards a settlement of the indemnities promised by the Treaty of Lunéville to the dispossessed princes of the left bank of the Rhine. The Reichstag had refused to let the question be settled by the Holy Roman Emperor, and had empowered a committee to discuss the indemnity with France. In vain did the Austrian Foreign Minister, Cobenzl, attempt to influence France with an offer of an alliance. Bonaparte and Alexander of Russia had already agreed to regulate the affair together. Actually, all the German princes, headed by the King of Prussia, negotiated at Paris and bribed Talleyrand with a combined sum of 10 to 15 million francs in their separate efforts to obtain choice lands. George III himself accepted the Bishopric of Osnabrück. Dalberg, Elector of Mainz, eagerly took part in the sport. Saxony, having no rightful claim, alone hung back. On June 3, 1802, France and Russia invited the Imperial Diet to ratify the plan worked out at Paris. Austria expressed her disapproval and took hold of Passau, which had been destined by the settlement for Bavaria; but she had to pull out in the face of unanimous protests. It was Bonaparte who rescued Austrian prestige in the end by reserving a place for her in the concluding agreement on December 26. On February 25, 1803, the Reichstag ratified the Imperial Recess.

The new imperial constitution abolished the ecclesiastical principalities and reduced the number of free cities from fifty-one to six, thus completing the process of secularization which had taken place in 1555 and 1648. Prussia acquired the Bishoprics of Paderborn, Hildesheim, Erfurt, and a substantial part of Münster; Bavaria received the Bishopric of Freising, and part of Passau; Baden obtained the towns of Mannheim and Heidelberg, and the right-bank territories of the Bishoprics of Speier, Strassburg, and Basle; other states participated in shares proportionate to their size. Austria, which was least favoured of all, ceded the Breisgau and Ortenau to the Duke of Modena, but gained the Bishoprics of Brixen and Trent and part of the Bishopric of Passau; through Austria's influence, the Grand Duke of Tuscany received the archbishoprics of

Salzburg and Eichstädt. Austria confiscated the lands and funds of princes dispossessed in her territories.

For the Catholic Church, the Recess was a catastrophe comparable to that of the sixteenth century: the Church lost nearly $2\frac{1}{2}$ million subjects and 21 million florins in annual revenue; eighteen universities and all monasteries were secularized; and of the clerical electors, only Dalberg of Mainz survived the redistribution, his seat having been transferred to Ratisbon. Austria, apart from her loss of prestige, was forced to contemplate the imminent doom of the Holy Roman Empire because the princes of Würtemberg, Baden, and Hesse-Cassel became electors, thus making the Protestant states the new majority in the electoral college as well as in the diet. The *Ritterschaft*** and the knightly orders were also destined shortly to disappear despite Austria's attempts to save them. France could only profit from this reshuffling of German territories, since all of the South German states had turned towards her to oppose the Hapsburgs. Prussia gained much but failed to fulfil all of her aspirations, having to turn down Hanover and a proffered French alliance in order to avoid falling out with England. With the advent of peace, Prussia had lost her domination over northern Germany. Frederick William III met the Russian tzar in Memel on June 10, 1802, this marking the beginning of Alexander's amorous friendship with Queen Louise, which bound him ever after to the Hohenzollerns. But the Prussian king sensed that he was the protégé, rather than the ally, of Russia, and so felt slighted.

England was an impotent witness to these upheavals, which, while they did not violate the Treaty of Amiens, were in her eyes clearly contrary to its spirit. Since Russia and Austria were concerned with the fate of Switzerland, and since Austria was disconsolate over the loss of Germany and Italy, the English were comforted and irritated at the same time: as Addington had foreseen, England would find allies. Until October 1802, relations with France remained satisfactory. Addington, who had complaints of his own about the *Moniteur*, even took cognizance of Bonaparte's protests and began civil action against the émigré journalist Peltier. As late as September 10 instructions received by Whitworth, the English

* See page 203. AUTHOR.

175

ambassador in Paris, were still wholly peaceful. But the annexation of Italian territory, and above all the intervention in Switzerland (which made quite as much of a stir as it had in 1798) caused an about face. Hawkesbury expressed his 'profound regret'. 'Although we wish for peace . . ., we must depend on the co-operation of the French government.' 'England desires for the continent the status quo as of the time of the Treaty of Amiens, and nothing but that.'* In his mind, the idea was being formed that every French gain would necessitate a *quid pro quo*.

The best interests of France were, at the very least, to play for time. She had only forty-three ships of the line, and while she planned to build twenty-three more, they would not be ready until 1804. Bonaparte anticipated war in his instructions to Decaen, but not before the fall of 1804. Nevertheless, he impolitically replied that England 'should have the Treaty of Amiens, and nothing but the Treaty of Amiens'. Talleyrand's threat that 'the first cannon shot could suddenly bring into being a Gallic Empire' and persuade Bonaparte to 're-establish the Empire of the West' only added fuel to the fire. Even so, Hawkesbury did not press matters and allowed the French and British ambassadors, Andréossy and Whitworth, to rejoin their posts. This apparent weakness only served to excite the First Consul more. On January 30, 1803, at the very moment that England was completing its evacuation of Egypt, he published in the *Moniteur* a report by General Sebastiani containing the notable remark that 'six thousand men would suffice to reconquer Egypt'. This kind of provocation is hard to explain. Although he would tell Lucien that he was thus counting on goading 'John Bull to fight', he was well aware that France was not ready. In October Talleyrand had also stated that if England was leading the world to believe that 'the First Consul had refrained from doing any particular thing because he had been prevented, he would do it forthwith'. Such statements were as subversive of the national interest as they were irrational.

Actually, Hawkesbury's peaceful posture was purely temporary. 'It would be impossible, under present circumstances,

---

* The translator has failed, despite extensive efforts, to locate the source of these quotes, and so has been unable to render them in their original English wording. TRANSLATOR.

even supposing it were wise policy,' he wrote to Whitworth on November 25, 1802, 'to engage England in a war over one or another of France's recent aggressions. Our policy must seek to use these aggressions to build a defensive system of alliance for the future, together with Russia and Austria.'* As early as October 27 he had tendered Russia a definite proposal of alliance for the preservation of the status quo in Europe. Alexander was then preoccupied in arranging German affairs together with France, and so at first turned a deaf ear. But Bonaparte's Eastern policy at last moved him too: as with the earlier French expedition to Egypt in 1798, it brought Russia and England closer together. Alexander reasoned that if he could not have Malta, it would be better for the English to have it than the French. On February 8, 1803, Hawkesbury therefore learned that the tzar wished the evacuation of Malta delayed. The news, coming as it did following the publication of Sebastiani's report in the *Moniteur*, could not have been better timed. On the 9th, Hawkesbury instructed Whitworth that before evacuating Malta England would demand 'a satisfactory explanation' of the conduct of the French government.

There ensued a series of stormy interviews between Bonaparte and the British ambassador, and on February 20, in a message delivered to the Legislative Body, Bonaparte denounced the schemes of the war party in London. On March 8, George III replied in a speech from the throne by drawing attention to French armaments; Parliament responded by calling up the militia. For the moment, England was committed to staying in Malta since the conditions stipulated in the Treaty of Amiens had not been fulfilled: Alexander was clouding his guarantee with reservations that presupposed a rewriting of the terms of the treaty, and Prussia followed suit. But Addington, having decided now to keep the island, took this opportunity to give events a sharp turn. On March 15, he demanded

* See the previous note. The diplomatic correspondence between Hawkesbury and Whitworth can be found in Oscar Browning: *England and Napoleon in 1803. Despatches of Lord Whitworth*, London, 1887. However, this collection neither contains any passages even remotely resembling the above quote, nor is a dispatch by Hawkesbury dated November 25, 1802, to be found anywhere in the book. Hawkesbury wrote to Whitworth on November 14 and on January 14, but these dispatches make no reference to a defensive system of alliance with Russia and Austria. TRANSLATOR.

occupation of Malta for ten years, as compensation for French territorial gains. Talleyrand replied by offering to negotiate within the framework of the Treaty of Amiens. Meanwhile, Hawkesbury learned on April 14 that Russia, while declining a new alliance, had promised its support if Turkey were attacked, and that Alexander had repeated his advice over Malta. On the 26th, Whitworth presented Bonaparte with an ultimatum.

This sudden resolve on the part of the English upset Bonaparte's entourage. Fouché was to tell him in the Senate, 'You, like us, are a product of the Revolution, and war places everything in doubt.' In March it was whispered in Whitworth's ear that in consideration for a bribe the First Consul's family could be persuaded to appease Bonaparte, and that Talleyrand would help provided he received his share. Bonaparte too was upset by Russia's fears: on March 11, he wrote the tzar to reassure him and to entreat him to pacify England. He now requested Russian mediation, and proposed to leave Malta in the hands of Great Britain for a year or two, after which time it would be turned over to Russia. Addington replied that this was unacceptable, and Whitworth left Paris on May 12. The British government reserved the option of treating the diplomatic break as a declaration of war, contrary to continental custom. British men-of-war began to capture French commercial vessels at sea without prior warning, an act which was regarded as one of unqualified piracy on the part of 'perfidious Albion'.

Alexander had in fact accepted the offer of mediation; aside from being flattered, he was well pleased with the prospect of occupying Malta, thus keeping both England and France out of the East. To Vorontsov, who demanded explanations, Addington answered that he had not had time to consult the king. This unyielding attitude, so contrary to previous policy, could only be explained by the intervention of the war party, and perhaps Pitt. It did not create a good impression at home, and the Whigs outdid themselves in denouncing it. It took some time for England to become equal to the occasion, but Bonaparte was so dangerous that national unity was welded much more quickly than it had been at the time of the Revolution.

The responsibility for the rupture has been a subject of much passionate argument. If Bonaparte's provocations are undeniable, it is nonetheless a fact that England broke the treaty and took the initiative to wage preventive war from the moment that she could hope for Russia's collaboration. Britain's justification was the preservation of the European balance of power, but this grave concern did not extend to the sea, since in her eyes God had created the oceans for the English. The conflict between Bonaparte and England was in reality a clash between two imperialisms.

THE ESTABLISHMENT OF THE EMPIRE IN FRANCE (1804)

The war, while benefiting neutral shipping, impeded English trade and caused a decline in the value of the pound sterling. It affected French trade even more. Bonaparte retaliated against attacks on French merchant vessels by sequestering enemy goods and incarcerating British subjects. Although he regarded British seizures of French merchantmen as justification, such counter-measures were considered outrageous and offered no practical help to French businessmen. After the Treaty of Amiens, entrepreneurs had gone heavily into shipbuilding, and many lost their fortunes, including Barrillon, a governor of the Bank of France. All of the banks were either directly or indirectly involved with maritime investments, and so were threatened with ruin. The stock exchange was also affected: 5 per cent bonds fell from sixty-five in March to forty-seven at the end of May. Bonaparte, aware of the danger ahead, had reorganized the Bank of France by the law of 24 Germinal, Year XI (April 14, 1803). Mollien, director of the *Caisse de Garantie*, unceasingly clamoured against the shareholders of the Bank, who enjoyed the privilege of discounting their own notes, and who paid themselves fat dividends and then speculated on the rise of the Bank's shares. Dividends were limited to 6 per cent by the new legislation, and the discount operation was entrusted to a committee of merchants, but without any real improvement as events in 1805 were to show. For Bonaparte, it was essential that the position of the Bank be strengthened. Its capital stock was raised to 45 million francs, and a reserve fund was created. It was granted the monopoly of issuing banknotes in Paris, and it absorbed the *Caisse d'Escompte du Commerce*

(Commercial Discount Bank), a rival bank. In return, the Bank agreed to discount all the rescriptions of the receveurs,* which were collectible after one or two months. Both trade and treasury were able, with the Bank's help, to weather the storm without excessive damage.

Bonaparte's prestige did not suffer. Since England had torn up the Treaty of Amiens, and had begun hostilities without bothering to declare war (as was her custom), he had every opportunity to place all of the blame on her without any fear of being contradicted. The French nation, under attack, was left with no alternative but to gather around its leader, and its determination was strengthened in the face of new Royalist plots, which were now being encouraged and subsidized by the British government. Thus the first consequence of the renewed war was that it yielded Bonaparte the imperial title and the hereditary succession.

Cadoudal had never ceased to keep his co-conspirators at the highest pitch; two of his agents had been imprisoned since the beginning of 1803. On August 21 he landed at Biville in Seine-Inférieure, and made his way to Paris where he was kept in hiding by numerous accomplices. By his own account he wanted to kidnap Bonaparte, not assassinate him; but having decided to kill him in case of resistance, his attempt would certainly have ended in murder. The arrival of the Comte d'Artois was to be the signal, but he never came. In the meantime, royalist unrest revived everywhere, and bands of marauders reappeared in the west. In another quarter, General Lajolais was trying to bring Pichegru and Moreau together. Relations between these two had already been established by a certain Abbé David, who had been arrested late in 1802. Lajolais left for London at the end of August 1803, and returned in December, followed shortly by Pichegru. Moreau agreed to a meeting, but did not commit himself to joining the conspiracy, seeing that the old Chouan leader, Cadoudal, had a hand in the affair. Finally, a third branch of the conspiracy was being uncovered by Méhée de la Touche, an ex-Jacobin turned agent provocateur; having contacted certain émigré circles in England, he proposed that they join hands with the republican conspirators. He then managed to make his way to

* See translator's note on p. 81.

Munich, where the English agent Drake informed him of his own schemes to raise the Rhineland in revolt and to keep open communications with Alsace in order to prepare the entry of the Duc d'Enghien at the head of a corps of émigrés.

The First Consul was in fact surrounded by treachery, of which he knew but a fraction. In Dresden, the Comte d'Antraigues, Alexander's spy, was being kept fully informed about Bonaparte's private life by *'l'amie de Paris'*, one of Josephine's intimates. Another source, *'l'ami de Paris'* (who seems to have been either Daru, future Intendant-General of the Grand Army, or his father—at any rate, an associate of Talleyrand), furnished d'Antraigues with diplomatic documents and information about Bonaparte's policies. Under the uninspired guidance of Chief Judge Régnier, the police had run up against a blank wall, and even though Fouché had put his intelligence system at the service of the First Consul, Bonaparte was still very much in the dark at the beginning of 1804. In February he decided to take action. Two prisoners revealed under torture the imminent arrival of 'a prince', and they also told of Moreau's treacherous negotiations. Moreau was immediately arrested, and terror became the order of the day: frontiers were closed, homes searched, the jury system suspended, and Murat became Governor of Paris. The police were not long in laying hold of Pichegru and Cadoudal. Meanwhile, Méhée de la Touche made it known that the Duc d'Enghien was residing at Ettenheim, in Baden, not far from Strasbourg, and that the émigrés were gathering at Offenburg. Bonaparte allowed that the Duc was the 'prince' whom the conspirators were awaiting, and on March 10, after holding a council which included both Fouché and Talleyrand, he decided to kidnap the Duc d'Enghien.

The kidnapping operation was entrusted to the former Marquis de Caulaincourt with General Ordener as his subordinate. Caulaincourt was unable to find any émigrés at Offenburg, but at Ettenheim Ordener arrested the Duc d'Enghien on the night of March 14. On the 20th, the privy council set the fatal machinery in motion. The duke was brought to Vincennes at five o'clock in the evening, dragged before a military commission at eleven, and shot at two in the morning. Although there was nothing in his papers to link him with Cadoudal, there was proof that he was in England's pay and that he yearned to lead an invasion of Alsace. He was condemned not as a conspirator but as an émigré being paid by a foreign nation to invade France. Had he been arrested on French soil or in enemy territory, the law would have prescribed the death penalty. But by kidnapping him on neutral soil, Bonaparte blatantly compromised the interests of France and provided the Continental Powers with the pretext for which they were searching.

The conspirators were now placed on trial. Twenty were condemned to death on June 9. Bonaparte pardoned twelve, most of them nobles, and the rest (including Cadoudal) were guillotined. Pichegru was found strangled in his cell. Moreau was acquitted, but a second verdict was ordered; this time the judges imposed a two-year sentence, which was commuted to banishment. During the course of the trial, the bourgeoisie and the salons seethed with ferment. 'The hate and vituperation aimed at the government,' wrote Roederer on June 14, 'have become as violent and pronounced as ever I saw them in the time before the Revolution.' Such sentiments were evidenced in the theatres and at the trial itself. The cause of national solidarity suffered a temporary setback; Chateaubriand, who had accepted a diplomatic post, resigned. But the dissidents did not consider going to the people, the press kept its silence, and the country as a whole either remained indifferent or supported Bonaparte.

Bonaparte's entourage, and Fouché who was anxious to regain favour, urged the First Consul to strike while the iron was hot. They suggested to him that the establishment of a hereditary succession would disarm the assassins: childish argument, for if Bonaparte had been murdered, the regime would surely have collapsed. What really put an end to the attempts on his life was the terror and the perfection of police surveillance. Nevertheless, the assemblies pretended to take the argument seriously, so as to preserve for themselves a place in the future order. The republicans, moreover, were not unsatisfied by the execution of the Duc d'Enghien: 'I am delighted,' said the Tribune Curée. 'Bonaparte is made of the same stuff as the Convention.' On March 23 the Senate announced that the time had come 'to change the institutions'. The Council of State, when consulted, objected to the principle of hereditary rule, but on April 23, Curée led the Tribunate in a resolution for its adoption. Bonaparte then made his reply to the Senate, saying, 'You have decided on the necessity for hereditary rule.' The Senate, which had done nothing of the kind, acquiesced. Between May 16 and 18, a new constitution was drafted, which was then promulgated by Senate decree on 28 Floréal, Year XII (May 18, 1804), and finally ratified by a plebiscite. The 'government of the Republic' was entrusted to a hereditary emperor who was to receive a civil list of 25 million francs and the revenues from crown lands, which were distinguished from his personal estate. He was given a free hand in the establishment of an imperial court and in the regulation of the affairs of the royal family.

The main problem was to define the rules for the succession. 'Hereditary' had always been synonymous with primogeniture, but Bonaparte had no male issue and was not even the eldest son of his family. The simplest solution would have been to permit the Emperor to designate his own successor, as in the time of the Roman Empire. In fact, Bonaparte reserved the right to adopt an heir, while it was denied to those who would succeed him. Even so, he was much too devoted to his family 'clan' to leave them completely out in the cold. His brothers, however, refused to renounce their rights in favour of Louis Bonaparte's son, Charles, the heir-presumptive. Overladen with riches and honours, they knew no gratitude, and with the support of their mother created a thousand difficulties. Lucien had just married Madame Jouberthou, the widow of a bankrupt speculator—a marriage hardly calculated to enhance the imperial dignity. Jérome, bound for the Antilles in a man-of-war, proceeded to the United States and married the daughter of a merchant. Maria-Paola, rechristened Pauline, took as her second husband the Prince Borghese without consulting her brother. Then there was Maria-Annunziata—now elegantly Caroline, the wife of Murat—and Maria-Anna—transformed into Elisa and married to that hopeless Corsican Bacciochi: both of these sisters raged because Bonaparte had not made them princesses. Finally, it was decided that failing a natural or an adopted heir the succession would fall to Joseph, and after him, Louis. Lucien, having refused to divorce his wife, was excluded and left for Italy.

France and England: The Struggle Renewed (1802–1805)

As in Year X, the Senate found this an opportune moment to express its wish (this time officially) for constitutional guarantees. The Senate wanted to become an hereditary body with a veto power which would enable it to protect the fundamental rights of citizens. As for the Legislative Body, Fontanes asked that it be granted the right to discuss laws, and that its presidency, which office he in fact occupied, be given some degree of permanence. The net result, however, was that the Senate alone obtained the right to appoint two permanent committees charged respectively with the maintenance of individual liberty and with the liberty of the press. They were empowered only to hear complaints, and to declare after conducting an investigation that there was a 'presumption' that these liberties had been violated. The police, on the other hand, were reorganized and brought under even greater central control; Fouché became minister again (July 10), and France was divided into four arrondissements headed by four councillors of state responsible to him. Apart from this, government institutions underwent little change. Napoleon took advantage of the occasion to assume the right to choose an unlimited number of senators, and he decreed that the princes, his brothers, together with the six Grand Dignitaries of the Empire, be made members of the Senate ex officio.

By instituting the Grand Dignitaries and the Grand Officers —the latter comprising eighteen marshals and numerous chamberlains—the Constitution of Year XII marked a stage in the creation of a new aristocracy. The imperial court burgeoned in the splendour of its luxury, and the decree of 24 Messidor, Year XII (July 13, 1804), concerning precedence, extended a protocol of etiquette to the entire administration. The cause of national solidarity was not long in resuming its course. Napoleon henceforth openly embraced the idea of creating a new nobility, and he wasted no time turning the Legion of Honour to that purpose: it became simply a decoration, much like the old chivalric orders. When ordaining that the representatives of the electoral colleges be invited to his coronation, he specified that they be chosen from among the ancient families which enjoyed public esteem. On the day of the ceremony he vented his contempt for the masses: 'The presidents of the cantons and the presidents of the electoral colleges, the army—these are the true people of France,' and not, '20,000 or 30,000 fishmongers and people of that ilk . . .; they are only the corrupt and ignorant dregs of society.'

Consequently, Napoleon could not regard the popular mandate as a sufficient foundation for the new legitimacy. Like Pippin the Short, he asked for the Pope's consecration so that divine right might be restored and written into the catechism. Negotiations were conducted in Paris between Caprara, the Pope's representative, and Talleyrand and Bernier; and in Rome between Cardinal Consalvi and Cardinal Fesch, the Emperor's uncle, who as a former constitutional priest had been appointed archbishop of Lyons, cardinal, and ambassador to the Vatican. In view of the recent execution of the Duc d'Enghien, Pius VII had reason enough to hesitate, fearing as he did to offend the great powers; but since he hoped to obtain modifications of the Organic Articles, and perhaps even the restoration of the Legations, he ended by giving his consent. The royalists broke out in furious uproar, and Joseph de Maistre wrote that the Pope had 'lowered himself to the point of being an inconsequential punchinello'. For all his trouble, Pius received nothing except the submission of the remaining constitutional bishops who had persisted in their recalcitrance; even so, Bishop Saurine of Strasbourg continued to refuse to disavow the civil constitution of the clergy. Pius was not even spared a final humiliation. At Notre-Dame on December 2, 1804, Napoleon seized the crown and placed it on his own head. Then, after the Pope had retired, the new Emperor took an oath to liberty and equality. Josephine too, was crowned by her husband, but on the eve of the coronation she had played the nasty trick of informing the Pope that her marriage had been only a civil one; and so Napoleon had to consent to a religious ceremony which would make divorce more difficult.

If the theatricality of the coronation ritual, which David was to depict, gave Napoleon the reassurance he wanted, it in no way added to his prestige. The French people watched with a sceptical eye the strange procession and the many celebrations that followed in the month of December. No one believed that Napoleon's power had been consolidated by all this. Having re-established the monarchy and heightened the aristocratic nature of the regime, he only served to widen still further the gulf between his own cause and the nation's. 'In those days,' said Chaptal, 'the history of the Revolution was as remote for us as the history of the Greeks and Romans.' Maybe so for Chaptal and his like, but among the people its spirit had not been extinguished! Napoleon had seduced the French nation with the promise of peace—he had finished by installing himself, while fanning the flames of war. Now there was nothing to restrain him from fulfilling his real desires. Imperial conquest, despotism, and the aristocratic principle would have their day, while the nation, stunned and troubled, was compelled to follow, lest it perish, the chariot of Caesar triumphant.

PROJECTS FOR AN INVASION OF ENGLAND. TRAFALGAR (1805)

The war between France and England dragged on for more than two years without any decisive result being achieved. Both sides had to endure more difficulties than they had anticipated. In 1803 England had fifty-five ships of the line, as against France's forty-two, of which only thirteen were ready for battle. This enormous advantage assured England's maritime dominance from the very start. French ports were once again blockaded and their commerce suppressed, whereas British merchantmen had scarcely anything to fear except corsairs, against which they were protected now that the use of escort convoys had been resumed. England wasted no time reoccupying Saint-Lucia, Tobago, and Dutch Guiana. Nevertheless, Addington was accused of waging the war feebly. Many of the ships were old, and few new ones were being built because St. Vincent was unable to reorganize the timber supply. Although indirect taxes had been raised, there were still financial difficulties. The Addington ministry continued to be on chilly terms with Russia ever since the affair of the Maltese mediation, and its role in the royalist plots of Year XII had weakened its reputation.

Napoleon pressed for armaments, but he lacked money. In Year XII the government began again to operate at a deficit. Confident of his power, Napoleon finally heeded the advice of Gaudin, his Minister of Finance, and restored indirect taxes. 'Do I not have my gendarmes, my prefects, and my priests?'

he thundered. 'If anyone should revolt, I will have five or six rebels hanged, and everyone else will pay.' On 5 Ventôse, Year XII (February 25, 1804), he founded the Excise Bureau (*Administration des Droits Réunis*) and appointed Français de Nantes as its director, but only a modest tax on liquor was imposed. As for the treasury, Barbé-Marbois was unable to keep its coffers filled, and so was forced to seek the assistance of bankers and contractors. In 1804, Després, a director of the Bank of France, and two financiers, Michel and Séguin, formed the 'Company of United Merchants'. To some extent this company was affiliated with Vanlerberghe's provisioning enterprise, but its leading spirit was none other than Gabriel Julien Ouvrard.* In 1805, it bought up all of the outstanding rescriptions. In April of that year, Ouvrard offered to advance the government 50 million francs at 9 per cent on condition that it would count as part of the loan the 20 million francs that it already owed him and had refused to pay, thus in effect bringing the interest to 15 per cent. In June Ouvrard lent 150 million francs, of which 42 million were to count toward the bad debt. In return, Barbé-Marbois pledged assignments of taxes and treasury obligations. Després saw to it that all of this paper was discounted at the Bank of France, which thus acquiesced to a disguised inflation. The allies were made to contribute. Beginning in April 1803 Flushing and Dutch Brabant were garnished, and Holland, while wishing to remain neutral, had to agree on June 25 to furnish 16,000 men and all the ships that might be required of her. It took an ultimatum to bring Godoy to heel, but on October 19 he promised to contribute 6 million francs every month; on December 19 the government in Lisbon also agreed to disburse 16 million francs. Nevertheless, neither Spain nor Portugal declared war. Elsewhere the French reoccupied the Neapolitan ports, and in May 1803, Mortier invaded Hanover from Holland, disarmed its army, and then seized Cuxhaven at the mouth of the Elbe and Meppen on the Ems. But all of this could not suffice to make England capitulate; and even if the naval war could have been waged successfully it would have offered only distant prospects.

---

* Being an association of purveyors and speculators, the company undertook, *inter alia,* to advance money to the French treasury and to supply the army with provisions. TRANSLATOR.

Therefore, Napoleon decided to threaten the enemy with an invasion.

Napoleon did not discount certain possibilities in Ireland: in 1803 there had been an insurrection, but it was crushed, and Emmett and Russell were hanged without France being able to intervene. It was to the project of 1801, however, that he devoted his greatest attention. The army was concentrated at the camp of Boulogne; on December 2, 1803, it was named 'The Army of England'. By thus massing his forces, Napoleon was able to separate the army from the nation and gain its personal loyalty through the promise of a grand enterprise. He was also keeping open the possibility of eventually swooping down on the Continent and striking a major blow. In January 1805 he maintained that this in fact was the army's only purpose, while in reality he was trying to conceal an obstacle which was all too apparent—the inescapable fact of seapower. There is no doubt that Napoleon on many occasions had been determined to cross the Channel—quite understandably in view of the military situation in the United Kingdom. Early in 1804 the English army numbered less than 100,000 regulars. The militia numbered 72,000 men, on paper, and volunteers again were pouring in to escape the draft, perhaps more than 300,000. On July 27, 1803, Parliament voted a mass levy compelling all men between the ages of 17 and 55 to drill; finally, on July 6, it was decided to create an 'additional force', recruited by lot. But all of these forces were worthless: it seems that the government, in case of a landing, planned to retire into the Welsh country to conduct guerrilla warfare. There can be no question that the French could have occupied London without firing a shot. This alone was enough to tempt Napoleon.

The English were well attuned to the danger. The nation became caught up in a movement more vibrant even than that of 1797, and about which Wordsworth left posterity a stirring account. In February 1804, Pitt set out to attack the ministry; the majority crumbled, and by the end of April Addington resigned. Pitt wanted a coalition government, but the king refused to accept Fox, whereupon Grenville, who had reconciled his differences with Fox, declined to take part in the new ministry. Pitt was thus forced to form his cabinet with Addington's colleagues, and he even had to bring in Addington himself in 1805. Pitt never recaptured the strong parliamentary position he had formerly enjoyed. He was further weakened by an inquiry into the Admiralty, which compromised certain speculators, including his intimate Dundas, now Lord Melville, and which forced the latter to resign. But Pitt nonetheless brought a firmness to English policy which it had previously lacked. He wove a new coalition in such a way that Russia, driven into the arms of England by Napoleon's policies, herself ended by proposing it. At the same time he organized the volunteers, putting them at last under state control, and he united the militia and the 'additional force' into a kind of reserve, from which 10,000 men were allocated as reinforcements to the regular army. In order to secure the co-operation of naval purveyors, he allowed them a free hand in provisioning the fleet, which was gradually brought to 115 ships of the line. He also took pains to assure that the coasts were defended, and he placed finances on a sound basis by restoring the income tax. His most felicitous act was the appointment of Sir Charles Middleton, Lord Barham, to succeed Dundas as First Lord of the Admiralty in April 1805. It was Middleton's masterly command of the naval operations of the squadrons that culminated in the battle of Trafalgar. Until this victory, English public opinion was in no way confident, but Pitt and Barham never lost their sangfroid. Now it was of little moment that Napoleon had an army: the great obstacle remained the crossing of the Channel.

On the one hand, Napoleon was evidently always willing to leave much to chance: had he not made it to Egypt and back, despite the English squadrons? On the other hand, he was so thoroughly Mediterranean that he failed to consider, initially, the problems posed by the Straits of Dover: its surging tides, turbulent currents, and treacherous winds. At first he had planned to clear the way by means of gunboats and flatboats, similar to the barges of the Flemish canals, which would be loaded with cannon and propelled by oars. The army was to be transported on merchant vessels; but the fact had to be faced that these were not in adqeuate supply, and in September 1803 it was decided that the troops would also be embarked on flatboats. Napoleon had them constructed everywhere along the length of the Channel, but the English squadrons never allowed them to be concentrated in one place. Nevertheless, in 1804, more than 1,700 flatboats were gathered at Boulogne and neighbouring ports, and facilities were constructed to enable them to load equipment. Decrès, the Minister of Marine, and Admiral Bruix, the chief of the flotilla, observed that no more than a hundred ships could leave Boulogne harbour in a single tide: they would have been at the mercy of the enemy squadrons. While a tempest or winds might prevent the enemy from intercepting them, these flatboats could not be risked at sea except in fair weather. And so, Napoleon was brought to the necessity of scouring the Channel with his warships; in short, he was forced to return to a war of naval engagement.

Here Napoleon's inferiority was all too obvious. The English possessed not only a superiority of numbers, but boasted a great many more three-deckers, which towered over the classical seventy-four-gun ship and carried carronades on the spar deck which enhanced their firepower even more. Sir Home Popham had introduced a new and effective system of signalling. English ships were in better condition, their crews more battle hardened, and their admirals, like Nelson, were selected from the ranks of fighting captains. French sailors and warships, shut up in their ports, could not be of the same quality. Nor could their admirals, who proved themselves capable only when commanding their own units. Notwithstanding this superiority, the English squadrons, divided as they were, risked being destroyed piecemeal. Brest was the only port they guarded closely, Rochefort being situated on the Bay of Biscay which was hard to contain, and Toulon being under the distant vigil of Nelson who tarried in the Neapolitan waters, lured by the proximity of Lady Hamilton. The French, then, were not being prevented from sailing. Had they done so, the British Admiralty had planned to rally the fleet at Ushant; as long as the British blocked the entrance to the Channel, they had nothing to fear. Still, the possibility of surprise could not be entirely discounted, however contemptible the idea might have seemed to some.

In May 1804 Napoleon decided that his squadrons, running the blockade, would rescue Ganteaume at Brest and then sweep the Channel. He arrived at Boulogne in August, where on the 16th he distributed medals of the Legion of Honour. The preparations, however, turned out to be insufficient. First Bruix, and then Latouche-Tréville died. From September 1804 to March 1805, Austria seemed to be poised for an attack, as a result of Napoleon's involvement in Italy, and the project for an invasion of England appeared to be scrapped. Napoleon ordered his squadrons to sail for the West Indies, where they were to attack the English colonies. But only Admiral Missiessy at Rochefort was able to effect a successful sortie (January 11, 1805); his expedition to the West Indies proved uneventful, and failing to meet the other French squadrons, he returned to France.

To all appearances, the danger of war on the Continent had now abated: it was not until July 15, 1805, that Napoleon realized the real intentions of the Coalition. Meanwhile, England, after having threatened Spain for a long time, seized several of her treasure galleons on October 5, 1804. In December, Spain finally declared war on England, and Godoy placed his fleet at the disposal of the French Emperor. Since his position at home was being menaced by the Princess of the Asturias, Godoy sent his agent, Izquierdo, to propose to Napoleon a partition of Portugal, all in the hopes of carving out a kingdom for himself. Thus encouraged, Napoleon returned to his grand design. The colonial expedition to the West Indies was now made part of a greater strategy: the various French squadrons were to effect a junction in the Antilles, and then, having sown confusion among the enemy, were to return to the Channel and if necessary give battle. In theory this plan may have been ingenious, but it presupposed a *matériel* and a leadership which simply did not exist. Moreover, Napoleon himself did not provide a consistent plan: having finally resolved on combat, he now forbade Ganteaume to break the blockade, thus reducing the latter to inactivity and throwing the whole crushing responsibility on the unenterprising commander of the fleet at Toulon, Admiral Villeneuve.

Sailing on March 30, 1805, with eleven ships (to which the Spaniards added six at Cadiz), Villeneuve first neglected to destroy Admiral Orde's force, which guarded the Straits of Gibraltar. He then set out for Martinique, which he reached only on May 14. Meanwhile, the English squadrons rallied at Ushant, with the exception of Nelson, who disobeyed orders.

Until April 15 Nelson scoured the Mediterranean looking for Villeneuve, whom he believed was on his way to Egypt; receiving information at last, he hastened to Gibraltar, where he learned that Villeneuve had sailed west. On May 11, he left for the Antilles under full sail. It was a huge gamble, for the enemy could have veered for the Channel or could have effected a juncture with other squadrons in the West Indies, and thus gained sufficient strength to defeat Nelson. The Admiralty, swayed by the public's alarm over Jamaica's safety, approved the audacious action. But however much Nelson may have been admired for his boldness, the fact remains that the outcome might have been disastrous. He gambled and won. In the Antilles, Villeneuve awaited the arrival of other French ships, but nothing came. He did however receive a dispatch from Napoleon in which the Emperor at last revealed the grand design and which instructed him to wait yet a month before proceeding back to rally the Ferrol and Rochefort squadrons in a concerted effort to break the blockade at Brest.

Arriving in Barbados on June 4, Nelson began searching for the French. Upon being apprised of this, Villeneuve decided to return to Ferrol immediately, hoping in vain to throw Nelson off his track. Nelson steered for Europe on June 13, after having sent off a fast brig to warn the Admiralty. But he was still obsessed by the danger to Egypt, and so went to Gibraltar; since Barham had ordered Admiral Calder to bar Villeneuve's passage off Cape Finisterre, the British once again found themselves dispersed. On July 22, Villeneuve met Calder's fleet. A battle ensued in which Calder captured two ships and then retreated, permitting the French to make port at Ferrol. In another quarter, Allemand, who had replaced Missiessy, put to sea from Rochefort and cruised for several months without encountering either friend or foe. From August 12 to 15, the English once again concentrated their forces near the isle of Ushant, but were immediately dispersed by Admiral Cornwallis who feared for the Convoy of the Indies and for General Craig, holed up in Lisbon with troops destined for Naples. Calder was sent back to Ferrol, and Nelson returned to England. Villeneuve knew nothing of this favourable opportunity, and so was unable to derive any profit from it. Sailing from Ferrol and Corunna on August 14, Villeneuve let himself be disheartened by the condition of his ships and by a false report that the enemy was coming up in full force. His instructions, dated July 16, were to head for Cadiz in the event that he should encounter insurmountable difficulties; this he did, anchoring there on August 18. Had he broken the blockade at Brest and beaten Cornwallis, he would still have arrived too late. On August 24 Napoleon set the Grande Armée on its march toward Germany and ordered the flotilla demobilized.

Villeneuve committed the mistake of not sailing immediately for Toulon and of allowing himself to be blockaded by Cornwallis and Calder, who were reinforced successively by other squadrons. On September 28, Nelson finally took command of the fleet off Cadiz. Nevertheless, the Franco-Spanish fleet was safe enough, sheltered in the harbour, and it was holding down thirty-three English vessels. Napoleon, however, played right into Nelson's hands by ordering the fleet to sail at all costs for an attack on Naples. Learning on October 19 that six enemy ships had departed for Tetuan to revictual, Villeneuve set sail with thirty-three vessels. On the 21st, off Cape Trafalgar, as they were sailing in a line six kilometres long, Nelson arrived to attack them. In a memorandum of October 9, he had indicated that he would take on the enemy perpendicularly, not side to side as was the custom. This was to be done by forming two columns which were to sever the enemy line in two places and break his centre, one column cutting off the van, the other destroying the rear. In actuality, the English ships did not preserve the intended formation. The attack was carried out rather confusedly since Nelson thought the allies were headed back to Cadiz. Nevertheless, his plan succeeded: the centre and rear were annihilated. Rear Admiral Dumanoir le Pelley, commanding the van with ten ships, was late in coming into the fray; four of his ships managed to elude the British, but were captured several days later. During the night, a storm crowned the disaster. Only nine ships of the line returned to port. The allies lost 4,398 killed, as against the British 449. Nelson, however, was mortally wounded. Villeneuve, taken prisoner and heaped with insults by the Emperor, committed suicide on his return to France.

England could breathe at last! True, the Coalition had made a landing impossible; but a victorious Napoleon could always return to his grand design. Nelson's triumph, however, postponed this indefinitely. It also put an end to the naval war. Eventually, this victory would make it possible for the English to carry the war on to the Continent with the help of the Spanish rebellion. But, for the time being, they were less inclined than ever to intervene on the Continent, so that the only positive effect of Trafalgar was to save Naples. Thus it seemed that the battle merely confirmed England's dominance of the seas, and one can readily understand Napoleon's view of Trafalgar as no more than a painful incident: as long as he remained victorious on land, England would never beat him.

THE CONTINENTAL BLOCKADE

The least that can be said of Napoleon's enterprises is that they guaranteed him the initiative. England, forced to defend herself, could no longer undertake fresh colonial conquests. The sole exception was Wellesley, the Governor-General in India. He had annexed part of Oudh, taken control of the Carnatic, and had established a protectorate over Surat and Tanjore. Taking advantage of civil strife among the Marathas, he undertook action there, too. Jaswant Rao Holkar, a Marathan prince, had expelled the Peshwa Baji Rao from Poona; Wellesley restored the latter to Poona in May 1803, thus making him a puppet of the East India Company. He then began to wage war against Daulat Rao Sindhia whose father, Madhoji Rao, had been on the verge of creating a vast empire when he conquered Delhi in 1788. He also attacked Raghuji Bhonsla, the Raja of Berar. He defeated Daulat Sindhia at the battle of Assaye on September 23, 1803, and Raghuji Bhonsla at Argaon, as a result of which both rulers surrendered a part of their territories. In 1804 Holkar took up the sword and succeeded in cutting Colonel Monson's column to pieces, but he in turn ended by being defeated. The following year, the Grand Moghul Shah Alam submitted to a British protectorate. These gains notwithstanding, Wellesley's independence and audacity irritated the East India Company and alarmed the English government, which had enough headaches without this one. Faced with dismissal, Wellesley resigned and sailed home on August 15, 1805.

Britain's main concern, as always, was to profit commercially from her maritime supremacy by laying claim to a monopoly of trade. She restored the terms of the blockade in full vigour. From 1803 to 1805 a sham blockade was enforced even against French-occupied Hanover. At the same time England began reissuing licences on May 18, 1803, and granted them even for the importation of enemy goods on neutral vessels. The 'Rule of 1756'* was applied once again to the enemy's colonial trade, but it was not strictly enforced against favoured neutrals. In Europe, circumstances created a certain amount of flexibility, but in the case of the United States, difficulties quickly came to the fore. The progress of American shipping was looked upon with increasing jealousy by England; James Stephen, in his book *War in Disguise* (1805), argued that the 'circuit'† lent itself to fraud and that so-called 'neutralized' enemy goods were not even unloaded or subjected to American tariffs. Since the British Admiralty never precisely defined the conditions under which neutralization would become effective, prize courts began to confiscate without restraint. On April 18, 1806, the United States Congress retaliated by declaring that the importation of British articles would be prohibited after November 15. But Napoleon launched his continental blockade at this time, and the entire situation was changed.

Since the Baltic and the Adriatic remained open, England was able to reorganize her commerce as she had in the previous war and she suffered little. Her exports fell from £25,500,000 to £20,400,000 in 1803, but rose to £23,300,000 in 1805. Re-exports suffered more, falling from £12,700,000 in 1802 to £7,600,000 in 1805. The production of sugar continued to increase in the English Antilles, the world's chief supplier, and the price continued to fall, for the market was glutted despite rising English consumption. The price of sugar declined from 55 shillings a quintal in 1805 to 32 in 1807. A series of good harvests, and the opening of new lands, made possible by the

---

* This regulation of the British Admiralty Courts declared, in effect, that colonial trade illegal in time of peace, would also be illegal in time of war. The Continental Powers whose ports were blockaded, viz., France, Spain, Holland, sought to relieve their situation by authorizing neutrals to trade in the exclusive fields to which these mother countries otherwise claimed a monopoly of trade in time of peace. The 'Rule of 1756' was simply designed to thwart neutrals, e.g., the United States, from doing this, by declaring such cargoes lawful prize. TRANSLATOR.

† For an explanation of this term, see p. 40, in text.

Enclosure Act of 1801, resulted in a decline in the price of bread to two pence a pound, which led to the landed proprietors demanding and receiving in 1804 a strengthening of the corn laws. Thus, England, relieved from the nightmare of a French invasion, fell into a state of apathy, and, until Tilsit, showed only a fitful interest in the affairs of the Continent.

Napoleon's economic policy during this period did not cause the British much concern. On June 20, 1803, he resumed the prohibitions on English goods; but hoping first to invade England and then absorbed by his continental campaigns, he never considered the prohibition as of more than secondary importance, despite what historians have often maintained. He did not even take the regulation very seriously. He remained faithful, in fact, to the moderate policy which he had substituted for that of the Directory ever since his rise to power. He did not put any restraint on neutral trade, which consequently continued to carry goods between the belligerents behind a façade of perfunctory neutralizations of cargoes. The continental blockade fell right in with the protectionism which formed part of Napoleon's mercantilistic thought. Moreover, the blockade was conceived to meet the desires of the industrialists; it excluded foreign competition without, however, excluding indispensable raw materials or hampering exports. The customs tariff indicates that England was not the sole target of this policy. In Year XI, refined sugar and molasses were prohibited without distinction of origin. On March 13, 1804, and on February 6, 1805, the rates on cotton fabrics and colonial goods were raised. The latter were again surtaxed on March 4, 1806. Since these items were primarily of English origin, the very existence of a duty on them belied the fact that the continental blockade was being strictly enforced and that Napoleon's policy was not basically military in intent but mercantilistic and protectionist.

As always, the most rabid protectionists were to be found in the cotton industries, especially the spinners, since imports of English yarn rose from 310,000 kilograms in 1804 to 1,368,000 in 1806. Likewise, the manufacturers of Lyons pressed desperately for the exclusion of Italian competition, and they demanded that Piedmontese silk be supplied to them exclusively. It can be concluded from the constantly rising tariff rates that the influence of manufacturers was decisive, and that they gradually extracted measures from Napoleon which he had not originally intended to grant. Chaptal disapproved, and so did the Paris merchants who, speaking through the Chamber of Commerce in 1803, condemned all prohibitions on trade and all measures directed against neutrals. Finally, on February 22, 1806, Napoleon banned the importation of bleached or printed calico, muslin, wick cotton, and hardware. But he continued to permit the importation of other yarns, notions, and ribbons, while surtaxing them. Cotton-spinning, which had already surpassed a million spindles by 1805, made yet greater progress, and the production of spindles rose from 2 million kilograms in 1806 to more than $4\frac{1}{2}$ million in 1808. The manufacturers of Lyons also were given concessions. Although the laws of 1803 and 1806 authorized the exportation of Piedmontese silks from Genoa and Nice, as well as from Lyons itself, the closing of the sea assured the Lyonnais a monopoly. They also sought advantages in the Kingdom of Italy, and in 1808 imposed a commercial treaty which lowered the duty on imported French goods and which, by a preferential adjustment of tariff rates, guaranteed Lyons the trade in Italian silks.

There were certain indications, however, that Napoleon, sliding down the same path as the Directory, was annoyed by the feeling that the blockade was not working as it should. On March 13, 1804, he prohibited the importation of goods 'coming directly from England', and decreed that neutrals should produce certificates of origin. His martial spirit blended perfectly with his instinct for economic nationalism: witness the sudden appearance of a tax on bale cotton on February 22, 1806—a measure which no doubt greatly displeased industrialists and which led to the increased use of flax and hemp. Finally, the anti-English policy was gradually imposed on the allies—on Holland, Spain, Italy, and even, in 1806, on Switzerland, where only yarn was excepted from the ban. As for British trade with Germany, it was impeded by the French occupation of Hanover and Cuxhaven, something the Directory had not been able to accomplish. The belief continued to be widely held that England could be defeated by stifling her export trade, and the writings of Montgaillard only served to express it once again.

All in all, however, no measures were taken against the English blockade, which overstepped the bounds of traditional mercantilist practice and the restrictive policies usually adopted in time of war. Napoleon patiently tolerated the authority which England claimed over neutrals. It can even be shown from his speech delivered to the Council of State on March 4, 1806, that, surprisingly enough, far from wishing to tighten the blockade at this time, he was waiting until peace was concluded before bringing his system of embargoes to perfection. 'Forty-eight hours after peace with England, I shall ban all foreign goods, and I shall promulgate a navigation act which will close our ports to all but French ships.' But all this was to change abruptly when Napoleon's continental successes, with his smashing victories and with the foundation of the Grand Empire, impassioned his lust for power.

THE ORIGINS OF THE THIRD COALITION

It cannot therefore be said that Napoleon's continental policy was the consequence of his war against England, and that finding it impossible to defeat England on the sea or by invasion he undertook to ruin her economically by shutting off her European market. He could not, of course, have been unaware of this possibility, but when it took shape it was because prior conquests had made such a policy workable. Nor can it explain the rash acts and encroachments which excited the hostility of the Continental Powers. It would be closer to the truth to say that although the European monarchs, no less than England, were aroused by Bonaparte's aggrandizements, and although they were still infused with an inner hatred for the leader of the revolutionary nation—whom they habitually referred to as 'the Corsican' and 'the usurper' or, like Maria Carolina, 'the successor of Robespierre', not to mention other sobriquets—they were unable to take arms, disunited and impoverished as they were, without the assistance of Great Britain. The rupture of the Peace of Amiens opened the possibility of obtaining that assistance, since England could finance a coalition and had the greatest reasons for doing so. In 1803, however, a spirit of belligerency was markedly lacking, at least in the Germanies, and Austria had even recognized on December

26, 1802, the changes which had taken place in Italy since the Treaty of Lunéville. If a coalition was possible, or even probable, it was not inevitable. To work to delay it, to wait patiently until England should be beset (as in 1801) by difficulties which were bound to come, and not just from France—this was what the national interest dictated. But such an inglorious and prosaic policy never even crossed Napoleon's mind. To spurn diplomacy for brute force was to precipitate a coalition and to run terrifying risks. It meant a commitment to hostilities whose end could only be the conquest of all Europe. No prospect could better have suited Napoleon's temperament.

Until 1803 the accord with Russia had been the keystone of Napoleon's foreign policy. It had been broken by the tzar, so that he might take the initiative in the formation of a coalition. Alexander I, aged 26, the grandson of a profligate queen and the son of a madman, carried within himself the seeds of a morbid instability which the circumstances of his upbringing and a premature marriage had accentuated even more. Entrusted by Catherine to the care of the Swiss La Harpe, who ranted of liberalism without imparting the spirit of it to his pupil, drilled by Paul in the tradition of Prussian corporalism, and exposed to the pitfalls of a heinous court—Alexander had become a tissue of contradictions: plain, yet refined; timid, yet obstinate; excitable, yet indolent; moralizing, yet corrupt; the 'Talma of the North', a seducer, a Byzantine to whom treachery was second nature. Once in power, he acquired the reputation of a liberal without doing much to deserve it. After promptly disgracing his father's murderers, Pahlen and Panin, he surrounded himself with men who had developed a certain taste for Western civilization, either at Geneva and London like Kochubei and Novosiltsev, or at Paris like Stroganov, the pupil of the French mathematician and revolutionary Gilbert Romme. To these he added his companion in pleasure, Adam Czartoryski, a Polish turncoat, clever and without character. These men constituted the 'committee of friends', or 'unofficial committee' (*neglasnyi komitet*) in which were bruited projects of constitutional reform, while the senatorial aristocracy clamoured for an important place in the government.

At the same time, Alexander counselled closely with partisans of the Old Regime—his aide-de-camp Prince Dolgorouki,

Arakcheev, the Director of Artillery, and Prince Golitsin, the Procurator of the Holy Synod who gradually won him over to mysticism. Since the liberal 'friends' did not deem Russia ripe for liberty, and had good reasons not to insist on the emancipation of the serfs, Alexander could with impunity shift his favour from one to the other group during the course of his reign, depending upon whether he leaned towards France or the Coalition, without ever ceasing to be an autocrat. On September 20, 1802, the Russian Senate saw itself established as the highest organ of judicial control, and it acquired in legislative matters a power of remonstrance which no sooner used was overridden. Eight ministries were instituted, but the ministers simply took their place at the head of the already existing administrative colleges. Nothing of consequence was done for the serfs, except in Livonia where Sievers granted them certain reforms by the ukase of February 21, 1804. The only real step forward was the creation by the new Ministry of Public Education of universities in Dorpat, Kharkov, and Kazan.

Conceited, not ambitious so much as vain, Alexander injected into his foreign policy a preference for liberal and humanitarian verbiage, and above all, a desire for showy popularity. He therefore regarded Bonaparte as a rival from the very beginning. He early surrounded himself with Germans who idolized him as the protector of their country and the future liberator of Europe. These were usually former admirers of the Revolution, who had been disillusioned by Bonaparte's restoration of monarchy. Notable among them was Klinger, who had formerly taken part in the *Sturm und Drang*, and who had been appointed by Paul I as his personal physician. 'The protector of humanity, justice, and enlightenment against the threats of impudent obscurantists and tyrants shall be none other than a prince arising from brutalized Europe . . . and it shall be he!' wrote Klinger. To the extent that he fell under the spell of mysticism, Alexander was persuaded that he was the new Messiah. He had no trouble reconciling this divine calling with the desire to preserve and to expand the Russian Empire. By the terms of the Treaty of Teschen, and as the guarantor of the Imperial Recess of 1803, he saw himself as the protector of the German states, with whose rulers he had many family ties. Czartoryski, following a family tradition of Russophilism, advised the tzar to restore Poland and proclaim himself king. But Alexander's ambitions coincided with Russia's historic mission against the Turks, and so Czartoryski, when he became foreign minister in 1804, drew up a plan to partition the Ottoman Empire. This he combined with a project for restoring Poland which would have involved a complete redrawing of the map of Europe. For the time being, Alexander compelled the sultan to recognize a kind of Russian protectorate in the Danubian principalities: in 1802, a firman excluded all Turks except garrisons from these territories; it was stipulated that all public officials would be Greek or Rumanian and that the hospodars could not be removed from office except with Russian consent. After the death of Heraclius in 1803, Georgia, whose prince had been under Russian protection for twenty years, was annexed outright, and so Russian rule bridged the Caucasus. Alexander's aggressive ambitions thus turned him against Bonaparte, conqueror of Egypt. He reasoned that Constantinople might well be endangered if Bonaparte were allowed to establish himself in Germany. If Alexander envisioned a partition of Europe with Napoleon, it was only with the intention of eventually taking it away from him.

The tzar, worried by Bonaparte's Eastern policy, made overtures to England and indirectly encouraged her to break the peace. But when France requested Russia's mediation, he cooled towards Britain: the offer was more than he could have wished for; not only could he play Solomon, but here was a chance to acquire Malta. Despite the fact that his ambassadors to Paris and London, Markov and Vorontsov, were pursuing a pro-English policy, he officially accepted the French offer on June 5, 1803. On July 19 he made his recommendations: Malta would receive a Russian garrison; England would occupy the small neighbouring island of Lampedusa; France would keep Piedmont on condition that its king were indemnified; and the neutrality of the Italian States, Holland, Switzerland, Germany, and Turkey would be guaranteed by the European powers. In short, he presumed to arbitrate for the whole Continent under colour of mediating between France and England. France had nothing to lose, since her natural frontiers were not being jeopardized, nor even her domination of Northern Italy. From the standpoint of Bonaparte, who did not want to have his hands tied by such conditions, agreement to these terms would have cost him nothing, for on June 27 England had announced that she would not surrender Malta. But Bonaparte had already occupied Hanover and the Neapolitan ports, a move which the tzar took as an affront, and on August 29 Bonaparte finally rejected the Russian proposal as being outrageously partial to England. He treated Markov very badly and demanded his recall. Alexander complied on October 28, leaving only Oubril in Paris as chargé d'affaires. Now that he realized that Bonaparte would never recognize him as the sovereign judge of Europe, he was profoundly irritated. The abduction of the Duc d'Enghien completed the rupture. As Germany's guardian, Alexander protested in the Diet against this violation of German neutrality. Bonaparte withdrew his ambassador from St. Petersburg and asked with insulting sarcasm whether Alexander, supposing that the English-paid assassins of his father had settled near the Russian frontier, 'would not have hastened to have them seized'. Oubril in turn requested his passport, and left for Russia at the end of September 1804.

At loggerheads with Bonaparte, Alexander turned of necessity to England. But since he still held a grudge against Addington, he did not make a firm approach until Pitt's return to power. And still it was not easy to come to an agreement. Consistent with the role he had assumed, the tzar wished to form a general alliance which would impose peace and completely redraw the map of Europe; he even suggested restoring freedom of the seas! On June 29, 1804, Pitt proposed simply an Anglo-Russian coalition for the purpose of taking Belgium and the Rhineland away from France. On September 11 Novosiltsev was sent to London with instructions for the negotiation of an alliance which were modelled on a memorandum of his assistant, the Abbot Piatoli. The proposals were still ambitious, but in order to make them palatable to Pitt they provided for a France reduced to her former frontiers. Leveson-Gower was dispatched to St. Petersburg in November, and the terms of the alliance began to take shape. Gustav IV of Sweden signed a secret convention with England on December 3, and a treaty of alliance with Russia in January 1805. Alexander demanded that England, in co-operation with the Russian troops at Corfu, rescue Naples, and in April 1805 General Craig embarked for the

Mediterranean. The treaty was not signed until April 11, however. England promised to pay Russia an annual subsidy of £1,250,000 for every 100,000 men contributed by the Continental Powers to the struggle against France. The division of conquests was to be settled at a later time, but it was understood that Holland would acquire Belgium and Prussia would get the northern stretch of the left bank of the Rhine. An effort would be made, short of outright imposition, to restore the French monarchy. Immediately Alexander sought to alter the agreement. Through Novosiltsev he made one last attempt to come to terms with Napoleon at the expense of the English, who totally failed to see the necessity for it.

And so negotiations went on while hostilities were being prepared. It was agreed that Russia and England would reinforce Gustavus' army in Pomerania, which was to invade Hanover and Holland. In Naples an understanding was reached with Maria Carolina, who had taken control of the government after Napoleon had demanded the dismissal of her Prime Minister, Sir John Acton, in May 1804. An agreement was signed in November, and an émigré, Baron Damas, took command of the Neapolitan army; meanwhile, Nelson was in control of Sicily. Pressure was also applied at Constantinople, where the Turkish sultan refused to recognize Napoleon as Emperor. However, it was not enough to threaten France from the north and the south: to secure victory, Russia had to have an assured route either through Germany or through Austria.

In Germany, the allies made no progress. The working out of the Imperial Recess of 1803 continued to align the German princes against Austria, which was attempting to redress the balance between Catholics and Protestants in the Diet. Austria defended the interests of the Imperial Knights (*Ritterschaft*); these comprised 350 seigneurs, many of them counts and barons, who ruled over 1,500 estates, a total area of over 110,000 hectares. Grouped into three circles—the Swabian, Franconian, and Rhenish—they owed their allegiance directly to the Holy Roman Emperor and were self-governing. Usually impoverished, their sons entered the Church or state service, preferably in Austria. This in fact was the origin of the Metternichs, Stadions, Dalbergs, and Steins. Already hurt by the secularizations, they now saw themselves the target of the greedy princes who were attempting to 'mediatize' them, that is to say make subjects of them. Prussia set the example in Franconia, and the other princes followed; on January 13, 1804, Stein protested against the annexation of two of his villages by the Duke of Nassau. Austria, acting perhaps on some knowledge of the conspiracy of Year XII, annulled these mediatizations as violations of the Imperial Recess and threatened Bavaria, which turned to France for help. On March 3, 1804, one week before ordering the arrest of the Duc d'Enghien, Bonaparte presented Vienna with an ultimatum; the Austrians disarmed immediately. The result of this crisis was that the Swedish and Russian protests against the violation of German territory were received with silence by the South German princes. In the fall of 1804, Napoleon visited the Rhineland, and some of the princes came to curry his favour at Mainz. There was an exchange of views on a confederation of the Rhine; Napoleon conceived the idea of marrying Eugène de Beauharnais to the Princess Augusta of Bavaria, who was however already affianced to the hereditary Prince Charles of Baden; Dalberg came with a proposal for an Imperial Concordat with the papacy, but the German states refused, preferring to strengthen their independence by treating separately with the Pope. In any case, the South German states now aligned themselves with France.

Things might have been different had Prussia clearly supported the South German states against Austria, but Frederick William III was pursuing a policy of pure self-interest. Moreover, a pro-French faction, whose leading light was the Cabinet-Secretary Lombard, continued to exert considerable influence in the king's immediate entourage; this group would gladly have accepted Bonaparte's offer of an alliance. The Foreign Minister Haugwitz was less committal and at times counselled firmness toward France, but he valued his position too much to press his views. Hardenberg, who replaced him at the beginning of April 1804, boasted a more energetic policy; in reality he was no more firm than his predecessor. The war between France and England placed Frederick William in a terrible predicament: in his capacity as Elector of Hanover, George III had declared his neutrality and, if worst came to worst, would have preferred a Prussian occupation to French conquest. This was indeed a magnificent opportunity for Prussia to revive the

League of Neutrality of 1795, which had gained her supremacy in North Germany, and also to reoccupy Hanover, as in 1801. The Prussian government cautiously decided to sound out the Russian tzar before taking any steps in that direction. Alexander, suspecting a secret agreement with France, protested. Haugwitz advised mobilization, coupled with a demand that France limit herself to a pecuniary levy in Hanover; this, the king refused to do. The minister returned to the charge on June 28, 1803, by pointing to the damage caused to Prussian commerce by the French occupation of Hanover and Cuxhaven. Frederick William chose instead to send Lombard to interview Bonaparte, then in Belgium, with a renewed proposal to enter into a three-cornered alliance with Russia on condition that French forces in Hanover be limited to their present level and that commerce be restored. The attempt failed. Haugwitz then proposed a Prussian guarantee of the neutrality of all Germany providing the French evacuate Hanover. Bonaparte consented only to reopen the ports, and even that only if Prussia became his ally. The king had no sooner resigned himself to this when Bonaparte asserted that the Prussian guarantee should cover the status quo in Italy and Turkey as well, which in effect would have enlisted Prussia against Austria and Russia, leaving her with only the hope of acquiring Hanover. In April 1804 the negotiations with France were abandoned: Prussia coveted Hanover passionately, but was willing to offer only her own neutrality in return.

At this point, the abduction of the Duc d'Enghien rekindled Frederick William's fears about the closeness of the French troops in Hanover, and he at last gave up trying to walk a tightrope between France and Russia. A defensive alliance, which Alexander had proffered as early as 1803, was finally signed on May 24, 1804, Russia promising to supply 50,000 men in the event that Napoleon should strengthen his forces in Hanover or engage in any fresh aggressions east of the Weser. Such a *casus belli* did in fact occur in October when Sir George Rumbold, the English envoy in Cuxhaven, was arrested on Fouché's orders who had hoped to find in his papers evidence linking him to the conspiracy of Year XII. Hardenberg wished to profit from this occasion by mobilizing and demanding the evacuation of Hanover, but Frederick William was content to insist upon the release of the prisoner, and when Napoleon did so, the whole affair blew over.

For a long time Austria offered no more hope than Prussia. After Lunéville, she had great difficulty in recovering. The Archduke Charles attempted to persuade his brother to reform the government machinery by allowing his ministers to make decisions on their own responsibility, and to deliberate in council. On September 12, 1801, a *Staatsministerium*, consisting of three departments, was created. It was to no purpose, for Francis still wished to exercise personal control over everything. At least he permitted the archduke, who was appointed president of the *Hofkriegsrath* on January 9, 1801, to reform the army with the help of his chief of staff Duka, and his adviser Fassbender. But funds were wanting: between 1801 and 1804, the public debt rose from 613 to 645 million guldens, and the paper *Bancozettel* (treasury notes) in circulation increased from 201 million to 337 million. An injurious inflation resulted; paper money, discounted at 16 per cent of its face value in 1801, was now discounted at 35 per cent. Prices rose, and it became necessary to increase wages and salaries. Speculation enriched a few and ruined the fixed-income classes. In 1804, a famine affecting all of Germany contributed to the general misery. Meanwhile, the privileged classes continued to enjoy tax exemptions which, had they been abolished, would have easily permitted the restoration of sound finances. Under such conditions, Austria, as Charles observed, needed peace above all else. The Foreign Minister Cobenzl and the influential Count Colloredo were of the same opinion; the former, who held great hopes of an alliance with France, worked hand in glove with the French ambassador Champagny and gave way every time Bonaparte raised his voice.

Nevertheless, there existed in Vienna a war party. Some Austrians like Count Starhemberg and Graf von Stadion belonged to it, but the chief role was played by the ambassadors of the powers already in coalition—the Russian Razumovsky, the Englishman Paget, and the Swede Armfelt—and it was in the salons of a few Russian grande dames that the intrigue took its course. Through the offices of Johann von Müller, then court librarian, they kept in touch with the Comte d'Antraigues, the tzar's agent in Dresden, who was not above taking Austrian money as well. Through Stadion and Metternich, then ambassador to Saxony, they had won Friedrich von Gentz over to their cause. Ruined by his debts at Berlin, Gentz accepted the post of counsellor to the chancellery in September 1802, without, however, ceasing to receive British subsidies. Although these men were compensated for their services, they truly hated the Revolution—particularly Armfelt, a fiery aristocrat whom Gentz would call 'the last of the Romans'. Gentz himself, having failed to enlist Frederick William in this crusade, still hoped to convert Francis. The Austrian ministers mistrusted him, and used him only as a publicist; thus treated as an inferior, he zealously attacked Cobenzl and Colloredo and exaggerated their feebleness.

In fact, Cobenzl was anything but inactive. He was uneasy about the Anglo-French conflict since he feared that Bonaparte, unable to win at sea, would seek revenge on the Continent at Austria's expense. At the same time he realized that this conflict placed him in a bargaining position, and in 1803 he began demanding subsidies in London, which were eventually received. The Franco-Russian break provided him with new opportunities. On September 1, 1803, Dolgorouki arrived in Vienna; he was given a warm reception and was invited to make proposals. In January 1804, Russia offered to supply 100,000 men to force France to return to the terms of the Treaty of Lunéville. Cobenzl rejected the offer as insufficient; besides, he had no desire to undertake the offensive, and the Emperor even less so: 'France has done nothing to me,' declared Francis.

The proclamation of the French Empire changed everything. The counter-revolutionaries screamed out their protests: 'The Revolution has been sanctioned, and very nearly solemnized by the incredible outcome of the bitter tragedy of our times,' wrote Gentz. The court in Vienna was also aroused by this event, but primarily because of the implied significance to the Holy Roman Empire and to Hapsburg interests. When Napoleon assumed the title of emperor and not that of king, he was not just placing himself at the forefront of the revolutionary tradition; his choice of title implied something of European dimension, for until now there had been only one emperor, the lawful heir of the Roman Empire and the theoretical head of Christendom. In the eyes of legal scholars, the Empire was not necessarily German, and coronation by the Pope (which the Hapsburgs had allowed to fall into desuetude) appeared as valid in Paris as in Rome. It did not make any difference that Napoleon had nationalized the dignity, calling himself Emperor of the French and denying all pretensions to universal dominion; everyone understood that the German Holy Roman Empire would not survive the birth of a new one. Therefore Francis II, although he consented to recognize Napoleon, demanded that he be accorded the same recognition in return when, on August 11, 1804, he took the title of Emperor of Austria. For the time being, he was still Holy Roman Emperor as well, but he evidently expected to be driven from Germany. Moreover, since tradition linked the Kingdom of Italy to the Holy Roman Empire, he also feared a fresh extension of French power in that quarter, and in this he was not mistaken. This being so, the creation of the French Empire hastened the formation of the Third Coalition.

Cobenzl's first move was to sound out Prussia, but since he offered her nothing, the attempt proved fruitless. When, in October, he learned that Novosiltsev was on his way to London, he reasoned that Russia, allied to England, would perhaps abandon Austria to her fate, and so he resolved on an agreement with Alexander. Although the convention, signed on November 6, 1804, was in the nature of a defensive pact, it nevertheless provided for joint action in the event that 'circumstances should be such as to require the use of mutual force in other ways'. Then in January 1805 news came that the Italian Republic was to become an hereditary kingdom. To free his own hands, Cobenzl determined to oust from power the Archduke Charles, who disapproved of the Russian alliance. Charles's independent ways had long ago earned him the Emperor Francis' displeasure, and the latter increased his chicaneries to such a point that the archduke resigned his offices. Duka and Fassbender were pushed aside, and General Mack, of whom the English had a high opinion, was recalled to head the general staff. Even so, Francis still refused to start an offensive, and Cobenzl himself hesitated, with the result that Russia impatiently threatened to renounce the agreement. It took new encroachments on the part of Napoleon to drive Austria into the arms of the Coalition.

None of the vassal and allied states behaved in accordance with Napoleon's expectations. Holland permitted smuggling to go on freely, and the Dutch deputies refused to vote either taxes or loans for armaments. In September 1804, Napoleon had indicated the necessity for a constitutional change. On March 22, 1805, Rutger Jan Schimmelpenninck received the title of Grand Pensionary along with complete executive power; legislative authority was bestowed upon an assembly of 'Their Eminent Powers' (*'Leurs Hautes Puissances'*), whose members were to be elected by the citizens from a slate proposed by the government; initially, Schimmelpenninck chose the candidates. This done, the Minister of Finance, Gogel, was able to undertake fiscal reforms.

Of much greater consequence was the death of the Italian Republic. As the Republic's vice-president, Melzi had organized the administration and judicial system on the French model, negotiated a concordat, founded an Institute, and reopened the universities. In order to suppress brigandage, he abolished the jury system, created a Prefect of Police and a gendarmerie, and set up special tribunals. Public works were increased, and the Simplon road completed. Prina, the energetic and able Minister of Finance, introduced indirect taxes, liquidated the debt, purged the personnel of his department, and improved the supervision of accounts. Finally, a native army was formed, conscription having at last been introduced in 1803 with success. But these reforms irritated much more than they pleased, and the population remained very hostile to the French. Although Melzi favoured the nobility, he received very little support; the Legislative Body proved recalcitrant, and rejected measures which would have introduced registry offices and a tax on inheritances. Melzi himself hoped for independence and for the evacuation of the French troops. In May 1803 he submitted to the Austrian government a strange proposal which would have placed all of northern Italy, including Venice, under the rule of the former Grand Duke of Tuscany. Knowledge of this aroused Bonaparte's suspicions and brought him to the conclusion that the affairs of the Italian Republic had to be taken into his own hands.

The proclamation of the French Empire imparted a most dangerous cast to Napoleon's designs on Italy. Ever since

Charlemagne, all of the Roman Emperors had been either kings of Lombardy or kings of Italy: so Napoleon must needs be, too. As early as May 1804, he notified Melzi of his intentions. A constitution was worked out by an Italian council, but the Emperor was irritated to find that some limits had been placed on his authority; he therefore summoned the council to Paris and dictated his own terms. He seems to have been aware of the risk he was taking in assuming the crown himself, for he offered it first to his brother Joseph, and on January 1, 1805, he wrote the Austrian Emperor to assure him that the new kingdom would forever be kept distinct from the French Empire. But Joseph, who was counting on eventually becoming ruler of France, refused the crown of Italy, and so did Louis, on behalf of his son. Consequently, Napoleon arranged for a senatus-consultum which was issued on March 18 and which summoned him to the throne of Italy. On May 18, he crowned himself at Milan, and nominated his stepson Eugène de Beauharnais as viceroy. With regard to Austria he simply promised that he would step down in favour of a relative when, with the coming of peace, Malta and Corfu would be evacuated. Thus the coronation in Milan constituted a breach of the Treaty of Lunéville. The treaty was again violated when, on June 6, Napoleon annexed the Ligurian Republic and created from it three new French départements after Saliceti, his representative in Genoa, prompted a vote for its incorporation with the French Empire. In addition, Napoleon bestowed the principality of Piombino upon his sister Elisa on March 18, and made his brother-in-law Bacciochi Prince of Lucca on June 23. These two domains were imperial fiefs, and by making such gifts, Napoleon made it evident that he regarded himself as the heir to the Roman Emperors.

Austria hesitated no longer. On June 17, the Aulic Council decided to join the Anglo-Russian alliance. At this very moment Novosiltsev was in Berlin en route to Paris with the authority to offer France the Rhineland and Belgium (except for Antwerp); on June 25, Alexander cancelled his mission. On July 16, General Winzingerode, then in Vienna, conferred with Mack and decided on a plan of operations. The Anglo-Russian Treaty, which had been signed in St. Petersburg on April 11, was finally ratified on July 28, without Pitt and Alexander coming to any agreement on the fate of Malta. Austria added her signature on August 9. Still, she made some final attempts in Paris to gain concessions which might have kept her out of the conflict. There being nothing forthcoming, Austria invaded Bavaria on September 11.

In the meantime, both sides exerted great efforts to persuade the German states. Frederick William remained obstinately deaf to the objurgations of the tzar, and on July 15 he refused passage to the troops massed in Pomerania, thus rendering an invaluable service to Napoleon. Alexander demanded in vain to see the king, and threatened to cut his way through Silesia. Czartoryski's hopes soared: on September 23 the tzar arrived at Pulawy, the Czartoryski family château; there he spoke of seizing Prussia's share of the Polish partitions and of restoring Poland. But Alexander was in reality deceiving his friend, for he only meant to frighten the King of Prussia and counted on winning him over.

Napoleon, after displaying some anxiety during the course of the winter over a concentration of troops in Venetia, suspected nothing more until the end of July and did not recognize the danger until August 23. Nevertheless, he tried once again to win Prussia to his side by offering Hanover on August 8 and by sending Duroc to Berlin on August 22. The king replied that he would only conclude an alliance to sustain the terms of the Treaty of Lunéville. In the Prussian court and in the army, a war party began to take shape; Queen Louise never flagged in her sympathy for Alexander nor in her hatred for Napoleon. The majority of Prussians, however, including the military, continued to favour a policy of neutrality. The Emperor, needing Bernadotte's corps elsewhere, decided to evacuate Hanover and to permit its occupation by the troops of Frederick William should the king wish to profit from the opportunity, which did not fail to arise. Napoleon foresaw that the king would be so satisfied, at least for a time, that he would abandon all warlike intentions: it was a sound calculation. Napoleon was even more successful in his dealings with the South German states, which were being menaced by Austria. On August 25 Bavaria allied herself with France, and on September 5 Württemberg adhered in principle. The disunion of Germany, which could have been foreseen since 1803, was thus accomplished.

France and England: The Struggle Renewed (1802–1805)

Napoleon manœuvred with similar dexterity in Italy. On September 10, Maria Carolina, Queen of Naples, concluded an alliance with Russia; eleven days later, the Emperor signed a treaty of neutrality with the Neapolitan ambassador, the Marquis de Gallo, providing for the evacuation of French troops which were needed on the Adige. He also occupied the Kingdom of Etruria, and even the port of Ancona over the protests of the Pope. Fearing an attack by Villeneuve, Ferdinand IV of Naples ratified the treaty. After Trafalgar, Maria Carolina threw off her mask and on November 19 an Anglo-Russian fleet landed 19,000 men at Naples. It was too late; Napoleon had won the game.

The Third Coalition has been called a deliberate attempt to deprive France of her natural frontiers. It goes without saying that if the allies had won, they would have taken back all or part of the French gains. But what remains to be shown is that England in 1803, and Russia and Austria in 1805, took up arms for that end alone—and this has never been demonstrated, not even in the case of England. In the first place, the spirit of aggression, while undeniable, was fostered by passions and interests which have been entirely ignored: England's economic interests and policy of maritime imperialism; Alexander's megalomania and personal jealousy; and the hostility of the European aristocracy, so influential in Vienna—a hostility whose roots lay in the very social order. Secondly, it is even clearer that Napoleon, as if daring the Powers, had inflamed this smouldering hostility, had alarmed them all, and had driven even the feeble Austrian monarchy to desperation. Aside from the interests of France, and speaking only of his personal policy, it was not indispensable to his authority to kidnap the Duc d'Enghien and to establish the Empire, to provoke England prematurely, to challenge Russia's Eastern ambitions, and above all, to create a hereditary kingdom out of the Italian Republic and to annex Genoa. Although he did not share the revolutionary ardour of the Girondins, he hurled defiances against kings and aristocrats in the same fashion for which they are blamed, and he pursued the turbulent policy of aggression which has earned the Directory so much contemptuous criticism.

Be that as it may, the formation of the Third Coalition after the rupture of the Treaty of Amiens pointed the way to Napoleon's final destiny. Not that his ultimate downfall was determined, as some have argued: it would yet require many more errors and unforeseeable accidents to checkmate him. But from now on, there was no choice other than the pursuit of world conquest.

CHAPTER EIGHT

Napoleon's Army

AFTER THE TREATY OF LUNÉVILLE, Bonaparte undertook to purge the army of its war-weary and untrustworthy elements. He discharged many officers, and released soldiers who had participated in at least four campaigns, a total of one-eighth of the effective force. Then between 1801 and 1805 he devoted more than four years to reorganizing his troops and to perfecting a system of warfare which would startle the world in 1805 and 1806. Bonaparte's inventive genius showed itself primarily in the elaboration of his principles of strategy and in the formation of a unified body of tactics essential to it. Otherwise, he remained substantially faithful to the methods of the French Revolution: the amalgame and promotion through the ranks were the most constant and important characteristics of his army. Although he displayed great executive ability and a meticulous care for detail in his preparations for war, Bonaparte still remained an incorrigible improviser.

RECRUITMENT AND PROMOTION

Recruitment was based on the law of Year VI, complemented by a great many administrative regulations, all of which were finally codified in 1811. This law subjected all Frenchmen between the ages of 20 and 25 to military service, but numerous exemptions were granted in order to save the government the expense of providing relief to wives and children. The first to be exempted were men who had been married, and men who had been widowed or divorced providing they had children, on or before January 12, 1798. Public opinion ignored the limiting date and took it for granted that the exemptions were permanent. But the text of the law was explicit, and until 1808 the levies, even retroactive ones, did not spare married men and widowed fathers. Nevertheless, recruiting officers were inclined to invalidate these categories or to register them in the '*dépôt*', that is to say, among the conscripts who had drawn a lucky number and who would be called only as replacements for regularly drafted men. Men in these categories were finally accorded dispensation by a senatus-consultum of September 10, 1808. Thus the number of hasty marriages became ever more frequent towards the close of the Empire. There was also a feeling of relative tolerance for breadwinners, and even more for seminarists after the Concordat. Lastly, the replacement of recruits by substitutes, which had constituted a mere privilege in Year VIII, became an established right by the law of 28 Floréal, Year X (May 18, 1802).

For financial and economic reasons stemming from a desire to conserve the labour force, the law of Year VI did not conscript all the men in each age group except in case of danger to the *patrie*. Instead, a fixed number of recruits was determined annually by the Councils, and was called up beginning with the lowest age group. Under the Consulate, recruiting operations were conducted much the same as during the French Revolution, although the quotas were much smaller. The annual contingent was voted by the Legislative Body, which then apportioned it among the départements. The general and district councils were to distribute the quota among the municipalities; these in turn examined the recruits with a doctor of their choosing, designated those who were to be discharged, admitted replacements into the ranks, and left appeals to the prefect.

This system evolved in the same direction as other institutions. From the very start the practice of 'replacement' favoured the wealthy middle class. On September 24, 1805, Napoleon fixed the quota by decree of the Senate, and henceforth the Legislative Body was stripped of its powers in this area. Moreover, there was much to complain about in the way of wilful negligence, incompetence, and scandalous abuses in many municipalities. And so the municipalities were deprived of their functions in the recruiting system, as they had already been deprived of their financial powers. Local recruitment was confided to a staff of professional civil servants, much to the benefit of the common people. Municipalities were prohibited from choosing recruits by vote, and were encouraged to resort to the drawing of lots. Prefects and subprefects intervened with increasing frequency in the operation of the system. On 18 Thermidor, Year X (August 6, 1802), there was established in every département an itinerant recruiting board, composed of the prefect and military officers, for the purpose of re-examining all exemptions based on physical disqualifications. The campaign of 1805 brought a new and decisive change: according to a decree of August 26 local councils were deprived of their distributory functions. From now on, the distribution of the quota devolved upon the prefect and the subprefects; the latter drew up the list of eligible recruits, chose them by lot, and presided over the medical examinations, which were still subject to review by the itinerant recruiting council, however. Having been selected, the recruits still retained the right to be replaced by a volunteer: this was called '*substitution*'; in addition, one could furnish a paid substitute: this was called '*remplacement*'. Even after joining his regiment, a recruit might be allowed to bring forward a paid substitute.

Assignment to regiments was determined by the Emperor or by his minister. Each regiment sent one of its officers as a consultant in the recruitment operations; accompanied by an escort detail, the officer brought his regiment's recruits to a military depot. Aside from the Bureau of Conscription, which was placed in the charge of Hargenvilliers in 1800 and subordinated to a director Lacuée de Cessac in 1807, the system of recruitment did not become a specialized institution. It made great progress nonetheless. As to corruption and the abuses of the wealthy middle class, Napoleon unquestionably reduced their importance but he did not succeed in suppressing them entirely.

Although this system made it possible to harness manpower in a rational way, it also introduced the drawback of altering the traditional character of French military service by doing away with equality and by transferring most of the burden to the poor. Between 1805 and 1811 the price of a substitute did not rise very much, but in the Côte-d'Or it fluctuated from 1,900 to 3,600 francs, so that only 5 per cent of the contingent was able to meet the cost of a paid substitute. Yet, if military enrollment became odious to the people, the reason can be found in the absence of peace after 1805. Drafted contingents were never destined for the barracks, but were rushed to battle with the briefest possible delay. Interminable warfare did not permit their discharge: a recruit returned home only when crippled. In 1803 the army still retained 174,000 men who had been called up between 1792 and 1799; their service was far from over. In addition, the numbers drafted kept increasing as the enterprises of the Emperor multiplied, and after 1806 the quotas were called in advance, even though the law contained no such provision. True enough, until 1813, no category was called up in its entirety, but those who drew lucky numbers and even those who had been replaced entertained no security in respect of their position. There was nothing to prevent an order for additional recruits to be obtained by way of recall of categories which had not yet been exhausted. As early as 1805 Napoleon called for 30,000 men from each age group of the classes 1800–1804.

To contemporaries these demands seemed unbearable because they had been unknown during the Old Regime. It must be noted, however, that from 1800 to 1812, Napoleon levied only a total of 1,300,000 men, of which slightly more than three-quarters were drawn from the old French territories. Even taking into consideration the enormous levies of 1812 and 1813 (over a million men), the proportion of those actually drafted to the eligible male population did not exceed 41 per cent. The Côte-d'Or supplied a total of only 11,000 soldiers out of 350,000 inhabitants, or 3·15 per cent; the Côtes-du-Nord 19,000 out of 500,000, or 3·80 per cent. Just as during the Revolution, Napoleon had to hunt down defaulters and deserters; as early as Year VIII, their parents were fined, and after 1807 they were subjected to new penalties. Both the gendarmerie and flying columns of the National Guard scoured the country. These measures were indeed effective, since the number of defaulters continued to be moderate until 1812: in the Côte-d'Or for example, they amounted to less than 3 per cent from 1806 to 1810. Three times—in Years VIII and X, and in 1810—Napoleon offered them amnesty. Thus the nation submitted to compulsory military service much more agreeably than has generally been maintained; it became restive only towards the end when mass levies were engendered by military defeats.

Incessantly waging war, the Napoleonic army obtained its recruits by a steady process of amalgamation, a principle derived from the Revolution. At the beginning of every campaign a contingent of raw recruits, dressed and armed for better or for worse, departed for the front in small groups. 'Conscripts need not spend more than eight days in training camp,' wrote the Emperor on November 16, 1806. They learned the essentials on the way to the battlefield if they were lucky. Once poured into the regiments, they mingled with the veterans and picked up whatever knowledge they could during the actual fighting. Drilling was regarded as useless and was consequently neglected during periods of respite. The Napoleonic soldier bore no resemblance to the soldier of the garrison: he was a warrior who improvised in the revolutionary tradition, and he retained that same quality of independence. Since the officers, risen from the ranks, were his comrades of yesterday, and since he might himself be promoted tomorrow, he took little notice of rank; for him, formal and mechanical discipline was unbearable; he would come and go as he pleased, and he obeyed only under fire. Few armies have ever tolerated insubordination to such a degree, where mass demonstrations, isolated rebellions, and mutinies were common currency. Napoleon thundered, but always proved more indulgent than the government; he regarded the soldier basically as a fighting man, and his great concern was that his men be eager for battle and plunge themselves into it desperately.

One of the legacies of the Revolution was this very fervour in the face of the enemy which inspired initiative, daring, and self-confidence in the individual, and which also gave the army its collective spirit. The passions of the Sans-culottes, love of equality, hatred of aristocracy, and ardent anti-clericalism were undoubtedly dulled by the passage of time, but these feelings were not extinguished, and in 1805, they were very much alive. In the opinion of the Old Guard, 'le Tondu', as

Napoleon was familiarly called, had never been a king, but the leader in a war against kings. From the French Revolution there also came a feeling of exalted nationalism, the pride of belonging to *La Grande Nation*. Bonaparte carefully nurtured these sentiments by issuing proclamations in the spirit of the Committee of Public Safety, which had made the war a democratic cause.

Like the armies of the Convention and Directory, the Napoleonic army drew its main strength from the social revolution which had opened careers to talent. In the world of the military, *égalité* meant promotion through the ranks. The Constitution of Year VIII allowed the commander-in-chief to choose his officers at his discretion. Napoleon, although he showed signs of wishing to reinstate a military aristocracy, was essentially guided by merit in making his appointments. Seniority was of no account, and intellect alone got little notice; success did not depend on education, but on daring and courage almost entirely. After every battle, the colonel, who was the officer in charge of promotions, filled the places of the fallen by drawing on men who had distinguished themselves in his regiment, and the regiment was the best judge of his fairness. Napoleon's appointments to the general staff were made on the same basis. In a society where hierarchy was tending to solidify everywhere else, it was the army which offered the greatest opportunity to merit, and it exerted, consequently, a passionate attraction on ambitious young men. Its finest elements instinctively sprang to battle and rushed to the front lines, carrying along the others or at least making up for their shortcomings. Napoleon never ceased to stimulate this craving for glory, at first by distributing ceremonial muskets and sabres, *armes d'honneur*, and later, medals of the Legion of Honour. At the same time, he greatly increased the number of elite companies and corps, of which the most exalted was the Imperial Guard, conspicuous by its glittering and multicoloured dress uniforms.

A consequence of this system was that the officers turned out to be as unschooled in war as the ranks. The disadvantage was minimal, since Napoleon never shared with anyone the responsibility for formulating strategic conceptions and issuing general orders; apart from this, it was sufficient to have daring generals, well trained in the art of manœuvres. The general staff was not an autonomous body, capable of exerting an influence over the course of operations; those who worked in the bureaus discharged only matter-of-fact tasks: the Emperor 'spoke' his instructions, and they relayed them. Their chief, Berthier, an irresolute and mediocre general, yet punctual and compliant, was in effect nothing but a major 'dispatching the orders of His Majesty'. 'Adhere strictly to the commands which I give you,' wrote Napoleon in 1806, 'I alone know what I have to do.' Berthier himself instructed a marshal: 'No one knows his thoughts, and your duty is to obey.' Napoleon's orderlies, like Marbot, Fesenzac, Castellane, Gourgaud, and his aides-de-camp like Duroc, Mouton, Rapp, Drouot, Savary, and Bertrand, were drawn from the regiments because of their qualities of rapid judgment and zeal. They possessed absolutely no authority over the corps commanders; they were simply so many eyes of their master. Always on mission, they surveyed the scene at a glance and reported back. If, however, Napoleon, who was unable to be everywhere at once, deemed it necessary to appoint persons to fill his place, he delegated his authority to men who had his confidence. Such were Murat, Lannes, Davout, and Masséna. Real lieutenant-generals, or temporary commanders of the army, they alone were empowered to take strategic initiatives. And so, there existed no necessity for an abundance of truly capable men.

Clearly then, the Napoleonic army was not institutionalized, and it continually underwent impromptu changes. Its strength lay in the importance it gave to individual valour and in the genius of its leader. Innovations in the organization of the various arms were negligible. The infantry remained divided into line and light infantry (or voltigeurs), and their tactics underwent no substantial change. On 1 Vendémiaire, Year XII (September 24, 1803), the cavalry received what was to be its classic division into light cavalry (hussars and chasseurs), line cavalry (dragoons), and heavy cavalry (cuirassiers). Thanks to the efforts of the Convention and the Directory, it was better trained than the infantry. Led by Murat and a host of intrepid horsemen, it had nothing to fear from its Austrian counterpart. The artillery was grouped according to horse and foot regiments, and infantry cannon was abolished. The engineers were organized into separate, independent battalions, to which were attached pontoniers. The Imperial Guard was formed on 10 Thermidor, Year XII (July 29, 1804), at which time two-thirds of the Guard were veterans; it comprised 5,000 foot soldiers and 2,800 cavalry, both of which were divided into grenadiers, chasseurs, and light-armed skirmishers (vélites). Added to these were more than 100 Mamelukes, a unit of light artillery, marines, gendarmes, and even a supply train, the only one in the French army.

Armaments underwent no change. The musket of 1777 was accurate up to 200 yards and at best fired four balls every three minutes. The Gribeauval cannons discharged solid balls of 4, 8, or 12 pounds at the rate of two a minute, and were excellent at a range of 600 yards. Shells and canisters, good at 400 yards, were infrequently employed. A 6-inch howitzer was also used. Napoleon attached much importance to firepower, and hence to the artillery. Yet his own artillery was quite small: until 1806 there were twelve pieces per division, and only in that year did there appear a general park of artillery consisting of about fifty-nine pieces. In 1808 field guns numbered less than two per thousand men. Marmont was partly responsible for this lag; in 1803 he had undertaken the work of recasting the entire ordnance, and he was forced to abandon the project when the war resumed in 1805. But there were also deeper causes: a shortage of tools, and above all, an insufficiency of transport; even so, it would have been impossible to procure enough gun carriages or to bring forward a sufficiency of munitions.

The energies of the Napoleonic army were gradually dissipated by war, extended conquests, and Napoleon's ever increasing aristocratic bent. As the veterans of the republican armies diminished in number, and as the draft increased, the amalgame became proportionately less and less effective, and in 1809 the army began to form entire divisions of raw recruits. For its efficacy, advancement through the ranks depended on a sufficient number of deaths in each campaign to open the way to new men: until 1812 at least, this did not happen. The higher ranks especially were becoming overcrowded. Once having attained their grade, the marshals sought only to preserve the money and honours which had been lavished upon them, and so aspired to peace and comfort. Had it been left solely to the Emperor, this evil might have progressed more rapidly, for it corresponded to his political designs and to his social ideal of a military elite of nobles, men of wealth, and officers' sons. He established a military academy (*prytanée*) for the sons of officers, a school of cavalry at Saint-Germain, and a school for cadets at Fontainebleau which was transferred to Saint-Cyr in 1808. Napoleon also contemplated re-establishing the *Gardes du corps* which had been dissolved in 1791: along these lines he created the *Volontaires de la réserve* in 1800 and the *Gendarmes d'ordonnance* in 1806. He encouraged the formation of local 'guards of honour' recruited from among the well-born members of the National Guard, and on September 30, 1805, he mobilized these parade corps as military units. Although officers enrolled their sons willingly in the military schools, the nobility and the upper stratum of the bourgeoisie were reluctant to follow suit. Napoleon, moreover, appreciated the danger of incurring the discontent of the army, and above all of the Imperial Guard. The Gendarmes d'ordonnance and the guards of honour were abolished in 1806, and only in 1813 were the latter revived. In the Kingdom of Italy alone, where their institution dated from June 26, 1805, the guards of honour formed a nursery for officers, thus revealing Napoleon's true intentions.

The national character of the army grew weaker as well. After 1800, a significant proportion of the French troops came from areas recently annexed, and this proportion increased with every new conquest. In addition, Napoleon revived a custom dating from the Old Regime of enrolling the greatest possible number of foreigners into the army. He had Swiss and Polish regiments, Hanoverian and Irish legions organized in 1803, and two 'foreign' regiments created in 1805. These also increased with time. Finally, the Imperial Army comprised soldiers from both subject and allied states: Italians, Dutch, and South Germans after 1805. So great was their increase that in 1812 Frenchmen were but a minority in the Imperial Army.

The very success of the system exposed certain concomitant weaknesses. Frequently, as the theatres of war increased, Napoleon's absence betrayed the fact that few of his lieutenants were fit to command in chief. Left to themselves, Ney, Oudinot, and Soult proved to be mediocre. Napoleon has been held responsible for this mediocrity because he deprived his commanders of all initiative. This accusation is baseless. Although like all great captains he retained complete control over the direction of the whole, he nonetheless left to his deputies considerable latitude in the choice of means. What he failed to do in forming his high command was to provide his officers with an intellectual indoctrination to grand strategy. Apart from this, every new conquest extended the lines of communications and the territories to be occupied, and this constituted yet another weakness. Devised as it was to end the war by a single decisive blow, the army lacked reserves. No recourse other than a levy in anticipation—summoning the yearly classes in advance of their turn—could bring it up to strength. Appeals were made to allies and to the most untrustworthy of vassals to help defend the occupied territories; at the front the proportion of effective combatants continuously declined. The National Guard, which the Constitution of Year VIII maintained on the basis of the law of 28 Prairial, Year III (June 16, 1795), could have supplied the elements of a territorial army. In 1805 it existed only on paper; on September 24 Napoleon decreed its reorganization and reserved to himself the right to choose its officers; but, in fact, he did no more than form elite companies and guards of honour. Later he partially mobilized the National Guard, as for example in the defence of the coasts: until 1812, however, he did not connect it closely with his military system.

In 1805 there appeared as yet no disquieting symptom. La Grande Armée, so baptized by Napoleon at the camp at Boulogne, began to march on Germany on August 26. It was the best army in the world. Nearly a fourth of its soldiers had fought in all the wars of the Revolution, another fourth, or thereabouts, had fought in the campaign of 1800, and the remainder, brought in during the Consulate, had gained time enough to fuse themselves solidly with the veterans. Almost all of the commissioned and noncommissioned officers had seen action, and if anything, they were too old: ninety lieutenants were over 50 years of age, some were over 60. The higher ranking officers, on the other hand, were very young, and full of spirit. It took only three years for this army to extend the frontiers of the Empire to the banks of the Niemen.

THE PREPARATION FOR WAR

Under the Old Regime, war had been a continual improvisation. Every time it broke out, officers and men had to be recruited. Army contractors, turned entrepreneurs, bought goods with which to fill their storehouses and stock supplies at any price. They sucked the king dry and fleeced his soldiers. Although efforts were made to organize a system of accounting, the army commissaries did not possess enough professional conscience to resist corruption. On the surface, these evils resulted from a lack of money; but the real explanation was rooted in the national economy, which was still too weak to supply the requirements of modern warfare and maintain an honest and competent bureaucracy. Thus the policies of the monarchy always overstepped the means with which to execute them. The Mountain, which was also committed to a policy of improvisation, made a superhuman effort to dispense with private contractors, to nationalize supply services, and to demand of civil servants devotion and honesty. After 9 Thermidor, the Republic found itself in the same position as the monarchy, and this situation became even more critical under Napoleon, as a result of the inordinate growth of the army and the permanence of hostilities.

Like the Jacobins, Napoleon harboured an intense dislike for the contractors, and, like them, he was compelled to make haste while lacking adequate funds and personnel. Since he relied on the notables, he could not resort to Jacobin methods. Just as he had been forced to seek the help of financiers to keep his treasury filled, he now found them indispensable in supplying his army. In 1805, Vanlerberghe and others guaranteed to furnish the home army with food and fodder. When the war broke out, certain companies took charge of monopolies of bread, meat, fodder, hospitals, and all transport services, including that of the artillery, all of which was operated at a guaranteed profit. A single battalion of artillery transport had been created in Year IX, and the Imperial Guard alone possessed its own baggage train.

Napoleon made great efforts to enforce the verification of accounts. In Year X the administrative services of the army were organized as the Ministry for Military Affairs, headed by Dejean. The treasury of the army became an independent office. As early as Year VIII, the task of verifying the number of troops had been taken away from the commissaries and conferred upon special officials called *inspecteurs aux revues*. The former, as well as the latter, were responsible to Villermanzy, the Intendant General of the Grande Armée, who was replaced by Daru in 1806. The Emperor himself took great pleasure in subjecting the profuse mass of accounts to his personal scrutiny and in uncovering errors. But he was unable to detect by these methods unregistered transactions or undue payments; these could come to his attention only by chance, never by a mere balancing of debits and credits. The commissaries of war, recruited at random, remained dishonest and odious. 'They make me pay all the dead soldiers,' wrote Napoleon on May 18, 1808. Moreover, he was never able to prevent his generals from levying contributions for their personal gain.

In 1805 Napoleon had amassed an army of nearly 400,000 foot, but it was beyond his capacity to maintain such a force properly in time of peace. The rank and file soldier received 5 sous per day, but the state merely allotted him bread and ammunition, and, in time of war, a ration of meat. Even this meagre pay was not disbursed regularly. On the very eve of departure, in 1805, Napoleon remarked that the soldiers' pay was lacking, and late in 1806 it was five months overdue. This shortage of funds made it impossible to accumulate food supplies, shoes, clothing, and the means of transport which were necessary to begin the campaign. Napoleon had to settle for weapons and munitions. In 1800 he had stated his need for a reserve stock of 3 million muskets, a total which he never received and which, in any event, would have been well beyond the nation's capacity to produce. In 1805 he was provided with 146,000 muskets, and it was estimated that a corresponding number would be lost during the course of a single campaign. Still less attention was given to the artillery, whose losses were made good only by ravaging enemy arsenals. If the supply of ammunition evoked no serious concern, the fact is it was used sparingly: at Jena, the 4th Corps fired only 1,400 cannon shots. Remounts, despite Napoleon's considerable pains, never became fully adequate. Since France was unable to guarantee enough horses, the shortage was made up from the conquered lands.

As for the remainder—food, shoes, clothing—it was expected that the army would live off the land. 'In a war of energetic offensives, such as the Emperor wages, storehouses do not exist,' wrote Berthier to Marmont on October 11, 1805; 'it is up to the commanders in chief of the army corps to obtain for themselves the means of subsistence in the countries they overrun.' It will be argued that on the eve of the campaign, Napoleon made a determined effort to supply his soldiers with bread, hardtack, and shoes; but time was too short, and these orders were only partially executed. Many soldiers crossed the Rhine in 1805 with only a single pair of shoes, and many left for Jena without overcoats in 1806; as for bread, they carried what they could. That Napoleonic warfare was, in part, based on the rapidity of forced marches, was in keeping with the general state of financial penury: given the available transport, supplies, even if they had existed, could not have kept up with the army. Soldiers departed ill-equipped, because in undertaking each campaign, Napoleon counted on an immediate and lightning-like victory. This victory became a question of life and death: nothing was organized in support of the war in the rear; if the army were forced to fight a retreating action, or even if a tenacious enemy were given time to ravage the land before surrendering it, the army would perish from sheer exhaustion.

When war is improvised, it is always at the expense of the soldier. Rare were the generals like Davout who took the trouble to supply their ceaselessly marching troops with regular requisitions. Usually the soldiers seized what they could from the population; but following each other in waves, they would end by finding nothing. Starved, often soaked to the skin, the soldier slept little. Alternating between total privation on the one hand and feasting and drunkenness on the other, he was condemned to a life of disease. No one cared about his health. The medical service continued to be utterly neglected. Although doctors and surgeons had been summoned to the colours as officers by the Convention, the Directory, for reasons of economy, decided that they could be dismissed outright in time of peace, and Napoleon allowed matters to stand unchanged. Apart from such eminent heads of the service as Larrey, Percy, and Coste, the medical staff was worse than mediocre. Having at their disposal only the most contemptible equipment, they set up ambulances and makeshift hospitals by requisitioning necessities from the local inhabitants and enlisting them as nurses. It was a hell whose gallery of horrors was depicted in Percy's diary: ghastly cannon-ball wounds, amputations without anaesthesia, gangrene and putrefaction, unspeakable filth, scabs, lice, and typhus. Napoleon absolutely forbade the shipment of the wounded far to the rear, and especially to France; they would have died en route anyway due to a lack of sanitary facilities. Understandably, the mortality rate for this epoch was for a long time pictured in terrifying terms. Taine still repeats that 1,700,000 men died under the Consulate and the Empire, and this number was confined to those from the boundaries of 1789. Since, however, the total number of soldiers from these territories never exceeded this figure, such an estimate would have precluded any survivors, let alone prisoners. The actual losses between 1800 and 1815 can in fact be estimated at less than 1 million, perhaps 40 per cent of the total, of which a third were missing and surely not all of these dead. To this must be added about 200,000 French from the post-1789 boundaries, and approximately as many others from allied and vassal territories. Above all, one must keep in mind that the number of men killed in action constituted only a small part of the total dead: 2 per cent at Austerlitz, and, the maximum, 8½ per cent at Waterloo. The remainder died either from wounds and diseases in hospitals or from exhaustion and exposure to the cold.

The manner in which Napoleon treated the problem of supply gave rise to many dire consequences. The French occupation grew increasingly unpopular. The widespread habit of pillaging and marauding led to a marked decline in soldierly discipline and morale. Forced marches left in their rear a gathering mob of cripples and stragglers who indulged in all kinds of excesses. Misery often bred mutinies. Worst of all, Napoleon's military strategy was predicated on the existence of fertile and populous lands, chiefly Lombardy, where he had waged his first two European campaigns. When he invaded North Germany, Poland, Spain, and Russia, geographical conditions made his system unworkable, and the army was imperilled.

THE CONDUCT OF WAR

In the closing years of the Old Regime, French writers on military affairs had demonstrated the disadvantages of the classical methods of warfare brought to perfection by Frederick II. An inflexible army, deploying slowly in file along a single road was incapable of encompassing the entire theatre of operations, and so could not compel the foe to fight or force him to abandon a strong defensive position. Nevertheless, it took the French Revolution to bring about a departure from the former practices. With the advent of mass warfare, involving very large numbers of troops, generals were forced to split their armies into divisions in order to render them manageable. Soon, however, these new groupings were found inadequate, for as they grew in number it became more difficult to co-ordinate their movements. Because the cavalry and artillery were attached to the separate divisions, it was impossible to concentrate their force. A higher organization, the army corps, had been haltingly attempted during the Directory, and in 1800 Moreau had commanded three corps of four divisions each, but without reserves. Napoleon derived his ideas of strategy from the teachings of Guibert and Bourcet, as well as from the practical experience of the Revolution; but it was at Marengo that he decided upon his final formula: two or three divisions per corps, with a minimum of cavalry; most of the cavalry organized separately, and a reserve of artillery directly under the commanding general. This organization was applied to the whole army under the Consulate.

The strength of these divisions and corps remained extremely variable. In 1805, the latter consisted of two to four divisions, totalling from 14,000 to 40,000 men. The divisions were made up of six to eleven battalions ranging from 5,600 to 9,000 men; regiments comprised one to three battalions. In the following year, the army achieved a more regular definition—divisions numbered 6,000 to 8,000, and every regiment was composed of two battalions.

Napoleon's military genius was best revealed in his ability to combine the movements of several army corps. The art lay in deploying and directing them so that the entire area of operations might be encompassed, making it impossible for the enemy to slip away. At the same time, the various army corps had to remain close enough together to be able to mass their forces for battle. The disposition of the corps generally took the shape of a flexible quincunx. Marching upon the enemy, the front progressively tightened as one or another of the corps found itself open to sudden attack. Sometimes, as at Eylau, they massed together on the battlefield itself, the corps having been aimed towards a distant point in such a way as to flank and envelop the enemy by their very advance. The arrangement of a campaign called for two different plans of action, depending upon whether Napoleon intended to fight a single army or occupy a central position in the midst of several adversaries, as in 1796–1797 around Mantua, or as in 1813. In any event, the pattern varied according to circumstances, and was never confined to one formula. Napoleonic strategy was an art which, while possessing certain principles, allowed neither tradition nor calculation ever to impoverish its inventiveness.

Victory was contingent upon the speed and daring of Napoleon's decisions, followed by a precipitate execution of troop movements. Surprise was an important element, and demanded the utmost secrecy. Always covered by cavalry, the army used rivers and mountains as a natural screen for its marches, whenever possible. But while cloaking its own movements, it was quite as essential to discover the enemy's: this was a function of the cavalry cover, as well as the intelligence service, which made use of diplomats, agents of all types (including in all probability the mysterious Countess Kielmannsegge), and above all, spies, who like the notorious Schulmeister were always ready to play a double game. Once the army was under way, Napoleon placed no great importance on lines of communication with France, since he invariably expected a short campaign. The lines of operations, on the other hand, were a matter of grave concern, and were to be protected at all costs. These were the roads connecting the army with the fortress where the headquarters was located, and whose location was shifted as the army advanced. Heavily travelled highways, dotted by postal relay stations guarded by a few soldiers, linked the army with France. Hence, fortifications had their place in the Napoleonic system. They served as a base of operations and could, by blocking rivers and passes, serve as a bridgehead and supporting cover for the army. They did not, however, play as important a role as in pre-revolutionary strategy. In campaigns aimed solely at forcing a decisive encounter and destroying the enemy, fortified places were never in themselves military objectives.

On the battlefield, Napoleon sought to compel the foe to exhaust his reserves by engaging him along the entire front. This was to be accomplished with a minimum of strength, so as to keep intact a concentrated striking force. Next, he would break the enemy's spirit with infantry and artillery fire, sustained by threats along his flank and line of retreat. Finally, when Napoleon felt that the enemy was sufficiently weakened, he would hurl forward his fresh troops, break all resistance, and pursue the beaten foe without mercy. This pursuit, which Frederick II with his small army never dared to order, was the most original feature of Napoleonic warfare. The battle plan, carried out with unparalleled precision, did not alter tactics at the unit level, a subject which Napoleon rarely touched upon. As a rule, the units adhered to the drill manual of 1791: the division was drawn up into brigades on two lines, one regiment deployed to the front, the other massed in columns. But, in fact, the methods of the revolutionary armies persisted: the infantry sent ahead a swarm of skirmishers, all picked men, who advanced under cover of the terrain. The first line of infantry gradually followed, often deployed in the same way. It was this kind of mobile shooting at will which so unsettled the enemy, who was accustomed to facing linear formations where soldiers, ranged elbow to elbow in three rows (the last two rows standing), offered perfect targets. At the signal to attack, the second line of infantry advanced in deep columns. They rarely had to use the bayonet; by this time the adversary was usually in flight.

Still, tactics underwent certain changes. Brimming with confidence, the French tended to replace much of the preliminary skirmishing by massed charges with naked weapons; officers became more partial to the use of columns as the number of untried recruits increased. But once the English, and even the Germans, adjusted to these new methods, the results were disastrous. Perhaps one of the weaknesses of Napoleonic warfare was the lack of attention to unit-level tactics and the failure to revise them in view of the improvements and advantages of the Coalition armies.

Owing to financial limitations, Napoleonic wars tended to be brief. This ensured the Emperor enormous prestige. The overpowering vigour of the campaigns, and the faultless dexterity with which they were brought to a swift finish, evoke our romantic admiration to this day. Their speed and daring bore the unmistakable imprint of Napoleon's fiery temperament. As in the case of provisioning the army, his ideas about the conduct of war were conceived in terms of the arena where he fought his first campaigns. The valley of the Po, hemmed in by a ring of mountains, allowed the enemy no chance of escape. It was small enough in area to be easily controlled by the army, cleverly deployed so that it might overrun the territory without taxing its strength. It was fertile enough to provide ample means of recovery. Already in South Germany the distances became greater and the army suffered accordingly. Yet this land, parcelled as it was, could still fit the original strategy. But once the army broached the limitless plains of North Germany, Poland, and Russia, things went differently. The enemy could now make his escape, vast distances required exhausting marches, and victualling became an insoluble problem. Soldiers were dropped off to act as occupation forces all along the way, and the army dissolved before it had even begun to fight. The economy failed to provide the required means of transport, and the organization of the military being what it was, reserves were lacking. Napoleon's strategy, which by its origin was totally Mediterranean, did not anticipate these new geographic conditions, and so never fully succeeded in adapting itself to them.

CHAPTER NINE

The Formation of the Grand Empire
(1805–1807)

THE CAMPAIGN OF 1805, undertaken within a year of Napoleon's coronation and in the midst of a grave financial crisis, exposed the Emperor to mortal danger. Saved by the victory at Austerlitz, he took control of Germany and began to organize the Grand Empire. This in turn provoked the formation of a new Coalition, whose defeat placed all of Central Europe in his hands and, by the Treaties of Tilsit, cemented the 'Continental System'.

THE FINANCIAL CRISIS OF 1805

Having set the Grande Armée on the road to Germany, Napoleon returned to Paris to improvise his campaign. He found businessmen greatly perturbed, the public panic-stricken at the doors of the Bank of France, and the treasury in utter ruin. The royalists were filled with hope. For a long time the Minister of the Treasury, Barbé-Marbois, had been desperately hard-pressed, and the Bank was rapidly succumbing to inflation. Besides the 27 million francs in rescriptions which the Bank had already directly discounted for the treasury, Desprès, one of the directors, had added 20 million more—these from the Company of United Merchants, who had received them from the treasury. This is not to mention paper accepted by the

Bank representing other delegations of taxes. But the evil reached unparalleled proportions as the result of Ouvrard's financial operations in Spain, the most grandiose speculative adventure of that time.

Charles IV's finances were in a pitiable state. Spain had been suffering from a serious shortage of food since 1804, and the flow of piastres from her treasury in Mexico had stopped. The annual subsidy promised to Napoleon was in arrears by 32 million francs as early as June 1804. Ouvrard advanced this sum to the French treasury, which handed over to him new obligations of the tax collectors as security. Having previously provisioned the Spanish fleet, Ouvrard held drafts on the Mexico treasury to the amount of 4 million piastres; his brother, who had founded a firm in Philadelphia, had personally verified that 71 million piastres lay in the vaults of the Mexico treasury and were only waiting to be shipped to Spain at the first available opportunity. Ouvrard now came forward with the assurance that he would find the means to have this treasure transferred to Europe for his own and France's benefit. Napoleon was naturally delighted with this prospect, and Ouvrard departed for Spain with the Emperor's approval in September 1804.

Arriving in Madrid, he proceeded to dazzle the court with his ostentation, eloquence, and presents. Godoy eagerly agreed to pay the arrears of the Spanish subsidy to Ouvrard, and accepted his bid to supply Spain with 2 million quintals of grain at 26 francs. Owing to a surplus of grain in France, particularly in the west, the cost to Ouvrard was 18 francs. Napoleon, who was always anxious to please the peasants and to divert the flow of specie into France, willingly granted export licences on condition that the French government receive half the gross profit. Ouvrard's next venture involved the *Caja de Consolidación*, a fund whose task it was to keep the rate of the vales reales from falling. He granted the Caja an immediate loan and arranged for additional credits over a period of five months. In return, he secured claims on the contemplated future sale of church properties, for which the Pope would have to grant his permission. In addition, Ouvrard was made the sole supplier of the government's tobacco monopoly and given the concession of the mercury mines, both of which had been in the hands of the Caja. When Spain declared war on England, Ouvrard provisioned the French and Spanish vessels harboured in the peninsular ports; to cover the cost, he negotiated a loan of 10 million florins from his friend P. C. Labouchère of the House of Hope in Amsterdam.

Having rendered so many services, Ouvrard was in a good position to tackle the problem of transferring the Mexican silver. To accomplish this, he exerted every effort to obtain a safe passage for the treasure from Pitt, who needed silver for commercial operations in India. On December 18, 1804, Ouvrard received from the Spanish government drafts on the Mexico treasury to the amount of 52½ million piastres; some of these he sent to Barbé-Marbois, who helplessly turned over to him more of the tax collectors' obligations. Charles IV, who had been completely won over, formed a partnership with Ouvrard covering all future shipments of specie from America. But Ouvrard was doing too well to stop there: he also secured the exclusive right to handle all of the trade for Spanish America and to undertake all shipments which the king might require, in return for which he was to receive a commission and the right to a third of the freight space on each ship while Charles would assume all the expenses and all the risks. Ouvrard obtained open licences in which the destinations of the ships were left blank; these he planned to sell to Americans. He then left for Amsterdam with the object of gaining the collaboration of the House of Hope. Labouchère was at first stupefied, but at last consented on May 6, 1805, to undertake the transfer of the Mexican treasure and to take over the traffic in the licences. Ouvrard, however, was forced to agree to give the House of Hope complete discretion, whatever the outcome, in the final settlement of accounts.

The whole affair consequently took on international proportions since Ouvrard counted on Labouchère—who was the son-in-law of Baring, the most influential London banker and a close friend of Pitt—to secure Great Britain's collaboration. Pitt, in fact, granted his approval, and even sent four English frigates to embark the initial cargo of silver, the value of which was then paid by the Bank of England to Labouchère. But in order to transfer the rest of the treasure and to take advantage of the valuable trade licences, Labouchère dispatched David

Parish (a son of the famous Hamburg banking house) to Phila-delphia, as well as two more agents, one to New Orleans and the other to Vera Cruz. They arranged for the Mexican piastres to be brought on American vessels to the United States, where they were advanced to merchants in exchange for bills drawn upon their European factors. Also, the trade licences were sold to American firms for a percentage of their net profit. This traffic could not get under way until 1806, and it was sus-pended by Jefferson's embargo in 1807. The entire transac-tion would have brought the House of Hope and Labouchère £900,000 or 225 million French francs; Ouvrard's share would have been only 24 million francs. In the meantime, Labouchère had to come to terms with Napoleon. Consequently, those who would defend Ouvrard's far-reaching plans have grounds to argue that they could have brought results; but they forget that the Emperor could hardly approve a scheme that enriched a foreign and, in fact, hostile banking house. Above all, they fail to recognize that it was France who was paying the bill.

It would take a long time for the transfer of the silver piastres and the trade in licences to bear fruit. Meanwhile, money was needed to pay for the grain which had been shipped to Spain and to provide the Caja with the credits and funds which it had been promised. The Bank of France now advanced the money by discounting some of the notes which had been issued by the Caja and the tax collectors' obligations which Barbé-Marbois had pledged, but only as security. Thus while Napoleon was congratulating himself on having concluded a good stroke of business, he was in effect financing the entire operation. Now Barbé-Marbois, for his part, had the Bank discount the Spanish bills which represented the silver reserves he had received from Ouvrard. To crown it all, Després and Vanlerberghe had not been paid by the treasury for their purveying services and, being short of funds, they resorted to the expedient of accepting accommodation bills enabling them to raise money and obtain additional credit. All of the members of the Company of United Merchants began drawing bills on each other, or even on themselves using fictitious entities, and the whole 'pack' con-verged on the Bank, which honoured all these bills without batting an eyelash. By September 1805, the Bank's note issue reached the staggering sum of 92 million francs. Such a pyramiding would have been inconceivable had Després not been a director of the Bank, and had Roger, Barbé-Marbois's secretary, not been bribed with over a million francs.

Ouvrard remained unshaken, believing that Spain would fulfil her obligations and that the credit situation in France would remain normal. In reality, Spain was very slow in paying for the grain shipments, and the Caja failed to honour any of its obligations since it was unable to carry through the sale of ecclesiastical properties in so short a time. In the summer of 1805, Barbé-Marbois demanded the money which Ouvrard had promised. To pacify him, Ouvrard began buying piastres with what little in the way of vales reales he was receiving; shortly thereafter, the vales reales lost 58 per cent of their face value, and Ouvrard stopped sending the money, considering the transfer impossible: his Spanish credits were frozen. On top of that, the bears on the Paris stock exchange were making money from the circumstance that war was imminent, and the public began a run on the Bank. Toward the end of September, the Bank's cash reserves fell to a mere $1\frac{1}{2}$ million francs. At first the Bank tried to play for time by resorting to various subterfuges, but it was finally forced to announce a partial suspension of payments. The panic quieted down a little after Ulm, but it resumed after Trafalgar and with the prospects of a prolonged war. In November, several private banks failed—the Banque Récamier and the Banque d'Hervas among others.

Ever since the end of August, the condition of the French treasury was causing Napoleon serious worry. The paymaster of the Pas-de-Calais département had been unable to meet the pay, and in Strasbourg it was necessary to borrow 12 million francs for which special guarantees had to be given. It is hardly surprising that a great many soldiers crossed the Rhine with only a single pair of shoes. They were the ones who ultimately paid, with their sufferings and even with their lives, the price of their master's improvisations and of the financiers' schemes. Before long, Vanlerberghe found himself unable to continue supplying the marching army and the garrisons with the necessary provisions; on September 23 he had to appeal for advances from the treasury, which was itself forced to turn to the Bank. To make matters worse, Vanlerberghe was given authorization to take directly from the tax collectors' tills by issuing a simple receipt, whatever cash he might find; consequently, as the tax collectors' obligations fell due, the Bank got back the receipts only. On January 1, 1806, Vanlerberghe was 147 million francs in the red and had to terminate his contract. Under the circumstances, one can well understand Napoleon's summary judgment of Barbé-Marbois: 'Had I been beaten, he would have been the best ally of the coalition.' But the minister's only sin had been his incapacity. The Emperor was making an allusion to a plot, supposedly hatched with Pitt's concurrence, whose purpose it was to place the former émigré Talon at the head of the Bank of France: unfortunately, we do not know any more about it. But in any event, we do have an indication of the fearful danger which the victory at Austerlitz averted.

If the crisis of 1805 was essentially a financial and banking one, it must not be forgotten that the whole economy suffered during this year of Austerlitz, in the agricultural as well as in the industrial sector. In the département of Meurthe, more or less the same old causes contributed to the crisis, but above all it harked back to the cyclical decline in agricultural prices which, as always in the past, adversely affected the purchasing power of the majority of the people. This resulted in a tightening of credit and in the growing importance of money lending. As usual, the most significant social consequence of all this was a corresponding increase in human misery.

THE CAMPAIGN OF 1805

Fortunately for Napoleon, Austria was not ready for war. The reforms which had been introduced by the Archduke Charles had hardly begun to take root. In 1802 he had substituted long-term military enrollment for life service, but this was not scheduled to take effect until 1805. Although he drew up rules governing exemptions, the annual contingent of recruits was still only 83,000 out of a population of 25 million. The Hungarian Diet had refused in 1802 to adopt compulsory service and conscription; it agreed to supply a mere 6,000 men yearly, plus 12,000 (granted only once) in case of war. Technically speaking, the Austrians were unable to create more than one regiment of Tyrolean chasseurs. When Mack took over the direction of the army, he enacted new regulations to increase the number of infantry and light cavalry and he instituted changes in the training manual, but he only succeeded in spreading confusion. Besides, the condition of Austrian finances reduced all of these efforts to nought. The peacetime establishment was short 83,000 men, 97,000 were on leave, and 37,000 cavalry and the entire artillery were without horses. The degree of improvisation was even greater than in France, and so the Austrian army marched to battle in a state of unpreparedness which was worse than that of its adversary.

Mack, moreover, was badly misled by the Russian General Winzingerode. Kutusov, who was in command of the 1st Russian Army, brought with him a force of only 38,000 men instead of the promised 50,000; Buxhöwden, who was to have followed hard by, did not arrive until November. Lastly, as in 1799, Austria's primary concern lay with Italy, and it was there that she sent her main concentration, the Archduke Charles with a force of 65,000 men, not counting the 25,000 in the Tyrol under the command of the Archduke John. The Archduke Ferdinand, who was rapidly subordinated to General Mack, was positioned in Germany with a force of only 60,000 men, plus 11,000 in the Vorarlberg, on the understanding that he would be reinforced by the advancing Russians. Ferdinand wanted to await them behind the River Lech, but Mack assured the Emperor Francis that Napoleon could not possibly cross the Rhine with more than 70,000 men. Having decided to push forward to the edge of the Black Forest, Mack crossed the Inn on September 11 and occupied Bavaria, whose army retreated behind the Main.

It was in Germany that the campaign would be decided after all. Napoleon's strategy consisted in moving his forces from Boulogne to Germany in such a way as to defeat the Coalition armies separately. On the Adige, Masséna kept to a holding action with only 42,000 men, for Italy was becoming restless and insurrections had broken out around Piacenza and in Piedmont. Napoleon had originally decided to mass the Grande Armée in Alsace: 176,000 men divided into six army corps, a cavalry reserve, and the Imperial Guard; a seventh corps, coming from Brest, did not arrive until the end of October. Then, on August 24-28, he decided that this plan would cause the advancing columns to lose time and that it would make it difficult for them to effect a juncture with Marmont and Bernadotte who were rushing in from Holland and Hanover. He therefore ordered them to veer toward the Palatinate where they crossed the Rhine on and after the 25th of September. The corps, covered by Murat's cavalry, then headed south-east toward various points on the Danube, downstream from Ulm. Having learned that the enemy was concentrated at Ulm, Napoleon ordered his men on October 7 to begin crossing the Danube near Donauwörth. He then lost contact with the enemy, and fearful lest Mack escape south into the Tyrol, he ordered his corps to deploy in fan order, sending Bernadotte toward Munich to cover the Russians, keeping Davout in the centre, and commanding the main body of his army to march on Ulm and the Iller. Actually, Mack, taken by surprise, was having great difficulty massing his troops, and two of his corps were badly beaten near Wertingen and Günzburg on October 8 and 9. Mack then decided to strike northward in the hopes of cutting the French communications. Ney, who had been sent to cover that side and whose main force was closing in on Ulm along the southern courses of the Danube, ordered only one division, commanded by Dupont, to cross the river. Dupont's division was severely tried at Haslach on the 11th, and Werneck's Austrian corps, together with the Archduke Ferdinand, managed to escape along the northern road. But Mack learned on the 14th that the French were marching westward towards the Iller, and thinking that they were beating a retreat to the Rhine, he returned to Ulm to intercept them. Napoleon rushed to envelop the enemy and ordered Ney to force a crossing of the Danube at Elchingen. The Austrian army, surrounded on all sides, capitulated on the 15th. Werneck's corps, pursued by Murat, surrendered on the 18th, the Archduke Ferdinand fleeing into Bohemia with only a handful of cavalry. A total of 49,000 Austrians fell prisoner to the French; Kienmayer's corps alone escaped. Nevertheless, the campaign did not come off as smoothly as some have maintained, and the army experienced more than one tactical reverse. The incessant rains and snows made the advance terribly difficult. 'At no other time, save in the Russian campaign,' wrote Fezensac, 'have I suffered as much, or seen the army in such a state of disorder.'

Ney now entered the Tyrol in pursuit of the Archduke John, and reached the valley of the River Drava; meanwhile, Augereau occupied the Vorarlberg. In Italy, Masséna fought an indecisive battle with the Archduke Charles at Caldiero, and Charles then withdrew his army in the direction of Laibach. Napoleon, wasting no time, drove straight for the Russian army, sending Kutusov, who had reached the Inn, on a headlong retreat. The pursuit was delayed, however, due to the sudden narrowing of the Danubian plain east of Enns. Marmont and Davout were forced to head into the mountains, while Mortier was shifted to the north bank to cut the Russian army's communications; but Kutusov managed to dodge Murat at Krems, and on November 11 he all but destroyed Mortier's leading division at Dürnstein. Pushing on to Vienna, Murat seized the Danube bridges by trickery, enabling the French army to advance beyond Brünn (Brno) in Moravia. However, Kutusov had already effected a junction in these parts with Buxhöwden's army and an Austrian corps; a third Russian army was in the offing.

Napoleon's position was rapidly becoming precarious. Already he knew that he was outnumbered. To the south there was always the possibility that the archdukes would succeed in combining their forces; to the north, there was the threat of Prussian intervention. Hungary refused to budge, annoyed that Francis should have denied her once again in October the use of the Magyar language in official life and the cession of Fiume; the Diet did not possess the means to equip a feudal levy —the traditional 'insurrection' of the Hungarian nation. The Hungarians were not hostile to Napoleon, and when Davout occupied Pressburg, Pälffy declared his neutrality; the Archduke Joseph was so hesitant in disavowing him that he was suspected of wanting to proclaim himself king. The Prussian threat was more dangerous. To save time, Bernadotte, on Napoleon's orders, had marched his troops through the neutral Prussian principality of Ansbach; it was a liberty which had been taken in previous campaigns. This time, Frederick William, who had not even been forewarned, reacted with great indignation. He immediately retaliated by giving the Russians permission to cross Silesia, and he then occupied Hanover without consulting Napoleon. Alexander, deeming the moment propitious, appeared in Berlin on October 25 where he was given an effusive reception. The war party began to gather momentum: Müller, now in the service of Prussia, and Hardenberg joined its ranks; Perthes, the Hamburg bookseller and publisher, appealed to Prussia not to abandon Austria to her fate; even Dalberg proclaimed in the Diet on November 9 the necessity of preserving the integrity of the Empire. On November 3 Alexander and Frederick William signed a convention at Potsdam wherein the Prussian king agreed to present Napoleon with an offer to mediate a peace along the lines of the Treaty of Lunéville. In addition, Frederick William promised, should the French reject this offer, to enter the conflict with an army of 180,000 men, not counting the Saxons, who had promised their assistance, or the Hessians, who were still hesitating but whose troops were already under Blücher's command. Meanwhile, Stein was finding the necessary resources to field this army: on October 15 he began resorting to paper money, and he paid the suppliers by means of treasury bills. Nevertheless, the king insisted on giving Napoleon until December 15 to declare his intentions. Haugwitz, the bearer of the ultimatum, travelled by short stages and did not reach Brünn until November 28; he was then sent on to Vienna where Talleyrand had been told to put him off. Actually, Frederick William had begun to waver again and had ordered Haugwitz to make every effort to preserve peace, as was his intention, no matter what the cost. Fearing lest Napoleon come to terms with Austria and turn against Prussia, he decided to await developments.

If Napoleon was unaware of the Potsdam Convention, he nevertheless felt the danger. Unable to pursue the enemy to Olmütz, he prayed that they would attack him: he simulated fear, drew back his outposts, retreated his troops, and attempted to negotiate with the tzar. Kutusov smelled out the ruse, but Dolgorouki and other close advisers persuaded Alexander to launch an offensive. At daybreak on December 2, the French army massed behind the Goldbach Brook west of Austerlitz, saw through the early morning mist the Austro-Russian forces advancing to the attack. The allies numbered 87,000 as against 73,000 French, but they were deployed along a wide seven-mile front aiming to sweep around the French right wing and sever its supposed retreat to Vienna. In accordance with their plan, the allies began to descend the heights of Pratzen, thus weakening the centre of their position. The French left under Lannes, and above all, the French right under Davout held fast against the enemy onslaught. Suddenly Napoleon, in the centre, ordered Soult to storm the heights. The French cut the enemy in two, turned their left, and put the army to flight. The combined Austro-Russian losses totalled 26,000 men; that of the French, 8,000 to 9,000. Alexander, furious and humiliated, announced that he was returning to Russia, and Austria signed a truce on December 6.

Now that the Coalition had broken up without waiting for Prussia's decision, Napoleon had no trouble isolating Austria. From December 10–12, he strengthened his alliances with Bavaria, Württemberg, and Baden. On the 7th he dealt harshly with Haugwitz; then on the 14th he again summoned the Prussian envoy, told him that Austria was asking that Hanover be given to the ex-Grand-Duke of Tuscany, and offered him a last chance to accept a French alliance. Thus cowed, Haugwitz gave in and signed the Treaty of Schönbrunn on December 15. According to the terms of the treaty Prussia finally annexed Hanover, but was forced to cede the Principality of Neuchâtel as well as the Margraviate of Ansbach which, the next day, Napoleon awarded to Bavaria in exchange for the Duchy of Berg. On December 24 Francis dismissed Cobenzl and Colloredo; on the 26th he acceded to the Treaty of Pressburg. Austria yielded all of the Venetian territory she had acquired at Campoformio (including Venetian Istria and Dalmatia) and all of her possessions in South Germany, as well as the Tyrol and the Vorarlberg; in return, Austria received Salzburg, which Ferdinand of Tuscany exchanged for Würzburg, taken from Bavaria. The Imperial Knights were thus delivered into the hands of their enemies. Bavaria and Württemberg, elevated to the status of sovereign kingdoms, were released (as was Baden) from all feudal ties with the Holy Roman Empire. As a consequence of the treaty, Austria was completely excluded from Italy, and aside from an empty title, she kept none of her possessions in Germany.

The Formation of the Grand Empire (1805–1807)

Returning to Paris on January 26, 1806, Napoleon first tackled the problem of restoring the nation's finances. This was done with the help of Mollien, who replaced Barbé-Marbois as Minister of the Treasury. On April 22 Napoleon passed a law placing the Bank under the direction of a governor appointed by the Emperor, thereby bringing it under state control. Mollien reformed the system of accountancy, forced the receveurs to make their rescriptions payable four months after date, and established on July 14 the *Caisse de Service* to regulate the flow of money; henceforth, the funds collected by the receveurs were not to earn interest unless they were actually deposited with the Caisse.

The settlement of the crisis itself proved considerably more arduous. The merchants, summoned before the Emperor on January 27 and threatened with their lives during the course of a memorable scene, were compelled to hand over all of their assets to Mollien; Ouvrard, who had been forewarned by Berthier, was nevertheless able to conceal some of his possessions. An accounting of the merchants' securities, credits, and warehouse stocks was drawn up, and they were forced to continue their provisioning services for which they were to be paid only half their due up to 18 million francs. Still, a balance of 60 million francs was found owing, a debt which Spain was made to bear despite the fact that she had only received 34 million francs. Charles IV was forced to seek an additional loan from Hope and Labouchère to pay France, and he obtained the Pope's permission to expropriate more Church properties. Labouchère himself had to abandon 10 million piastres for which he had not yet secured drafts. The whole affair dragged on for years. In the end, Vanlerberghe and Ouvrard, unable to make the Spanish debt good, declared themselves bankrupt; Ouvrard was thrown into prison for debt in 1809. But this enormous task of restoring the nation's finances did not prevent the Emperor from undertaking the work of domestic reorganization: there were still various codes to be prepared, and it was in 1806 that the Imperial University was established.

All of these things were mere trifles, however, compared with the new flights of Napoleon's imagination which the victory at Austerlitz had occasioned. In the South German states, upheavals followed each other in rapid succession. The Austrian possessions were distributed among the King of Bavaria who received the Bishopric of Eichstädt, the Tyrol, and the Vorarlberg, the King of Württemberg who took Ulm, in addition to other territories, and the Margrave of Baden who annexed the Breisgau, the Ortenau, and Constance. In November 1805, Württemberg began mediatizing the domains of the Imperial Knights, thus giving the signal for other German princes who also hastened to absorb them. Now that they enjoyed full sovereign power, they strove to fashion their institutions on the Napoleonic model, and the King of Württemberg finally succeeded in getting rid of his *Landtag*. But Napoleon had no intention of allowing Germany to crumble into dust. In January 1806 he proposed the formation of a new confederation of states which would recognize him as their protector. The rights and obligations of the member states were to be set forth in a constitution and enforced by a diet with the necessary power. Napoleon had already compelled his German allies to grant the mediatized territories a privileged position in their states—an excellent pretext for intervening in their affairs—and he expressed the keen desire that they adopt the *Code Civil*. The new monarchs were indignant that he would thus wish to mutilate their recently acquired sovereignty. 'This is a fatal blow to my political existence,' cried out Frederick I of Württemberg; Montgelas, the Bavarian minister, did not want to go beyond a temporary alliance. Not daring to break away, the states gave in. On July 12, 1806, sixteen princes announced their separation from the Holy Roman Empire and formed the Confederation of the Rhine, promising to supply their Protector with a military contingent of 63,000 men.

Napoleon could not dispose of the German princes just as he liked, for he could not rely on Prussia. While the act of union provided for a constitution and a diet, they were postponed indefinitely and never saw the light of day. Moreover, the submission of the princes was compensated by a fresh distribution of territories: the free cities of Augsburg and Nürnberg were annexed by Bavaria; Frankfurt was allotted to Dalberg. Several minor sovereigns entered the confederation by virtue of their personal connections only in order to escape being mediatized. Such, for instance, was the Count of Leyen who became a prince because he was Dalberg's nephew and who was made to contribute a contingent of only 29 men out of a population of 4,000 subjects; also in this category was the Princess Hohenzollern-Sigmaringen whose husband was a friend of the Beauharnais and whose son, married to the niece of Murat, was the ancestor of the kings of Rumania. All of the other petty rulers lost their sovereign rights: the houses of Schwarzenberg, Kaunitz, Ligne, and Thurn and Taxis, to name a few. There were also promotions: Baden, Berg, and Hesse-Darmstadt were elevated to the rank of grand duchies; Nassau became a duchy; and Dalberg received the title of Prince Primate of the Confederation of the Rhine.

All that remained was to abolish the last vestiges of the Holy Roman Empire. For Austria, resistance was unthinkable because Napoleon had used the Russian seizure of the Dalmatian harbour of Cattaro as a pretext for keeping his troops in Braunau. The Grande Armée remained in Germany, living at the expense of the allied states. While this provided Napoleon with a singular opportunity to alleviate the condition of French finances, the army of occupation generated a great deal of resentment. 'I was fond of the French who drove out our enemies and who returned our legitimate rulers,' wrote Madame de Montgelas to Talleyrand, 'but I detest those who live like leeches at the expense of my poor country.' A sense of national consciousness was beginning to pervade the German states; Palm, a Bavarian bookseller, began circulating anti-French pamphlets and Napoleon had him shot. On August 1, 1806, the Diet at Ratisbon announced its separation from the Empire. Given formal notice, Francis II renounced his title and prerogatives as Holy Roman Emperor on August 6. Thus ended the final act of the drama begun by the Treaty of Basle.

Bringing Holland into harmony with the new political conditions was child's play by comparison. On February 6 Talleyrand pointed out the necessity for a change to Schimmelpenninck, and on March 14 Napoleon revealed his intentions to Admiral Verhuell: his brother Louis would be King of Holland, otherwise he would annex the country. An extraordinary session of the executive council was summoned ('The Great

Task') and bowed its acceptance on May 3, Schimmelpenninck alone dissenting. A treaty guaranteed the integrity of the kingdom and its separation from France, and Louis took the throne on June 5, 1806.

In Italy, Venetia was annexed to the kingdom; Massa and Carrara were given to Elisa; Guastalla was conferred upon Pauline, who then sold it to the Kingdom of Italy. Of novel significance was the downfall of the Neapolitan Bourbons, whose fate was decided on December 27, 1805, by a celebrated military decree proclaiming that 'The dynasty of Naples has ceased to reign'. The sentence was easily carried out by Masséna: the Russian force abandoned Naples and returned to Corfu; the English were content to hold on to Sicily, which they used as a place for military exercises; and the royal family sought refuge in Palermo. Gaëta held out until July 18. In Calabria, bands of native insurgents rose up at once. Napoleon nevertheless believed, at least until July, that everything had been settled, and on March 30 he handed the crown of Naples to his brother Joseph. And yet he readied himself for a guerrilla warfare, like in the later Peninsular War. Maria Carolina had not given up the fight. Commanding but 6,000 men, she fomented an insurrection. Its ranks were filled with leaders of all types, from the nobleman Rodio to the highwayman Pezza (styled Fra Diavolo), most of whom had led the revolt in 1799. Many priests aided them. The Calabrians lacked a sense of national self-consciousness and were almost indifferent to the fate of the Bourbon dynasty, but the French occupation overburdened them and they were angry that they had been disarmed. The population was accustomed to brigandage fostered by the economic conditions of the country, by smuggling, and by a powerful mafia. The herdsmen and peasants held the bourgeoisie and the nobility as the ones most favourable to the French and to modern ideas, and so they regarded the queen's appeal as a licence to pillage the towns and the property of the upper classes.

The English looked disapprovingly upon this appeal to popular insurrection, which they believed to be of doubtful military value; but having seized Capri and the Pontine Islands, they decided to risk a landing, and by so doing, unleashed the uprising. On July 1, a British force of 5,200 men under Sir John Stuart landed in the Gulf of Santa Eufemia. They were met at Maida on July 4 by a division of more than 6,000 men under General Reynier who, without preparation, ordered a charge with naked swords. The English infantry stood firm, waiting for their approach, and routed them by means of successive volleys. This was the first example of a tactic that Wellington would demonstrate from Talavera to Waterloo, and which Napoleon, unfortunately for him, completely ignored. The French defeat became a signal for a widespread uprising marked by unspeakable horrors. Masséna and Reynier reconquered Calabria inch by inch, and were merciless in their reprisals. The town of Lauria was completely destroyed, Fra Diavolo was hung, and prisons and galleys were filled beyond capacity. Nevertheless, the insurrection had its effects: it proved to be very costly to the French, the British remained in possession of Reggio until 1808, and 40,000 French soldiers were kept immobilized. Meanwhile, Napoleon occupied the port of Leghorn, closing it to the English, and he placed a division of Spaniards in the Kingdom of Etruria. Now the only remaining independent territories in Italy were the Papal States.

Long before the coronation, Pius VII had been apprehensive about the progress of France in Italy. He had been forced to consent to the application of the Concordat in Piedmont, annexed to France in September 1802, and then he had to sign yet another Concordat with the Italian Republic. The latter convention was not devoid of advantages, however: it recognized Catholicism as the state religion, treated the clergy favourably, and referred undecided questions to the Church. But in January 1804, Melzi issued a decree maintaining the former laws which the Concordat did not expressly forbid. Pius VII protested against the imposition of these new organic articles; the Emperor replied with vague promises. In the meantime, a month after being crowned at Milan by Caprara (May 26, 1805), Napoleon issued two decrees which, without the prior approval of Rome, reorganized the life of the clergy. While increasing their revenues, he reduced the number of parishes, suppressed monasteries, and set a limit to their numbers. Much worse, he extended the Code Civil to Italy on January 1, 1806. Except in the Kingdom of Etruria where the sovereign was under the sway of Rome, everywhere in Italy—in

Lucca, Parma, Piacenza, and Naples—the Church became the object of offensive encroachments. Having tolerated secularizing trends in France as the lesser evil, Pius VII feared lest they be introduced by the Code Civil in Italy, which he regarded as his preserve, at least in a spiritual sense.

Conditions in Germany were no less disconcerting to the Pope. The Imperial Recess of 1803 had aggravated the situation, since rulers were secularizing Church properties and extending their control over the clergy without consulting Rome. Caesaro-papism was even winning in Bavaria. Now that they ruled over peoples of diverse religions, the princes renounced the principle of *cuius regio, eius religio,* and openly espoused tolerance, thus making rapid strides in the direction of the secular state. At first the papal court thought to negotiate a German Concordat with Vienna, but it finally rejected the idea because there was no way to force the German sovereigns to accept it except under pressure from France. Particularly after Austerlitz, there was always the fear that the Grand Empire, the symbol of a claim to universal domination, might someday challenge the priesthood, and this deterred Pius VII from implicitly recognizing Napoleon as the temporal head of the Roman Church.

And yet despite these trials and tribulations, the Church derived so great a benefit from Napoleon's protection that Pius VII would never have broken with the Emperor had he not himself been a temporal ruler. But such he was, and Napoleon could not permit the Pope to imperil his earthly domination. In vain did the pontiff invoke his neutrality: the fact remained that his dominions stood between the French and the Kingdom of Naples, an accomplice of the Coalition. When the English and Russians landed there in 1805, they were in a position to invade the Kingdom of Italy, and Pius VII would have been powerless to bar their passage across his territories, an eventuality which his court would have welcomed.

Consequently, the French occupied Ancona, and later Civita Vecchia. In answer to the protests of Pius VII, Napoleon replied on February 13, 1806, by summoning him to enter into his 'system', expel the English, and close his territories to them. When the Pope refused, the Emperor recalled Fesch, the French ambassador at Rome. Consalvi's policy was wrecked, and he resigned. The rupture was final, and Napoleon never again wrote to Pius VII.

In April Marmont entered Dalmatia, and Dandolo was appointed commissioner there. However, a Russian force from Corfu seized the harbour of Cattaro with Austrian complicity, and at Ragusa the French General Molitor was attacked by Montenegrins. Napoleon availed himself of the occasion to compel Vienna to grant him a right of way across Austrian Istria. No sooner had he thus reached the threshold of the Ottoman Empire when he decided to interfere in its affairs, and the year 1806 marked the reawakening of his Eastern ambitions. Pouqueville, the consul at Janina, was already busy with intrigues; Reinhard was sent to Moldavia; David was charged with a mission to the Pasha of Bosnia, who was in the midst of a conflict with the Serbs. The victory at Austerlitz had strengthened French influence with the sultan, who finally recognized the Emperor and sent him an embassy; in return, Sebastiani was dispatched to Constantinople, where he arrived on August 9. At the same time, relations between Turkey and Russia, supported by England, became strained. Nevertheless, the fact remained that like the army in Italy, Marmont's 2nd Corps was immobilized in Dalmatia.

The war of 1805 inordinately extended the range of Napoleon's enterprises, and so made the French Empire merely the core of the 'Grand Empire' which itself began to evolve through legislative acts. The Emperor regarded his new creatures as constituting 'federated states or a veritable French empire'. Although he made free reference to historical examples, the organization he adopted was original. At the top were the kings and princes, hereditary and sovereign in their domains: Joseph, Louis, and Murat, who was made Grand Duke of Berg on March 15. Next came the vassal princes, also sovereign and even entailed, but whose domains held in 'fief', were subject to a fresh investiture at each change of ownership: such were Elisa in Piombino, and Berthier who became Prince of Neuchâtel. Below them were princes with neither an army nor money: Talleyrand, Prince of Benevento, and Bernadotte, Prince of Ponte Corvo—two domains which had hitherto been disputed by the Pope and the King of Naples. At the bottom were the simple fiefs, which carried with them no sovereign powers: six duchies which Napoleon reserved to himself in the Kingdom of Naples, and twelve which were created in Venetia, all of which were destined for deserving Frenchmen.

Nor was this all. The princes and kings, while theoretically independent, were vassal to Napoleon as persons, even though their states were not fiefs. In effect, they formed part of the Imperial Family which the Constitution of Year XII had made subject to a special law promulgated on March 31, 1806. The statute created a special civil status for the family; it conferred upon the head of the Empire wardship over its minors and patriarchal power over its adults, including the power to allow or disallow their marriages and the power to imprison them. Moreover, the princes, even the sovereign ones, remained Grand Dignitaries of the Empire. Thus the edifice was founded, in good part, on the notion of a family pact, at once recalling the traditional network of Bourbon alliances and reflecting Napoleon's attachment to his clan. Family ties were for him the strongest ones. He also extended this policy to the allied states. On January 15, Eugène de Beauharnais finally married Augusta, Princess of Bavaria, and was at the same time adopted by the Emperor, although he was excluded from all rights to the French succession. Stephanie de Beauharnais, Josephine's niece, was also adopted, and given in marriage to the heir of the Grand Duke of Baden. Berthier had to abandon his liaison with Madame de Visconti and marry a widowed Bavarian princess. The following year, Jerome married into the house of Württemberg. This same motif, added to Napoleon's anxiety to provide a direct heir for the Empire, now suggested the feasibility of a second marriage for the Emperor.

The Grand Empire, tailored to fit the occasion, was nonetheless a first manifestation of the Roman imperial idea which was implicit in the title which Napoleon assumed in 1804. He now no longer hesitated to pose publicly as the restorer of the Western Roman Empire and to lay claim to the prerogatives of Charlemagne, his 'illustrious predecessor'. It stands to reason that these historically rooted pretensions seriously undermined the position of the papacy. Napoleon's letter of February 13, 1806, reminded Pius that although Charlemagne had been consecrated Roman Emperor by the Pope, he had nevertheless regarded the latter as his protégé, and that he had established the temporal dominions of the Church only as an integral part of his own empire. So too Napoleon: 'Your Holiness is sovereign of Rome, but I am its Emperor,' he wrote to Pius VII. This admirable formula, truly imperial in its brevity, already indicated that the Grand Empire, even before it had been established, would be but the beginning of a world domination.

THE BREAK WITH PRUSSIA (1806)

Such a policy could scarcely be expected to bring about a general peace. However, circumstances left room for discussion with the two Coalition powers who remained in the field. In England, Pitt died heartbroken on January 23, 1806, immediately after the disastrous failure of his policy and the sharp attacks of the opposition. The Whigs once again demanded that the Continent be left to its own fate, and they argued that peace was the only means of putting an end to French expansion. 'If we cannot cut down her enormous power,' Fox would say, 'it would at least be something to arrest her progress.'* In other words, he proposed to try Addington's experiment again, even though nothing about the present situation recalled the crisis of 1801. While not all of his friends may have shared his illusions, they were disposed to negotiate, if only to justify their accession to power. To form a ministry, the king called upon Grenville, who insisted on Fox's participation: this time he succeeded in bringing Fox in, giving him the Foreign Office. The Whig administration—Grenville, Lord Petty, the son of Shelburne, Lord Howick, the son of Lord Grey, and Erskine— was joined by Addington, now Lord Sidmouth, to form the 'Ministry of All the Talents'.

The domestic policy of the Whigs inflamed the British public: martial law in Ireland was lifted and Catholic emancipation was once again brought under consideration. No one, however, objected to an attempt to make peace. The war party was frustrated by the attitude of Prussia, who had accepted a French alliance in order to acquire Hanover. When England declared war on May 11 and placed the German North Sea coast under blockade, Prussia closed her Baltic ports to British

---

* Here again, the translator was unable to locate the source for this quote in order to render it in its original (English) version. TRANSLATOR.

trade to the alarm of the mercantile establishment. As early as the end of February, Fox had reopened channels with Paris by warning of a plot on the Emperor's life; Talleyrand in turn communicated to him Napoleon's desire to explore negotiations for peace. Lord Yarmouth, who had been interned in France and who was the intimate of several highly placed persons, set out for London and returned to France on June 17 with full power to act as intermediary. Fox refused to negotiate any agreement unless Russia were made a party to it, nor would he accept the Treaty of Amiens as the basis for a settlement. He insisted on the rule of *uti possidetis* with the reservation that Hanover would have to be restored to England. Napoleon did not object in principle, thinking that some compensation could be found for Prussia; nevertheless, he kept Prussia ignorant of these developments, knowing she would certainly protest.

Meanwhile, Alexander also decided to negotiate. The defection of Prussia had increased the influence of Czartoryski, who in January advised the tzar to abandon his vast projects of arbitration for Europe and to concentrate instead on the interests of Russia, that is to say, on the East. He regarded the situation in the Ottoman Empire as very promising. There, the Janissaries had been restless ever since March 1805 when Selim III had officially established his new standing army (the *Nizam Djedid*). At the same time, the Rumelian pashas, fearing for their authority, had taken up arms with the connivance of Ypsilanti and the other hospodars who were in league with Russia. The Serbs were in open revolt. In March 1804 Nenadovich, who had been negotiating with Austria, was put to death, and his compatriots rose up under the leadership of Kara George. Supported by the tzar, they demanded independence. In the summer of 1805 they elected a popular assembly (*Skupshtina*) which created a senate and petitioned the Sultan. The Turks were unable to subdue them. Czartoryski realized that a victorious Napoleon would be sure to thwart Russia's foreign ambitions, and the proof was not long in coming. Selim refused to renew his treaty of 1798 with Russia, and he also refused to negotiate a trade agreement. In June he revoked the *berats*, by which the Powers were authorized to grant the immunities and privileges of their own citizenship to Ottoman subjects. Ever since May 1806, a Russian army had been concentrating on the Dniester, and the English ambassador to Constantinople, Arbuthnot, urged that a squadron be sent. Czartoryski counselled keeping on the defensive in the West and entering into talks with Napoleon: if the latter were willing to give Russia a free hand in the East, a deal could be concluded and Russia could proceed to dismember Turkey. He broached the subject with Lesseps, the French consul, and on May 12 informed him of the departure for Paris of the Russian ambassador, Oubril, who journeyed by way of Vienna. After all, Napoleon's policy in Italy and Germany portended the renewal of a war against Austria in which she might disappear altogether: Oubril always maintained afterwards that he had received instructions to negotiate peace at any price in order to save Austria.

When Napoleon learned of this mission, he changed his attitude. He had been treating with Fox in the hope of isolating Russia; but the opposite alternative interested him much more, since of the two England was the more difficult to defeat. He immediately demanded that Sicily be surrendered to Joseph, adding that Ferdinand IV could be compensated elsewhere. Yarmouth expostulated and the talks were broken off. When Oubril arrived on July 6, he was at once cajoled, menaced, and subjected to unremitting pressure: Russia, he was told, could keep the Ionian Islands and enjoy free passage of the Straits; Albania and Dalmatia might even be given to Ferdinand to create a buffer state friendly to Russia between France and Turkey. Yarmouth did not reject this proposal when he was informed of it, although he had hitherto refused to discuss the question of Sicily. The creation of the Confederation of the Rhine brought Oubril to a decision; convinced that Austria would otherwise be lost, he signed a treaty of peace on July 20. At the last minute, Napoleon substituted the Balearic Islands for the Balkan provinces which had been destined for Ferdinand. Russia obtained at least a consolidation of her position: although she lost Cattaro, she held on to the Ionian Islands, saved Ragusa, and placed Turkey under the mutual protection of herself and France; in addition, Napoleon undertook to evacuate Germany. Alexander would not obtain so much at Tilsit!

For a moment the English were staggered. 'A mortifying agreement,' admitted Fox, finding England abandoned once again. Yarmouth, following in Oubril's steps, submitted a peace proposal which Napoleon returned on August 6 without making any essential changes: England would keep Malta and the Cape, regain Hanover, accept the Balearics for Ferdinand, and recognize Joseph, thereby implicitly giving up Sicily. It seemed that Napoleon's game at separate negotiations was about to succeed. Writing to Joseph, he already saw himself as master of the Mediterranean, 'the chief and constant objective of my policy'—at least for the time being, for he had many other plans in mind.

Suddenly the wind changed. There were many reasons to doubt that Alexander would ratify the treaty for he had just dismissed Czartoryski, whose policies exasperated the anglophile nobility of Russia which was passionately hostile to Napoleon. On July 9 the tzar appointed a new foreign minister, Baron Budberg, a Baltic German who was interested only in continental affairs and who was very sympathetic to Prussia. England could only expect to profit from this. Moreover, Fox had changed his attitude, and his colleagues condemned the Yarmouth agreement even more severely than he. Lauderdale, a new negotiator but one still quite friendly to France, was sent to Paris to demand once again the principle of uti possidetis, while nevertheless allowing for the surrender of Sicily provided that a less contemptible compensation could be found for Ferdinand. Napoleon refused to reopen the discussion, counting on Russian ratification to make the English back down. But now the attitude of Frederick William III caused the tzar to refuse to ratify the treaty. Perhaps his only reason for having r.egotiated with France had been to lure Prussia.

There can be no doubt that the Emperor was far from wanting a break with Prussia; when it came he was profoundly disappointed and vexed. The Prussian alliance, which had long been sought by the revolutionary governments and by himself, rendered Austria and Russia powerless and kept Germany closed to the English. Therefore his attitude toward Prussia was entirely benevolent, provided that she, like Spain, entered into his 'system', that is to say became a vassal state, and Napoleon made this perfectly clear to her. The king had stuck to the unfortunate idea, despite the warnings of Haugwitz, of not accepting the Treaty of Schönbrunn on its original terms;

he did not want to annex Hanover before a general peace had been concluded, but only wished to occupy it in order to avoid a break with England. As his appetite grew, he claimed that it was his right to keep Ansbach and to obtain the Hanseatic towns as well. When Napoleon received these handsome proposals on February 1, 1806, he had just been apprised of Pitt's death. He declared that Prussia's counter-proposition annulled the Treaty of Schönbrunn, and on February 15 he made Haugwitz sign a substitute treaty which compelled Prussia to annex Hanover immediately and close its ports to the English, surrender not only Ansbach and Neuchâtel but also that part of the Duchy of Cleves which lay east of the Rhine and which now was joined to the Duchy of Berg, and permit the French to install a garrison at Wesel. Frederick William III capitulated; it was a terrible chastisement which he never forgave.

The Prussian war party would prove even more vindictive. Momentarily disheartened after Austerlitz, it soon grew in strength. Still, there remained in Prussia admirers of Napoleon up to the very end: Bülow, brother of the future hero of the war of liberation, who wrote a book on the campaign of 1805 in which he treated Prussia very harshly; Buchholtz, who in his *New Leviathan*, turned Hobbes' philosophy into a eulogy of imperial despotism; and in the army there was Massenbach, a Württemberger. The court, on the other hand, was in favour of war. Queen Louise, comparing Napoleon to her dear Alexander, was full of proposals against the 'monster', the 'scum from Hell'. These sentiments were echoed by the king's first cousin Louis Ferdinand, by his sister, who was married to Prince Radziwill, by Countess Voss, and by her sister, Madame Berg. Schleiermacher, Alexander Humboldt, Johann Müller, and Merkel had all turned against France. In the military there were many like Phull, Scharnhorst, and Blücher who pressed for action. Hardenberg supported them, and in April, Stein asked the king to dismiss Lombard and Beyme, his favourite advisers; this request was again put forward by the royal princes on the eve of the war. Frederick William took offence; however, he was so concerned that he made secret efforts to win back the friendship of the tzar. He dispatched Brunswick to assure Alexander that despite Prussia's alliance with Napoleon she would never make war on Russia; when, on June 23, he learned of Oubril's mission, he repeated these assurances in writing. Hardenberg, for his part, negotiated secretly with the Russian ambassador Alopeus, and concluded an agreement along those lines, which the tzar signed on July 24.

The creation of the Confederation of the Rhine added to the discontent. True, the Emperor maintained that nothing prevented Prussia from forming that Confederation of the North which had been her great dream between 1795 and 1801. But he forbade the Hanseatic towns to become members and he told Saxony that she was entirely free to refuse her adherence. The elector of Hesse, too, did not dare to join. To make matters worse, early in August Yarmouth disclosed to the Prussian ambassador in Paris, Lucchesini, that Hanover would be taken away from Prussia. A false rumour finally brought Frederick William to a decision: Blücher reported a concentration of French troops on the Rhine, and a similar alarm was heard from Franconia. The king believed that Hanover was in danger, and without verifying the facts, mobilized on August 9 after notifying the tzar. During the whole month of August he was in agony, not knowing what the result of Oubril's treaty would be. Actually, Frederick William's own resolution had rendered the Oubril treaty nugatory, and the tzar refused to ratify it. Informed of this fact, the king wrote to Alexander on September 6, 'I have no other choice but to go to war.'

Just as in 1805, Napoleon would not believe what was happening up to the very last moment. On August 17 he even gave the order to prepare the return of the Grand Armée to France now that the German question had been settled with the abdication of Francis. As late as August 26 he called the Prussian mobilization 'ridiculous', but when it was shortly followed by Alexander's refusal to ratify the Oubril treaty, he saw the light. Now he was convinced that a new Coalition was being formed. On September 5, he issued his first orders; general instructions did not appear until the 19th. After Fox's death on September 13, his colleagues, confident of Russia and Prussia and much heartened by the fall of Buenos Aires, increased their demands. On September 26, they insisted on obtaining Dalmatia for Ferdinand IV; Napoleon put an end to the negotiations by his refusal on October 5. He was by then already at Bamberg, en route to annihilate Prussia. He improvised this campaign as airily as the preceding one. When he arrived in Franconia, his orders had not even been carried out, and he dismissed the Intendant General Villemanzy, replacing him with Daru. The soldiers set out lacking greatcoats, most of them without a second pair of shoes, and with only a few days' supply of bread and biscuit. Nevertheless, the campaign was so lightning-like that this time they suffered much less. The Prussian ultimatum demanding the retreat of the French troops to the west bank of the Rhine was submitted on October 1; Napoleon received it in Bamberg on the 7th; by the 14th the Prussian army no longer existed.

JENA AND AUERSTÄDT. THE WINTER CAMPAIGN (1806–1807)

Prussia had full confidence in her army, and all Europe shared it. Even in France, there were many who did not consider Napoleon's fame enduring until after the destruction of the army of Frederick the Great. It did not appear to have changed since its days of glory. Although recruitment of foreigners had become nearly impossible ever since the Low Countries and Germany had dried up as sources of manpower, there were still at least 80,000 of them in the ranks. The rest of the army was made up of 'cantonists' drafted from the peasantry; the nobility and the bourgeoisie were exempt from service, while the Junkers furnished most of the officers. This army, which had no national character, was admirably prepared by drill for combat in linear formation and in the open field. The infantry was made up of battalions of fusiliers, but they were not trained to fight as skirmishers. The cavalry was still adequate, but the artillery's equipment was worthless. The engineers and medical services were almost nonexistent, and notions of conducting a war had made scarcely any progress at all. The regiments did not have divisions. Marches were planned according to the location of military storehouses, and the army was always encumbered by an enormous baggage train. No one realized that this army, when faced with the soldiers of the Revolution, would be singularly outdated, or that its worse fault would be loss of its disposition for fighting. The captains in charge of the companies earned money in peacetime, thanks to extended leaves, and they regarded a campaign as a calamity. The generals were too old and lacked resolution. So the troops, although brave and well trained, were defeated by want of good leadership.

If the Prussians had not been urged on by their own vainglory to cross the Elbe, they would have been able to avoid disaster by remaining behind the river and waiting for the Russians. For his part, Alexander was much more tardy than he had been in 1805 because he was keeping an eye on Turkey. On August 24, Selim had unilaterally deposed the hospodars; frightened by an ultimatum, he restored them on October 15. At the same time, Michelson's army was ordered to occupy the Principalities. Consequently, not only were the preparations for war against Napoleon slackened; the Russians would also be fighting on two fronts.

The Prussians converged on Thuringia in three main columns: the Duke of Brunswick and the king, with 60,000 men; Hohenlohe's army of 50,000, which went through Dresden in order to mobilize the Saxons; and Rüchel with 30,000 Hanoverians who passed through Hesse. Brunswick, who had been vanquished at Valmy, had little authority over his subordinates and was unable to effect a concentration, screen his army, or even impose a plan of campaign. He wanted to advance on the Main in order to threaten the French line of operations, whereas Hohenlohe advised meeting the French head on by marching through the Franconian Forest. Ultimately, Hohenlohe, leaving two corps at the River Saale, moved toward Jena thus drawing closer to Brunswick's army, but he never did reach him. The Prussians were attacked before they could unite their forces.

Napoleon left Louis and Mortier to guard the Rhine; his German allies held the rear. Around September 25 his main army was concentrated in the vicinity of Nürnberg behind a cover consisting of the length of the Main and the Franconian Forest. There were six corps in all plus the cavalry reserve and the Guard, about 130,000 men. It was imperative for Napoleon to defeat the Prussians before the arrival of the Russian army, and he feared lest they were holding themselves behind the

Elbe. When he heard that they were on the march, he assumed that they were heading for Mainz or Würzburg: in that case, he would have engaged them on the Main, and turning their left would have rolled them back toward the Rhine. Seeing that they remained stationary, he crossed the Franconian Forest in three columns on October 7–9 in order to cut them off from the Elbe. Ney and Soult debouched into the village of Hof without encountering resistance; Murat, Bernadotte, Davout, and the Guard hustled Tauenzien's division out of Schleiz; and on the left, Lannes and Augereau fell on Saalfeld, where Prince Louis Ferdinand was defeated and killed on the 10th. Next the army advanced north, then wheeled westward, while Murat dashed toward Leipzig where he had heard the Prussians were beating a retreat. The Saale was fordable at two main points: Kösen and Kahla. Davout took possession of the first; Lannes and Augereau seized the second and then, moving up the left bank of the river, reached Jena and occupied the Landgrafenberg, a height overlooking the plain where Hohenlohe was camped. Thinking that the bulk of the Prussian army was there, Napoleon ordered Ney, Soult, the Guard, and part of the cavalry to mass on the height; the rest of the army, under Bernadotte, was summoned back from Naumburg to Dornburg with the order to march toward the roar of the cannon fire, in case of need.

In fact, Brunswick and the king were advancing on Kösen with 70,000 men, and Hohenlohe had but 50,000 men who were not even concentrated. Against the latter, Napoleon engaged 56,000 on October 14. Lannes and Soult, rushing down from the Landgrafenberg, crumpled the enemy's first line, attacked the second, and turned its left flank. Augereau, delayed by bad terrain, finally succeeded in threatening the Prussian right which, after a sharp resistance, took flight. Rüchel, who hastened with reinforcements, reached the battle-field only to suffer the same fate. All this time, Davout, with 26,000 men, was taking the weight of the main Prussian army near Auerstädt; Brunswick was mortally wounded, and his troops, retreating in disorder, collided with the streams of fugitives from Jena who engulfed them in the rout. As for Bernadotte, although he did indeed cross the Saale at Dornburg, his customary ill will kept him at a distance from the two battlefields. The Prussians lost 27,000 killed and wounded, 18,000 prisoners, and nearly all their field guns.

Murat, Ney, and Soult pursued the remnants of the enemy through the Harz country, capturing 20,000 prisoners, but letting several corps escape. The main body of the French army marched from Leipzig straight to Berlin, which Davout was the first to enter on the 25th; from there, he and Augereau crossed the Oder, where they forced the capitulation of the fortress of Küstrin. The pursuit now became more methodical, and Hohenlohe, cut off from Stettin, surrendered at Prenzlau on the 28th. Blücher managed to reach Lübeck where he was captured on November 6. All that remained now of the Prussian army was Lestocq's corps in East Prussia. Fortresses as far as the Vistula opened their gates, all except the Silesian towns, and Colberg, defended by Gneisenau. The populace made no resistance, and the civil functionaries took an oath to Napoleon. The conquered territory was rapidly organized and subjected to war contributions amounting to 160 million francs, not to mention requisitions which were imposed to procure supplies of all kinds which the army utterly lacked.

Napoleon immediately began to pluck the fruits of his victory. As early as September 27, the Grand Duke of Würzburg had become a member of the Confederation of the Rhine; on December 11, the Elector Frederick of Saxony also joined and received the title of king; on the 15th the Saxon dukes, and ultimately the other princes of Central Germany followed suit. Hesse-Cassel and the Duchy of Brunswick were forfeited, along with Fulda, whose ruler, the Prince of Orange, had fought on the Prussian side. Frederick William III himself seemed willing to accept vassalage in order to save his throne. Lucchesini and Zastrow negotiated a peace treaty with Duroc, which ceded all Prussian territories west of the Elbe except Altmark and closed the Baltic ports to the English. Signed on October 30, the treaty was ratified by the king on November 6.

But the situation had already changed. When Napoleon entered Berlin on October 27, he had discovered in the archives the evidence of an entente between Prussia and Russia, and he commented scandalously about the relations between the Prussian queen and the Russian tzar. It was soon clear that Russia would come to the aid of Prussia: an outburst of military wrath roused the Petersburg nobility, and the Orthodox Church excommunicated Napoleon. On November 9 the Emperor decided to postpone the signing of the peace treaty, and he substituted an armistice in which he demanded the Vistula–Bug line; the king's troops were to be quartered in East Prussia, whence they would drive out the Russians if necessary. In addition, he declared that he would not evacuate the realm until a general peace had been concluded, including restitution of the French colonies and a guarantee of Turkey's integrity. On November 21, these intentions were publicly announced in a message to the Senate. In effect, Prussia was made a hostage, and it seemed likely that her captivity would endure for some time.

As the army advanced it sequestered English goods systematically; with the occupation of the Hanseatic towns, Germany was now closed to British trade. In the famous Berlin Decree of November 21, Napoleon declared the British Isles 'in a state of blockade', that is, he turned against them their own weapon, the paper blockade. Consequently, no vessel whose voyage originated in Great Britain or her colonies would any longer be admitted to the ports of the Empire.

The continental blockade has been called 'the raison d'être of the Grand Empire'. This is simply not so; it spread naturally as a result of imperial conquest. Since Napoleon did not control the sea, the resounding Berlin Decree in itself added nothing to the already existing prohibitions on English goods. The new and significant circumstance was that since the neutrals were implicitly affected the blockade would lose that essentially protectionist character which Napoleon had given it when he came to power. Henceforth, it became an offensive weapon. By an abrupt and decisive turnabout, victory led Napoleon back to the policy of the Directory in 1798. The desire to unite the Continent against England had been formulated, thereby giving the 'imperial' and 'Roman' idea a real meaning in contemporary politics. 'I intend to conquer the seas with my land armies,' wrote Napoleon. This is why the Berlin Decree marks an important turning point.

The Prussian negotiators, not seeing so far, accepted the armistice on November 16, but the king rejected it and found himself bound to the Coalition against his will. Not waiting to hear the king's decision, Napoleon advanced his army to the Vistula: it reached Warsaw on November 27. The Emperor was obliged, however, to stay in Berlin for a month to see to the reinforcement and re-equipment of his soldiers. Mortier was sent to occupy Swedish Pomerania and to blockade Stralsund. Jerome, who had shown repentance and had allowed his American marriage to be annulled, went with his South German contingents to besiege the Silesian fortresses. The class of 1806 conscripts departed for the front. Meanwhile, the march to the Vistula had opened the Polish question. As the French advanced, the Poles rose and drove out the Prussian administrators. The movement principally attracted the bourgeoisie and the nobility, yet they were not of one mind: there was a Prussian party headed by Prince Radziwill—for more than one nobleman made use of the mortgage banks founded on the Prussian example—and above all, there was a Russian party. Czartoryski had once again advised Alexander to forestall Napoleon by proclaiming himself King of Poland, and he was supported by Niemcewicz and by Archbishop Siestrzencewicz who inveighed against 'the perjured conscience of Bonaparte'. Poniatowski himself hesitated until the end of December. The Polish Grandees feared reprisals in case of defeat; scarcely less did they fear a French victory which would emancipate their serfs.

Napoleon, in any event, compelled to fight the Russians, could not refuse the help offered. As early as September 20 he had authorized General Zajonczek to form a legion from the Poles who would desert the Prussian ranks. After Jena, Generals Dombrowski and Wybicki were entrusted with the formation of three legions in the insurgent territories. Kosciuszko, also summoned, demanded guarantees. Napoleon had no intention of undertaking a restoration of Poland, a project which would have enraged the tzar and incited Austrian intervention. Kosciuszko blamed the Emperor's silence on his egoism: 'He thinks of nothing but himself. He detests every great nation, and he detests even more the spirit of independence. He is a tyrant.' A deeply penetrating judgment, but a misinterpretation of the Emperor's reserve: he was not averse to reviving the Polish state in order to make a vassal of it if such a project were possible. Would the Poles be capable of governing themselves? He doubted it, and some of his marshals denied it outright. Moreover, it was too soon now. Nor did he make any promises, despite the persistent demands of the Countess Walewska, who passed the winter with him and whom he loved passionately. All he did was create a temporary administration at Posen for Dombrowski, then in Warsaw on January 14, 1807, a temporary commission which elected Malachowski president. Under the supervision of Talleyrand and Maret, the commission entrusted the administration to five directors, undertook the supplying of Napoleon's army and the formation of a national Polish army, and began to reorganize the judicial system on the French model.

Bennigsen and his 35,000 men had retreated before the Grande Armée to a position between the Narew and Wkra Rivers to await the arrival of Buxhöwden's 40,000 reinforcements. At the end of December, Napoleon began an offensive against Bennigsen. With Davout, he forced a crossing of the Wkra at Czarnowo on the 23rd, and he ordered Lannes to advance on Pultusk. The rest of the army, coming from Thorn and Plock, were to roll up the enemy centre and right and envelop them. But the weather was dreadful and the broken roads slowed up the advance. Bernadotte fell behind, and Ney strayed in pursuit of the Prussians. Napoleon strove to re-establish order, but in vain. On December 26, the French, in Napoleon's absence, launched a disorderly attack at Pultusk and Golymin; the Russians held firmly and were able to withdraw. The Emperor decided that it would be impossible to pursue them into the forests and swamps with soldiers who lacked greatcoats, shoes, and food, and he established his winter quarters from the banks of the Passarge to Warsaw.

A line so far extended invited surprise. Bennigsen, who was situated behind the forests, now moved northward. At the end of January he crossed the Passarge, intending an offensive against Bernadotte, who retreated on Thorn. Meanwhile, Lestocq advanced as far as Graudenz. But Napoleon was already gathering his other forces, and marched north to cut the enemy's line of retreat. Bennigsen, informed of Napoleon's plans by the capture of a courier, was able to hold out on the Passarge long enough to make his escape. Hotly pursued, he accepted battle at Preussisch-Eylau in order to save Königsberg.

On February 8, 1807, Napoleon attacked him, even though he had only 60,000 men against the enemy's 80,000. First he turned the Russian left, and then attacked the centre, but Augereau's corps strayed in the midst of a blinding snowstorm and suffered very heavy losses. Bennigsen then took the initiative, and was repulsed only with great difficulty by repeated cavalry charges. The arrival of Lestocq made matters worse, but at last Ney, who was pursuing him, reached the battlefield at seven o'clock in the evening and turned Bennigsen's right; Bennigsen then ordered a retreat. Twenty-five thousand Russians and 18,000 French had fallen. Napoleon called off any attempt at pursuit and led his army back behind the Passarge. He set up his own headquarters at Osterode, then, on April 1, at the castle of Finkenstein.

He had won a bloody battle, but his plans had again proved abortive and he would be compelled to fight a summer campaign. Once again he was in a precarious situation, so very far from France where the war was causing an industrial crisis which, in turn, necessitated large increases in government orders and loans in order to avoid the spread of unemployment. Meanwhile, Austria might enter the fray, and England could contemplate undertaking action on the Continent. Eylau caused a sensation throughout Europe, and reinforced the impression already left by the Polish campaign. It was said that Napoleon's strategy and the resources of the Grande Armée were ill adapted to the topography and climate of East-Central Europe. The Breidt company had to confess its inability to guarantee transports; the countryside could not provide the needed supplies; and the troops melted away. Of those who remained only a quarter could be brought into battle—the rest were needed to guard the rear. A prodigious effort, both military and political, would be necessary to triumph over Russia.

THE SUMMER CAMPAIGN AND THE TREATIES OF TILSIT (1807)

The easiest task was to procure soldiers. From September to November 1806 the reserves and half of that year's draft contingent were brought to the Rhine, whence Kellerman sent them to the front, unit by unit. The rest of the contingent was used up in the same way between October and December. Just as he departed for war, Napoleon called up the Contingent of 1807 ahead of its time; it too was sent to the front during the course of the winter. Finally, in April 1807, the class of 1808 was summoned, and scarcely had it arrived in camp when it was sped off, half outfitted and totally lacking in military instruction. The behaviour of the new conscripts becoming difficult, they were for the first time mingled with soldiers of fortune in 'provisional regiments'. Altogether, the Empire called up 110,000 men; the allies—Germans, Dutch, Poles, Spaniards under the Marquis de la Romana, and the Army of Italy—furnished 112,000, an increase of 72,000 over the previous year. On July 15, 1807, the Grande Armée in Germany numbered 410,000 men, twice as many as in September 1806. Around 100,000 men fought in the Friedland campaign. In addition, the Emperor kept a force of 120,000 in Italy to watch over Austria and Sicily, and another 110,000 (some of them National Guardsmen) for coastal defence.

The organization of transport and supply proved considerably more difficult. The failure of the private companies led the Emperor to militarize these services, in principle at least. The artillery train was expanded, baggage wagon battalions were created, and the general victualling of the army was placed under state control and entrusted to Maret's brother. Thus the war of 1807 resulted in an extension of the government's activities. But it would be wrong to conclude that the features of Napoleonic warfare were much changed by all this. The new organizations were never adequate, and most of the wagons were still procured along the line of march. The director of the food supply was scarcely ever concerned with the army while it was fighting, otherwise the army would have ceased to live off the land and campaigning would have been even more expensive. During the campaign of 1807 Napoleon took only 30,000 horses from France to replenish his remount depots at Potsdam and Kulm; it was much more economical and expedient to requisition everything on the spot. Workshops were set up in Germany, and arrangements were made with local bargemen and carters. For the most part, the difficulties remained insurmountable. It did little good to keep production in high gear when the goods could not be transported. The combatants, crammed in the area east of the Vistula—the bleakest spot in Europe—obtained just enough supplies to keep from starving. Up to July the French received only 26,000 greatcoats, 52,000 jackets, and as many trousers; an enormous stock of shoes remained unused in the rear. The Russians as usual suffered cruelly, and for the same reasons. Nor did their allies fare any better, even though they fought on native soil: wretched East Prussia was ravaged and despoiled from end to end.

On the diplomatic front, Napoleon conducted negotiations while attempting to sow discord among the Coalition powers and to keep Austria neutral. Frederick William's resolute posture was short-lived. On December 16, he offered the portfolio of Foreign Affairs to Stein, but the latter refused (to the king's great displeasure) because Frederick William would not dismiss his intimate nonministerial advisers and appoint a responsible cabinet. Zastrow, who was left in charge of foreign affairs, was very eager to treat with France, for he feared the loss of his estates. Since Napoleon had declared after the failure of the armistice of November 16 that he would not negotiate except on the issue of a general peace, the king let himself be persuaded to ask for the consent of Russia and England, which they granted, provided that France first be obliged to state her conditions. During this time Napoleon, because of his difficulties, was once again entertaining the possibility of that separate peace with Prussia whose breakdown he had previously provoked. He made overtures at the end of January, and after Eylau sent Bertrand to Königsberg to confirm them. In return, the king dispatched Colonel Kleist to Finkenstein. While insisting upon his own terms, Napoleon admitted the possibility of a congress, and when in April Prussia submitted an official proposal for one,* he accepted it. On June 9 the king informed England; by that time, the campaign was almost over.

Napoleon rejoiced at the discomfort these negotiations caused Alexander. On April 2 the tzar journeyed to Memel and persuaded the king to replace Zastrow with Hardenberg; on April 23 he induced him to sign the Convention of Bartenstein, strengthening their alliance. Up until then, the Prussians

* The author probably meant *Austria*, not *Prussia*. See below. TRANSLATOR.

had not lost hope, for the Russians were making great efforts to save Danzig. However, the fall of that fortified town and the plaints of the Junkers against the excesses of the allied troops led to cooler relations. And so Alexander began to formulate ever so dimly the ideas which would ultimately lead him to Tilsit.

Austria could favour only peace. Stadion, the new chancellor, burned with desire to attack Napoleon, but he judged the French still too formidable, and he was apprehensive about Prussian and Russian ambitions. So Austria armed herself and awaited events. Ever since October Napoleon had been cajoling and menacing by turns, proposing an alliance without offering anything but an exchange of Galicia for Silesia, and insisting that Austria cease arming. Stadion was studiously evasive; however, in January he sent Baron Vincent to Warsaw to talk with Talleyrand, who easily caught the Baron in his nets. It was more difficult to resist, and still not annoy, the other negotiators: the Russian ambassador Razumovsky, joined by Pozzo di Borgo, an émigré in the service of the tzar, and the English representative Adair. The project of a peace conference deftly rescued Austria from her embarrassment. On March 18, Stadion made an offer to mediate which upon Talleyrand's approval became official on April 7.* When all sides had accepted the mediation, Napoleon suddenly fell silent, summoned Talleyrand to his side, and left Vincent without any word for the whole month of May. In this manner he was able to reopen the campaign before Austria had taken a position in the mediation.

Alexander found Austria's action unforgivable, but even more exasperating to him was England's attitude. After Fox's death, his colleagues had remained in power, Lord Howick moving to the Foreign Office. English policy became more and more insular. After the fall of Buenos Aires, the public's only concern was with South America; the forces sent there, and the expeditions to the Levant tied up the available regiments, so that the tzar called in vain for a continental diversion. Sicily would have offered an excellent base against Italy, but General Fox, who was the butt of Maria Carolina's hostility and who received no reinforcements, declared himself unable to undertake

* See previous note. TRANSLATOR.

any action. Nor was the British government any the less sparing of money, and it refused to guarantee a Russian loan.

England had lost her touch in the field of diplomacy. She demanded the evacuation of Hanover as a condition of peace with Prussia, which was concluded only on January 28; even afterwards she snubbed Prussia. Her ambassadors at Königsberg and St. Petersburg, Hutchison and Douglas, lacked both amiability and adroitness, and revealed themselves as warm admirers of Napoleon. Finally, the 'Ministry of All the Talents' became seriously compromised in February over the Catholic question; the king at last consented to the abolition of the Test Act, but he still refused to admit papists to higher ranks, especially in the Navy. On March 7 the cabinet resigned; the Tories returned to power and called for a general election with the slogan of 'No Popery'. The government was only nominally headed by the Duke of Portland; the principal ministries fell to Pitt's disciples who would resume their dead leader's continental policy and display the same dauntless determination in its pursuit: Perceval, son of Lord Egmont, who became Chancellor of the Exchequer; Bathurst, who took over the Board of Trade; and above all Canning, the Foreign Secretary, and Castlereagh, the Secretary for War. However, since little was known about these men, their rise made hardly any impression. Canning delayed naming a new ambassador to Russia, Leveson-Gower, until May 16. He remained distrustful of Prussia, suspecting her of wanting to recover Hanover in order to dominate North Germany; moreover, he felt that there was nothing to be gained by substituting Prussian militarism there for that of Napoleon. His principal activity was to badger Gustavus IV of Sweden into breaking the armistice he had concluded with France on April 18. Among the Coalition Powers, irritation with England stood at its peak as the summer campaign began.

While Alexander was waiting in vain for the English to intervene, he found himself obliged to divert part of his army to continue the struggle against Persia and to maintain the war inopportunely begun against Turkey. Napoleon seized this chance to reach an understanding with the tzar's enemies, and so the European conflict was extended to the Levant, just as in the days of the Directory. Russia's General Michelson had occupied Moldavia and taken Bucharest without firing a shot, but part of his army was recalled and he had to come to a halt. Although Selim III had been encouraged by Napoleon to declare war on Russia, the Pasha of Rustchuk, Mustapha *Bairakdar* ('the flag-bearer') who commanded the Danubian army, remained inactive until the end of May. The uprising of the Serbs thus took on great significance, especially since they captured Belgrade on December 12. The Turks granted the Serbs all their demands, but now the influence of the Russian agents prevailed. In March, the Pasha Suleiman and his troops were massacred while retreating, and the Serbian popular assembly (*Skupshtina*) voted an alliance with the tzar. Napoleon did his best to help the sultan; he made peace with Ali Pasha of Janina, and induced him to attack the Ionian Islands of Corfu and Levkas (Santa Maura); Marmont sent cannons and artillery instructors to the Pasha of Bosnia; one officer went to Bairakdar at Rustchuk, another to the successor of the just deceased Pasvan Oglu at Vidin. The Emperor even offered to send the Army of Dalmatia to the Danube. But Muslim opinion was affronted by this news, and Selim himself refused to tie himself too closely to France; the embassy which reached Napoleon in March concluded no alliance. At the end of May Russia invaded Little Wallachia in order to aid the Serbs, who were advancing toward the Danube by way of the Krajina; they had to retreat precipitantly, for Bairakdar at last crossed the river. He did not get far, however. On May 25 the Janissaries revolted in Constantinople, massacred the ministers, abolished the Nizam Djedid, and deposed Selim in favour of his cousin Mustapha IV. Bairakdar retreated, and the Russians were able to join up with the Serbs under the walls of Negotin on July 17.

The English came to the rescue of the Russians in the East, intending, however, to work for their own interests. After a fruitless appeal to the sultan to renew the alliance of 1798 and to declare war on France, a squadron under Admiral Duckworth forced the passage of the Dardanelles on February 19 and appeared the next day at Constantinople. Selim's envoys played for time in order to allow Sebastiani to organize the defence of the city; then on the 26th, the mask was thrown off. Duckworth had to beat a hasty retreat through the Straits on

March 3, with considerable losses. England did not pursue the matter, not caring in the last analysis to insist on a policy which was of advantage primarily to Russia; instead, the British government decided that it would be preferable to reoccupy Egypt. There, ever since the departure of the French, the sultan had not succeeded in re-establishing his authority. The Mamelukes had defeated Khosrev Pasha, and the Albanian troops, led by their chief Mehemet Ali, had asserted their independence. The initiative passed to Mehemet Ali because the Mamelukes were divided: Osman Bey Bardisi came over to his side; Mohammed Bey el-Elfi allied himself with the English; and both Mameluke chiefs conspired with the French consul Drovetti. Finally in 1804, Mehemet Ali drove Bardisi out of Cairo, broke with the Turks, and compelled the sultan to recognize him as lieutenant of the country (Kaimakam) and in 1805, as pasha. English intervention at Constantinople brought about his replacement by el-Elfi, but Mehemet Ali held his ground; the two Mameluke chieftains then died, leaving him a free hand. To counter this failure, Duckworth landed a detachment of soldiers from Sicily at Alexandria; they occupied Rosetta where they were soon defeated in a surprise attack by Mehemet Ali. On April 22, 1807, the pasha laid siege to Alexandria, and on September 15, the English agreed to evacuate their forces.

For the moment, they were also checked in Persia. The shah had been fighting the Georgians and Russians since 1804, and a defeat had cost him Baku and Daghestan in 1806. Simultaneously he asked for help both from Napoleon and the Viceroy of India. French agents were sent to negotiate for an alliance, and a Persian embassy visited the Emperor at Finkenstein, where a treaty was signed on May 4. France agreed to take Persia under her protection and to send weapons and instructors; Persia, in return, promised to help in a proposed expedition to India. On May 10, instructions were drafted for General Gardane who was dispatched on mission to Teheran.

In short, everything had turned in Napoleon's favour, but the fact remained that only a decisive victory over Russia could destroy the Coalition. It was Bennigsen who made such a victory possible. Now that Danzig and all of the Silesian fortresses except Kosel had fallen, it was expected that Königsberg would succumb to the first French offensive. Early in June, Bennigsen tried to save the city by a surprise manœuvre, suddenly advancing to the Passarge in the hopes of crushing Ney who was encamped on the right bank of the river. Ney extricated himself and withdrew across the river where he was joined by Davout, while the rest of the French army advanced on June 9 against the Russian right in order to cut it off from Lestocq's 24,000 Prussians. Bennigsen then fell back on Heilsberg, a fortified position on the Alle. Murat, who should have fixed him there while the army emerged on the only available road, rashly ordered a full-scale attack on June 10 which needlessly lost about 10,000 men and enabled Bennigsen to retreat down the right bank of the Alle. Napoleon now threw himself against the Prussians who were retreating toward Königsberg. On June 13 Bennigsen, crossing the Alle at Friedland, attempted to create a diversion on their behalf. He probably intended no more than that, for when he encountered Lannes' corps on the following morning, he made no attempt to take advantage of his superior forces. Thus he gave the Emperor enough time to rush to the field with three army corps. The Russian left, after repulsing two of Ney's assaults, was finally totally battered by artillery fire. The bridges were burned, and Bennigsen's army, driven to the river, lost 25,000 men. Its fragments retreated to Tilsit, pursued by the French. Dazed by this blow, the Russian generals deemed an armistice absolutely necessary, and envoys from Alexander were sent to ask for one on June 19. They were favourably received, and a truce was signed on June 21. More than that, Duroc had already offered them a final peace on the 19th.

Napoleon needed peace: if Russia continued to resist, he would have to cross the Niemen; once again enormous preparations would be necessary, and Austria might take advantage of the delay. Alexander, for his part, was unhappy with his allies, and was in no humour to stake everything. He conferred with his brother Constantine, a devoted partisan of peace, and was undoubtably convinced by him that in case of an invasion, anything might happen: a revolt of the military, a conspiracy of the nobles, an insurrection of the Polish provinces, perhaps even a serf rebellion. Alexander then met with Frederick

William, and on June 22 Hardenberg seized the opportunity to submit a truly startling proposal: Prussia, which no longer existed, advised the tzar to change his entire policy and to offer Napoleon a three-cornered alliance whose purpose it would be to fight England and to redraw the map of Europe; Russia and Austria would divide Turkey and would abandon, together with Prussia, their Polish territories; the King of Saxony would be installed at Warsaw and give up his kingdom to Prussia. Thus it was Prussia who guided the tzar towards an alliance with France and a rupture with England. Alexander, who was infuriated with England, was very receptive to such advice. Moreover, Hardenberg's plan would again set him up as Europe's mediator, jointly with Napoleon as in 1801; for in her present condition, Prussia could scarcely count at all. This coincided exactly with Napoleon's mood; renouncing for the time being all ideas of conquering Russia, he now contemplated taking her as an ally in the place of Prussia. The offer, transmitted to Alexander on June 23, touched the tzar's vanity. He probably also thought that he would seduce Napoleon, as he had so many others, and so Alexander proposed a personal interview which took place on June 25, on a raft moored in the middle of the Niemen River. There the two emperors held prolonged discussions in the solitude of their own privacy. We shall never know what they said to each other: it is the 'mystery of Tilsit'.

The peace and the alliance presented no difficulty; what remained was to settle the fate of Prussia. Napoleon had never for a moment considered admitting her as a third party. He treated Frederick William with disdain and kept him at a distance. Queen Louise came to see him on July 6; she was heard out politely and went away empty handed. Having agreed in principle to Hardenberg's plan, Alexander did his best to defend his ally, but ended by signing the alliance without him. For this he would be accused of treachery. He probably found that Napoleon was immovable, and yielded to his reasons: the Emperor argued that he held Prussia by right of conquest and could, if he wished, keep her; nevertheless, out of regard for the tzar, he would grant her an armistice and restore a part of her territory. It is likely that Napoleon also dazzled his new ally with the prospects which would open up in the East once they had brought England to her senses, if not sooner. In short, he swept the tzar off his feet.

The instruments signed at Tilsit on July 7, 1807, consisted of a peace treaty, certain secret articles, and an alliance pact. A separate treaty with Prussia was added on July 9. Russia emerged unscathed; Prussia, on the other hand, lost all of her possessions west of the Elbe, except that she might recover 300,000 to 400,000 souls should England cede Hanover to Napoleon. East Frisia had already been reunited with Holland, and the Westphalian lands were taken over by the Grand Duchy of Berg. The rest—Minden, Hildesheim, Halberstadt, Magdeburg—were incorporated with Brunswick, Hesse-Cassel and a part of Hanover, Osnabrück, and Göttingen to form the Kingdom of Westphalia which was to be ruled by Jerome. Napoleon kept under his own hand the rest of Hanover, together with Erfurt, Hanau, and Fulda. Prussia also lost all of her Polish territories except for a small stretch of West Prussia, an isthmus 30 kilometres wide connecting Brandenburg and Pomerania with East Prussia. Thus mutilated and reduced to four provinces, the Prussian realm was to be handed back to Frederick William; but a convention signed on July 12 made the evacuation of Prussia conditional upon the payment of a war indemnity. Since the tzar was not made a party to this agreement, he had no right to any say in its execution. For the time being, Napoleon held on to all of Prussia.

The key to the future of the Franco-Russian alliance lay in the disposition of the Polish provinces (apart from Danzig which, now isolated in Prussian territory, was made a Free City, but continued to be under the occupation of the French General Rapp). Unfortunately, it is precisely on this point that the Tilsit talks remain shrouded in the deepest obscurity. There is no doubt that Napoleon freely invited Alexander to take part in the dismemberment of Prussia; in fact, he had already proposed that Russia expand to the Niemen. The tzar, it appears, was offered the Polish provinces overrun by Napoleon in exchange for the French acquisition of Silesia. As the offer was phrased it was turned down, and of the Polish provinces formerly held by Prussia, Russia annexed only Bialystok. Perhaps Alexander would have accepted it if Napoleon had renounced Silesia and permitted Prussia to keep her territories in Central

Germany. Instead, Prussia's Polish provinces were converted into the Grand Duchy of Warsaw. This solution may have been suggested by the tzar himself as a temporary compromise; or again, it may have been Napoleon's idea. In any event, the Grand Duchy of Warsaw, with a population of 2 million inhabitants, was given to the King of Saxony to rule. While passing through Dresden on July 22, the Emperor granted the Poles a constitution. Like Westphalia, the new grand duchy became a member of the Confederation of the Rhine, and 30,000 French soldiers were garrisoned there. Thus Poland was resurrected in all but name. In reality, she was no more than a military march against Russia, and so contributed from the very beginning to the eventual failure of the Franco-Russian alliance.

While Napoleon was extending the French Empire to the banks of the Niemen, Alexander was renouncing the gains which Paul I had amassed in the Mediterranean. He ceded Cattaro and the Ionian Islands to France, and he even evacuated the Danubian Principalities which he had just occupied on the sole condition that the Turks should not reoccupy them until peace had been concluded. In this matter, Napoleon was to act as mediator; if the sultan refused to make peace within three months, France would make common cause with Russia to deprive the Porte of all her European possessions, with the exception of Rumelia. As for England, it was Alexander who undertook to mediate by summoning her to restore her colonial conquests and to recognize the freedom of the seas. If he failed in this attempt, measures would be taken to compel Sweden, Denmark, and Portugal to enter into the Continental System. Thus the agreement of 1801 was both renewed and expanded. The tzar could look forward to the conquest of Finland and Turkey; for Napoleon, there was Portugal and a confederated continent closed to English trade. Prussia had adhered to the blockade; Austria, isolated, could hardly refuse to do as much. Caught in the crossfire of the Franco-Russian alliance, these two German powers were reduced to helplessness, effectively ruling out any possibility of a coalition.

For Napoleon, Tilsit was thus a brilliant success, albeit a temporary one. While Alexander appears to have been seduced by Napoleon, whom he thought was under his sway, his vanity and inconstancy stood guarantee that such a state of affairs could not long endure. He would make no honest effort to share the management of Europe's affairs with a man whose temperament brooked no equal partnership. Surely Alexander, artful deceiver that he was, concealed his intentions. He extricated himself from a nasty situation without loss and he calculated that France, more readily than England, would allow him to despoil Sweden and Turkey. Meanwhile he remained absolutely free to take up arms again at his own convenience. Therefore it has been said that it was he who duped Napoleon.

This is simply not so. Napoleon, at the time of Tilsit, remarked to Meneval that he had resolved never to turn Constantinople over to the Russians: 'It is the centre of world empire.' As far as he was concerned, the alliance had not been concluded on an equal basis. Russia was entering into his system, and was thereby becoming a vassal. It could not have escaped him that the war might someday be resumed, but he lived for the present, not the future; he knew that peace was necessary in order for him to rebuild his army, disarm Austria, and complete the submission of Western Europe. The alliance made this possible, for the moment at least; perhaps it would even permit him to conquer England. Time alone would tell. If Russia went to war before England succumbed, then he would conquer Russia. But as long as he had Alexander's support, if only temporarily, Napoleon was gaining time to amass the force he would need to defeat him.

BIBLIOGRAPHY

Note

THE FOLLOWING BIBLIOGRAPHY, prepared and revised by Georges Lefebvre and subsequently expanded by Professor Albert Soboul, is presented as it appeared in the 5th (1965) edition of *Napoléon*. In some instances, the translator has made corrections, brought publication facts up to date, and indicated the existence of English translations. No new items have been added.

The fifty-eight titles listed below, most of them published since 1953, were compiled by the translator. They do not pretend to be a full bibliography, but constitute only a selection of recent useful works in the field of Napoleonic studies. For a more complete survey of current works, the reader should consult J. Godechot's *Bulletins Historiques*, Vols. 213 (1955), 221 (1959), 227–28 (1962), 236–37 (1966–1967), and the University of North Carolina periodical, *French Historical Studies*.

J. BAELEN. *Benjamin Constant et Napoléon*. Paris, 1965.

M. BALDET. *La vie quotidienne dans les armées de Napoléon*. Paris, 1965.

P. BARTEL. *La jeunesse inédite de Napoléon*. Paris, 1954.

P. BESSAND-MASSENET. *Le 18 Brumaire*. Paris, 1965.

R. CAMERON. *France and the Economic Development of Europe, 1800–1914*. Princeton, N.J., 1961.

R. CAVALIERO. *The Last of the Crusaders: the Knights of St. John and Malta in the Eighteenth Century*. London, 1960.

A. CHATELLE. *Napoléon et la légion d'honneur: au camp de Boulogne, 1801–1805*. Paris, 1962.

A. COBBAN. *The Social Interpretation of the French Revolution*. New York and Cambridge, 1964.

H. COLE. *Josephine*. London, 1962.

O. CONNELLY. *Napoleon's Satellite Kingdoms*. New York, 1965.

G. CRAIG. *The Politics of the Prussian Army*. Oxford, 1955.

A. CROSBY. *America, Russia, Hemp, and Napoleon: American Trade with Russia and the Baltic, 1783–1812*. Columbus, Ohio, 1965.

B. DELACROIX. *Réorganisation de l'Église de France après la Révolution*. Paris, 1962.

R. DELDERFIELD. *Napoleon's Marshals*. New York, 1966.

J. DROZ. *Le romantisme allemand et l'État: résistance et collaboration dans l'Allemagne napoléonienne*. Paris, 1966.

V. ESPOSITO and J. ELTING. *A Military History and Atlas of the Napoleonic Wars*. New York, 1964.

O. FESTY. *Les mouvements de la population française du début de la Révolution au Consulat*. Paris, 1954.

Bibliography

H. GAUBERT. *Conspirateurs sous Napoléon Ier*. Paris, 1962.

D. GEORGE. *English Political Caricature*. Oxford, 1959.

B. GILLE. *Les sources statistiques de l'histoire de France, des enquêtes du XVIIe siècle à 1870*. Geneva and Paris, 1964.

M. GONTARD. *La question des écoles normales primaires, de la Révolution de 1789 à la loi de 1879*. Toulouse, 1962.

A. GUÉRARD. *Napoleon*. London, 1957.

E. HALES. *Revolution and the Papacy*. London, 1960.

—— *Napoleon and the Pope*. London, 1960.

F. HEALEY. *Rousseau et Napoléon*. Geneva, 1957.

—— *The Literary Culture of Napoleon*. Geneva, 1959.

W. HENDERSON. *The Industrial Revolution on the Continent, Germany, France, Russia, 1800–1914*. London, 1961.

A. HERIOT. *The French in Italy, 1796–1799*. London, 1957.

C. HEROLD. *The Mind of Napoleon*. New York, 1955.

—— *Madame de Staël*. London, 1959.

—— *Bonaparte in Egypt*. London, 1963.

E. HOBSBAWM. *The Age of Revolution*. London, 1962.

R. HOLTMAN. *Napoleonic Propaganda*. Baton Rouge, La., 1950.

J. HOWARD. *Letters and Documents of Napoleon*. Vol. I: *1769–1802*. London, 1961.

M. KUKIEL. *Czartoryski and European Unity*. Princeton, N.J., 1955.

J. LACRETELLE et al. *Talleyrand*. Paris, 1964.

M. LEWIS. *The History of the British Navy*. London, 1959.

—— *A Social History of the Navy*. London, 1960.

—— *Napoleon and his British Captives*. London, 1962.

J. MASSIN. *Almanach du Premier Empire, du 9 thermidor à Waterloo*. Paris, 1965.

S. MCCLOY. *French Inventions of the Eighteenth Century*. Lexington, Ky., 1952.

B. MELCHIOR-BONNET. *Le duc d'Enghien*. Paris, 1961.

B. NABONNE. *La diplomatie du Directoire et Bonaparte*. Paris, 1952.

The New Cambridge Modern History, Vol. IX: *War and Peace in an Age of Upheaval, 1793–1830*, C. W. Crawley, ed. Cambridge, 1965.

R. VON OER. *Der Friede von Pressburg: Ein Beitrag zur Diplomatie-Geschichte napoleonische Zeitalters*. Münster, 1965.

R. R. PALMER. *The Age of the Democratic Revolution: A Political History of Europe and America, 1760–1800*. Princeton, N.J., 1959.

J. PALOU. *La Franc-maçonnerie*. Paris, 1964.

D. POPE. *England Expects: Trafalgar*. London, 1959.

A. RÉMOND. *Les prix des transports marchands de la Révolution au Ier Empire*. Paris, 1956.

A. ROGER. *The War of the Second Coalition, 1798–1801: A Strategic Commentary*. New York and Oxford, 1964.

T. ROPP. *War in the Modern World*. Durham, N.C., 1959.

G. RUDÉ. *The Crowd in History, 1730–1848: A Study of Popular Disturbances in France and England*. New York, 1964.

—— *Revolutionary Europe, 1783–1815*. London, 1964.

T. RUYSSEN. *Les sources doctrinales de l'internationalisme*, Vol. III: *De la Révolution française au milieu du XIXe siècle*. Paris, 1961.

Bibliography

W. SHANAHAN. *Prussian Military Reforms, 1786–1813.* New York, 1945.
J. THIRY. *Eylau, Friedland, Tilsit.* Paris, 1965.
J. VIDALENC. *Les émigrés français, 1789–1825.* Caen, 1963.
M. WEINER. *The French Exiles, 1789–1815.* London, 1960.

Bibliography

PART ONE. THE LEGACY OF THE REVOLUTION

Chapter I. The Conflict between the Old Regime and the Revolution

General works: For the present chapter as well as for the entire Part I, see the preceding volume in this series and its bibliography, Vol. XIII of 'Peuples et Civilisations' published under the direction of L. Halphen and P. Sagnac: G. Lefebvre, *La Révolution française* (Paris, 3rd ed., 1963, this being the latest revised edition). English translations appear in two volumes by E. Evanson, *The French Revolution: from Its Origins to 1793* (London: Routledge & Kegan Paul, and New York: Columbia University Press, 1962); J. Stewart and J. Friguglietti, *The French Revolution: from 1793 to 1799* (London: Routledge & Kegan Paul, and New York: Columbia University Press, 1964).

The above mentioned work by G. Lefebvre will henceforth be cited as EVANSON *or* STEWART, *and page references will apply to its English translations.*

Among the general histories (and their selected bibliographies) on the period covered by this volume, see *Histoire générale du IVᵉ siècle à nos jours,* published under the direction of E. Lavisse and A. Rambaud, Vol. IX (Paris, 1897); *The Cambridge Modern History,* Vol. IX (Cambridge, 1906); *Weltgeschichte in gemeineverständlicher Darstellung,* published under the direction of L. M. Hartmann, Vol. VII, Pt. II (Stuttgart and Gotha, 1925); *Propyläen Weltgeschichte,* published under the direction of W. Goetz, Vol. III: *Die grosse Revolution, Napoleon und die Restauration, 1789–1848* (Berlin, 1929); C. Barbagallo, *Storia universale,* Vol. V, Pt. II: *Dall'età napoleonica alla fine della prima guerra mondiale* (Turin, 1950–1954); R. R. Palmer, *A History of the Modern World* (New York, 1950; 2nd ed., 1956), with an extensive bibliography chiefly for works in English; *Histoire générale des civilisations,* M. Crouzet, ed., Vol. V: *Le XVIII siècle. Révolution intellectuelle, technique et politique (1715–1875)* by R. Mousnier and E. Labrousse, with the collaboration of M. Bouloiseau (Paris, 1953); *Destins du Monde,* L. Febvre and F. Braudel, eds.: *Les bourgeois conquérants* by C. Morazé (Paris, 1957); *Historia Mundi,* F. Kern, ed., Vol. IX: *Aufklärung und Revolution* (Berne–Munich, 1950); F. Markham, *Napoleon and the Awakening of Europe* (London, 1954); W. Andreas, *Das Zeitalter Napoleon und die Erhebung der Völker* (Heidelberg, 1955); M. Göhring, *Napoleon, von alten zum neuen Europa* (Göttingen, 1959).

Bibliography

Among the general histories of France during the Napoleonic rule, see: A. Thiers, *Histoire du Consulat et de l'Empire*, 20 vols. (Paris, 1845–1862); G. Pariset, *Le Consulat et l'Empire* (Paris, 1921), Vol. III of *Histoire de France contemporaine*, published under the direction of E. Lavisse and containing valuable bibliographies; H. Taine, *Origine de la France contemporaine*, 2 vols. (Paris, 1891–1894), see Pt. III which, however, was never completed; L. Madelin, *Histoire du Consulat et de l'Empire*, is now complete with the appearance of the final volume, Vol. XVI: *Les Cent Jours. Waterloo* (Paris, 1954); L. Villat, *La Révolution et l'Empire*, Vol. II: *Napoléon* (Paris, 1936, in the collection 'Clio: introduction aux études historiques'), extensive bibliographies follow a brief account.

THE SOCIAL AND POLITICAL CONFLICT

See the first few references cited above and especially Stewart, pp. 318–40 and corresponding bibliographies, pp. 393–94. In addition see J. Gode-chot, *La Grande Nation. L'expansion révolutionnaire de la France dans le monde, 1789–1799*, 2 vols. (Paris, 1956) and *La contre-révolution. Doctrine et action, 1789–1804* (Paris, 1961).

THE CONFLICT OF IDEAS

See Stewart, pp. 328–40, 394.

On rationalism and the sciences, see Evanson, pp. 57–59, 302–3.

On philosophic currents, see the recasted great work by Kuno Fischer, *Geschichte der neuern Philosophie* (Heidelberg, 1854, 6 vols.; 1897–1904, 10 vols. in 11; 5th ed., 1909–1912, 2 vols.); W. Windelband, *Die Geschichte der neuern Philosophie in ihrem Zuzammenhange mit der allgemeinen Kultur*, 2 vols. (Leipzig, 1878–1880; 7th ed. rev., 1922), refer to Vol. II; É. Bréhier, *Histoire de la philosophie*, Vol. II (Paris, 1930).

On political thought, P. Janet, *Histoire de la science politique dans ses rapports avec la morale*, 2 vols. (Paris, 1872; 4th ed., 1913); G. Sabine, *A History of Political Theory* (New York, 1937; rev. ed., 1955); J. Touchard, with the collaboration of L. Bodin, P. Jeannin, G. Lavau, and G. Sirinelli, *Histoire des idées politiques*, Vol. II: *Du XVIII siècle à nos jours* (Paris, 1959, coll. 'Thémis'); F. Ponteil, *La pensée politique depuis Montesquieu* (Paris, 1960).

On literature, P. Van Tieghem, *Histoire littéraire de l'Europe et de l'Amérique de la Renaissance à nos jours* (Paris, 1941); W. Scherer, *Geschichte der deutschen Literatur* (Berlin, 1883; 15th ed., 1922); J. Schmidt, *Geschichte der deutschen Literatur von Leibnitz bis auf unsere Zeit*, Vol. III (Berlin, 1886); O. Walzel, *Deutsche Dichtung von Gottsched bis zur Gegenwart* (Berlin, 1926); *The Cambridge History of English Literature*, Vol. IX (Cambridge, 1914); E. Legouis and L. Cazamian, *Histoire de la littérature anglaise* (Paris, 1924); *Histoire de la langue et de la littérature française*, published under the direction of Petit de Julleville, see Vol. VI (Paris, 1909); G. Lanson, *Histoire de la littérature française* (Paris, 1895, often re-edited), resumed under the title of *Histoire illustrée de la littérature française*, 2 vols. (Paris, 1923–1924), see Vol. II; J. Bédier and P. Hazard, *Histoire de la littérature française illustrée* (Paris, 1923–1924; rev. ed. published under the direction of P. Martino, Paris, 1950), see Vol. II; P. Hazard, *La*

Bibliography

Révolution française et les lettres italiennes (Paris, 1910); F. de Sanctis, *A History of Italian Literature*, 2 vols. (New York, 1931).

On German thought, F. Schnabel, *Deutsche Geschichte in neunzehnten Jahrhundert*, Vol. I (Freiburg-im-Breisgau, 1929; 4th ed., 1949); L. Lévy-Bruhl, *L'Allemagne depuis Leibnitz* (Paris, 1890); the noteworthy synthesis by J. E. Spenlé, *La pensée allemande* (Paris, 1934, no. 171 in the collection 'Armand Colin'); G. P. Gooch, *Germany and the French Revolution* (London, 1920); A. Stern, *Der Einfluss der französischen Revolution auf das deutsche Geistesleben* (Berlin, 1927), with an important bibliography; R. Aris, *History of Political Thought in Germany from 1789 to 1815* (London, 1936); J. Droz, *L'Allemagne et la Révolution française* (Paris, 1949); Xavier Léon, *Fichte et son temps*, 3 vols. (Paris, 1922–1927); V. Basch, *Les doctrines politiques des philosophes classiques de L'Allemagne. Leibnitz, Kant, Fichte, Hegel* (Paris, 1927); M. Guéroult, *L'évolution et la structure de la doctrine de la science chez Fichte*, 2 vols. (Strasbourg, 1930, Vols. 50 & 51 in 'Publications de la Faculté des Lettres de Strasbourg'); R. Leroux, *Guillaume de Humboldt. La formation de sa pensée jusqu'en 1794* (Strasbourg, 1932, Vol. 59 in 'Publications de la Faculté des Lettres de Strasbourg'); N. Wallner, *Fichte als politischer Denker* (Halle, 1926); E. Vermeil, 'La pensée politique de Hegel' in *Revue de métaphysique et de morale*, Vol. XXVIII (1931), pp. 441–510; J. Ritter, *Hegel und die französische Revolution* (Cologne–Opladen, 1957).

On the beginnings of Romanticism, see P. Van Tieghem, *Le pré-romantisme*, 2 vols. (Paris, 1924 and 1931) and *Le romantisme dans la littérature européenne* (Paris, 1948).

On the social origins of Romanticism, H. Brunschwig, *La crise de l'État prussien à la fin du XVIIIe siècle et la genèse de la mentalité romantique* (Paris, 1947).

On the mystical origins of Romanticism, two very fine treatments may be found in: R. Berthelot, *Un romantisme utilitaire*, 3 vols. (Paris, 1911–1922); A. Viatte, *Les sources occultes du romantisme*, 2 vols. (Paris, 1928); J. Droz, 'La légende du complot illuministe et les origines du romantisme politique en Allemagne' in *Revue historique*, Vol. CCXXVI, 1961, pp. 313–38; Renzo de Felice, *Note e ricerche sugli 'Illuministi' e il misticismo rivoluzionario, 1789 1800* (Rome, 1960).

On Romanticism in Germany, see R. Haym, *Die romantische Schule* (Berlin, 1870; 4th ed. by O. Walzel, 1920); Ricarda Huch, *Die Romantik*, 2 vols. (Leipzig, 1911; 7th ed., 1918–1920); O. Walzel, *Deutsche Romantik*, 2 vols. (Leipzig and Berlin, 1908; 4th ed., 1918); a good synopsis may be found in P. Kluckhohn, *Deutsche Romantik* (Bielefeld and Berlin, 1924); for an excellent résumé, see J. E. Spenlé, *La pensée allemande* (Paris, 1934, No. 171 in the collection 'Armand Colin').

On the combined features of German Romanticism, F. Strich, *Deutsche Klassik und Romantik* (Munich, 1922; 2nd ed., 1924); J. Petersen, *Die Wesensbestimmung der deutschen Romantik* (Leipzig, 1926).

On the early German Romantics, F. Rouge, *Frédéric Schlegel et la genèse du romantisme allemand, 1791–1797* (Paris, 1904); J. E. Spenlé, *Novalis* (Paris, 1906), and *Rahel. Histoire d'un salon romantique en Allemagne* (Paris, 1910); A. Schlagdenhaufen, *Schlegel et son groupe. La doctrine de l'Atheneum, 1798–1800* (Strasbourg, 1934, Vol. 64 in 'Publications de la Faculté des Lettres de

Bibliography

Strasbourg'); R. Minder, *Ludwig Tieck* (Paris, 1936, Vol. 72 in 'Publications de la Faculté des Lettres de Strasbourg').

On English Romantics, see É. Legouis, *La jeunesse de Wordsworth* (Paris, 1897); C. Cestre, *La Révolution et les poètes anglais* (Paris, 1906); P. Berger, *William Blake* (Paris, 1907); J. M. Middleton, *William Blake* (London, 1933); J. Aynard, *Coleridge* (Paris, 1907); J. H. Muirhead, *Coleridge as Philosopher* (London, 1930); R. Huchon, *George Crabbe* (Paris, 1907).

On Romanticism in France, A. Monglond, *Histoire intérieure du pré-romantisme français de l'abbé Prévost à Joubert*, 2 vols. (Paris, 1929); P. Van Tieghem, *Ossian en France*, 2 vols. (Paris, 1917). For a regional study, see L. Trénard, *Histoire sociale des idées. Lyon, de l'Encyclopédie au Préromantisme*, 2 vols. (Paris, 1958).

On the counter-revolution, see J. Morley, *Edmund Burke* (London, 1898); B. Newman, *Edmund Burke* (London, 1927); A. Cobban, *Edmund Burke and the Revolt against the Eighteenth Century* (London, 1929); F. Braune, *Edmund Burke in Deutschland* (Heidelberg, 1917, Vol. 50 in 'Heidelberg Abhandlungen zur mittleren und neueren Geschichte'); G. Krüger, 'Die Eudämonisten' in Vol. CXLIII of *Historische Zeitschrift* (1930), pp. 467–500; A. Robinet de Cléry, *Frédéric de Gentz* (Paris, 1917); E. Guglia, *Friedrich von Gentz* (Vienna, 1901); preferably, see P. R. Sweet, *Friedrich von Gentz, Defender of the Old Order* (Madison, Wisconsin, 1941); H. Moulinié, *Bonald* (Paris, 1915); P. Rohden, *Joseph de Maistre als politischer Theoretiker* (Munich, 1929); also see J. de Maistre, *Des constitutions politiques et autres institutions humaines*, critical edition by R. Triomphe (Strasbourg–Paris, 1959, 'Publications de la Faculté des Lettres de Strasbourg'); O. Karmin, *Sir Francis d'Ivernois* (Geneva and Paris, 1920); B. Mallet, *Mallet du Pan and the French Revolution* (London, 1902); N. Matteucci, *Jacques Mallet du Pan* (Naples, 1957); also by the same author, 'Mallet du Pan, genevois et européen' in *Bulletin de la Société d'histoire et d'archéologie de Genève*, 1957, Vol. XI, pp. 153–68; M. Moechli-Cellier, *La Révolution française et les écrivains suisses-romands* (Paris, 1931); F. Baldensperger, *Le mouvement des idées dans l'émigration française*, 2 vols. (Paris, 1925); J. Godechot, *La contre-révolution. Doctrine et action, 1789–1804* (Paris, 1961).

On rationalist thought, F. Picavet, *Les idéologues* (Paris, 1890); É. Halévy, *La formation du radicalisme philosophique*, Vol. II (Paris, 1901); and on the sciences, see Vols. XIV and XV of *Histoire de la nation française*, published under the direction of G. Hanotaux: *Histoire des sciences en France*, 2 vols. (Paris, 1924); *Histoire générale des sciences*, R. Taton, ed., Vol. II (Paris, 1958). Also see Evanson, pp. 57–59.

On Freemasonry and on theosophy, see Evanson, pp. 54–57.

On the religious renaissance, Abbé F. Mourret, *Histoire générale de l'Église*, Vol. VII (Paris, 1913); W. Dilthey, *Leben Schleiermachers* (Berlin, 1870); F. Lichtenberger, *Histoire des idées religieuses en Allemagne depuis le milieu du XVIIIᵉ siècle*, 3 vols. (Paris, 1873), see Vol. I; G. Goyau, *L'Allemagne religieuse. Le catholicisme*, 4 vols. (Paris, 1905–1909), see Vol. I; P. Brachin, *Le cercle de Munster (1779–1801) et la pensée religieuse de F. A. Stolberg* (Paris, 1950, typewritten thesis); É. Halévy, *Histoire du peuple anglais*, Vol. I: *L'Angleterre en 1815* (Paris, 1913), Eng. tr. by E. I. Watkin and D. A.

Bibliography

Barker, *A History of the English People in the Nineteenth Century*, Vol. I (New York, 1949); P. Pierling, *La Russie et le Saint-Siège* (Paris, 1912); M. de Taube, 'Le tsar Paul I et l'ordre de Malte en Russie' in *Revue d'histoire moderne*, 1930, pp. 161–77; P. de La Gorce, *Histoire religieuse de la Révolution française*, Vol. III (Paris, 1919); A. Latreille, *L'Église catholique et la Révolution française*, Vol. I: *Le pontificat de Pie VI et la crise française, 1775–1799* (Paris, 1946); also see bibliography in Vol. II (Paris, 1950); Chanoine J. Leflon, *La crise révolutionnaire, 1789–1846*, Vol. XX of *Histoire de l'Église*, published under the direction of A. Fliche and V. Martin (Paris, 1949); J. Leflon, *Monsieur Émery*, Vol. I: *L'Église d'Ancien Régime et la Révolution* (Paris, 1944). Also see Evanson, pp. 54–57; A. Latreille, J.-R. Palanque, E. Delaruelle, R. Rémond, *Histoire du catholicisme en France*, Vol. III: *La période contemporaine* (Paris, 1962).

On the arts, see *Histoire générale de l'art*, published under the direction of André Michel, Vol. VIII, Pt. I (Paris, 1926); P. Lavedan, *Histoire de l'art*, Vol. II: *Moyen Age et temps modernes* (Paris, 1944, in the collection 'Clio', Vol. X); F. Benoit, *L'art français pendant la Révolution et l'Empire* (Paris, 1897); J. Combarieu, *Histoire de la musique*, Vol. II (Paris, 1913; 2nd ed., 1919); Romain Rolland, *Beethoven*, 2 vols. (Paris, 1929). Also see Evanson, pp. 67–70.

THE AWAKENING OF NATIONALITIES

See Evanson, pp. 70–72, 306, and Stewart, pp. 328–40, 394; F. Schnabel, *Deutsche Geschichte in neunzehnten Jahrhundert*, Vol. I (Freiburg-im-Breisgau, 1929; 4th ed., 1949); F. Meinecke, *Weltbürgertum und Nationalstaat* (Berlin, 1908; 4th ed., 1917), and *Geschichte des Historismus im XVIII^ten und XIX^ten Jahrhundert*, 2 vols. (Berlin, 1927); O. Vossler, *Der Nationalgedank von Rousseau bis Ranke* (Munich and Berlin, 1937); O. Tschirch, *Geschichte der öffentlichen Meinung in Preussen im Friedensjahrzehnt vom Basler Frieden bis zum Zusammenbruch des Staates*, 2 vols. (Weimar, 1933); R. Reinhold Ergang, *Herder and the Foundation of German Nationalism* (New York, 1931, Vol. 341 in 'Publications of the Columbia University'); J. Godechot, *La Grande Nation. L'expansion révolutionnaire de la France dans le monde, 1789–1804*, 2 vols. (Paris, 1956); A. Soboul, 'De l'Ancien Régime à l'Empire: problème national et réalités sociales' in *L'Information historique*, 1960, nos. 2 and 3.

Chapter II. The Consequences of the War and the Terms of the Peace

General works: H. von Sybel, *Geschichte der Revolutionszeit*, 5 vols. (Düsseldorf, 1853–1879), Eng. tr. by W. C. Perry, *History of the French Revolution*, 4 vols. (Leipzig, 1867–1869), Fr. tr. by Mlle Dosquet, *Histoire de l'Europe pendant la Révolution française*, 6 vols. (Paris, 1869–1888); A. Sorel, *L'Europe et la Révolution française*, 8 vols. (Paris, 1885–1904); A. Wahl, *Geschichte des europäischen Staatensystems im Zeitalter der französischen Revolution und der Freiheitskriege* (Munich and Berlin, 1912, in the collection 'Handbuch der mittelalterlichen und neueren Geschichte' under the general editorship of G. von Below and F. Meinecke); Émile Bourgeois, *Manuel historique de politique*

Bibliography

étrangère, Vol. II (Paris, 1900; 6th ed., 1920); R. Guyot, *Le Directoire et la paix de l'Europe* (Paris, 1911); H. Fugier, *La Révolution française et l'Empire napoléonien* (Paris, 1954), Vol. IV of *l'Histoire des relations internationales*, P. Renouvin, ed.; J. Godechot, *La Grande Nation. L'expansion révolutionnaire de la France dans le monde, 1789–1804*, 2 vols. (Paris, 1956).

THE CONTINENTAL POWERS

See Evanson, pp. 72–78 and 91–93, and corresponding bibliographies on pp. 307–9 and 311–12; see Stewart, pp. 322–25, and corresponding bibliography on p. 393.

Also see L. Häeusser, *Deutsche Geschichte vom Tode Friedrichs des Grossen bis zur Gründung des Bundes, 1786–1815*, 4 vols. (Berlin, 1854–1857; 4th ed., 1869); K. von Heigel, *Deutsche Geschichte vom Tode Friedrichs des Grossen bis zur Auflösung des alten Reiches*, 2 vols. (Stuttgart, 1899–1911, Vols. X and XI in 'Bibliothek deutscher Geschichte', published under the direction of H. von Zwiedineck-Südenhorst); *Die französiche Kriege und Deutschland 1792 bis 1815* (Berlin, 1958), a collective work; J. Streisand, *Deutschland, 1789–1815* (Berlin, 1959; *Lehrbuch der deutschen Geschichte*, published by Prof. Dr. Meusel, Vol.V); M. Philippson, *Geschichte des preussischen Staatswesens vom Tode Friedrichs des Grossen bis zu den Freiheitskriegen*, 2 vols. (Leipzig, 1880–1882), unfinished, stops with the death of Frederick William II; P. Bailleu, *Preussen und Frankreich von 1795 bis 1807. Diplomatische Correspondenz*, 2 vols. (Leipzig, 1881–1887, Vols. XXVIII and XXIX in 'Publikationen aus den klg. preussischen Staatsarchiven') with an introduction; W. Trummel, *Der norddeutsche Neutralitätsverband, 1795–1801* (Hildesheim, 1918, Vol. VII, fasc. 41 in 'Beiträge für die Geschichte Niedersachsens und Westfalens'); G. S. Ford, *Hanover and Prussia, 1795–1803* (New York, 1903); H. Brunschwig, *La crise de l'État prussien à la fin du XVIII siècle et la genèse de la mentalité romantique* (Paris, 1947); O. Tschirch, *Geschichte der öffentlichen Meinung in Preussen im Friedensjahrzehnt vom Basler Frieden bis zum Zusammenbruch des Staates*, 2 vols. (Weimar, 1933); F. Krones, *Handbuch der Geschichte Oesterreichs*, 5 vols. (Berlin, 1876–1879); K. and M. Urlisz, *Handbuch der Geschichte Oesterreichs und seiner Nachbarländer Böhmen und Ungarn*, 3 vols. (Graz and Vienna, 1929); I. Beidtel, *Geschichte der oesterreichischen Staatsverwaltung*, 2 vols. (Innsbrück, 1896–1898); E. Wertheimer, *Geschichte Oesterreichs und Ungarns im ersten Jahrzehnt des XIX Jahrhunderts*, 2 vols. (Leipzig, 1884–1890); *Histoire de Russie*, published under the direction of C. Seignobos, P. Miliukov, and L. Eisenmann, see Vol. II (Paris, 1933); V. Gitermann, *Geschichte Russlands*, Vol. II (Zurich, 1947); N. Kirchner, *Geschichte Russlands* (Stuttgart, 1950); K. Waliszewski, *Catherine II* (Paris, 1893), and *Le fils de la grande Catherine: Paul I* (Paris, 1912); N. Iorga, *Geschichte des osmanischen Reiches*, Vol. V (Gotha, 1913, Vol. 37 in 'Geschichte der europäischen Staaten' founded by Heeren and Ukert).

THE ENGLISH WAR EFFORT

W. Hunt, *Political History of England from the Accession of George III to the Close of Pitt's First Administration* (London, 1905, Vol. X in *Political History of England*, published under the general editorship of W. Hunt and R. L. Poole); Sir C. G. Robertson, *A History of England under the Hanoverians*

Bibliography

(London, 1911; 17th ed., 1958, Vol. VI in *History of England*, founder editor, Sir C. Oman); J. S. Watson, *The Reign of George III, 1760–1815* (Oxford, 1960), Vol. XII of *The Oxford History of England*; D. G. Barnes, *George III and William Pitt, 1783–1806* (Stanford, Calif., 1939); J. Dechamps, *Entre la guerre et la paix. Les Iles britanniques et la Révolution française, 1789–1803* (Brussels, 1949); J. Holland Rose, *Pitt and the Great War* (London, 1911); A. Bryant, *Years of Endurance, 1793–1802* (London, 1942); A. W. Ward and G. P. Gooch, *The Cambridge History of British Foreign Policy* (Cambridge, 1922–1923), see Vol. I; R. W. Seton-Watson, *Britain in Europe, 1789–1914* (Cambridge, 1937); A. T. Mahan, *The Influence of Sea Power upon the French Revolution and Empire*, 2 vols. (London, 1892); W. James, *The Naval History of Great Britain* (London, 1824, 5 vols.; new ed., 1886, 6 vols.); J. W. Fortescue, *History of the British Army*, 12 vols. (London, 1899–1938), Vol. IV; H. McAnally, *The Irish Militia* (Dublin and London, 1949); É. Halévy, *Histoire du peuple anglais*, Vol. I: *L'Angleterre en 1815* (Paris, 1913), Eng. tr. by E. I. Watkin and D. A. Barker, *A History of the English People in the Nineteenth Century*, Vol. I (New York, 1949); A. F. Freemantle, *England in the Nineteenth Century*, 2 vols. (London, 1929–1930), see Vols. I and II for the years 1801–1810; J. Tramond, *Manuel d'histoire maritime de la France des origines à 1815* (Paris, 1912; 3rd ed., 1947).

FRANCE AND HER ALLIES

For the history of the Directory, see Stewart, pp. 167–360, and corresponding bibliographies on pp. 378–95. Also, J. Godechot, *Les institutions de la France sous la Révolution et l'Empire* (Paris, 1951, in 'Histoire des institutions', published under the direction of L. Halphen).

On economic and social history, consult H. Sée, *Französische Wirtschaftsgeschichte*, 2 vols. (Jena, 1936, in 'Handbuch der Wirtschaftsgeschichte', G. Brodnitz, ed.), see Vol. II, Fr. tr. with bibliographies by R. Schnerb: *Histoire économique de la France*, 2 vols. (Paris, 1939–1942); M. Marion, *Histoire financière de la France depuis 1715*, 6 vols. (Paris, 1914–1931), see Vols. III and IV; P. Sagnac, *La législation civile de la Révolution française (1789–1804)* (Paris, 1898), and 'La division du sol pendant la Révolution et ses conséquences' in *Revue d'histoire moderne et contemporaine*, Vol. V (1903–1904), pp. 456–70; G. Lefebvre, *Les paysans du Nord pendant la Révolution française*, 2 vols. (Lille, 1924: 2nd ed. with statistical appendix abridged); G. Lefebvre, 'La place de la Révolution dans l'histoire agraire de la France' in *Annales d'histoire économique et sociale* (1929), pp. 506–23, and 'La Révolution française et les paysans' in *Annales historiques de la Révolution française* (1933), pp. 97–128, in *Cahiers de la Révolution française* (1934), pp. 7–49, and in *Études sur la Révolution française* (Paris, 1954; 2nd ed., 1963); R. Laurent, *Les vignerons de la Côte-d'Or au XIX siècle*, 2 vols. (Paris, 1958; Vol. XIV of 'Publications de l'Université de Dijon'); P. Bois, *Paysans de l'Ouest. Des structures économiques et sociales aux options politiques depuis l'époque révolutionnaire dans la Sarthe* (Le Mans, 1960); E. Levasseur, *Histoire des classes ouvrières et de l'industrie en France depuis 1789 jusqu'à nos jours*, 2 vols. (Paris, 1862; 2nd rev. ed., 1903), and *Histoire du commerce en France*, Vol. II (Paris, 1912); P. Chauvet, *Les ouvriers du livre en France, de 1789 à la constitution de la Fédération du Livre* (Paris, 1956); L. Chevallier, *Classes laborieuses et classes dangereuses* (Paris, 1958; describes the situation in Paris); C. Ballot, *L'introduction du machinisme dans l'industrie française* (Lille, 1923, Vol. IX of 'Comité des travaux historiques: notices, inventaires et documents'); T. S. Ashton, *La révolution industrielle, 1760–1830* (Paris, 1955); F. Ponteil, *La situation économique du Bas-Rhin au lendemain de la Révolution française* (Strasbourg, 1927, Vol. III in the 'Collection d'études sur l'histoire du droit et des institutions de l'Alsace, publiée par les Facultés de droit et des lettres de Strasbourg'); P. Léon, *La naissance de la grande industrie en Dauphiné (fin du XVII siècle—1869,)* 2 vols. (Paris, 1954).

On the movement of prices, see F. Simiand, *Recherches anciennes et nouvelles sur le mouvement général des prix du XVIe au XIXe siècle* (Paris, 1931), and *Le salaire, l'évolution sociale et la monnaie*, 3 vols. (Paris, 1932), applies only to France; A. Chabert, *Essai sur le mouvement des prix et des revenus en France de 1798 à 1820*, 2 vols. (Paris, 1945 and 1949); R. Schnerb, 'La dépression économique sous le Directoire' in *Annales historique de la Révolution française*, 1934, pp. 27–49.

On the history of the 'départements réunis', see H. Pirenne, *Histoire de Belgique*, 6 vols. (Brussels, 1900–1926), Vol. V; P. Verhaegen, *La Belgique sous la domination française, 1792–1814*, 5 vols. (Brussels, 1922–1929), Vols. IV and V on the Consulate and Empire; for a recent bibliography of the period, see P. Gérin, *Bibliographie de l'histoire de Belgique, 1789–21 juillet 1831* (Louvain-Paris, 1960; cahier no. 15 of 'Centre universitaire d'histoire contemporaine'); P. Sagnac, *Le Rhin français pendant la Révolution et l'Empire* (Paris, 1917), with a bibliography; A. Conrady, *Die Rheinlande unter die französische Herrschaft* (Bonn, 1922); M. Springer, *Die Franzosenherrschaft in der Pfalz, 1782–1814* (Stuttgart, 1926); E. Chapuisat, *Genève et la Révolution française* (Geneva, 1912) and *L'influence de la Révolution française sur la Suisse*; *le département du Léman* (Paris, 1934, fasc. 2 of *Cahiers de la Révolution française*, published by the 'Centre d'études de la Révolution'), contains a bibliography.

On France's allies, see H. F. Colenbrander, *Gedenstukken der algemeene Geschiedenis van Nederland van 1785 tot 1840*, Vol. I: *Introduction: Nederland en de Revolution, 1789–1795*, Vols. II and III: *1795–1801* (The Hague, 1905–1907, 4 vols.), containing a great many new documents which have not yet been made the object of a proper study; P. Blok, *Geschiedenis van het nederlandsche volk*, Vol. VII (Groningen, 1892–1908, 8 vols.; 3rd ed., enlarged, Leyden, 1923–1926, 4 vols.), Ger. tr., *Geschichte der Niederlande*, Vol. VII (Gotha, 1925, in 'Geschichte der europäischen Staaten', founded by Heeren and Ukert), Eng. tr., *History of the People of the Netherlands*, 5 vols. (New York, 1898–1912); L. Legrand, *La Révolution française en Hollande* (Paris, 1894); A. Pingaud, *Bonaparte président de la République italienne*, 2 vols. (Paris, 1914), see Vol. I; St. Canzio, *La prima republica cisalpina e il sentimento nazionale italiano* (Modena, 1944, Vol. 33 in 'Collezione storica del Risorgimento italiano'); M. Roberti, *Milano capitale napoleonica; la formazione di un stato moderno, 1796–1814*, 3 vols. (Milan, 1946–1947); G. Candeloro, *Storia dell'Italia moderna*, Vol. I: *Le origini del Risorgimento (1700–1815)* (Milan, 1956); L. Dal Pane, *Storia del lavoro in Italia dagli inizi del secolo XVIII al 1815* (Milan, 2nd ed., 1958; Vol. IV of *Storia del lavoro in Italia*, A. Fanfani, ed.); G. Vaccarino, 'Da Vittorio Amedeo III al congresso di Vienna' in *Storia del Piemonte*, pp. 245–71 (Turin, 1960); E. His, *Geschichte des neueren schweizerischen Staatsrechtes*,

Bibliography

Vol. I: *1798–1803* (Basel, 1920); W. Oechsli, *Geschichte der Schweiz im XIX Jahrhundert*, Vols. I and II: *1798–1830* (Leipzig, 1903–1913, 2 vols.); A. Rufer, *Pestalozzi, die französische Revolution und die Helvetik* (Bern, 1928); H. Schenkel, *Die Bemühungen der helvetischen Regierung um die Ablösung der Grundlasten, 1798–1803* (Affoltern a. A., 1931); M. Salamin, *Histoire politique du Valais sous la République helvétique (1798–1802)* (Sierre, 1957; extract from *Vallesia*, Vol. XII); R. Altamira, *Historia de la nación y de la civilisación española*, 4 vols. (Barcelona, 1906–1911; 5th ed., 1935), Vol. IV; A. Muriel, *Historia de Carlos IV*, 6 vols. (Madrid, 1893–1895, Vols. 29–34 of *Memorial histórico español*, published by the Royal Academy of History); R. Herr, *The Eighteenth Century Revolution in Spain* (Princeton, 1958); M. Defourneaux, *Pablo de Olavide ou l'Afrancesado (1725–1803)* (Paris, 1959); G. Demerson, *Don Juan Meléndez Valdés et son temps (1754–1817)* (Paris, 1962); P. Vilar, *La Catalogne dans l'Espagne moderne. Recherches sur les fondements économiques des structures nationales*, 3 vols. (Paris, 1962); A. Fugier, *Napoléon et l'Espagne*, 2 vols. (Paris, 1930), Vol. I, introduction; also, by the same author, *Napoléon et l'Italie* (Paris, 1947).

THE BLOCKADE AND THE NEUTRALS

See A. T. Mahan, *The Influence of Sea Power upon the French Revolution and Empire*, 2 vols. (London, 1892); E. F. Hecksher, *The Continental System* (Oxford, 1922); L. Amé, *Étude économique sur les tarifs de douane et les traités de commerce* (Paris, 1860); W. Freeman Galpin, *The Grain Supply of England during the Napoleonic Period* (New York, 1925, Vol. VI in 'Publications of the University of Michigan, History and Political Sciences'); R. G. Albion, *Forests and Sea Power; the Timber Power of the Royal Navy, 1652–1862* (Cambridge, Mass., 1926, No. 29 in 'Harvard Economic Studies'); J. Holland Rose, 'British West India Commerce as a Factor in the Napoleonic Wars' in *The Cambridge Historical Journal*, Vol. 3 (1929), pp. 34–46; J. Kulischer, *Russische Wirtschaftsgeschichte* (Jena, 1925, in 'Handbuch der Wirtschaftsgeschichte', G. Brodnitz, ed.); E. Baasch, *Holländische Wirtschaftsgeschichte* (Jena, 1925); A. Nielsen, *Dänische Wirtschaftsgeschichte* (Jena, 1933); J. B. Manger, *Recherches sur les relations économiques de la France et de la Hollande pendant la Révolution française* (Paris, 1923); J. G. Büsch, *Geschichtliche Beurteilung der am Ende des XVIII Jahrhunderts enstandenen grosses Handelsverwirrung* (Hamburg, 1800); A. Wohlwill, *Neuere Geschichte der Freien und Hansestadt Hamburg, inbesondere von 1789 bis 1815* (Gotha, 1914); R. Ehrenberg, *Grossen Vermögen, ihre Entstehung und ihre Bedeutung* (Jena, 1902), on the banking houses of Hope and of Parish; K. von Eichborn, *Das Soll und Haben von Eichborn und C° in 200 Jahren* (Leipzig, 1928), for Silesia; A. Dietz, *Frankfurter Handelsgeschichte*, Vol. V (Frankfurt, 1910), stops in 1792; E. Hasse, *Geschichte der Leipziger Messen* (Leipzig, 1885); E. Gothein, *Geschichtliche Entwickelung der Rheinschiffahrt im XIX Jahrhundert* (Leipzig, 1903, No. 101 in 'Schriften des Vereins für Sozialpolitik'); A. König, *Die sächsische Baumwollenindustrie am Ende des vorigen Jahrhunderts und während der Kontinentalsperre* (Leipzig, 1899, fasc. 3 of 'Leipziger Studien auf dem Gebiete der Geschichte', Buchholtz, Lamprecht, Marcks, and Seelinger, eds., Vol. V); E. Buron, 'Statistics on Franco-American Trade, 1778–1806' in *The Journal of Economic and*

Bibliography

Business History, 1932, pp. 571–80; S. E. Morison and H. S. Commager, *The Growth of the American Republic*, Vol. I (New York, 1930; 4th ed. rev., 1950); S. M. Bemis, *A Diplomatic History of the United States* (New York, 1936; rev. ed., 1950); H. Adams, *History of the United States*, 9 vols. (New York, 1890–1917), Vols. I and II; E. Channing, *History of the United States*, 6 vols. (New York, 1905–1925), see Vol. IV: 1789–1815.

For France, see works cited above in Pt. I, Ch. II, sec. 2.

THE STRENGTH AND DANGERS OF BRITISH CAPITALISM. EUROPEAN EXPANSION IN THE WORLD

See bibliographical references in Evanson, pp. 291–96, 300–1 (sections entitled 'British Society' and 'The Proletariat'), and in Stewart, p. 395. Also see works by Hecksher, Galpin, and Albion cited at the beginning of the preceding section, 'The Blockade and the Neutrals'.

For British finances, see J. Clapham, *The Bank of England*, 2 vols. (Cambridge, 1944); on the subject of private banks, there are several pages on the beginnings of Baring in R. W. Hidy, *The House of Baring in American Trade and Finance, 1763–1861* (Cambridge, Mass., 1949, No. 14 in 'Harvard Studies in Business History'); R. G. Hawtrey, *Currency and Credit* (London, 1919); see especially the outstanding studies by N. J. Siberling, 'Financial and Monetary Policy of Great Britain during the Napoleonic Wars' in *Quarterly Journal of Economics*, Vol. 38 (1924), pp. 214–333 and 397–439; A. Hope-Jones, *Income Tax in the Napoleonic Wars* (Cambridge, 1939); W. Smart, *Economic Annals of the Nineteenth Century, 1801–1820*, 2 vols. (London, 1910).

On prices, N. J. Siberling, 'British Prices and Business Cycles, 1779–1850' in *Review of Economics and Statistics*, Vol. V (1923), pp. 223–61, uses an index of 100 for the year 1790; Elizabeth Schumpeter, 'English Prices and Public Finance, 1660–1822', *ibid.*, Vol. 20 (1938), pp. 21–99, uses an index of 100 for the year 1700; W. B. Smith, 'Wholesale Commodity Prices in the United States, 1795–1824', *ibid.*, 1927, pp. 171–83.

On the economic and social development of Great Britain, P. Mantoux, *La révolution industrielle en Angleterre* (Paris, 1905; 2nd ed., 1959, the text corresponds to the English edition revised by the author, with a bibliographical supplement by A. Bourde), Eng. tr. by M. Vernon, *The Industrial Revolution in the Eighteenth Century* (London, 1928); T. S. Ashton, *The Industrial Revolution, 1760–1830* (Oxford, 1948; Fr. tr., Paris, 1955) and *An Economic History of England. The Eighteenth Century* (London, 1955); J. Clapham, *An Economic History of Modern Britain*, Vol. I: *The Early Railway Age, 1820–1830* (Cambridge, 1926; 2nd ed., 1930), provides much information on the preceding period; H. D. Gayer, W. W. Rostow, A. J. Schwartz, and I. Frank, *The Growth and Fluctuations of the British Economy, 1790–1850. An Historical, Statistical and Theoretical Study of Britain's Economic Development*, 2 vols. (Oxford, 1953).

On agricultural history, see Lord Earle (before 1919, R. E. Prothero), *English Farming Past and Present* (London, 1912; 5th ed. published by A. D. Hall, 1936); W. Curtler, *The Enclosure and Redistribution of Land* (Oxford, 1920); E. Davies, 'The Small Landowner, 1780–1832' in *The Economic History Review*, Vol. I (1927), pp. 87–113; D. Grove Barnes, *A History of the English Corn Laws, 1660–1846* (New York, 1930); J. L. and B. Hammond,

Bibliography

The Village Labourer, 1760–1832 (London, 1911), *The Town Labourer* (London, 1917), and *The Skilled Labourer* (London, 1919); C. R. Fay, *Great Britain from Adam Smith to the Present Day* (London, 1928); E. Cannan, *A History of the Theories of Production and Distribution in English Political Economy from 1776 to 1848* (London, 1893).

For British trade, see W. Schlöte, *Entwicklung und Strukturwandlungen des englischen Aussenhandels von 1700 bis zur Gegenwart* (Jena, 1938), Eng. tr. by O. Henderson and W. H. Chaloner, *British Overseas Trade from 1700 to the 1930's* (Oxford, 1952); see especially A. H. Imlah, 'Real Values in British Foreign Trade' in *The Journal of Economic History*, Vol. VIII, 1948, pp. 133–52.

Our statistical knowledge of exports and imports for Great Britain derives from valuations of the customhouse, based on a scale of prices prevailing at the end of the seventeenth and at the beginning of the eighteenth century. Consequently these 'official values' do not correspond exactly with 'real values'. A. H. Imlah has worked out the 'real values' for importations, exportations, and re-exportations, but he was able to do this beginning with 1798 only. He concluded that with very rare exceptions, Great Britain's balance of trade was adverse, contrary to current opinion. For a critical comparison of studies by Gayer, Schlöte, and Imlah, see F. Crouzet, *L'économie britannique et le blocus continental, 1806–1813*, 2 vols. (Paris, 1958).

On the British Empire and European expansion, see *The Cambridge History of the British Empire*, Vol. II: *The Growth of the New Empire, 1783–1870* (Cambridge, 1940), Vol. IV: *British India, 1497–1858* (1929; also appeared as Vol. V of *The Cambridge History of India*), Vol. VI: *Canada and Newfoundland* (1930), Vol. VII: *Australia and New Zealand* (1933); V. A. Smith, *The Oxford History of India* (Oxford, 1919; 2nd ed., 1923); C. H. Philips, *The East India Company, 1784–1834* (Manchester, 1940); C. Northcote Parkinson, *Trade in the Eastern Seas, 1793–1813* (Cambridge, Mass., 1937), and *The Trade Winds. A Study of British Overseas Trade during the French Wars, 1793–1815* (London, 1948); J. W. Fortescue, *History of the British Army*, 12 vols. (London, 1899–1938), Vol. V; W. J. Gardner, *History of Jamaica* (London, 1873; 2nd ed., 1909).

For the Portuguese, Spanish, and Dutch colonies, see Evanson, pp. 288–290; for discoveries, *ibid.*, p. 287; for foreign civilizations, *ibid.*, pp. 290–91. Also see H. Cordier, *Histoire générale de la Chine et de ses rapports avec l'étranger*, Vol. III (Paris, 1920); C. B. Maybon, *Histoire moderne du pays d'Annam* (Paris, 1919); J. Murdoch and J. Yamagata, *History of Japan*, 3 vols. (London, 1925), Vol. III.

For missions, F. Mourret, *Histoire générale de l'Église*, Vol. VII (Paris, 1913); J. Leflon, *La crise révolutionaire, 1789–1846*, Vol. XX of *Histoire de l'Église*, published under the direction of A. Fliche and V. Martin (Paris, 1949); J. Schmidlin, *Katholische Missionsgeschichte* (Steyl, 1924), containing an appendix on Protestant missions; R. Lovett, *The History of the London Missionary Society*, 2 vols. (London, 1899); E. Stock, *The History of the Church Missionary Society*, 3 vols. (London, 1899); E. Descamps, *Histoire générale et comparée des missions* (Brussels and Paris, 1932).

For the United States, see works by H. Adams and E. Channing cited at the bottom of the preceding section, 'The Blockade and the Neutrals'.

Bibliography

Also see Thurman W. Van Metre, *Economic History of the United States* (London, 1925); L. C. Gray, *History of Agriculture in the Southern United States to 1860*, 2 vols. (Washington, 1933); K. W. Porter, *John Jacob Astor Businessman*, 2 vols. (Cambridge, Mass., 1931, Vols. I and II of 'Harvard Studies in Business History'); J. B. MacMaster, *The Life and Times of Stephen Girard, Mariner and Merchant*, 2 vols. (Philadelphia, 1918).

England's difficulties are generally seen in the light of her struggle with France, as though the internal crises of capitalism and the clash of interests which could have brought Great Britain in conflict with the other powers were of no account.

THE TERMS OF THE PEACE

See 'general works' cited for Chapter II above and titles listed in the section 'France and her Allies' in the present chapter.

Chapter III. The Coming of Napoleon Bonaparte

THE DICTATORSHIP IN FRANCE

See Stewart, pp. 252–56 and 316–17, and corresponding bibliographies on pp. 388–89 and 393. In addition, see A. Vandal, *L'avènement de Bonaparte*, Vol. I: *La genèse du Consulat, Brumaire* (Paris, 1903); A. Meynier, *Les coups d'État du Directoire*, Vol. III: *Le 18 brumaire an VIII* (Paris, 1928).

NAPOLEON BONAPARTE

For the origins of the Bonaparte family, see F. Pomponi, *Essai sur les notables ruraux en Corse au XVII siècle* (Aix-en-Provence, 1962, publication No. XX of 'Annales de la Faculté des Lettres d'Aix-en-Provence').

On the early career of Bonaparte, see Stewart, pp. 167–256, particularly 183–85, and corresponding bibliographies in the relevant sections, pp. 378–389. Also see F. Masson and G. Biagi, *Napoléon inconnu*, 2 vols. (Paris, 1895); A. Chuquet, *La jeunesse de Napoléon*, 3 vols. (Paris, 1897–1899); V. Marcaggi, *La genèse de Napoléon* (Paris, 1902).

On his private life, A. Cabanès, *Au chevet de l'Empereur* (Paris, 1924), and *Dans l'intimité de l'Empereur* (Paris, 1924); Arthur-Lévy, *Napoléon intime* (Paris, 1893); F. Masson, *Napoléon et les femmes* (Paris, 1893); F. Masson, *Napoléon chez lui; la journée de l'Empereur* (Paris, 1894).

On the relations of Napoleon to his family and intimates, see the relevant works cited below under Pt. II, Ch. IV, sec. 2, and also the works listed in G. Lefebvre, *Napoléon* (Paris, 1935, 5th ed., 1965), Pt. IV, Ch. II, sec. 5, 'Le mariage autrichien' (p. 314, 5th ed.) and Pt. V, Ch. II, sec. 1, 'L'organisation politique du système (p. 435, 5th ed.). See also A. Decaux, *Laetizia, mère de l'empereur* (Paris, 1959).

The best way to get to know Napoleon is to read the *Correspondance de l'empereur Napoléon Ier*, 28 vols. (Paris, 1858–1869), published by order of Napoleon III, followed by 4 vols. (XXIX–XXXII) containing the writings of Napoleon at St. Helena (1870). This collection is incomplete, and has since been supplemented by the appearance of several other collections of letters, particularly: L. Lecestre, *Lettres inédites de Napoléon Ier, 1799–1815*,

Bibliography

2 vols. (Paris, 1897); L. de Brotonne, *Lettres inédites de Napoléon I*ᵉʳ (Paris, 1898) and *Dernière lettres inédites de Napoléon I*ᵉʳ (Paris, 1903); E. Picard and A. Tuetey, *Correspondance inédite de Napoléon I*ᵉʳ *conservée aux Archives de la Guerre*, 4 vols. (Paris, 1912–1913, publication of the 'Section historique de l'État-Major'); A. Chuquet, *Ordres et apostilles de Napoléon*, 4 vols. (Paris, 1911–1912); *Lettres de Napoléon à Joséphine et lettres de Joséphine à Napoléon* (Paris, 1959); *Lettres inédites de Napoléon I*ᵉʳ *à Marie-Louise écrites de 1810 à 1814*, L. Madelin, ed. (Paris, 1935); *Marie-Louise et Napoléon. Lettres inédites (1813–1814)*, collected by C. F. Palmstierna, with commentaries (Paris, 1955), replies to the letters of Napoleon published in 1935 and fortunately re-edited in this volume.

The memoirs relate many characteristic utterances of the Emperor. The most trustworthy appear to be the following: A. C. Thibaudeau, *Mémoires sur le Consulat*, 2 vols. (Paris, 1826); J. A. Chaptal, *Mes souvenirs sur Napoléon* (Paris, 1893); P. L. Roederer, *Journal* (Paris, 1909); C. F. de Méneval, *Mémoires*, 3 vols. (Paris, 1894; Eng. tr., London, 1894–1895) and A. J. F. Fain, *Mémoires* (Paris, 1909), both of whom were secretaries of Napoleon; F. N. Mollien, *Mémoires*, 4 vols. (Paris, 1837; 3 vols., 1898); H. de Noailles, *Le comte Molé*, Vol. I (Paris, 1922), fragments of Molé's *Mémoires*; A. A. L. de Caulaincourt, *Mémoires*, 3 vols. (Paris, 1933). The *Mémoires* of Mme C. E. J. de Rémusat, 3 vols. (Paris, 1879–1880), although famous, are hostile and unreliable (extracts in *Mémoires de Mme de Rémusat, 1802–1808*, Paris, 1957, with an important critical preface by C. Kunstler); Charles de Rémusat, *Mémoires de ma vie*, Vol. I: *Enfance et jeunesse, la Restauration libérale (1797–1820)*, introduced and annotated by Charles-H. Pouthas (Paris, 1958). Also see *Bourrienne, Bonaparte intime, tiré des 'Mémoires'* by B. Melchior–Bonnet (Paris, 1961).

There exist countless biographies of Napoleon. The most notable are: A. Fournier, *Napoleon I: eine Biographie*, 3 vols. (Vienna and Leipzig, 1886–1889; 2nd ed., 1904–1906; Fr. tr. by E. Jaeglé, incomplete, 2 vols., Paris, 1891–1892, and Eng. tr., London, 1911); J. Holland Rose, *The Life of Napoleon I*, 2 vols. (London, 1901; 11th ed., 1929, in one vol.); P. Lanfrey, *Histoire de Napoléon I*ᵉʳ, 5 vols. (Paris, 1867–1875), stops in 1810, penetrating but utterly lacking in good will. The more recent biographies are: É. Driault, *Napoléon le Grand*, 3 vols. (Paris, 1930); J. Bainville, *Napoléon* (Paris, 1931); F. Kircheisen, *Napoleon I: sein Leben und seine Zeit*, 9 vols. (Munich and Leipzig, 1911–1934), and *Napoleon I, ein Lebensbild*, 2 vols. (Stuttgart, 1927–1929); Fr. tr. by J. Guidau, *Napoléon. Une Vie*, 2 vols. Paris, 1934), Eng. tr.: *Napoleon* (New York, 1932); E. Tarlé, *Napoléon*, which is a French tr. of the Russian volume by C. Steber (Paris, 1937), Eng. tr. by J. Cournos: *Bonaparte* (London, 1937); J. M. Thompson, *Napoleon. His Rise and Fall* (Oxford, 1952); E. Tersen, *Napoléon* (Paris, 1959); L. Salvatorelli, *Leggenda e realtà di Napoleone* (Turin, 1960). One hesitates to class as a work of history the brilliant and celebrated psychological study, *Napoleon* (1924), by the German writer, Emil Ludwig.

On Napoleonic historiography in France, see the critical study by P. Geyl, *Napoleon voor an tegen de Franse Geschiedschryving* (Utrecht, 1946), Eng. tr. by Olive Renier: *Napoléon For and Against* (New Haven, Conn., 1949).

Bibliography

On Napoleonic historiography in England, see W. Moilahn, *Napoleon in der englischen Geschichtsschreibung von den Zeitgenossen bis zur Gegenwart* (Berlin, 1937).

PART TWO. THE PACIFICATION OF FRANCE AND EUROPE (1799–1802)

Chapter IV. The Organization of the Dictatorship in France

General works: First and foremost, see F. Kircheisen, *Bibliographie napoléonienne* (Berlin, 1902; 2nd ed., Paris, 1908–1912, 2 vols.), which is incomplete. Also see the general histories of the period and the biographies of Napoleon listed under general works at the beginning of Pt. I, Ch. I, in this volume, and in Pt. I, Ch. III, sec. 2, immediately above. In addition, on the Consulate, see F. A. Aulard, *Histoire politique de la Révolution française* (Paris, 1901; 5th ed., 1921), Pt. IV; A. Vandal, *L'avènement de Bonaparte*, Vol. II (Paris, 1905); L. de Lanzac de Laborie, *Paris sous Napoléon Ier*, Vol. I: *Le Consulat provisoire et le Consulat à temps* (Paris, 1905–1913, 8 vols.); G. Hanotaux, 'Du Consulat à l'Empire: issue napoléonienne de la Révolution' in *Revue des Deux Mondes*, 7th series, Vol. XXVI (1925), pp. 66–106, and 'Comment se fit l'Empire', *ibid.*, pp. 344–77, 573–609, 774–807; J. Godechot, *La contre-révolution. Doctrine et action, 1789–1804* (Paris, 1961).

THE PROVISIONAL CONSULATE AND THE CONSTITUTION OF YEAR VIII

See works listed immediately above.

On the preparation of the constitution, see the thesis by J. Bourdon, *La constitution de l'an VIII* (Rodez, 1941), which introduces new documents and presents original views.

On the constitution itself, see P. Poullet, *Les institutions française de 1795 à 1814* (Brussels and Paris, 1907); M. Deslandres, *Histoire constitutionelle de la France de 1789 à 1870*, Vol. I (Paris, 1932); J. Godechot, *Les institutions de la France sous la Révolution et l'Empire* (Paris, 1951); M. Duverger, *Constitutions et documents politiques* (Paris, 1957, coll. 'Thémis').

THE ORGANIZATION AND EXTENSION OF BONAPARTE'S POWERS

See works by Aulard, Vandal, Poullet, and Godechot cited at the beginning of this chapter under 'general works' and in the section immediately above.

On the organization of Bonaparte's work, see F. Masson, *Napoléon chez lui; la journée de l'Empereur* (Paris, 1894); A. J. F. Fain, *Mémoires* (Paris, 1909). Also see the studies by J. Bourdon on the central administration and on the Ministry of Justice in the works dealing with judicial reform cited below in this section.

On Bonaparte's collaborators, see P. Vialles, *L'archichancelier Cambacérès*

Bibliography

(Paris, 1908); F. Papillard, *Cambacérès* (Paris, 1961); J. Bourdon, 'Le rôle de Cambacérès sous le Consulat et l'Empire' in *Bulletin de la Société d'histoire moderne*, 1928, pp. 71–72; L. Madelin, *Fouché*, 2 vols. (Paris, 1901), and *Mémoires* of Fouché, which were re-edited and annotated by L. Madelin in 1945; G. Lacour-Gayet, *Talleyrand*, 3 vols. (Paris, 1930–1934). Vols. I and II; E. Tarlé, *Talleyrand* (Moscow, 1958); E. Dard, *Napoléon et Talleyrand* (Paris, 1935); A. A. Ernouf, *Maret, duc de Bassano* (Paris, 1878); J. Pigeire, *La vie et l'œuvre de Chaptal* (Paris, 1931).

On the Council of State, the basic work is now that of C. Durand, *Études sur le Conseil d'État napoléonien* (Paris, 1949); by the same author, *Le fonctionnement du Conseil d'État napoléonien* (Gap. 1954, Bibliothèque de l'Université d'Aix-Marseille, Droit-Lettres, no. 7), *Les auditeurs du Conseil d'État de 1803 à 1814* (Aix-en-Provence, 1958), *La fin du Conseil d'État napoléonien* (Aix-en-Provence, 1959, extract from *Annales de la Faculté de Droit d'Aix-en-Provence*, new series, no. 51); L. Aucoc, *Le Conseil d'État* (Paris, 1876); A. Gazier, 'Napoléon au Conseil d'État' in *Revue de Paris*, Vol. II (1903), pp. 160–74; A. Marquiset, *Napoléon sténographié au Conseil d'État* (Paris, 1913); J. Bourdon, *Napoléon au Conseil d'État. Notes et procès-verbaux inédits de Jean-Guillaume Locré, secrétaire général du Conseil d'État* (Paris, 1963); J. Pelet, *Opinions de Napoléon* (Paris, 1833; Eng. tr., Edinburgh, 1837); A. C. Thibaudeau, *Mémoires sur le Consulat*, 2 vols. (Paris, 1826); H. de Noailles, *Le comte Molé* (Paris, 1922), Eng. tr., *Life and Memoirs* (London, 1923).

On the organization and functions of the government powers, see C. Durand, *L'exercice de la fonction législative de 1800 à 1814*, and *Le régime de l'activité gouvernementale pendant les campagnes de Napoléon*, 2 vols. (Aix-en-Provence, 1955 and 1957, extracts from *Annales de la Faculté de Droit d'Aix-en-Provence*, nos. 48 and 49).

On the administrative work of the government, see F. Ponteil, *Napoléon I et l'organisation autoritaire de la France* (Paris, 1956, coll. 'A. Colin').

The general features of the Napoleonic administration are skilfully delineated by J. Bourdon, 'L'administration militaire sous Napoléon I et ses rapports avec l'administration générale' in *Revue des études napoléoniennes*, Vol. XI (1917), pp. 17–47. In addition, see A. Aulard, *La centralisation napoléonienne; les préfets*, in Vol. VII of his *Études et leçons* (Paris, 1913), pp. 113–95; J. Bourdon, 'L'administration communale sous le Consulat' in *Revue des études napoléoniennes*, Vol. V (1914), pp. 289–304, and 'Les conditions générales de nomination des fonctionnaires au début du Consulat' in the *Bulletin de la Société d'histoire moderne* (1931), pp. 31–33.

There exist several good monographs on the prefectural administration: L. Passy, *Frochot, préfet de la Seine* (Paris, 1867); E. Dejean, *Un préfet du Consulat: Beugnot* (Paris, 1897), on the administration of the Seine-Inférieure département; G. Saint-Yves and J. Fournier, *Le département des Bouches-du-Rhône de 1800 à 1810* (Paris, 1899); *Les Bouches-du-Rhône*, an encyclopedia published under the direction of P. Masson, Vol. V: *Vie politique et administrative* by R. Busquet and J. Fournier (Marseille, 1929); G. Chavanon and G. Saint-Yves, *Le Pas-de-Calais de 1800 à 1810* (Paris, 1907); P. Darmstädter, 'Die Verwaltung des Unter-Elsass [Bas-Rhin] unter Napoleon I' in *Zeitschrift für die Geschichte des Ober-Rheins*, Vol. XVIII (1903) pp. 283–330,

Bibliography

538–63, and Vol. XIX (1904), pp. 122–47, 284–309, 631–72; L. Pingaud, *Jean Debry* (Paris, 1909), on the administration of the département of Doubs; H. Parisot, 'De l'organisation départementale et communale par un préfet de la Meurthe (Marquis)' in *Annales de l'est et du nord*, 1908, pp. 399–412 and 578–91; P. Viard, *L'administration préfectorale dans le département de la Côte-d'Or sous le Consulat et l'Empire* (Lille, 1914); L. Benaerts, *Le régime consulaire en Bretagne; le département d'Ille-et-Vilaine durant le Consulat* (Paris, 1914); R. Durand, *L'administration des Côtes-du-Nord sous le Consulat et l'Empire*, 2 vols. (Paris, 1925), the only complete study; F. L'Huillier, *Recherches sur l'Alsace napoléonienne de brumaire à l'invasion* (Strasbourg, 1944); G. Rocal, *De brumaire à Waterloo, en Périgord*, 2 vols. (Paris, 1942); J. Godechot, 'Les premiers préfets de l'Aude' in *Actes du Congrès régional des Fédérations historiques du Languedoc* (Carcassonne, 1952). Much information will also be found in H. Contamine, *Metz et la Moselle de 1814 à 1870*, 2 vols. (Nancy, 1932).

On the organization of the central power, see also A. Outrey, 'L'administration française des Affaires étrangères' in *Revue française de science politique*, 1953 (separate reprint, Paris, 1954).

The reorganization of justice has been made the subject of a study by J. Bourdon, *La réforme judiciaire de l'an VIII*, and *Les premières nominations judiciaires*, 2 vols. (Rodez, 1941).

On the police, see L. Madelin, *Fouché*, 2 vols. (Paris, 1901); E. d'Hauterive, *Napoléon et sa police* (Paris, 1943).

For finances, see the excellent work by R. Stourm, *Les finances du Consulat* (Paris, 1902); F. N. Mollien, *Mémoires*, 4 vols. (Paris, 1837; 3 vols., 1898); M. M. C. Gaudin, *Mémoires, souvenirs, opinions et écrits*, 3 vols. (Paris, 1826–1834; new ed., 1926); M. Marion, *Histoire financière de la France depuis 1715*, 6 vols. (Paris, 1914–1931), see Vol. IV (1925); G. Ramon, *Histoire de la Banque de France* (Paris, 1929); C. Ballot, 'Les banques d'émission sous le Consulat' in *Revue des études napoléoniennes*, Vol. VII (1905), pp. 289–323; R. Bigo, *La Caisse d'escompte et les débuts de la Banque de France* (Paris, 1927), and *Les origines historiques de la finance moderne* (Paris, 1933, No. 161 in the collection 'Armand Colin'); L. de Lanzac de Laborie, *Paris sous Napoléon*, Vol. VI (Paris, 1910); G. Weill, 'Le financier Ouvrard' in *Revue historique*, Vol. CXXVII (1918), pp. 31–61; Arthur-Lévy, 'Ouvrard' in *Revue de Paris*, Vol. IV (1929), pp. 500–31, 899–930, and Vol. V, pp. 116–47; O. Wolff, *Die Geschäfte des Herrn Ouvrard* (Frankfurt, 1932; Eng. tr. by Stewart Thomson, London and New York, 1962); M. Payard, *Le financier Ouvrard, 1770–1846* (Reims, 1958).

On the royalist opposition, C. L. Chassin, *Études sur la Vendée et la Chouannerie*, 11 vols. (Paris, 1892–1900), see third series: *Les pacifications de l'ouest*, Vol. III, *1796–1815*; L. Dubreuil, *Histoire des insurrections de l'ouest*, Vol. II (Paris, 1930); J. Godechot, *La contre-revolution. Doctrine et action, 1789–1804* (Paris, 1961); L. de La Sicotière, *Louis de Frotté*, 3 vols. (Paris, 1888); E. Daudet, *La police et les chouans sous le Consulat et l'Empire* (Paris, 1895); E. d'Hauterive, *La contre-police royaliste en 1800* (Paris, 1931).

On the republican opposition, Mlle A. Gobert, *L'opposition des assemblées pendant le Consulat* (Paris, 1925); A. Guillois, *Le salon de Madame Helvétius, Cabanis et les idéologues* (Paris, 1894), and *La marquise de Condorcet* (Paris,

Bibliography

1897); J. Gaulmier, *Un grand témoin de la Révolution et de l'Empire, Volney* (Paris, 1959); P. Gaffarel, 'L'opposition militaire sous le Consulat' in *La Révolution française*, Vol. XII (1887), pp. 865–87, 982–97, and 1096–1111; by the same author, 'L'opposition républicaine sous le Consulat', *ibid.*, Vol. XIII (1887), pp. 530–50, Vol. XIV (1888), pp. 609–39; by the same author, 'L'opposition littéraire sous le Consulat', *ibid.*, Vol. XVI (1889), pp. 307–26, 397–432; P. Gautier, *Madame de Staël et Napoléon* (Paris, 1902); Lady Blennerhassett, *Frau von Staël*, 3 vols. (Berlin, 1887–1889; Fr. tr. by A. Dietrich, Paris, 1891, 3 vols.; Eng. tr., London, 1889, 3 vols.); P. S. Larg, *Madame de Staël* (Paris, 1924). See also the works on Benjamin Constant and Mme de Staël cited in G. Lefebvre, *Napoléon* (Paris, 1935, 5th ed., 1965), Pt. V, Ch. I, sec. 4, 'L'évolution sociale et l'opinion' (p. 422, 5th ed.).

THE IMPROVISATION OF THE CAMPAIGN OF 1800

See the works cited at the beginning of this chapter under 'general works' and those listed in the preceding section immediately above. Also see the works bearing on the campaign cited below in Ch. V, sec. 1, 'The Campaign of 1800 and the Treaty of Lunéville'.

Chapter V. The Pacification of Europe

General works: For diplomacy, see the works by Sybel (stops with the treaty of Lunéville), Sorel (Vol. VI), Bourgeois, and Wahl cited at the beginning of Pt. I, Ch. II, above, under 'general works'. Also see É. Driault, *Napoléon et l'Europe*, Vol. I: *La politique extérieure du Premier Consul* (Paris, 1910); A. Hermann, *Der Aufstieg Napoleons. Krieg und Diplomatie von Brumaire bis Lunéville* (Berlin, 1912): H. Fugier, *La Révolution française et l'Empire napoléonien* (Paris, 1954), Vol. IV of *l'Histoire des relations internationales*, P. Renouvin, ed.

For the general history of the campaigns, see Col. E. Bourdeau, *Campagnes modernes, 1792–1815*, 3 vols. with an atlas (Paris, 1912–1921); Gen. H. V. Descoins, *Étude synthétique des principales campagnes modernes* (Paris, 1901; 7th ed., recast, with sketches by Gen. Chanoine, 1928); Lt. Col. J. Colin, *Napoléon Ier* (Paris, 1914).

THE CAMPAIGNS OF 1800 AND THE TREATY OF LUNÉVILLE

See works listed immediately above. Also see H. Hüfer, *Quellen zur Geschichte des Zeitalters der französischen Revolution*, Pt. I: *Quellen zur Geschichte der Kriege von 1799–1800*, and Pt. II; *Quellen zur Geschichte von 1800* (Leipzig, 1901); O. Tschirch, *Geschichte der öffentlichen Meinung in Preussen im Friedensjahrzehnt vom Basler Frieden bis zum Zusammenbruch des Staates*, 2 vols. (Weimar, 1933); É. Driault, *Napoléon en Italie* (Paris, 1906). In addition, see works by Haeusser, Heigel, Bailleu, Ford, Trummel, Krones, Urlisz, Beidtel, and Wertheimer, all cited above in Pt. I, Ch. II, sec. 1, 'The Continental Powers'.

On the campaign in Italy, see Capt. de Cugnac, *La campagne de l'armée de réserve en 1800*, 2 vols. (Paris, 1900–1901, publication of the 'Section historique de l'État-Major'), or the abridged version by the same author, *La campagne de Marengo* (Paris, 1904); A. Hermann, *Marengo* (Münster, 1903).

Bibliography

On the campaign in Germany, see the following works published by the Historical Section of the French General Staff under the general title *La campagne de 1800 en Allemagne*: E. Picard, *Le passage du Rhin* (Paris, 1907); P. Azan, *Du Rhin à Ulm* (Paris, 1909); E. Picard, *Hohenlinden* (Paris, 1909), see A. Chuquet, *Historiens et marchands d'histoire*, pp. 161–85 (Paris, 1914); E. Picard, *Bonaparte et Moreau* (Paris, 1903).

On the official version of events by Napoleon, see M. Reinhard, 'L'historiographie militaire officielle sous Napoléon Ier: étude d'une origine méconnue de la légende napoléonienne' in *Revue historique*, Vol. CXCVI (1946), pp. 165–84.

On the peace negotiations, L. M. Roberts, 'The Negotiations Preceding the Peace of Lunéville' in *Transactions of the Royal Historical Society*, Vol. XV (1901), pp. 47–130.

THE LEAGUE OF ARMED NEUTRALITY AND THE ENGLISH CRISIS

For Bonaparte's foreign policy, see works cited above at the beginning of this chapter under 'general works'.

For Russia, see K. Waliszewski, *Le fils de la grande Catherine: Paul I* (Paris, 1912); *Histoire de Russie*, published under the direction of C. Seignobos, P. Miliukov, and L. Eisenmann, Vol. II (Paris, 1933); an excellent summary in T. Schiemann, *Geschichte Russlands unter Kaiser Nicolas I*, 3 vols. (Berlin, 1904), Vol. I. Also see works dealing with Alexander I cited below in Pt. III, Ch. VII, sec. 5, 'The Origins of the Third Coalition'.

On the League of Armed Neutrality, see J. Brown Scott, *The Armed Neutralities of 1780 and 1800* (New York, 1908, 'Publication of the Carnegie Endowment for International Peace').

For the history of England, see bibliographies in this book, Pt. I, Ch. II, secs. 2, 4, and 5. Also see H. Furber, *Henry Dundas, First Viscount Melville* (Oxford, 1931).

For Egypt, F. Rousseau, *Kléber et Menou en Égypte* (Paris, 1900, publication of the 'Société d'histoire contemporaine'); G. Rigault, *Le général Abdallah Menou et la dernière phase de l'expédition d'Égypte* (Paris, 1911); F. Charles-Roux, *L'Angleterre et l'expédition française d'Égypte*, 2 vols. (Cairo, 1925, publication of the 'Société royale de géographie d'Égypte'); Comdr. de La Jonquière, *L'expédition d'Égypte*, 5 vols. (Paris, 1899–1907, publication of the 'Section historique de l'État-Major'), stops with the return of Bonaparte.

THE PEACE OF AMIENS (MARCH 25, 1802)

See works listed under 'general works' at the beginning of this chapter and those cited in sec. 2 immediately above. Also see M. Philippson, 'La paix d'Amiens' in *Revue historique*, Vol. LXXV (1901), pp. 236–318, and Vol. LXXVI (1901), pp. 48–78; by the same author, *Die äussere Politik Napoleons I: der Friede von Amiens* (Leipzig, 1913); O. Brandt, *England und die napoleonische Weltpolitik, 1800–1803* (Heidelberg, 1916, fasc. 48 of 'Heidelberg Abhandlungen zur mittleren und neueren Geschichte'); H. Bowman, 'Preliminary Stages of the Peace of Amiens, 1800–1801' in *University of Toronto Studies*, 2nd series, Vol. I (1899), pp. 75–155; C. Gill, 'The Relations between England and France in 1802' in *The English Historical Review*, Vol.

XXIV (1909), pp. 61–78; T. Ebbinghaus, *Napoleon, England und die Presse, 1800–1803* (Munich, 1914, fasc. 55 of 'Historische Bibliothek', published by the *Historische Zeitschrift*).

THE REORGANIZATION OF THE VASSAL STATES

See works cited at the beginning of this chapter under 'general works'. For Italy, É. Driault, *Napoléon en Italie* (Paris, 1906). Also see works by Pingaud, St. Canzio, Roberti, and Fugier cited above in Pt. I, Ch. II, sec. 3, 'France and her Allies'. Also P. Marmottan, *Le royaume d'Étrurie* (Paris, 1896), and *Bonaparte et la république de Lucques* (Paris, 1896); G. Drei, *Il regno d'Étruria, 1801–1807* (Modena, 1937); Boulay de la Meurthe, *Histoire de la négotiation du Concordat* (Paris, 1920); *I carteggi di Francesco Melzi d'Eril, duca di Lodi: La vice-prezidenza della Republica italiana*, 5 vols. (Milan, 1958–1961), covers the period from January 26, 1802, to January 27, 1804.

For Holland, Switzerland, and Spain, see works cited above in Pt. I, Ch. II, sec. 3 of this book. Also see A. Wyss, *Alois Reding Landeshauptmann von Schwyz und erster Landamman der Helvetik, 1765–1818* (Stanz, 1936); A. Rufer, 'Pestalozzi auf der Konsulta in Paris' in *Neue schweizer Rundschau*, 1953.

On the Recess, see K. von Heigel, *Deutsche Geschichte vom Tode Friedrichs des Grossen bis zur Auflösung des alten Reiches*, 2 vols. (Stuttgart, 1899–1911, Vols. X and XI in 'Bibliothek deutscher Geschichte', published under the direction of H. von Zwiedineck-Südenhorst).

Chapter VI. Bonaparte Consul for Life

General works: See works cited above at the beginning of Pt. II, Ch. IV under 'general works' and in Ch. IV, sec. 2, 'The Organization and Extension of Bonaparte's Powers'.

THE CRISIS OF YEAR IX

In addition to general historics, especially J. Godechot, *La contre-révolution. Doctrine et action, 1789–1804* (Paris, 1961), see F. Masson, 'Les complots jacobins au lendemain de brumaire' in *Revue des études napoléoniennes*, Vol. XVIII (1922), pp. 5–28, and 'L'affaire Becdelièvre, l'affaire Duchâtellier: la contre-police de Cadoudal', *ibid.*, Vol. XX (1923), pp. 57–112; E. d'Hauterive, *L'enlèvement du sénateur Clément de Ris* (Paris, 1925); J. Lorédan, *La machine infernale de la rue Saint-Nicaise* (Paris, 1924); G. Hue, *Un complot de police sous le Consulat: La conspiration de Ceracchi et d'Arena* (Paris, 1909); J. Destrem, *Les déportations du Consulat et de l'Empire* (Paris, 1885); R. Cobb, 'Note sur la répression contre le personnel sans-culotte de 1795 à 1801' in *Annales historiques de la Révolution Française* (1954), pp. 23–49.

On the judicial repression, see the works by Poullet and Godechot cited above in Pt. II, Ch. IV, sec. 1, 'The Provisional Consulate and the Constitution of Year VIII'.

THE CONCORDAT

See works by Mourret, Leflon, and Latreille cited above in Pt. I, Ch. I, sec. 2, 'The Conflict of Ideas'. Also see P. de La Gorce, *Histoire religieuse de la*

Bibliography

Révolution française, Vol. V (Paris, 1923); A. Debidour, *Histoire des rapports de l'Église et de l'État en France de 1789 à 1870* (Paris, 1898); G. Constant, *L'Église de France sous le Consulat et l'Empire* (Paris, 1928); J. Schmidlin, *Papstgeschichte der neuesten Zeit*, Vol. I: *Papsttum und Päpste im Zeitalter der Restauration, 1800–1846* (Munich, 1933), Fr. tr.: *Histoire des papes de l'époque contemporaine*, Vol. I: *Pie VII* (Paris, 1938); J. Boussoulade, *L'Église de Paris du 9 thermidor au Concordat* (Paris, 1950); A. Latreille, *L'Église catholique et la Révolution française*, Vol. II: *L'ère napoléonienne et la crise européenne, 1800–1815* (Paris, 1950). On Pius VII before his pontificate, and while awaiting the sequel to this work, J. Leflon, *Pie VII*, Vol. I: *Des abbayes bénédictines à la Papauté* (Paris, 1958). The indispensable works are those of Boulay de la Meurthe, *Documents sur la négociation du Concordat et sur les autres rapports de la France avec le Saint-Siège*, 6 vols. (Paris, 1891–1905), and *Histoire de la négociation du Concordat* (Paris, 1920); G. Pariset, *Le Consulat et l'Empire* (Paris, 1921, Vol. III of *Histoire de France contemporaine*), provides a very lengthy summary and an extensive bibliography.

On Protestantism, C. Durand, *Histoire du protestantisme français pendant la Révolution et l'Empire* (Paris, 1902); A. Lods, 'Étude sur les origines des articles organiques des cultes protestants' in *Revue illustrée des provinces de l'ouest*, Vol. XV (1895), pp. 53–64, 112–16, and 177–91; B. C. Poland, *French Protestantism and the French Revolution. A Study in Church and State, Thought and Religion, 1685–1815* (Princeton, 1957). The indispensable work is that of D. Robert, *Les églises réformées de France, 1800–1830* (Paris, 1961). On the relations between Geneva and French Protestantism, see by the same author, *Genève et les églises réformées de France de la 'réunion' (1798) aux environs de 1830* (Geneva and Paris, 1961), and also *Textes et documents relatifs à l'histoire des Églises réformées en France (période 1800–1830)* (Geneva and Paris, 1962).

On theophilanthropy, A. Mathiez, *La théophilanthropie* (Paris, 1903).

THE TRIBUNATE PURGED AND THE LIFE CONSULATE ESTABLISHED

See the works cited above at the beginning of Pt. II, Ch. IV under 'general works' and in Ch. IV, sec. 2 of this book, particularly those by Aulard, Vandal, Poullet, and Godechot. Also see P. Sagnac, 'Le Consulat à vie' in *Revue des études napoléoniennes*, Vol. XXIV (1925), pp. 133–54 and 193–211; the articles by P. Gaffarel cited above in Ch. IV, sec. 2 of this book; E. Guillon, *Les complots militaires sous le Consulat et l'Empire* (Paris, 1894); Gilbert Augustin-Thierry, *Conspirateurs et gens de police: le complot des libelles* (Paris, 1903), and *La mystérieuse affaire Donnadieu* (Paris, 1909); A. Aulard, 'Le centenaire de la légion d'honneur' in his collection of *Études et leçons*, Vol. IV (Paris, 1904), this article first appeared in *Revue de Paris*, Vol. III (1902), pp. 539–66; E. L'Hommedé, 'Les sénatoreries' in *Revue des études historiques*, 1932, pp. 19–40.

BONAPARTE'S SOCIAL POLICY

G. Hanotaux, 'La transformation sociale à l'époque napoléonienne' in *Revue des Deux Mondes*, 7th period, Vol. XXIII (1926), pp. 89–123, 562–97.

On the Civil Code, P. Sagnac, *La législation civile de la Révolution française* (Paris, 1898), and *Le Code civil, livre du centenaire*, 2 vols. (Paris, 1904);

Bibliography

M. Leroy, *L'esprit de la législation napoléonienne* (Nancy, 1898), and 'Le centenaire du Code civil' in *Revue de Paris*, Vol. V (1903), pp. 511–33 and 762–80; J. Ray, *Essai sur la structure logique du Code civil français* (Paris, 1926), and *Index du Code civil* (Paris, 1926); P. Viard, *Histoire générale du droit privé français de 1789 à 1830* (Paris, 1931); M. Garaud, *Histoire générale du droit privé français (de 1789 à 1804)*, Vol. I: *La Révolution et l'égalité civile* (Paris, 1953), with a foreword by G. Lefebvre, and Vol. II: *La Révolution et la propriété foncière* (Paris, 1959).

On the application of the Concordat, Boulay de la Meurthe, *Histoire du rétablissement du culte de 1802 à 1805* (Paris, 1925); A. Latreille, *Napoléon et le Saint-Siège, 1801–1808. L'ambassade du cardinal Fesch à Rome* (Paris, 1935); A. Mathiez, 'Les prêtres révolutionnaires devant le cardinal Caprara' in *Annales historiques de la Révolution française* (1926), pp. 1–15; C. Latreille, *L'opposition religieuse au Concordat*, 2 vols. (Paris, 1910); L. Lévy-Schneider, *L'application du Concordat par un prélat d'Ancien Régime: Monseigneur Champion de Cicé, archevêque d'Aix et d'Arles, 1802–1810* (Paris, 1921); J. Leflon, *Étienne Alexandre Bernier, évêque d'Orléans, et l'application du Concordat*, 2 vols. (Paris, 1938), and *Monsieur Émery*, Vol. II: *L'Église concordataire et impériale* (Paris, 1947); P. Mouly, *Le Concordat en Lozère-Ardèche* (Mende, 1942). On the application of the Concordat in the bishopric of Liège in annexed Wallonia, see *La correspondance de Mgr Zaepffel, 1801–1808* (without place of publication, 1951). In addition, see works listed in G. Lefebvre, *Napoléon* (Paris, 1935; 5th ed., 1965), Pt. V, Ch. I, sec. 3 (p. 409 in 5th ed.).

On the lower classes, see E. Levasseur, *Histoire des classes ouvrières et de l'industrie en France depuis 1789 jusqu'à nos jours*, 2 vols. (Paris, 1862; 2nd ed., 1903), and *Histoire du commerce en France*, Vol. II (Paris, 1912).

On the famine of Year X, see L. de Lanzac de Laborie, *Paris sous Napoléon*, Vol. V (Paris, 1908); P. Viard, 'Les subsistances en Ille-et-Vilaine sous le Consulat et l'Empire' in *Annales de Bretagne*, Vol. XXII (1917), pp. 328–352, 471–88, and Vol. XXIII (1918), pp. 131–54; *Tableaux des prix moyens de l'hectolitre de blé de 1800 à 1870*, published by the Ministry of Agriculture and Commerce (Paris, 1873).

On education, see the bibliography and the account in G. Pariset cited in Pt. I, Ch. I under 'general works' above. Also see A. Aulard, *Napoléon et le monopole universitaire* (Paris, 1911); L. de Lanzac de Laborie, *Paris sous Napoléon*, Vol. IV (Paris, 1907), and 'La haute administration de l'enseignement sous le Consulat et l'Empire' in *Revue des études napoléoniennes*, Vol. X (1916), pp. 185–219; M. Gontard, *L'enseignement primaire en France de la Révolution à la loi Guizot, 1789–1833* (Paris, 1959).

On relief, see J. Imbert, *Le droit hospitalier de la Révolution et de l'Empire* (Paris, 1954; 'Publications de l'Université de la Sarre'); A. Cherubini, *Dottrine e metodi assistenziali dal 1789 al 1848, Italia, Francia, Inghilterra* (Milan, 1958).

On the court and morals, P. Lacroix, *Directoire, Consulat et Empire. Mœurs et usages, lettres, sciences et arts* (Paris, 1883); R. Peyre, *Napoléon et son temps* (Paris, 1888); P. Bondois, *Napoléon et la société de son temps* (Paris, 1895); F. Masson, *Madame Bonaparte* (Paris, 1920); É. Herriot, *Madame Récamier et ses amis*, 2 vols. (Paris, 1904); L. de Lanzac de Laborie, *Paris sous Napoléon*,

Vols. III, VII, VIII (Paris, 1906, 1911, 1913); G. Thibault-Laurent, *La première introduction du divorce en France, 1792–1816* (Clermont-Ferrand, 1938); see also the bibliographies of memoirs and foreign travellers' accounts in G. Pariset, cited in Pt. I, Ch. I under 'general works' above.

PART THREE. THE IMPERIAL CONQUEST TO THE TREATY OF TILSIT (1802–1807)

General works: The principal interpretations of Napoleon's foreign policy are those of A. Thiers, *Histoire du Consulat et de L'Empire*, 20 vols. (Paris, 1845–1862); A. Sorel, *L'Europe et la Révolution française*, Vols. VI–VIII (Paris, 1903–1904); É. Bourgeois, *Manuel historique de politique étrangère* (Paris, 1900; 6th ed., 1920); É. Driault, *Napoléon et l'Europe*, 5 vols. (Paris, 1910–1927); Arthur-Lévy, *Napoléon et la paix* (Paris, 1902). These interpretations are summarized and discussed by Pierre Muret, 'Une conception nouvelle de la politique étrangère de Napoléon I' in *Revue d'histoire moderne et contemporaine*, Vol. XVIII (1903), pp. 177–200 and 353–80.

For Thiers, the main objective of Napoleon's foreign policy was to defeat England, the fomenter of anti-French coalitions; but he recognized that the Emperor's ambition helped to provoke these coalitions. Bourgeois also saw in Napoleon a dynamic will, which he sought to explain in terms of his Eastern ambitions (the 'oriental mirage'). Driault discovered in Napoleon's foreign policy the expression of a grand design: the desire to reunify all of Europe, at first in the image of the Carolingian Empire, and later, the Roman Empire. For Sorel, Napoleon was only defending the natural boundaries, whose conquest entrained ever-recurring coalitions; the French annexations were intended to protect the natural boundaries from subsequent aggression (this thesis was taken up, purely and simply, by Jacques Bainville in his study *Napoléon*, Paris, 1931). Arthur-Lévy even went so far as to maintain that Napoleon always wished for peace.

Pierre Muret pointed out in his remarkable article that none of these hypotheses took into account all of the facts, and he concluded that it would be impossible to explain Napoleon's policies in terms of a unique and precisely defined goal which once reached would have completely satisfied him. Essentially, Muret was right: time alone could have mellowed Napoleon's temperament and made him suspend his conquests. Even so, each of these interpretations has its value. Surely the Napoleonic Wars sounded the final curtain in the Anglo-French rivalry for the domination of the seas, and in fact the world; and there can be no doubt that all of the powers shared in the desire to deprive France of her conquests, given the opportunity. From 1806 on, the tendency on the part of the Emperor to manage the affairs of the Continent is quite evident; one could even concede that Napoleon would have willingly kept peace, had he been left free to do everything he wished. Lastly, Europe's hostility is also explainable by the aristocracy's intense hatred for Revolutionary France and for the parvenu. It is indeed strange that no historian has ever dwelled on this point. As for the role of the 'oriental mirage', it appears to have been the least important. The question has been taken up again by H. C. Deutsch in *The Genesis of Napoleonic Imperialism* (Cambridge, Mass., 1938), which does not formulate any original arguments, and by A. Fugier in Vol. IV of *l'Histoire des relations internationales*, P. Renouvin, ed.: *La Révolution française et l'Empire napoléonien* (Paris, 1954), which stresses the concept of 'national enmities' and emphasizes the deeply social nature of the struggle between Old Europe and Napoleon.

Chapter VII. France and England: The Struggle Renewed (1802–1805)

General works: See bibliographies in Pt. II, Ch. IV (general works); Pt. II, Ch. IV, sec. 2; Pt. II, Ch. V, sec. 2 of this book.

BONAPARTE'S ECONOMIC POLICY AND THE RUPTURE OF THE TREATY OF AMIENS

See works cited above under Pt. II, Ch. V, sec. 3, especially that of M. Philippson. See also the important article by H. Beeley, 'A Project of Alliance with Russia in 1802' in *The English Historical Review* (1934), pp. 497–501.

On the economic situation, see F. Crouzet, 'Les conséquences économiques de la Révolution. Un inédit de sir Francis d'Ivernois' in *Annales historiques de la Révolution française* (1962), pp. 183–217 and 336–62 (the article concerns 'A Memorandum on the Advantages and Disadvantages of a Treaty of Commerce with the French Republic', dated 1802); *Documents sur l'état de l'industrie et du commerce de Paris et du département de la Seine (1778–1810), publiés avec une étude sur les essais d'industrialisation de Paris sous la Révolution et l'Empire*, B. Gille, ed. (Paris, 1963; 'Documents pour servir à l'histoire économique de Paris', fascicle I); J. Vidalenc, 'La crise économique dans les départements méditerranéens pendant l'Empire' in *Revue d'Histoire moderne et contemporaine* (1954), No. 3; F. Roques, *Aspects de la vie économique niçoise sous le Consulat et l'Empire* (Aix-en-Provence, 1957; extract from *Annales de la Faculté de droit*, No. 49); O. Festy, *Les délits ruraux et leur répression sous la Révolution et le Consulat. Étude d'histoire économique* (Paris, 1956).

On economic policy, see L. Amé, *Étude économique sur les tarifs de douane et les traités de commerce* (Paris, 1860); F. Braesch, *Finances et monnaies révolutionnaires*, fasc. 5: *La livre tournois et le franc de germinal* (Paris, 1936); M. Reinhard, 'La statistique de la population sous le Consulat et l'Empire. Le bureau de statistique' in *Population* (1950), pp. 103–20; A. de Saint-Léger, 'Les mémoires statistiques des départements pendant le Consulat et l'Empire' in *Le bibliographe moderne* (1918–1919), Nos. 1–3; A. Fabre, *Les origines du système métrique* (Paris, 1931); P. Darmstaedter, 'Studien zur napoleonischen Wirtschaftspolitik' in *Vierteljahrschrift für Sozial- und Wirtschaftsgeschichte*, Vol. II (1904), pp. 559–615, Vol. III (1905), pp. 112–41; E. Tarlé, 'Napoléon I et les intérêts économiques de la France' in *Revue des études napoléoniennes*, Vol. XXVI (1926), pp. 117–37; J. Holland Rose, 'Napoleon and the British Commerce' in his *Napoleonic Studies* (London, 1904), pp. 166–203; A. Cunningham, *British Credit in the Last Napoleonic Wars* (Cambridge, 1910);

Bibliography

J. Chaptal, 'Un projet de traité de commerce avec l'Angleterre sous le Consulat' in *Revue d'économie politique*, Vol. VI (1893), pp. 83–98.

On economic doctrines, see C. Gide and C. Rist, *Histoire des doctrines économiques depuis les physiocrates*, 2 vols. (Paris, 1909; 3rd ed., 1920); G. Dionnet, *Le néo-mercantilisme au XVIIIe siècle et au début du XIXe* (Paris, 1901); E. Allix, 'La méthode et la conception de l'économie politique dans l'œuvre de J. B. Say' in *Revue d'histoire des doctrines économiques et sociales*, Vol. IV (1911), pp. 321–60.

On colonial policy, J. Saintoyant, *La colonisation française pendant la période napoléonienne* (Paris, 1931); E. Wilson Lyon, *Louisiana in French Diplomacy, 1759–1804* (Oklahoma, 1934); Col. Nemours, *Histoire militaire de la guerre d'indépendance de Saint-Domingue*, 2 vols. (Paris, 1925–1928), and *Histoire de la captivité et de la mort de Toussaint-Louverture* (Paris, 1929); E. D. Charlier, *Aperçu sur la formation historique de la nation haïtienne* (Port-au-Prince, 1954); A. Césaire, *Toussaint-Louverture. La Révolution française et le problème colonial* (Paris, 1960; coll. 'Portraits de l'Histoire', No. 26); G. Roloff, *Die Kolonialpolitik Napoleons I* (Munich and Leipzig, 1899, fasc. 10 of 'Historische Bibliothek' of *Historische Zeitschrift*).

For the negotiations on the eve of the rupture, see C. L. Lokke, 'Secret Negotiation to Maintain the Peace of Amiens' in *American Historical Review*, Vol. XLIX (1943), pp. 55–64.

THE ESTABLISHMENT OF THE EMPIRE IN FRANCE (1804)

See works cited in Pt. II, Ch. IV (general works) and Pt. II, Ch. IV, sec. 2 above. Also see F. Masson, *Napoléon et sa famille*, 13 vols. (Paris, 1897–1919), Vol. II.

On the relations between Napoleon and Pius VII at the time of the coronation, and on the submission of the constitutional clergy, see the works by A. Latreille and J. Leflon cited above in Pt. I, Ch. I, sec. 2 and in Pt. II, Ch. VI, sec. 4; also see other relevant works cited under Pt. I, Ch. I, sec. 2 and Pt. II, Ch. VI, sec. 2. In addition, see F. L'Huillier, 'La doctrine et la conduite d'un évêque concordataire, ci-devant assermenté, Saurine' in *Revue historique*, Vol. CLXXXV (1939), pp. 286–317.

On the conspiracy of Year XII, G. Caudrillier, 'Le complot de l'an XII' in *Revue historique*, Vol. LXXIV (1900), pp. 278–86, Vol. LXXV (1901), pp. 257–85, and Vol. LXXVIII (1902), pp. 45–71; Boulay de la Meurthe, *Correspondance du duc d'Enghien et documents sur son enlèvement et sa mort*, 4 vols. (Paris, 1904–1913, publication of the 'Société d'histoire contemporaine'); see G. Pariset cited in Pt. I, Ch. I of this book for a bibliography and lucid account; J. Godechot, *La contre-révolution. Doctrine et action, 1789–1804* (Paris, 1961).

PROJECTS FOR AN INVASION OF ENGLAND. TRAFALGAR (1805)

See E. Chevalier, *Histoire de la marine française sous le Consulat et l'Empire* (Paris, 1886); J. Tramond, *Manuel d'histoire maritime de la France des origines à 1815* (Paris, 1916; 3rd ed., 1947); E. Desbrières, *Projets et tentatives de débarquement aux Iles Britanniques*, 5 vols. (Paris, 1900–1902), *Le blocus de Brest de 1793 à 1805* (Paris, 1903), and *La campagne maritime de 1805. Trafalgar*

Bibliography

(Paris, 1907); J. Holland Rose, *Pitt and the Great War* (London, 1911); A. T. Mahan, *The Influence of Sea Power upon the French Revolution and Empire*, 2 vols. (London, 1892), Vol. II, and *Life of Nelson*, 2 vols. (London, 1897); F. B. Wheeler and A. M. Broadley, *Napoleon and the Invasion of England*, 2 vols. (London, 1910); J. Corbett, *The Campaign of Trafalgar* (London, 1919); H. C. Deutsch, 'Napoleonic Policy and the Project of a Descent upon England' in *The Journal of Modern History*, Vol. II (1930), pp. 541–68; Adm. Castex, *Théories stratégiques*, Vol. II: *La manœuvre stratégique* (Paris, 1930); A. Thomazi, *Trafalgar* (Paris, 1932), and *Napoléon et ses marins* (Paris, 1950); P. Mackesy, *The War in the Mediterranean* (London, 1957).

THE CONTINENTAL BLOCKADE

See works cited above under Pt. I, Ch. II, sec. 4 of this book. Also see A. Stephen, *War in Disguise or the Fraud of Neutral Flags* (London, 1805; re-edited in 1917); F. Crouzet, *L'économie britannique et le blocus continental, 1806–1813*, 2 vols. (Paris, 1958), see Vol. I.

THE ORIGINS OF THE THIRD COALITION

See the general histories cited under Pt. I, Ch. III, sec. 2 and at the very beginning of Pt. III, the works on Prussia and Austria cited under Pt. I, Ch. II, sec. 1 and the works on England cited under Pt. I, Ch. II, sec. 2. In addition, see G. Brodrick and J. Fotheringam, *The History of England from Addington's Administration to the Close of William IV's Reign, 1801–1837* (London, 1906, Vol. XI of *Political History of England*, published under the direction of Hunt and Poole); A. Bryant, *Years of Victory, 1802–1812* (London, 1944); A. Fournier, *Gentz und Cobenzl. Geschichte der æsterreichischen Diplomatie in den Jahren 1801–1805* (Vienna, 1880); H. Ullmann, *Russisch-preussische Politik unter Alexander I und Friedrich-Wilhelm III bis 25 Februar 1806* (Leipzig, 1899); P. Bailleu, *Briefwechsel König Friedrich-Wilhelm's III und der Königin Luise mit Kaiser Alexander I* (Leipzig, 1900, publications of the Royal Archives of Prussia, Vol. LXXV); M. H. Weil, *D'Ulm à Iéna. Correspondance inédite du chevalier de Gentz avec F. J. Jackson, ministre de Grande-Bretagne à Berlin, 1804–1806* (Paris, 1921); J. Holland Rose, *Select Dispatches Relating to the Formation of the Third Coalition against France* (London, 1904).

On Alexander I, see the histories of Russia cited above in Pt. I, Ch. II, sec. 1 of this bibliography. Also see Grand Duke Mikhailovitch, *Les relations de la Russie et de la France d'après les rapports des ambassadeurs d'Alexandre Ier et de Napoléon Ier*, 6 vols. (St. Petersburg, 1905), and *Le tsar Alexandre Ier* (Paris, 1931); K. Waliszewski, *Le règne d'Alexandre Ier*, 3 vols. (Paris, 1923–1925); N. Brian-Chaninov, *Alexandre Ier* (Paris, 1934); L. Czartoryski, *Alexandre Ier et le prince Czartoryski. Correspondance particulière et conversations*, with an introduction by C. de Mazade (Paris, 1905); *Mémoires et correspondance du prince Czartoryski avec l'empereur Alexandre Ier*, C. de Mazade, ed. (Paris, 1887); H. Schaeder, *Die dritte Koalition und die Heilige Allianz* (Königsberg, 1934, Vol. XVI of *Osteuropäischen Forschungen*).

For Eastern policy, see N. Iorga cited above in Pt. I, Ch. II, sec. 1; B. Mouravieff, *L'alliance russo-turque au milieu des guerres napoléoniennes*

Bibliography

(Neuchâtel, 1954); V. J. Purgear, *Napoleon and the Dardanelles* (Berkeley and Los Angeles, 1951); G. Lebel, *La France et les principautés danubiennes (du XVI siècle à la chute de Napoleon I)* (Paris, 1955; 'Publications de la Faculté des Lettres d'Alger', Vol. XXVII); M. Samic, *Les voyageurs français en Bosnie à la fin du XVIII siècle et au début du XIX et le pays tel qu'ils l'ont vu* (Paris, 1962); C. Yaktchich, *L'Europe et la résurrection de la Serbie, 1804–1834* (Paris, 1907); E. Haumant, 'Les origines de la liberté serbe d'après les mémoires du protopope M. Nénadovitch' in *Revue historique*, Vol. CXVIII (1915), pp. 54–69.

On Russian expansion in the East, T. Schiemann, *Geschichte Russlands unter Kaiser Nicolas I* (Berlin, 1904), Vol. I.

On Italy, see A. Fugier cited above in Pt. I, Ch. II, sec. 3; also, C. Auriol, *La France, l'Angleterre et Naples, de 1803 à 1806*, 2 vols. (Paris, 1905); J. von Helfert, *Maria-Karolina von Œsterreich, Königin von Neapel und Sicilien* (Vienna, 1884); A. Bonnefous, *Marie-Caroline, reine des Deux-Siciles* (Paris, 1905).

For Sweden, R. Carr, 'Gustavus IV and the British Government' in *The English Historical Review*, Vol. LX (1945), pp. 36–66.

Chapter VIII. Napoleon's Army

General works: J. Morvan, *Le soldat impérial*, 2 vols. (Paris, 1904–1907); P. Cantal, *Études sur l'armée révolutionnaire* (Paris, 1907), a very instructive work.

RECRUITMENT AND PROMOTION

G. Vallée, *La conscription dans le département de la Charente* (Paris, 1936), despite its title, this work describes the general evolution of this institution, stopping in 1807; G. Vallée, *Compte général de la conscription de A. A. Hargenvilliers* (Paris, 1937), and *Population et conscription, 1798–1814* (Rodez, 1938, 31 pages). Also see P. Viard, 'Études sur la conscription militaire napoléonienne' in *Revue du Nord* (1924), pp. 287–304, and (1926), pp. 273–302, devoted exclusively to the Nord region.

On conscription in the Belgian departments, see E. Fairon and H. Heuse, *Lettres de grognards* (Liège, 1936); H. Lachouque and A. S. K. Brown, *The Anatomy of Glory, Napoleon and his Guard, a Study in Leadership* (Providence, U.S.A., and London, 1961), especially valuable for its plates; P. Conard, 'Napoléon et les vocations militaires' in *Revue de Paris*, Vol. VI (1902), pp. 345–65; E. Bucquoy, *Les gardes d'honneur de l'Empire* (Nancy, 1908); Lt. Col. Sauzay, *Les Allemands sous les aigles françaises*, 6 vols. (Paris, 1902–1912).

On the general staff, Lt. Col. Philip, *Études sur le service d'état-major pendant les guerres du premier Empire* (Paris, 1900); also see works by Lechartier and Guignes cited below in sec. 2 of this chapter.

G. Six, *Dictionnaire biographique des généraux et amiraux français de la Révolution et de l'Empire, 1792–1814*, 2 vols. (Paris, 1934–1935), and *Les généraux de la Révolution et de l'Empire* (Paris, 1947); J. Valynseele, *Les maréchaux du Premier Empire, leur famille et leur descendance* (Paris, 1957).

Among the biographies of the marshals, see S. J. Watson, *By Command of the Emperor, a Life of Marshal Berthier* (London, 1957), and the more personal

Bibliography

account by J. Courvoisier, *Le maréchal Berthier et sa principauté de Neuchâtel* (*1806–1814*) (Neuchâtel, 1959); Marquise de Blocqueville, *Le maréchal Davout*, 4 vols. (Paris, 1879–1880); Gen. H. Bonnal, *La vie militaire du maréchal Ney*, 3 vols. (Paris, 1910–1914); Gen. C. Thomas, *Le maréchal Lannes* (Paris, 1891); P. Saint-Marc, *Le maréchal Marmont, duc de Raguse, 1774–1852* (Paris, 1957); H. Aureas, *Un général de Napoléon, Miollis* (Paris, 1961; 'Publications de la Faculté des Lettres de l'Université de Strasbourg', fascicle 143); *Les cahiers du général Brun, baron de Villeret, pair de France, 1773–1845*, collected by P. Desachy (Paris, 1953); *Les cahiers du colonel Girard, 1766–1846*, edited by L. de Saint-Pierre (Paris, 1951).

THE PREPARATION FOR WAR

J. Bourdon, 'L'administration militaire sous Napoléon I et ses rapport avec l'administration générale' in *Revue des études napoléoniennes*, Vol. XI (1917), pp. 17–47; see the work by J. Morvan cited above at the beginning of this chapter; Capt. Lechartier, *Les services de l'arrière à la Grande Armée* (Paris, 1910), deals with the years 1806 and 1807; Col. Guignes, *L'organisation des services de la Grande Armée* (Paris, 1939). On the Intendant General of the Grand Army, and in the absence of a good biography, see *Les Archives Daru aux Archives nationales*, inventory by S. d'Huart (Paris, 1962); G. Nigay, 'Le comte Pierre Daru, intendant général de la Grande Armée. Documents inédits' in *Cahiers d'histoire* published by 'Les Universités de Clermont-Lyon-Grenoble', Vol. VII, 1962. Also see the following works connected with the campaigns: A. Meynier, 'Levées et pertes d'hommes sous le Consulat et l'Empire' in *Revue des études napoléoniennes*, Vol. XXX (1930), pp. 26–51, this article, revised and perfected, was published separately under the title *Une erreur historique. Les morts de la Grande Armée et des armées ennemies* (Paris, 1934, 34 pages); P. Triaire, *D. Larrey et les campagnes de la Révolution et de l'Empire* (Paris, 1902).

THE CONDUCT OF WAR

Lt. Col. Grouard, *Maximes de guerre de Napoléon* (Paris, 1898); Col. Vachée, *Napoléon en campagne* (Paris, 1913); York von Wartenburg, *Napoleon als Feldherr*, 2 vols. (Berlin, 1885–1886; 2nd ed., 1901; Fr. tr. by Comdt. Richert, Paris, 1899, 2 vols.; Eng. tr., 2 vols., London, 1902); H. Delbrück, *Geschichte der Kriegskunst im Rahmen der politischen Geschichte*, Vol. IV (Berlin, 1920), and *Historische und politische Aufsätze über den Unterschied der Strategie Friedrichs und Napoleons* (Berlin, 1897; 2nd ed., 1907). In addition to the last mentioned work, the following three books by Capt. (later Lt. Col.) J. Colin are highly recommended: *L'éducation militaire de Napoléon* (Paris, 1900), *Les transformations de la guerre* (Paris, 1912), and *Napoléon Ier* (Paris, 1914).

On the military organization of Napoleon, see E. G. Léonard, *L'armée et ses problèmes au XVIII siècle* (Paris, 1958); Matti Lauerma, *L'artillerie de campagne française pendant les guerres de la Révolution; évolution de l'organisation et de la tactique* (Helsinki, 1956; 'Annales Academiae Scientiarum Fenicae', series B, Vol. 96); somewhat more precise is R. S. Quimby, *The Background of Napoleonic Warfare. The Theory of Military Tactics in Eighteenth Century France* (New York, 1957).

Bibliography

Chapter IX. The Formation of the Grand Empire (1805–1807)

General works: The same as for Pt. III of this book.

THE FINANCIAL CRISIS OF 1805

See the works dealing with Ouvrard cited in Pt. II, Ch. IV, sec. 2; A. Fugier cited in Pt. I, Ch. II, sec. 3; V. Labouchère, 'P. C. Labouchère' in *Revue d'histoire diplomatique*, Vol. XXVII (1913), pp. 425–55 and Vol. XXVIII (1914), pp. 74–97.

On Labouchère's business operations in America see V. Nolte, *Fünfzig Jahre in beiden Hemisphären*, 2 vols. (Hamburg, 1854).

On the general economic crisis, and as a regional study, see M. Lacoste, *La crise économique de 1805 dans le département de la Meurthe* (complementary thesis presented at the Faculté des Lettres de l'Université de Paris, 1951; typewritten copy).

THE CAMPAIGN OF 1805

See the 'general works' cited above at the beginning of Pt. III; for diplomacy, see the works cited under Pt. III, Ch. VII, sec. 5; for the campaign, see the general works cited at the beginning of Ch. V.

P. C. Alombert and J. Colin, *La campagne de 1805 en Allemagne*, 6 vols. (Paris, 1902–1908, publication of the French General Staff), stops on November 11. The account was continued by the following anonymous articles, which appeared under the same title as the one above, in *Revue d'histoire*, published by the General Staff: Vol. XXIV (1906), Vols. XXV, XXVI, XXVII (1907). Also see E. Mayerhoffer von Vedropolje, *Der Krieg der dritten Koalition gegen Frankreich* (Vienna, 1905), and *Die Schlacht bei Austerlitz* (Vienna, 1912); D. Guerrini, *La manovra napoleonica d'Ulm* (Rome, 1925, publication of the Italian General Staff); A. Slovak, *La bataille d'Austerlitz* (Paris, 1912; Fr. tr. by E. Leroy).

On the Austrian army, M. von Angeli, *Erzherzog Karl als Feldherr und Heeresorganisator*, 6 vols. (Vienna, 1895–1897), Vols. III and V.

THE GRAND EMPIRE

See works cited above under Pt. I, Ch. II, sec. 1; Pt. III (general works); Pt. III, Ch. VII, sec. 5. Also see A. Rambaud, *La domination française en Allemagne*, Vol. II: *L'Allemagne sous Napoléon Ier* (Paris, 1874; 4th ed., 1897); E. Denis, *L'Allemagne de 1789 à 1810: fin de l'ancienne Allemagne* (Paris, 1896); T. Bitterauf, *Geschichte des Rheinbundes*, Vol. I [only one volume appeared]; (Munich, 1905); A. Müller, *Der letzte Kampf der Reichsritterschaft um ihre Selbstständigkeit* (Berlin, 1910, fasc. 77 'Historische Studien', Ebering, ed.); E. Hölzle, 'Das napoleonische Staatssystem in Deutschland' in *Historische Zeitschrift*, Vol. CXLVIII (1933), pp. 277–93. For the official documents which marked the end of the Holy Roman Empire, see E. Walder, *Das Ende des Alten Reiches* (Berne, 1948). Also see J. E. d'Arenberg, *Les princes du Saint-Empire à l'époque napoléonienne* (Louvain, 1951), valuable for its lists of names and statistical information, particularly in regard to the mediatized lands.

For Naples, see relevant works cited above under Pt. III, Ch. VII, sec. 5,

Bibliography

as well as J. Rambaud, *Naples sous Joseph Bonaparte* (Paris, 1911); H. Acton, *The Bourbons of Naples (1734–1825)* (London, 1956); M. Caldora, *Calabria napoleonica (1806–1815)* (Naples, 1960). On relations with the pope, see works cited above under Pt. I, Ch. I, sec. 2; Pt. II, Ch. VI, sec. 2; A. Fugier, *Napoléon et l'Italie* (Paris, 1947); E. Dard, 'Entretien de Napoléon et de Monseigneur Arezzo, 9 novembre 1806' in *Revue de Paris*, Vol. III (1935), pp. 606–26. On Talleyrand, see works by Lacour-Gayet, Tarlé, and Dard, cited above in Pt. II, Ch. IV, sec. 2.

THE BREAK WITH PRUSSIA (1806)

See 'general works' at the beginning of Pt. III and works listed in the previous section immediately above; Heigel and Bailleu cited in Pt. I, Ch. II, sec. 1; *The Cambridge History of British Foreign Policy* cited in Pt. I, Ch. II, sec. 2; the works dealing with Alexander I cited in Pt. III, Ch. VII, sec. 5. In addition, see E. Heymann, *Napoleon und die grossen Mächte im Fruhjahr 1806* (Berlin, 1910); P. Bailleu, *Königin Luise* (Berlin, 1908; 3rd ed., 1926). On public opinion in Prussia and Germany, see O. Tschirch cited in Pt. I, Ch. I, sec. 3.

JENA AND AUERSTÄDT. THE WINTER CAMPAIGN (1806–1807)

For diplomatic history, see works cited at the beginning of Pt. III under general works and in the section immediately above. Heigel (cited in Pt. I, Ch. II, sec. 1) carries the narrative up to August 1806; for the continuation, see H. von Zwiedineck-Südenhorst, *Deutsche Geschichte von der Auflösung des alten bis zur Errichtung des neuen Kaiserreiches*, Vol. I: *Die Zeit des Rheinbundes, 1806–1815* (Stuttgart, 1897).

For the campaigns, see works listed in Pt. II, Ch. V, under 'general works'. Also see Comdt. P. Foucart, *Campagne de Prusse, 1806* (Paris, 1890), *La cavalerie pendant la campagne de Prusse* (Paris, 1880), *Campagne de Pologne, 1806*, 2 vols. (Paris, 1882), and *Iéna* (Paris, 1887, publications of the General Staff); Gen. Bonnal, *La manœuvre d'Iéna* (Paris, 1904); P. Grenier, *Les manœuvres d'Eylau et de Friedland* (Paris, 1901).

On the Prussian army, C. von der Goltz, *Rossbach und Iena* (Berlin, 1883; 2nd ed., 1906; Fr. tr. by Comdt. Chabert, Paris, 1890); C. Jany, *Geschichte der königlichen preussischen Armee bis zum Jahre 1807*, 3 vols. (Berlin, 1928); O. von Lettow-Vorbeck, *Der Krieg von 1806–1807*, 4 vols. (Berlin, 1891–1896, publication of the Prussian High General Staff).

On the Polish question, M. Handelsman, *Napoléon et la Pologne, 1806–1807* (Paris, 1909); Count d'Ornano, *Marie Walewska 'l'épouse polonaise' de Napoléon* (Paris, 1938); 'La Pologne du siècle des Lumières au duché de Varsovie', special issue in *Annales historiques de la Révolution française* (1964), devoted to Poland during the period of the Revolution and Empire, and containing a bibliography of recent Polish works on this period.

THE SUMMER CAMPAIGN AND THE TREATIES OF TILSIT (1807)

See works listed in the preceding section immediately above; for diplomacy, see works listed at the beginning of Pt. III under 'general works'; for

Bibliography

Russia, see Pt. III, Ch. VII, sec. 5; in addition, see the excellent study by H. Butterfield, *The Peace Tactics of Napoleon I, 1806–1808* (Cambridge, 1929). On the East, É. Driault, *La politique orientale de Napoléon. Sébastiani et Gardane* (Paris, 1904); P. Shupp, *The European Powers and the Near East Question, 1806–1807* (New York, 1931, fasc. 349 of 'Publications of Columbia University'); V. J. Purgear, *Napoleon and the Dardanelles* (Berkeley and Los Angeles, 1951); N. Iorga, *Geschichte des osmanischen Reiches*, Vol. V (Gotha, 1913, Vol. 37 of the collection 'Geschichte der europäischen Staaten', Heeren and Ukert, eds.); B. Mouravieff, G. Lebel, and C. Yaktchich, cited above in Pt. III, Ch. I, sec. 5; B. V. Kallay, *Die Geschichte des serbischen Aufstandes, 1807–1810* (Vienna, 1910); A. Boppe, *L'Albanie et Napoléon* (Paris, 1914); C. Rados, *Napoléon Ier et la Grèce* (Athens, 1921); E. Rodocanacchi, *Bonaparte et les îles ioniennes, 1797–1816* (Paris, 1899); J. W. Fortescue, *History of the British Army*, 12 vols. (London, 1899–1938), see Vol. VI, which deals with the Egyptian expedition; A. T. Mahan, *The Influence of Sea Power upon the French Revolution and Empire*, 2 vols. (London, 1892); A. W. Ward and G. P. Gooch, *The Cambridge History of British Foreign Policy* (Cambridge, 1922–1923); É. Driault, *Mohammed Ali et Napoléon* (Cairo, 1927); G. Drouin, *L'Égypte de 1802 à 1804* (Cairo, 1925), and *Mohammed Ali pacha du Caire* (Cairo, 1926); G. Drouin and Mme Fawtier-Jones, *L'Angleterre et l'Égypte; la campagne de 1807* (Cairo, 1928), these four last-mentioned works were published by the 'Société royale de géographie d'Égypte'.

For the military preparations of the campaign, see Lechartier, cited in Pt. III, Ch. VIII, sec. 2.

For the campaign itself, see E. Bourdeau, cited in Pt. II, Ch. V under 'general works' and P. Grenier cited in the preceding section of this chapter.

On the treaties of Tilsit, the most recent study is that of H. Butterfield cited in this section above. Also see A. Vandal, *Napoléon Ier et Alexandre Ier*, 3 vols. (Paris, 1891–1896), Vol. I.

On the indemnity exacted from Prussia by the Convention of Bayonne, see T. Mencel, 'Les sommes de Bayonne' in *Roczniki Historyczne* (Poznan, 1950; with a synopsis in French).

Index

311

Index

Index

Index

Index

Index

Index

Index

Index

Index

Index

Index

Index

Index

Index

navy
English, *see* England
French, 176, 186, 192–4
Spanish, 191, 193
See also flatboats
Neapolitan ports, 172, 187, 202
See also Naples
Neipperg, Adam-Adalbert, Count of, 100
Nelson, Horatio, 8, 33, 105, 190, 191–3, 203
forced passage of the Sound, 111
Nenadovich, 252
Neuchâtel, Principality of, 242, 255
Neufchâteau, François de, 167
neutralization of cargoes, 195–6
See also pavillon neutre
New Orleans, 170
newspapers, *see* press
Ney, Michel, Duke of Elchingen, 158, 173, 222, 239, 240, 259–60, 263–4, 271
Nguyen Anh, 53
Nice, 56, 96, 197
Niemcewicz, 262
Niemen River, 271–4
Nizam Djedid, 269
Nizam of Hyderabad, 53
nobility, *see* aristocracy
Norinaga, Motoori, 24
Notability, Lists of, 74, 148
notables, 75–6, 89, 116, 118, 130, 155
in assemblies, 149
under Constitution of Year VIII, 120–1
dictatorship of, 73
in Helvetic Republic, 119
in Legion of Honour, 144
under monarchy of 1802, 143
monopoly of, 149
notaries (*notaires*), 87, 151
Notre Dame cathedral, Paris, 144, 185
Novalis (Baron von Hardenberg), 15, 16
Hymns to the Night, 15
Novara, 103
Novosiltsev, Nikolai Nikolayevitch, 199, 202–3, 208, 210
Nuremberg, 29
Nürnberg, 244, 258

Oberkampf, Christopher-Philip, 44
Oberlin, Jean Frédéric, 19

occultism, 19
octrois (municipal tolls), 35 & *n*, 93, 131
Oder River, 260
Offenburg, 181
Oglio River, 98
O'Higgins, 52
Ohio, 54
Old Guard, 162, 218
Old Regime, ix, 88, 133
army in, 222, 224, 228
attempts to restore, 116
bishops' privileges under, 138
in conflict with Revolution, 3 *ff*
Corporate bodies of, 150
men of, under Bonaparte, 77
oligarchy, 4–5, 150
See also England
Olivenza, 106
Olmütz, 241
Olona, 116
Opéra, the, 125, 158
Orange, Prince of, 4, 113, 115, 121, 260
See also Holland
Orde, Admiral, 91
Ordener, General Michel, 181
Order of Malta, 17
Order of St. John, 114
Organic Articles, *see Articles organiques*
Orléans, bishopric of, 139
Orléans, Duke of, Louis-Philippe, 94
Ortenau, 174, 244
Orthodox Church, 261
Osman Bey Bardisi, 270
Osnabrück, Bishopric of, 174
Ossian, 12, 20
Osterode, 264
Otranto, 104
Ottoman Empire, 201, 249, 252
See also Turkey
Oubril, 202, 253–4, 256
Oudh, 194
Oudinot, Nicolas-Charles, Duke of Reggio, 222
Ouvrard, Gabriel-Julien, 38, 94, 106, 133, 187, 233–6, 243
Overberg, Bernhard, 17
Owen, Robert, 48

Paderborn, Bishopric of, 174
Paget, Henry William, 1st Marquis of Anglesey, 206
Pahlen, Count Peter, 110, 199

329

Index

Index

Index

Index